C000141360

AA

Explorer
Brittany

Lindsay Hunt

AA Publishing

Front cover
*Top: Buildings, old city area
of St Malo (Steve Day);
Centre (left to right): (a) St
Malo Cathedral rose window
(Steve Day); (b) Fishing
boats, Camaret (Rick
Strange); (c) Mont-St-Michel
(Steve Day); (d) half-timbered
house, Rennes (Barrie Smith);*
Spine *house, Morlaix
(R Strange);*
Back cover
*Left: Playing boule, Erquy (R
Victor); Right: Vitré, house
(Steve Day).*
Page 2: *A traditional Breton
lace* coiffe
Page 3: *The granite shoreline
at Pointe du Grouin, Cancale*
Page 4: *Fishing boats
moored at Douarnenez,
Cornouaille*
Page 5 (top): *Half-timbered
houses, Rennes*
Page 5 (bottom, left): *A
detail from the calvary at
Guéhenno*
Page 5 (bottom, right):
*Stone Age Alignement
de la Lande de Cojoux, near
St.-Just*
Page 6 (top): *A sunset over
the sea at St.-Briac-sur-Mer*
Page 7 (bottom): *The beach
at Paramé, near St.-Malo*
Page 8: *Craggy rocks at
Pointe du Raz, Cap Sizun,
Finistère*
Page 9: *St.-Malo—the Fort
National at sunset*
Page 29: *The moated ruins
of Hunaudaie castle*
Page 265: *Le Gand Hôtel
Barrière, Dinard*

Written and revised by Lindsay Hunt
Original photography by Rick Strange and Steve Day

Published by AA Publishing, a trading name of Automobile
Association Developments Limited, whose registered office is
Fanum House, Basing View, Basingstoke, Hampshire RG21 4EA.
Registered number 1878835.

ISBN-10: 0-7495-4823-1
ISBN-19: 978-0-7495-4823-1

All rights reserved. No part of this publication may be
reproduced, stored in a retrieval system, or transmitted in any
form or by any means—electronic, photocopying, recording or
otherwise—unless the written permission of the publishers has
been obtained beforehand. This book may not be sold, resold,
hired out or otherwise disposed of by way of trade in any form of
binding or cover other than that in which it is published without
the prior consent of the publisher.

The contents of this publication are believed correct at the time
of printing. Nevertheless, AA Publishing accepts no responsibili-
ty for errors, omissions or changes in the details given, or for the
consequences of readers' reliance on this information. This does
not affect your statutory rights. Assessments of the attractions,
hotels and restaurants are based upon the author's own experience, and contain subjective opinions that may not reflect the
publisher's opinion or a reader's experience. We have tried to
ensure accuracy, but things do change, so please let us know if
you have any comments or corrections.

A CIP catalogue record for this book is available from the British
Library.

Colour separation by M.R.M. Graphics Ltd, Bucks, UK
Printed and bound in Italy by Printer Trento Srl

Find out more about AA Publishing and the wide range of travel
publications and services the AA provides by visiting our website at www.theAA.com/bookshop.

Revised fourth edition 2006
First published 1995

© Automobile Association Developments Limited 1995, 1999,
2003, 2006. Automobile Association Developments Limited
retains the copyright in the original edition © 1995 and in all subsequent editions, reprints and amendments.

Titles in the Explorer series:
Australia • Boston & New England • Britain • Brittany
California • Canada • Caribbean • China • Costa Rica • Crete
Cuba • Cyprus • Egypt • Florence & Tuscany • Florida
France • Germany • Greek Islands • Hawaii • India • Ireland
Italy • Japan • London • Mallorca • Mexico • New York
New Zealand • Paris • Portugal • Provence • Rome
San Francisco • Scotland • South Africa • Spain • Thailand
Tunisia • Turkey • Venice • Vietnam

A02698

How to use this book

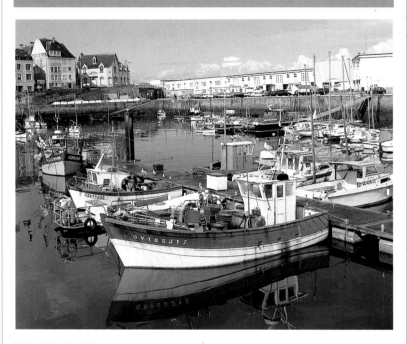

ORGANIZATION

Brittany Is, Brittany Was
Discusses aspects of life and culture in contemporary Brittany and explores significant periods in its history.

A–Z
Breaks the area down into regions, and covers places to visit, including walks and drives. In addition, Focus On articles consider a variety of topics in greater detail.

Travel Facts
Contains the strictly practical information that is vital for a successful trip.

Hotels and Restaurants
Lists recommended establishments throughout Brittany, giving a brief summary of their attractions.

ADMISSION CHARGES
An indication of an establishment's admission charge is given by categorizing the standard, adult rate as:

Inexpensive: up to €4
Moderate: €4–8
Expensive: over €8

ABOUT THE RATINGS
Most places described in this book have been given a separate rating. These are as follows:

▶▶▶   **Do not miss**

▶▶   **Highly recommended**

▶   **Worth seeing**

MAP REFERENCES
To make the location of a particular place easier to find, every main entry in this book is given a map reference, such as 176B3. The first number (176) indicates the page on which the map can be found, the letter (B) and the second number (3) pinpoint the square in which the main entry is located. The maps on the inside front cover and inside back cover are referred to as IFC and IBC respectively. A red square denotes a place of interest.

Contents

5

6

7

After a year living and working in Spain, Lindsay Hunt got hooked on travel. Since then, she has been a regular contributor to a consumer magazine and has written a number of hotel and destination guides. She is familiar with many parts of France, from Flanders' fields to the Savoy Alps, and has paced the length and breadth of Rivieran strands, clambered up innumerable Parisian hotel staircases, and toured round Burgundy's vineyards on a bicycle.

My Brittany

For decades, Brittany eluded me. Somehow my visits to France always by-passed this ragged, northwestern peninsula. In dim corners of my mind's eye, images of standing stones lingered, shrouded in Celtic legends and Atlantic mists. Gradually, this unexplored piece of the Gallic jigsaw grew more and more tantalizing, and when the opportunity came, I jumped at the chance to visit. So the truth is out: I am an enthusiastic but comparative newcomer to Brittany's charms.

The best of the region's attractions lie around its dog-toothed coast. Here you'll find a hugely varied coastline of weirdly shaped granite boulders, wave-dashed promontories and placid lagoons. Fishing boats jostle for turning space with cross-Channel ferries and laden freighters in the enticing harbour towns of St-Malo and Roscoff. Lonely, seaweed-strewn shores contrast with the hubbub of an early morning market. Stray inland via estuarine tentacles to discover the irresistible medieval towns of Dinan and Quimper, the remarkable religious art in the ornate parish closes of Finistère and the mighty Breton border castles.

Francophiles should be warned. In some ways, Brittany doesn't feel like France at all, something that many of its inhabitants regard with pride. In medieval times this was a separate duchy, and even after several centuries of integration, Bretons chafe under the reins of Parisian government. You still hear the Breton language spoken in the western regions of Finistère, and Breton hymns sung at the annual festivals and *pardons*, age-old local celebrations that still play a central role in Breton culture. Consider Brittany, then, not just as an isolated corner of France, but as a new-found land, and enjoy it as much as I did.

Lindsay Hunt

Brittany Is

The rocks of Brittany are among the oldest on earth. The Armorican Massif emerged from a sea that covered France over 500 million years ago. It formed two giant crystalline backbones that were taller than the Alps. Now time has filed them down to mere molehills less than 400m (1,300ft) high.

A HEART OF STONE Few regions are as geologically uniform as Brittany. Schist covers two-thirds of the land mass, the source of those ubiquitous grey-slate roofs. There are sparkling outcrops of quartz and feldspar, cliffs of blood-red porphyry, lodes of silver, lead and tin, sediments of kaolin and river-silt. Never far beneath the surface, though, is Brittany's true heart of solid granite, the primitive, elemental force that the artist Paul Gauguin admired. Granite influences Brittany's landscapes, its buildings and, perhaps, the rugged

Granite locks on a stretch of the Nantes–Brest Canal

stoicism of its people. But Breton granite takes protean forms: wave-sculpted boulders, mysterious standing stones like marching soldiers, timeworn calvaries blotched with lichen, lace-fretted church spires…

THE BRETON LANDSCAPE Erosion over millennia has reduced Brittany's grand mountains to low stumps. The contours of the granite hills are gently rounded, like pudding basins. The sharper, toothier crests of upland regions such as the Monts d'Arrée and the Montagnes Noires are outcrops of schist or slate. Inland, much of the countryside was once covered in forest, which the ancient Celts called the *argoat* ('land of the woods'). Today the woodlands have been depleted by man for fuel or ship timber, or to make way for usable agricultural land, and have dwindled to small patches.

Moorland or brushwood predominate in uncultivated areas, but most of the region is an undulating plateau of fields divided by countless rivers, hedges, pollarded trees and stone walls. Granite boulders dumped by meltwater in glacial valleys form chaotic rockeries of moss and ferns.

Where the Breton interior lacks visual drama, the jagged coastline amply compensates. Its shore presents a spectacularly varied scene of cliffs, estuaries, beaches, marshes and dunes. Most striking of all are the granite rocks of the north coast, glowing fiery at sunset and worn by the elements into weirdly organic shapes that seem almost alive.

BUILDING IN GRANITE By far the commonest building material in Brittany is granite. The earliest shelters of all were probably the huge rounded boulders that lie tumbled in river gorges, some as big as houses, where remnants of very early prehistoric settlements have been discovered. When tools developed sufficiently to work the hard stone, granite was used through the

Elven, one of Brittany's many granite castles

ages in many types of structure, from the dolmens of the megalith-builders, through the fortresses of the Middle Ages, to today's whitewashed holiday homes. The stone appears in street cobbles and paving slabs, in the earth-covered banks around fields and, perhaps most

memorably, in the churchyards, where gravestones, ossuaries and elaborately carved calvaries all consist of local rock. Breton churches are nearly always granite, too. The few cathedrals built of alien stone make a dramatic impact in Brittany: the jaundiced limestone of St.-Pol-de-Léon or the pale tufa of Nantes startle amid the monochrome grey.

A MULTIFACETED STONE Granite can seem gloomy and dark, lending itself only to squat, crouching buildings and coarse-grained sculpture. But when cut and dressed it takes on a new sparkle. The pink granite of the north coast is the colour of expensive bathrooms and exclusive boutiques. Kersanton stone, used in so many of the region's churches, is the stuff of intricate rood screens, altarpieces and tombs. Malleable when worked, it hardens over time, preserving the mason's chiselled outlines. However, most granite is notoriously stubborn, and ambitious projects such as large churches often took several centuries to complete. Many craftsmen abandoned the laborious task of vaulting in stone and turned instead to wood panelling, often vividly carved or decorated with frescoes.

11

The parish close at Guimiliau

On a map, Brittany's jagged profile looks something like a savage animal snarling at the Atlantic, but in reality it is the sea that snarls, battering its rocks with storms and gales. 'The sea is English by nature…she breaks our ships,' wrote the 19th-century historian Michelet in his Tableau de la France.

A CHANGING SHORE Aeons ago Brittany was one of the few parts of what is now France to lie above the waves, but prehistoric megaliths and fossilized tree trunks discovered below the waterline indicate that sea levels subsequently fell, then rose again. The drowned valleys (*abers*), inland seas and tidal marshes that characterize parts of the coast were created after the last Ice Age. What were once parts of the mainland are now islands and offshore reefs. Twice daily the tides strike deep into Brittany's land mass through its many estuaries. On the Rance they do so with sufficient force to generate 600 million kWh of electricity each year (see page 62).

A WAY OF LIFE Before the Romans arrived, the inhabitants of Brittany were already experienced seafarers. The Gaulish Veneti were intrepid traders, loading their sturdy, leather-sailed boats with cargoes of tin to sell in distant lands. Throughout the centuries that followed, Bretons earned a living from the sea in many different ways. Fishing became a vital source of food and

income for thousands of families. Whale and cod from the northern seas, and tuna and sardines from the south, have all brought prosperity at various periods. Traditional fishing fleets still cast their nets, but increasingly the fishing industry relies more on farming the seas than on hunting them. Oysters, mussels and salmon can be raised more or less predictably now, in captivity. Important subsidiary industries such as fish-canning or processing also depend on the sea. Shore-based livelihoods practised for centuries can still be earned today, including evaporating sea water for salt and gathering seaweed.

In the days of sailing ships and merchant adventurers, Bretons hunted the high seas for more than fish. Many ventured great distances in search of new territory: Jacques Cartier, discoverer of Canada, was one of the most famous Breton explorers. Other seafarers became corsairs (see page 68), the state-registered pirates based in St.-Malo who plagued English, Spanish and Dutch fleets. Even less honourable scavengers were the wreckers of Finistère, who lured shipping on to their deadly reefs with false lights.

French fleets (merchant and naval) have always been manned by a large proportion of recruits from Brittany, and going to sea remains a strong tradition for many. So too is shipbuilding, once a thriving industry in St.-Nazaire, Nantes and Lorient. Breton forests supplied much of the timber for

Inspecting the previous night's catch at Concarneau's criée *(fish auction)*

12

Cap Fréhel's lighthouse guards the Emerald Coast

navigation equipment. The most notable shipwreck in recent decades was that of the oil tanker *Amoco Cadiz,* wrecked off Finistère in 1978. The disaster was remarkable not for the loss of human life but for the hideous effect on the environment. Oil slicks ravaged the beaches, threatening countless seabirds and Brittany's vital tourist industry.

❏ Brittany has several excellent museums dedicated to various aspects of the sea. Among the best are Brest's Océanopolis (see page 99), Douarnenez's Port-Musée (see pages 152–153), Le Guilvinec's Haliotika (see page 159), Concarneau's Musée de la Pêche (see page 149), the Musée des Marais Salants in Batz-sur-Mer (see page 230) and the port museums of St.-Nazaire. Some lighthouses are open to the public. Creac'h on the island of Ouessant has a lighthouse museum (see page 109). One of the museums in the citadel of Port-Louis commemorates Brittany's sophisticated coastal rescue service. ❏

France's early sailing ships' and its famous hempen sailcloth flew from most of Europe's rigging.

COASTAL RESCUE The west Breton coast is studded with lighthouses and warning beacons to head shipping off its treacherous rocks. Despite these precautionary measures, disasters still occur, even with all the assistance of modern

13

Sea-rescue services play a vital role on the Breton coast

Brittany has become ever more industrialized since World War II, but its economic base is obvious to even the most casual observer of its well-tended artichoke fields or pedigree dairy herds. Today over a million Bretons (about one-third) are actively engaged in farming, and over 60 per cent of the land is cultivated.

14

THE MANAGED COUNTRYSIDE

The great natural forests that once covered the *argoat* (Breton interior) have steadily dwindled to coppices and stands of conifers over the centuries. Marshlands submerged by neap tides have been drained and reclaimed as pasture for *pré salé* lambs, whose meat has a distinctive salty flavour (see pages 16–17); unproductive heath has succumbed to the plough. Breton soils are acidic and not naturally very fertile; they need considerable coaxing to produce high yields. Seaweed and *maërl* (estuary mud) are used as fertilizers.

From high vantage points in the Monts d'Arrée or the Montagnes Noires you get a clear impression of

typical Breton farm is still relatively small, and usually family-run. There are no vast prairies or Texan-sized ranches, yet Brittany manages to produce a huge proportion of France's total agricultural output. Ille-et-Vilaine is its top milk producer; Fougères hosts the biggest cattle market in Europe. The region as a whole raises about half of all the pigs and chickens in France and grows the lion's share of its market vegetables. Artichokes, cauliflowers, peas and beans are the main crops, but carrots, onions, salad vegetables and brassicas also figure high on the list. Many of Brittany's cabbages, grown extensively around Lorient, end up as German sauerkraut. Even the

the modern countryside. It is unquestionably man-made, a chequered landscape known as *bocage*, tamed by hedges, tree-lined dikes and banks of earth and stone. There is little true wilderness, nor in most places is it especially picturesque.

THE MARKET GARDEN
Though land units have increased in size, the

Testing the potato crop at Cancale, on Brittany's Emerald Coast

humble potato, once falsely accused of spreading cholera in Brittany, now occupies many fields.

One of the most fertile areas of Brittany is the Ceinture d'Orée (Golden Belt) which runs along the north coast, in particular around

St.-Pol-de-Léon. Fertilized for centuries with seaweed, the alluvial soils are exceptionally productive. A trip through the region close to harvest time reveals a purposeful hum of activity, as laden tractors and trucks roar along the roads taking produce to the marketplaces or the docks at Roscoff. The scale of the operation, and the perfection of these splendid crops, can hardly fail to impress.

About a third of the cultivated land is devoted to cereals and animal fodder. Apples are grown around Fouesnant and the Rance valley, mostly for cider or juice, while Plougastel is famed for its strawberries. The crops on which Brittany once grew rich (flax for linen and sailcloth and buckwheat) no longer figure largely, and vines thrive only in the southeastern corner, near Nantes.

POLITICAL CLOUT These days the vote of the small farmer is crucial to the survival of any French government, and the agricultural lobby influences many political decisions, both in Paris and more significantly in Brussels. Even industrial workers have a keen vested interest in the well-being of the farming community; about a third of the Breton factory workforce is involved in food processing of one sort or another.

As the world's second largest

The artichoke season near Roscoff

Visitors to Brittany should expect to see many tractors around harvest time

exporter of agricultural produce after the US, France pays careful heed to its farming interests, whose antagonism to European Union (EU) quotas and anger at surpluses periodically manifests itself in strikes and violent confrontation. Indeed, the French government's support of the industry is sometimes at the expense of goodwill among its EU neighbours. While Brittany exports its cabbages and crustaceans, it has aggressively resisted low-priced foreign imports. This trend towards protectionism may have far-reaching effects. Will new EU agricultural policies, aimed at regulating production, be accepted?

The range and quality of foodstuffs produced in Brittany indicates its importance to everyday life. There is much to enjoy, particularly seafood and pancakes, a range of charcuterie, *and delicious cakes like* kouign amann— *more readily eaten than pronounced.*

The ubiquitous crêperie

COCKLES AND MUSSELS Breton seafood is predictably superb; Brittany is one of France's foremost fishing regions, and the range available in markets and restaurants is staggering. Visit a *criée* (fish auction), or commercial fish farm for some idea of this marine cornucopia. Those less keen may be unable to look another *moule* in the eye by the end of their trip to Brittany, dreading the prospect of yet another *assiette de fruits de mer.*

Enjoying oysters at Cancale

They are daunting sights, those platefuls of seaweed and crushed ice, piled so precariously with curious sea creatures that extracting any one threatens a deluge. Whatever else you find on your plate there are almost certain to be mussels and oysters, which are prime local products. Winkles, crayfish, clams, crabs and scallops may also put in an appearance.

If you prefer your fish hot, try a traditional Breton *cotriade*, or fish stew. Freshwater species of fish reach the kitchens too, such as *brochet au beurre blanc*, a classic dish of pike in the Nantais white butter sauce. Most Breton of all, though, is lobster, often prepared in a special sauce of tomato, shallots and cognac (*homard à l'armoricaine*). On many menus it appears as *homard à l'américaine*, a misspelling attributed to a mistake made by a Parisian restaurant.

MEAT PRODUCTS Perhaps steak Chateaubriand is the most widely known Breton meat dish. But Brittany is more famous for its dairy produce than its beef. More typical meat products include the *pré salé* (salt meadow) lambs raised on the briny marshes of Ouessant and Mont-St.-Michel, with a characteristic salty flavour. *Gigot à la bretonne* (roast leg of lamb with haricot beans) is a local delicacy. Pork is also produced in great quantities and *charcuterie* takes many forms, especially sausages, black pudding and *andouille*, a sort of pork haggis. Hearty peasant soups and casseroles such as *kig-ha-farz* often contain ham or bacon. Some of France's most succulent chickens come from around Rennes, while the *challan* is a delicious duck from the Nantes region.

PANCAKES Once, pancakes were a staple of the Breton diet, replacing bread in poor homes. You will find *crêperies* everywhere in Brittany, and crêpes are an inexpensive, quick way of satisfying hunger pangs. The variety of fillings offered is legion, and imaginative to the point of eccentricity. Two names are used for them: crêpe and *galette*. Generally, crêpes are made with a batter of wheat flour and usually have sweet fillings, while the more traditional *galettes* are made with the heavier buckwheat flour and are most often savoury. The distinctions between the two are, however, blurred in different parts of Brittany. You can buy them ready made in packets or tins, though they are much nicer warm and fresh. Crêpes

Terrace dining in Rennes

dentelles are paper-thin, lacy pancakes, a delicacy of Quimper.

CAKES AND PUDDINGS Like many Breton dishes, desserts tend to be rich and heavy. One famous local dessert is *far breton*, a solid flan which normally contains prunes or raisins. Others include *kouign amann*, a delicious cake of sugar, butter and almonds, and *galettes de Pont-Aven* (not to be confused with pancakes) are buttery biscuits like shortbread.

❏ A recipe for *far breton*: 125g (1 cup) wheat flour, 125g (0.75 cup) sugar, 4 eggs, 750ml (3.5 cups) milk, 250g (8oz) prunes, 2 tbsp rum, 2 sachets vanilla sugar, pinch of salt. Sift the flour into a basin and add sugar, salt, and vanilla sugar; make a well and add the eggs. Stir to a smooth paste. Heat the milk with the rum and prunes. Pour on to the paste and mix vigorously. Pour this batter into a buttered dish and bake at 240°C/465°F/gas mark 8 for 10 minutes, then at 200°C/390°F/gas mark 6 for 30 minutes, until well browned. Serve warm. ❏

Like all Celtic regions, Brittany is a land of storytellers, legends and folklore. Intense piety and religious fervour often go hand in hand with a belief in fairies, demons and witches that stretches back to pagan times.

18

THE ARTHURIAN MYTH When Celtic settlers arrived in the 6th century AD from Wales and Cornwall they brought with them shadowy tales of the saintly protector-king who fought the invading tribes of Saxons. The legends of Arthur became established in the mysterious forests of Brittany, where they still live on today. The forest of Paimpont (see pages 216–217) is identified as the

Detail of a painting showing a scene from the opera Tristan and Isolde

Brocéliande of the ancient stories, where the Knights of the Round Table began their Quest for the Holy Grail, and where the great wizard Merlin was ensnared by Viviane, Lady of the Lake. Other legends of Brocéliande tell of the magic Fontaine de Barenton, whose water splashed on a nearby stone and summoned storms and a fierce knight in black armour, or of the Val sans Retour, where Morgan le Fay imprisoned faithless lovers. Today these vivid associations are by no means discouraged by the Breton tourist industry.

TRISTAN AND ISOLDE The most famous version of the Tristan legend filters through Wagnerian opera. Tristan, prince of Lyonesse, was sent to Ireland by his uncle, King Mark of Cornouaille, to fetch Mark's betrothed princess, Isolde. On their return, Tristan and Isolde accidentally drank a magic love potion intended for Mark and Isolde on their wedding night, and the inevitable happened. The star-crossed lovers fled from Mark's wrath to a friendly kinsman, the Duke of Hoel, where (depending on which particular version you follow) they either lived happily ever after or died tragically of broken hearts.

THE LOST CITY OF YS This is one of Brittany's most enduring legends, a subject beloved by 19th-century Romantic painters. In the 6th century King Gradlon ruled Brittany from Ys, a beautiful island city in the bay of Douarnenez. This was protected from the sea by sluicegates, which only the king could unlock. The king's daughter, Dahut, fell in love with a handsome young man (the Devil in disguise), who persuaded her to steal the keys one night. The Devil unlocked the gates at high tide and

Merlin's spell haunts the Fontaine de Barenton

□ Elves known as *korred* are the equivalent of the 'little people' of other Celtic traditions. They are hunchbacked dancers and magicians less than a metre (3ft) high, with cats' claws for hands and goats' hooves for feet. Folklore declares they brought the standing stones to Brittany on their backs, and they help mortals by sharpening knives or lending oxen. Unfortunately, today's tourists have driven them all away! □

story tells of the blacksmith in Ploumilliau who spent all night sharpening Ankou's scythe in an effort to placate him, instead of attending midnight mass. Next day he discovered that he, too, was destined for Ankou's cart. On dark nights crossing lonely moors, many a Breton peasant has been horrified by the sound of rumbling wheels.

the city began to flood. Gradlon woke in the nick of time, raised the alarm, mounted his horse and fled across the causeway, with Dahut clinging behind. But the waves were swift, and the horse grew weary of the extra load. A heavenly voice commanded Gradlon to drop his wicked daughter in the sea and immediately the waves subsided, allowing the inhabitants to escape to the mainland. But Ys, like Atlantis, vanished for ever. Gradlon set up a new court in Quimper, while Dahut turned into a mermaid and lured many sailors to their doom.

ANKOU, DEATH'S COACHMAN
Ankou is the Breton incarnation of death, a skeletal figure with a scythe depicted on tombs, charnel-houses and calvaries throughout the region. He drives a creaking cart piled high with bodies and spares no one. One

Ankou reaps the harvest of souls in Ploumilliau church

Few regions of France are as overtly pious as Brittany and Mass is well attended in rural communities. Breton churches and enclos paroissiaux (parish closes) are well cared for, and the shrines of the region's seven thousand, seven hundred, seven score and seven saints are revered.

BRETON SAINTS Brittany's many saints appear sculpted in countless churches or wayside shrines, in local legends and in hundreds of place-names. Some are undoubtedly apocryphal, and a large proportion have never been formally recognized by the Church. Miraculous or super-natural events were associated with them, and many were attributed specific healing or protective powers against the ills of everyday life. The Seven Healing Saints celebrated at the Chapelle Notre-Dame-du-Haut near Moncontour (see page 213) are typical examples. Some saints looked after animals, such as St. Golgan (sick horses), St. Cornély and St. Herbot (guardians of horned cattle). Others warded off lightning (St. Barbe) or brought rain (St. Vio).

Many Breton saints date back to the early wave of Celtic settlers fleeing Anglo-Saxon invaders in Britain during the 5th and 6th centuries. Evangelist monks then appeared in

St. Yves, patron saint of lawyers, ~~lies~~ buried in Tréguier

great numbers on Breton shores. The Seven Founding Saints set up the first seven dioceses of Brittany: Samson (Dol), Maclow (St.-Malo), Brieuc (St.-Brieuc), Tugdual (Tréguier), Paul the Aurelian (St.-Pol), Corentin (Quimper) and Patern (Vannes).

ST. ANNE The cult of St. Anne began to be venerated in western Europe around the time of the crusades. Anne, mother of the Virgin Mary, was enthusiastically adopted as a patron and spiritual guardian of Brittany. She was (of course) a Breton, who is said to have journeyed to Judea to give birth to Mary, then came back to her native land, where Jesus and Peter visited her. Her name embraces aeons of Breton tradition; she is hazily identified with the all-powerful Celtic deity Ana, and also with the beloved Duchess Anne, an icon of Breton independence (see pages 36–37). Two famous *pardons* celebrate her, in Ste.-Anne-la-Palud and in Ste.-Anne-d'Auray (the largest and most revered shrine in Brittany).

ST. PAUL THE AURELIAN St. Paul travelled with St. Samson to Brittany in the 6th century, and is one of the most famous of the Seven Founding Saints. His bishopric was St.-Pol-de-Léon, where his relics are still kept in the cathedral. His final island refuge was Batz near Roscoff, where he captured a troublesome dragon

St. Anne is revered in many parts of Brittany

with his stole and threw it into the sea. He died on Batz at the great age of 104.

ST. YVES Yves Helori (1253–1303) was born at Minihy-Tréguier. The patron saint of lawyers, Yves combined religious duties with his work as a magistrate and advocate in Tréguier, and was famously incorruptible in an age when most lawyers took bribes. He was a champion of the poor, and is often depicted standing between a well-dressed client and a man in rags, an image which relates to the most famous story about him: A rich man sued a beggar for loitering by his kitchen door and 'stealing' his cooking smells. St. Yves heard the evidence, declared the rich man had won his case, and awarded him appropriate damages: the sound of a coin rattling in a tin. Yves led an ascetic life and died at the age of 49. He is buried in Tréguier cathedral.

❏ A medieval joke relates how St. Yves died and arrived at heaven's gates at the same time as a group of nuns. St. Peter said to the nuns, 'You'll have to wait a while; we're crammed with nuns already.' Then he turned to St. Yves, and asked who he was. 'A lawyer, sir,' replied St. Yves. 'Then come straight in,' said St. Peter. 'You're the first one we've had.' ❏

Though Brittany is a fierce defender of Celtic traditions, comparatively few people still use Breton as their everyday language. Music, however, is thriving, and new interpretations of the old folk tunes produce a widespread awareness of Breton culture.

22

THE LIVING LANGUAGE Breton belongs to the so-called Brythonic group of Celtic languages, closely related to Welsh and Cornish in the UK. Some words have very similar counterparts in Welsh—*menez/ mynydd* (mountain), *yenez/ynys* (island), and so on. Some prefixes to place-names, such as *'pen'* or *'lan,'* are the same. The Breton hymn *Bro Goz Ma Tadon* translates exactly into the Welsh national anthem, *Hen Wlad fy Nhadau* ('Land of My Fathers'), and is even sung to the same tune. Rumours that the Bretons and the Welsh can understand each other are, however, greatly exaggerated, though canny Breton onion-sellers taking the boat from Roscoff may have looked up a few words of Welsh before reaching Wales, the better to sell their wares.

There are four distinct dialects in Brittany, spoken in Côtes-d'Armor, North Finistère, Cornouaille and the Morbihan. Like other Celtic languages, Breton has been subjected to great changes of attitude in the last couple of centuries. After Brittany officially became part of France, the Paris-based government attempted

Breton mingles with French on many signposts in Brittany

The Breton flag (Gwen ha Du, meaning 'White and Black') was designed in 1923 by the architect Morvan Marchal

to suppress Breton language and culture, which it perceived (sometimes accurately) as a subversive influence. Since the inauguration of the Institut Culturel de Bretagne in 1981, which was set up to safeguard all aspects of Breton culture, the language has experienced a slight revival. It is now an optional subject at schools and universities, heard on radio and television, and published in books and

ROC - TREVEZEL
Altitude : 364 m,62

magazines. Despite this, many would say that the native language is in decline, and that efforts to revive it in the face of a continual onslaught from French-speaking mass media are artificial. About 600,000 people still speak Breton, mostly the elderly in Trégor and Finistère (Basse Bretagne), or separatists. Eastern Brittany (Haute Bretagne) has always allied itself more closely with French culture for obvious geographic reasons.

MUSIC AND DANCE Music is a strong social bond in Brittany. The Celts brought with them their bardic traditions of singing and storytelling. Long songs or poems (*lais*) were accompanied by musical instruments, often harps. Oral traditions went through a revival during the 18th century, and collections of folksongs began to be published.

Today's musicians continue this trend, encouraged by the spread of Celtic festivals and a renewed tourist interest in folk music. Music is now

Piping Celtic themes at a local festival

Brittany's most vigorous and versatile transmitter of Celtic culture, transcending the language barrier. You can see typical Breton instruments such as the *bombarde* (oboe), the *biniou* (bagpipes) or the *vielle* (hurdy-gurdy) in many museums, but try to hear them being played. All through the summer, concerts and festivals offer an opportunity to hear or even take part in Breton musical events (see page 28).

BRETON SEPARATISM Nationalist groups have existed in Brittany ever since the Act of Union lumped it with France in 1532. So far, luckily, terrorism has not played a great part in Breton politics (though the occasional statue has been blown up and, in 1977, the mirrors of Versailles were smashed by a Breton activist), but there are extreme voices, committed to more than putting a BZH (*Breizh* or Brittany) sticker on their cars. Some disaffected groups overtly ally themselves with terrorist organizations such as the IRA or the violent Basque separatists ETA.

23

The Celtic temperament adores competitive activities, and trials of strength and team games have an enthusiastic following. For visitors, too, Brittany offers endless opportunities to enjoy active outdoor pursuits.

24

BRETON GAMES The local form of wrestling (known as *ar gouren* in Breton) can be seen at a number of summer festivals, such as the Fête de Locmaria at Belle-Isle-en-Terre. Breton wrestling is a bit like oriental judo. The wrestlers wear a voluminous garb of long shorts and loose shirts, and exchange three smacking ritual kisses before commencing battle. Other trials of strength are similar to those that can be seen at the Scottish Highland Games or in Spain's Basque country: tug-of-war, lifting a heavy stone, caber-tossing or discus-throwing. *Tire-baton* is a typical Breton sport, where the contestants attempt to lift each other with a pole. Brittany also has its own forms of those other popular Celtic team games, hockey and rugby. Breton sports are mostly conducted in a spirit of good humour and fun today, but in earlier times post-*pardon* games could degenerate into deadly interparish rivalries resulting in drunken brawls and broken heads.

TOURIST ACTIVITIES Brittany's changeable climate has always encouraged a fair degree of seaside activity rather than torpid sunbathing. Dinard's Victorian visitors used to amuse themselves by playing croquet on the sands. Today, however, the range of activities available to holidaymakers is much more extensive, with specialist sports such as hang-gliding, jet-skiing, windsurfing and sand-yachting, as well as the more traditional resort pastimes of golf, riding, bicycling and tennis.

Watersports All types naturally proliferate in the region's coastal areas, though Brittany's inland waterways and lakes also provide many opportunities to canoe, cruise, sail and fish. Windsurfing (*planche à voile*) is especially popular along the south coast, though experts head for the Plage de la Torche on the Penmarc'h peninsula. The Golfe du Morbihan offers excellent scuba-diving. Quiberon is one of Brittany's best sailing bases, and the clear waters of the Îles de Glénan are a marvellous place to practise sailing or diving.

Angling There are about 9,200km (5,500miles) of shoreline or river bank in Brittany, offering sea, river or lake angling; there is even underwater

Checking the score at palet. *Who won that round?*

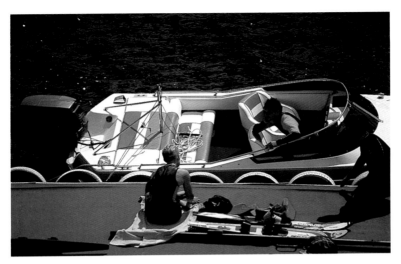

Brittany's inland waterways offer an endless source of relaxation

spear fishing off shore. Ask at the local tourist office about regulations on permits and the like. Alternatively, you can join in the simple pleasure enjoyed by countless Breton families of *pêche à pied* (searching for shellfish in rockpools at low tide). All the equipment you will need (spades, rakes, nets or buckets) should be available locally.

Golf Brittany now has more than 30 golf courses, many on the coast in lovely scenery. Dinard is the oldest and most fashionable, but golf is a more sociable, family-oriented game in France than in many other countries, and course etiquette is generally unstuffy, though fees can be quite high.

Bicycling Each *département* has a local *Comité Départemental de Cyclotourisme* which dispenses information and organizes cycling events, and in most towns you can rent a

bicycle from a cycle shop or the railway station for a day's outing.

Riding Brittany has many *centres équestres*, and organized riding holidays (by yourself or in a group with a guide) are easily arranged. Some of these treks include overnight accommodation. Like canal cruising, riding through Brittany adds a whole new dimension to the countryside. If driving seems too pressurized you can opt for lower levels of horsepower in a *roulotte*, Brittany's version of a Romany caravan.

❏ In the evenings in quiet town squares you often see a sight familiar to visitors to all parts of France—all-male gatherings of local elders playing what looks like *boules* or *pétanque*. In Brittany, however, flat discs like quoits are thrown at the target instead of a ball. This Breton game is known as *palet*. ❏

The Celtic love of dressing up and making merry shows through in Brittany's festivals, which provide a continual backdrop of pageantry to any summer visit. Originally the festivals were religious events, but now they reflect many aspects of local culture.

PARDONS The *pardon* is one of the most distinctive aspects of Breton life, and virtually every parish holds one at some time during the year (some places have several). The word *pardon* implies forgiveness of sins, which was the purpose of the original medieval ritual. The inspiration for local *pardons* is still a fervent communal expression of spiritual contrition, followed up in a lighter vein by feasting and fun. Increasingly, *pardons* are used as occasions to cement Breton solidarity with some sort of festival or fair, and inevitably more than half an eye is cocked towards the tourist trade and an associated fresh influx of revenue. The *pardons* also present an opportunity to wear those elaborate costumes now stuck in the wardrobe for special occasions.

In some *pardons* darker echoes of the ancient Celtic gods can be heard. At Plougastel's midsummer festival young children are passed over the flames of a bonfire, a tradition that harks back to rituals of human sacrifice. Some Christian *pardons* are held at the same times of year as older pagan festivals (harvests, or the summer and winter solstice, for example), and the forms of worship reflect the Celtic belief that gods or saints returned to earth at certain auspicious seasons.

FOLKLORE FESTIVALS After the solemn hymns and long religious services, *pardons* generally take on a much more cheerful tone. Locals in bright costumes parade embroidered banners and statues of their patron saint through the streets, while stall-holders sell all kinds of crafts, souvenirs, crêpes and cider. Afterwards there may be dancing and traditional music, or a sports competition featuring typical 'trials of strength' such as Breton wrestling or a tug-of-war.

Many secular folk festivals have appeared in the past century. Largest of all is Quimper's Festival de Cornouaille, a massive gathering of Celtic artists, musicians and dancers. This is one of the best places to see regional costumes and enjoy Breton music. Rennes holds its Tombées de la Nuit in July, another huge celebration of all things Breton, with modern rock music thrown in. Lorient's Festival Interceltique is a further

Stepping out in style at one of Cornouaille's popular festivals

The male version of the coiffe

chance for Celtic cousins to join hands and dance a gavotte to the harp, the *bombarde* and the *biniou*. Dinan's medieval Fête des Remparts or Pont-Aven's Fête des Fleurs d'Ajoncs (Gorse-flower Festival) have been immensely popular in recent years. Châteauneuf-du-Faou and Guingamp both hold annual festivals of traditional dancing.

Several festivals have charitable origins, such as Concarneau's Fête des Filets Bleus (Blue Nets Festival) that began as a fundraising exercise for the distressed families of redundant sardine fishermen. Others celebrate local livelihoods: Fouesnant's Fête des Pommiers (Apple-tree Festival) honours its cider industry, and Paimpol remembers its Icelandic fishermen in a Fête des Terre-Neuvas et des Islandais. Blessings of the Sea ceremonies (for example, at Carantec or Douarnenez) propitiate the gods of the deep.

Many Breton communities now rely heavily on tourist revenue and promote colourful spectacles or *fest-noz* (night festivals) as a way of attracting summer visitors. Some of the more famous annual events are a great draw, and accommodation fills up fast If you are planning to visit a particular town in high season, check its diary for crowd-pulling junkets, and book well ahead.

The calendar of events overleaf gives a selection of the larger festivals and *pardons*. Any tourist office can provide advice about events happening locally, though they may be vague about those taking place farther afield. The French Government Tourist Office website (www.franceguide.com) and the websites of any of Brittany's Comité Départemental du Tourisme have more comprehensive details about festivals and events.

Pont-l'Abbé is one of the best places to see traditional costumes

27

Calendar of events Most of Brittany's cultural events and festivals are geared to the short tourist season. Little happens between November and April. Here is a small selection.

Some of the following events are moveable feasts and vary from year to year, so if there is one you particularly wish to see, check precise dates with the local tourist office.

May
Quintin *Pardon*
Tréguier *Pardon* de St. Yves

June
Le Faouët *Pardon* de Ste. Barbe
Nantes Quinzaine Celtique
St.-Brieuc Art Rock Festival

July
Binic Fête de la Morue
Dinan Fête des Remparts (every two even-numbered years)

Traditional Breton costumes are worn with pride on festival days

Fouesnant Fête des Pommiers
Lamballe Festival Folklorique des Ajoncs d'Or
Locronan Petite (annual) or Grande Troménie (every sixth year, next one takes place in 2007)
Morlaix Les Mercredis de Morlaix
Nantes Festival International d'Été
Paimpol Fête des Terre-Neuvas et des Islandais
Pont-l'Abbé Fête des Brodeuses (embroidery festival)
Quimper Festival de Cornouaille
Redon Fête de la Batellerie (canals festival), Festival de l'Abbaye
Rennes Les Tombées de la Nuit
Ste.-Anne-d'Auray *Grand Pardon*
St.-Malo Tall Ships Race

August
Carantec Blessing of the Sea
Carnac Grande Fête des Menhirs
Châteauneuf-du-Faou Festival International de Danses et Traditions Populaires
Concarneau Fête des Filets Bleus
Erquy Festival de la Mer
Fédrun Fête de la Brière
Fougères Festival du Livre Vivant (historical pageant)
Guingamp Festival de la Danse Bretonne
Lorient Festival Interceltique
Perros-Guirec Fête des Hortensias (hydrangeas)
Plomodiern Fête du Menez-Hom
Pont-Aven Fête des Fleurs d'Ajoncs (gorse flowers)
St.-Briac-sur-Mer Fête des Mouettes (seagulls)
Ste.-Anne-la-Palud *Pardon*
Cap Sizun Fête des Bruyères (heather)
Vannes Grandes Fêtes d'Arvor

September
Camaret Blessing of the Sea
Le Folgoët *Grand Pardon*
Josselin *Pardon*
Hennebont *Pardon*
Penhors *Pardon*
Tronoën Notre-Dame de Tronoën *Pardon*

Brittany Was

Very little is known about the enigmatic people who raised those standing stones around Carnac over 6,000 years ago. After wrestling with all the theories it is tempting to assume that the alignments are an elaborate Stone Age joke, constructed simply to baffle posterity.

EARLIEST INHABITANTS Scarcely anything remains of any civilization before the megalith-builders. The earliest signs of human settlement in Brittany date from the Old Stone Age (about 8000BC, well before the megalithic period). Brittany seems to have been more sparsely populated at this stage than other more fertile

30

Reconstructed necropolis at St.-Guénolé's Musée de la Préhistoire

regions of France, perhaps because there were so few caves to provide natural shelters (Brittany has virtually no limestone). What communities there were seem generally to have lived on or near the coast, subsisting on a monotonous diet of shellfish eked out with scraps of meat from captured game. A few signs of ritual graves and domestic hearths have been unearthed from the mesolithic or Middle Stone Age period (about 6000–3500BC), mostly in Morbihan and Cornouaille.

SETTLING DOWN As time went on, the hand-to-mouth existence of these early peoples became more ordered and settled. The climate grew colder, and the lack of natural caves may have encouraged them to create their own shelters by piling up stones and earth. Gradually, the possibilities of building more complex structures opened up. When the climate grew more favourable again, farming techniques were developed. Wild plants were cultivated and improved, including wheat, barley, lentils and a primitive kind of apple.

ARCHITECTS IN STONE Monuments similar to those found in Brittany can be found all over the world, dating from widely differing periods. Not all, even within Brittany, can clearly be related to each other, nor do they all have a common purpose. The earliest Breton megaliths can be identified with reasonable certainty as burial places. These are dolmens (literally 'table stones'), or passage graves. They usually consist of flattish slabs of rock assembled into a roofed chamber with an entrance at

❑ If you visit any of Brittany's museums you will almost certainly see dozens of metal axe heads. These smooth, greenish artefacts are so beautifully shaped that it is easy to suspect some modern factory is churning them out. Weapons of smelted metal were once as precious as jewels. Nearly 400 Bronze Age hoards have been unearthed all over Brittany, containing about 20,000 axes made of 10 tonnes of bronze. ❑

Standing stones, Carnac

one side. Some are enclosed in mounds of earth and stone (cairns).

A second group of similar but more extended monuments are called gallery graves (*allées couvertes*). The third and most mysterious type of all are the menhirs, or standing stones, in some places solitary, elsewhere arranged in rows, or *alignements*. These are thought to date from between 4500 and 1800BC, the neolithic (New Stone Age) period. By far the most impressive and numerous of these *alignements* stand near Carnac (see pages 184–185).

At some time during the Bronze Age (1800–600BC), new settlers appeared who were known as the Bell-Beaker

people because of their style of pottery. Brittany's most recent megalithic monuments date from this period, by which time both tools and skills had developed considerably. Ornate gold jewellery, shaped axe heads and decorated pottery reveal great artistry and craftsmanship, and indicate a knowledge of metalworking.

THEORIES Some historians believe the stone lines were masterminded by a caste of priest-kings in order to determine the dates for sowing and harvesting crops from the movements of the stars. Although it is known that the stones were used by later cultures for ritual purposes, no current theory about their original function is entirely convincing.

Alignement at Cojoux

The first wave of Celtic peoples arrived in Brittany during the Iron Age, calling their new home Armor or 'The Land by the Sea.' After the Romans left, the Celts returned in the 5th and 6th centuries AD, this time from Britain.

THE EARLY CELTS It seems likely that the new arrivals merged gradually with the previous inhabitants rather than conquering and supplanting them. The Bronze Age dragged on late in Brittany, and full 'Celticization' of the population did not take place until around 500BC. The Celts were skilled metalworkers and potters. They built hill forts surrounded by earthworks to protect themselves from interlopers, and barrows to bury their dead. Some were farmers and stock-breeders, while others were adventurous seafarers who traded Armor's mineral wealth as far as the Mediterranean.

The Celts were a warlike people, and their military exploits were often ill-advised. After they dared to attack Rome in 387BC, the Romans resolved to quell them. The task was made easier by the Celts' lack of any sense of political nationhood. They were essentially a tribal people who allied themselves around strong, individual leaders but frequently fought among themselves. Thus divided, they fell. The Romans steadily picked them off all over Europe using a subtle mixture of diplomacy and military action.

By the time Julius Caesar launched his Gallic Wars in 58BC, Brittany (or Armorica, as the Romans called this outpost of Gaul) was inhabited by five identifiable Celtic tribes. The powerful Veneti, who spearheaded the resistance movement against the Roman invasion, inhabited the Morbihan area. Their epic sea battle against Caesar's fleet marks the turning point of Roman supremacy in Gaul.

Looking through moss-covered rocks of the Gouffre to the Argent River flowing below at Huelgoat, part of the Armorique Regional Park

32

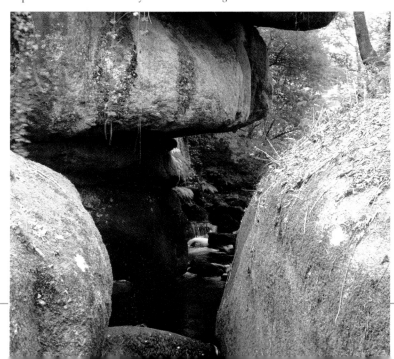

THE BATTLE OF THE VENETI By 56BC one of the few remaining pockets of Gaul yet unconquered was Armor, a wild and infertile but potentially rich metal-producing region. Caesar attempted bloodless infiltration by taking Armorican hostages. Most tribes acquiesced, but the proud Veneti seized Roman envoys in reprisal. Caesar determined to teach them a lesson. The Veneti were a seafaring race who controlled the tin mines and the lucrative Atlantic trade. Their sturdy sailing ships were designed for rough seas and heavy cargoes, and numerically and structurally they far outstripped the slow, oar-propelled Roman galleys. However, a period of dead calm left the Veneti's sailing ships helpless, while the lighter Roman craft rowed towards their bows, hurled grapnels at the rigging and pulled down their sails. Thus immobilized, the Veneti were soon captured.

The battle took place somewhere off the Rhuys peninsula in the Golfe du Morbihan, and was allegedly watched by Caesar himself from a nearby hill. Caesar was not a magnanimous victor; the Veneti were ruthlessly massacred, mutilated or sold into slavery.

Gaius Julius Caesar (100–44BC), Roman general and statesman

The 4th-century BC Celtic Kermaria Stone, found just north of Pont-l'Abbé, Finistère

ROMAN BRITTANY The Romans left no great reminders of their existence in Armorica. They improved the roads and replaced the camps of the old Celtic tribes with stoutly walled cities (Rennes, Vannes and Nantes), but their purpose in occupying Armorica was more to take from it than to add. There are no aqueducts or amphitheatres to admire in Brittany, and evidence of the Gallo-Roman period is mostly confined to museums. Rennes' Musée de Bretagne (see page 221) has a good Roman section; so too does Corseul's town hall museum, near Dinan (see page 50).

THE FALL OF THE EMPIRE Roman supremacy in Gaul and neighbouring Britain brought a peace that lasted until the 5th century AD, when the legions were hurriedly recalled to defend Rome from barbarian hordes. Thus unprotected, Great Britain was subjected to Viking raids and invasions by Angles and Saxons, who steadily drove the indigenous Celts westwards to Wales and Cornwall, whence they set sail for Armorica and their long-lost Celtic cousins. Many of their leaders became the saints of the new Celtic dawn. They renamed Armorica after their old homeland: Brittany (Little Britain).

33

The old gods were supplanted by Christianity after the arrival of the British Celts, who also brought their language (unadulterated by the Low Latin which later turned into French) and their Arthurian myths. Under continual threat of invasion, the disparate Celtic groups were gradually forged into a nation.

34

FRANKS AND NORSEMEN In AD799 the petty kingdoms of Brittany were easily subjugated by the Franks and placed under a governor, Nominoë, a Breton noble and a protégé of Charlemagne. At Redon in AD845, Nominoë expelled the Franks and made Brittany an independent state under his ducal authority. Nominoë's son and heir, Erispoë, took the title of King of Brittany.

Another heroic leader, Alain Barbe-Torte (Crookbeard), repelled the Norse invasions of the 10th century and became the last Breton king. He took measures to strengthen Brittany's defences against invasion, and built many fortresses. After Barbe-Torte's death, dissent among the nobles plunged Brittany into a long period of fighting and confusion.

THE WAR OF SUCCESSION When Duke Jean III (1312–1341) died childless, the succession for the Duchy of Brittany was contested by his half-brother, Jean de Montfort, and his niece, Jeanne de Penthièvre, wife of Charles de Blois, the French king's nephew. The English under Edward III supported Jean de Montfort, while the French allied themselves with Charles de Blois and his wife. The confusing struggle lasted 24 years, complicated by the wider issues of the Hundred Years War. One of the most memorable incidents of the long campaign was the Battle of the Thirty in 1351, a chivalric fight between 30 knights from each side near Josselin (see panel on page 188). The French side won this epic tournament, but not the war. The Montforts eventually claimed victory when Charles de Blois was killed at the Battle of Auray in 1364. Jean IV (son of Jean de Montfort) succeeded to a much impoverished duchy.

BERTRAND DU GUESCLIN (1320–1380) This great medieval warrior was born of minor nobility near Dinan, the eldest of ten children. He came of age, conveniently for a military man, just as the Hundred Years War began. Bertrand's interests were thoroughly active: hunting, hawking and fighting. He detested academic pursuits and remained illiterate all his life. Apparently he was so ugly and boorishly

Jean de Montfort, head of a new dynasty

aggressive that his parents disowned him when he was young. He became the leader of a lawless peasant gang, and thus honed his fighting skills. At a tournament to celebrate the marriage of Jeanne de Penthièvre and Charles de Blois in 1338, Bertrand appeared in disguise and acquitted himself so well in the lists that when his identity was revealed his father was instantly reconciled with him.

Du Guesclin seized the chance of military adventure during the War of Succession, when he backed Charles de Blois and tormented the English supporters of the Montforts. When he was captured after the Battle of Auray, the French ransomed him for a massive 100,000 crowns. After many more adventures in Spain and elsewhere, mostly fighting the English, Du Guesclin became Constable of France in 1370. He died of fever, still on active service, in the Massif Central. Du Guesclin wanted

Du Guesclin rides roughshod over Dinan's main square

Bertrand du Guesclin, hero of the Hundred Years War

to be buried in his native Dinan, but the journey was long and the summer hot, and bit by bit the great warrior's decomposing corpse was interred en route: entrails at le Puy, flesh at Montferrand, and his skeleton at St.-Denis. Finally, his heart reached Dinan, where it lies in the church of St.-Sauveur (see page 52).

❏ Du Guesclin was immensely courageous, and knew all the 'rules' of medieval chivalry. But he didn't always play by them; he fought to win. He was a master of cunning guerrilla tactics, and developed the use of gunpowder and new methods of siege warfare. His soldiers were taught to fight on foot, hand to hand, using ambushes and subterfuge. ❏

35

After the exhausting struggles of medieval times, the Duchy of Brittany entered its most glorious phase under the House of Montfort (1364–1532). But the seeds of Brittany's downfall lay dormant in its greatness, which represented a threat to French supremacy.

THE MONTFORT RECOVERY Things soon picked up under the firm Montfort leadership and trading possibilities blossomed, bringing a new wave of prosperity to Brittany. Salt and textiles were the economy's mainstays—linen and sailcloth were particularly important commodities. Art and architecture also flourished, and many of Brittany's most memorable Gothic cathedrals and castles date from this period.

36

The Montfort dukes reinforced their independence from France with a mighty chain of fortresses along the Breton Marches. By the end of the 15th century the strength of the Breton duchy was beginning to alarm the French monarchy, and the newly wealthy province looked an increasingly attractive prize. Duke François II, sensing which way the wind blew, sought allies abroad, and entered into a coalition against the powerful Anne de Beaujeu, then Regent of France on behalf of the young Charles VIII. Anne invaded Brittany, and François II was defeated at the Battle of St.-Aubin-du-Cormier in 1488. He was forced to sign a treaty and died (of shame, it is said) just two weeks later.

ANNE DE BRETAGNE (1477–1514)
François II was succeeded by his daughter, Anne, who became Brittany's best-loved heroine but its last duchess. Anne lived only to the age of 37, but her dynastic marriages and astute personality had a huge influence on Brittany's destiny. When she entered the political arena she was very young. One of the terms of the treaty her father had signed after his defeat was that the French king should choose Anne's future husband. Even at the tender age of 12 she had already been

Though not physically prepossessing, Charles VIII won Anne's heart

betrothed by proxy twice for political reasons: once to the English Prince of Wales (King Edward IV's successor), then to a Habsburg prince, heir to the Holy Roman Empire. Both these powerful alliances represented a threat to French interests. Although pledged to another, Charles VIII of France broke off his engagement and made a determined play for Anne. He captured Nantes, besieged Rennes and then proposed. The spirited Anne was in no mood to be browbeaten into marriage, but the pleas of her starving people swayed her and she finally agreed to meet Charles. Amazingly, the two got on well, and Anne soon became not simply Duchess of Brittany but also Queen of France. Brittany remained independent, but inevitably the bonds with France grew tighter.

Anne is described as small and frail, with a limp. Though not especially pretty, she was charming and intelligent, and very determined.

Charles was neither physically nor mentally prepossessing, but they seem to have been genuinely fond of each other. No heir survived the marriage; they watched all four of their children die in infancy, which caused them both enormous grief.

After seven years, Charles died of an accidental blow to the head. A clause in the terms of their alliance stated that Anne should marry Charles's successor in the event of his death, and this she duly did. Louis XII hastily extracted an annulment from his first marriage and married Anne. Again, she made the best of her arranged match and lived on good terms with her kindly but ailing husband, who treated her with great affection. Anne devoted herself tirelessly to the administration of Brittany and attempted to ensure its future independence. She toured the province and endowed it with great wealth. Once again, her desire for a healthy male heir for the duchy was thwarted; of her four later children, only two daughters survived. When Anne died in 1514, exhausted by her fruitless confinements, the whole of Brittany mourned.

Anne in characteristically devout pose, surrounded by patron saints

Despite Anne de Bretagne's endeavours, Brittany was irrevocably absorbed into the French kingdom when her daughter, Claude, married François d'Angoulême, the future king of France. The rights and privileges that Anne had fought so hard to retain were subsequently ignored and dishonoured.

UNION WITH FRANCE The Treaty of Vannes in 1532 proclaimed the 'perpetual union of the Country and Duchy of Brittany with the Kingdom and Crown of France.' In theory, Brittany was still permitted to control taxes and maintain its own army. In practice, however, its destiny now lay in French hands. The title of Duke of Brittany became obsolete, and the province was ruled by an appointed governor. Brittany's interests were represented by the *états*, a legislative parliamentary assembly based first at Nantes, then later at Rennes. Meanwhile, the region's assets and resources were stripped and its autonomy eroded. Many Breton citizens developed a lasting sense of grievance against central government.

BRITTANY IN THE 16TH CENTURY
The new era of union began auspiciously enough for Brittany. The Breton explorer Jacques Cartier dis-covered Canada for the French Crown just two years later, in 1534; St.-Malo, Nantes and Lorient grew enormously rich from seaborne trade and privateering; and architecture flourished with a profusion of elegant castles and country mansions. Popular religious art also reached great heights and many parish closes were constructed during this period (see pages 136–137). Later in the 16th century, however, the Wars of Religion caused terrible hardship and disruption in some parts of France. Brittany was not seriously affected because very few of its population

Jacques Cartier meeting the native people of Canada (top)
Jacques Cartier (left) added Canada to France's colonial possessions

Cardinal Richelieu had a marked influence on Brittany's destiny

were Protestants, but the Breton *Ligue* (a band of fanatical Catholics) implicated Brittany in various political plots. One of these *Ligueurs* was the cruel bandit La Fontenelle, who ravaged the Penmarc'h peninsula (see panel on page 153). The Edict of Nantes put a temporary end to religious strife by granting Protestant Huguenots civil rights. It was signed by Henri IV in 1598 at Nantes castle, where he is alleged to have exclaimed in amazement at the Duchess Anne's mighty fortress: 'God's teeth, they are no small beer, these Dukes of Brittany!'

THE *ANCIEN RÉGIME* In 1610 the accession of Louis XIII (1610–1643) ushered in a new era. He appointed as Governor of Brittany Cardinal Richelieu, who lost no time in making his mark on the province. Fortifications were dismantled at Richelieu's behest to discourage any insurrection. France's imperial ambitions dictated a massive upgrading of its naval defences, and the port of Brest underwent a startling transformation after 1636 when work began on the dockyards. Port-Louis on the south coast also became an important naval stronghold, though the first India Company founded by Richelieu failed. The Breton landscape began to

change too. Huge quantities of timber were felled for the French fleet of sailing ships and the great forests of the *argoat* dwindled. Some trees reappeared, however, for it was during this period that the cider apple was imported to Brittany from neighbouring Normandy, changing its drinking habits for ever. The vines that once struggled in Brittany's damp climate were confined to the region around Nantes and the Loire Valley (on the spurious grounds that the Bretons were habitual drunkards).

In 1643 Louis XIII died, a year after Richelieu, and was succeeded by the redoubtable Sun King, Louis XIV, then only four years old. After a period of regency under his Sicilian mentor, Mazarin, Louis XIV decided at the age of 23 that he preferred absolute power. He appointed his finance minister, Colbert, Governor of Brittany, and once again the province was exploited. So lavish were the king's tastes that new sources of revenue were constantly sought. Besides continuing Richelieu's plan of building up the French fleet, Colbert had to find finance for palaces, colonial adventures and foreign wars.

Brittany provided a convenient cashbox for Louis XIV's extravagance, but not a docile one. Smouldering resentment erupted into violent protest against unjust and draconian taxation. The scene was set for wide scale revolt.

THE BONNETS ROUGES One of Colbert's first attempts to balance the Sun King's budget resulted in the so-called 'Stamped Paper Revolt'. Colbert decreed in 1675 that to be legally valid all documents must be recorded on special stamped paper. There was, of course, a stiff duty on the stamps, and payments filled the royal coffers. Tobacco and pewter, other commodities dear to the Breton

Louis XIV, the Sun King, reigned from 1643 to 1715

heart, were also heavily taxed, despite an 'amnesty' Brittany had obtained at a massive cost of 2 million *livres* absolving it from further increases in taxation. Riots broke out in Rennes, Nantes and St.-Malo, and troops were dispatched to punish the truculent Bretons. The local aristocracy joined in on the king's side and helped to crush the rebels.

The situation deteriorated when Colbert threatened to impose further taxes, including the hated *gabelle*, or salt tax. Armed peasants calling themselves the Bonnets Rouges (Red Caps) rampaged through 40 parishes, ringing the church bells to call supporters to arms. They attacked local châteaux and drank the cellars dry, demanding an end to long lists of grievances. Under the leadership of Sébastien Le Balp, a lawyer, 30,000 insurgents sacked Carhaix, but the revolt collapsed abruptly after Le Balp was killed. Dreadful reprisals followed, and the remaining ringleaders were broken on the wheel or sent to the gallows. Madame de Sévigné, observing these events, wrote that the frightened peasants destined for the scaffold had spirit left only to plead for a drink and a quick death. French troops were then billeted in Brittany, where their appalling behaviour, including rape and pillage, went unchecked. Rebellion was quelled temporarily.

THE FRENCH REVOLUTION When the Bastille fell in July 1789, Brittany rejoiced, hoping for an end to the injustice it had felt since being annexed by France. The optimism was short-lived, however. The Breton temperament, though fiercely independent, was not naturally radical, and was quickly appalled by the godless excesses of the French

Jean-Baptiste Colbert, appointed superintendent of finances in 1661

secret counter-Revolutionary movement called the Association Bretonne, set up by the Marquis de la Rouerie after the execution of Louis XVI in 1793. The rebels became known as the Chouans (see page 179) from their use of a screech-owl signal, and their rallying cry was '*Vive le roi, vive la bonne religion.*' ('Long live the King, long live the true religion.')

THE AFTERMATH
After some of the grim memories of the Revolution had been expunged in a brief decade of Napoleonic glory, Brittany settled down to lick its wounds. In the 19th century, canals and railways were built and the roads improved. A cultural revival took place, bringing a renewed interest in the music, folklore and language of Brittany. Pont-Aven became an artists' haven, and several local writers put Brittany on the map, notably Chateaubriand and Jules Verne. This new awareness of Breton identity took a political turn with the founding of the first separatist party, Strollad Broadel Breiz, in 1908. Economic unrest rumbled in some quarters, resulting in strikes and industrial riots among the fishing community in the early 20th century, when cod and sardine prices slumped. But before long, a much greater disaster engulfed the region.

Revolution. It also became clear that the Revolutionary ideals promised less, not more, autonomy for Brittany. The native language was discouraged in favour of French, and administration focused on Paris. Even the name of Brittany disappeared, submerged into five *départements*. Armies garrisoned in Brittany requisitioned rations from already depleted local stocks, and conscription was introduced.

One of the least successful ambassadors of the Revolutionary ideal was Jean-Baptiste Carrier, whose atrocities in Rennes and Nantes shocked even his Convention paymasters (see page 179). The scene was set for the emergence of a

The novelist Jules Verne, born in Nantes in 1828

By the end of World War I the Breton country-side had changed little compared with some parts of France, but its communities were devastated. World War II was less costly in terms of human lives, but the destruction it wrought changed the face of Brittany's coastal cities for ever.

THE GREAT WAR The huge memorial at Ste.-Anne-d'Auray commemorates the dead of all modern wars, but the names of the dead of World War I make awesomely lengthy reading. More than 250,000 perished, the highest death toll per head of population of any region in the world. Brittany's maritime tradition meant that many of those killed were naval recruits.

The lost generation had a profound impact on both the region's psyche and its economy. The birth rate dropped dramatically, and emigration was rife between the wars. After World War I many disillusioned survivors turned to separatist organizations to impart some meaning to their colossal sacrifice. Among the more militant of these groups were Gwenn ha Du (White and Black, taking its name from the Breton flag), a secret society responsible for a number of protest bombings, and Bezenn Perrot, which declared itself as a Breton army and whose aim was to eject the French from Brittany. The separatists attracted support by claiming that the valiant Breton war effort had been made on behalf of a government that had destroyed Brittany's autonomy and suppressed Breton culture.

WORLD WAR II After the pounding Brittany had received in the Great War, few expected its people would have the heart for another global conflict. Yet the Bretons provided one of the most spirited bastions of resistance against the German invasion. They accounted for a quarter of the Free French Forces summoned by General de Gaulle, and bravely endured a massive aerial onslaught.

At first the fighting seemed a distant rumble beyond the eastern borders, but once Holland and Belgium had fallen Brittany was all

The moving war memorial at Ste.-Anne-d'Auray

too close to the Maginot Line. By June 1940 the first German occupying troops arrived. Some expected the Bretons to welcome them as allies against their French oppressors; they were disappointed. By this time General de Gaulle had broadcast his stirring call to arms from England, and many Bretons were already on their way to join him—the Île de Sein was deserted except for women, children and old men. An effective Resistance network was set up all over Brittany, to which many Allied servicemen owe their lives.

By 3 August, 1944, when the Liberation of Brittany began under

43

An emotional welcome for American troops entering Rennes in 1944

the command of George Patton's US VIII Corps, 30,000 Bretons were in arms. Six weeks later several historic Breton ports, including St.-Malo, Brest, Lorient, St.-Nazaire, lay in unrecognizable fragments.

Although the structural damage of the war has long since been repaired, bitter memories linger in some areas and can been seen expressed on gravestones and memorials throughout Brittany. Many older Bretons, who lived through the war and remember the hard times, simply never speak of that period of their lives.

The submarine pens at St.-Nazaire

❏ From Plage Bonaparte beach near Paimpol, a massive rescue operation codenamed Shelburne was mounted by the Resistance and the British Royal Navy during World War II. Allied aircrew shot down over German-occupied territory, or escaped prisoners-of-war, were smuggled across France to the north coast of Brittany to await a coded message relayed by BBC radio transmitters: '*Bonjour à tous dans la maison d'Alphonse.*' This was the signal to assemble beneath the cliffs on Plage Bonaparte, where a Dartmouth gunboat would slip quietly past enemy defences to collect them. Moonless nights were chosen for the escape missions, but even so they were extremely risky: 'To right and left of us were German listening posts…Ten miles away, there was a radar installation and a battery of medium guns…' Memorials near the beach and on the surrounding cliffs now commemorate the brave participants in Operation Shelburne. ❏

Since World War II, Brittany has slowly recovered, its economy boosted by tourism, though many farmers and fishermen still feel they get a raw deal from Paris. While rural populations drift to the towns in search of work, weary citydwellers gaze longingly towards the countryside, dreaming of rustic bliss.

44

DOWN ON THE FARM During the 1960s agricultural prices slumped and, with no organized marketing strategy to protect them, farmers suffered badly. In time-honoured fashion they took the source of their grievances to Paris and dumped them in the streets—an episode that became known as the Artichoke War. One unexpected by-product of this farming tussle was the creation of Brittany Ferries (see page 113). Since the 1960s, agriculture has enjoyed a great renaissance in Brittany, bolstered by enormous windfalls of cash from the European Union (EU). Protests still recur, though, sometimes erupting in violent confrontation against imported produce.

POWER LINES Brittany has new industries, too, from space-age telecommunications and high-tech

Nuclear and tidal power help generate Brittany's electricity

Pleumeur-Bodou, hub of French telecommunications

electronics to controversial nuclear power stations. The Bretons have complained vociferously (and sometimes successfully) about having nuclear power plants dumped in their quiet backwaters, comfortably distant from France's more populated areas. Much more enthusiastically received was the innovative Rance estuary dam near St.-Malo, the world's first tidal power station, inaugurated in 1967 (see page 62).

DIVERTING THE LOIRE In 1973 France underwent one of its periodic bureaucratic upheavals and redrew the map, leaving Brittany with just four *départements* instead of the former five. Loire-Atlantique in the southeast joined the neighbouring region of Pays de la Loire. Psychologically, many Bretons have never accepted this change, and regard it as just another idiotic imposition by Parisian pen-pushers. Most inhabitants of Loire-Atlantique still regard themselves as Bretons, at least as far as that great natural divide, the River Loire. Economically, however, the transition cannot be ignored. Nantes, Brittany's old capital and one of its most populous and prosperous cities, now heads another region, taking with it the lucrative Muscadet wine trade and a significant proportion of tourism. La Baule, formerly Brittany's most sophisticated seaside resort, and Brière Regional Nature Park, now pay dividends elsewhere.

FORGING AHEAD In 1962 Brittany basked briefly in a welcome glow of world attention when the giant radar antennae at Pleumeur-Bodou transmitted (and received) the first transatlantic satellite broadcast via *Telstar*. Today Brittany is still the centre of the French telecommunications industry. Other large employers are Citroën, near Rennes, and Renault, which has a plant near Lorient. Massive amounts of money have been poured into Breton cities such as Brest, which were badly damaged during World War II. The Brest Charter, ratified in 1988, encouraged large-scale investment in new city facilities and in education. This has resulted in the creation of new roads and bridges and the development of the Technopôle

Brest-Iroise, a vast complex including research centres, higher education establishments and businesses.

Road, rail and air links with the rest of France have also become a major priority. The regional airline, BritAir, and the advent of the high-speed train (TGV or Train à Grande Vitesse) have done much to make Brittany less isolated. New road bridges, particularly at St.-Nazaire, provide a gateway to the south.

World recession, though, has hit the region badly. Unemployment is still high, and rural depopulation is a problem. Traditional industries such as shipbuilding and steel have dwindled to a fraction of their former importance. Fishing is also suffering from aggressive foreign competition and the cutbacks caused by EU attempts to conserve fish stocks. One other maritime harvest is being investigated with great interest, however, that of offshore oil. So far Brittany has experienced only the minus side of the drilling business, when laden tankers founder against its reefs and spoil its precious beaches. But the region looks enviously towards its Celtic relatives in Scotland, hoping that somewhere off Finistère lies similar buried treasure.

45

A power provider: the Rance tidal dam

The Emerald Coast

See drive page 54

3

Baie de
St-Brieuc

Côte   de   Penthièvre

Côte de Emeraud

Cap Fréhel

Fort la
Latte

Pléhérel-
Plage

Sables-d'Or-
les Pins

St-Cast-
le-Guildo

St-Malo

Dinard ★

St-Lunaire

St-Briac-
sur-Mer

Lancieux

Usine
Marémotrice

Erquy

Plurien

Baie de la Frênaye

Pen Guen

Caroual

Matignon

St-Jacut-
de-la-Mer

la Richardais

Pointe de Pordic

Pointe de Pléneuf

le Val-André

Château de
Bienassis

Dahouet

Pléneuf-
Val André

Henanbihen

St-Pôtan

Trégon

Ploubalay

Pleurtu

les Rosaires

Plérin

Pointe des
Guettes

Morieux

Planguenoual

D768

Pludun

Crehen

Plancoët

Plouër-sur-Ranc
Moro

Gouët

ST-BRIEUC

Hillion

Landébia

Languenan

D766

Trégueux

Yffiniac

Arguenon

St-Samson-
sur-Rance

Dinan

Län

Pommeret

Haras
National

Lamballe

Château de
la Hunauday

Corseul

Temple
de Mars

D700

Épon

Plédéliac

Ferme
d'Antan

Léhon

Plédran

Guessant

N176-E401

Quessoy

Tritte

Plestan

N12-E50

Jugon-les-Lacs

Languédias

Brusvly

CÔTES-D'ARMOR

Château de
la Touche-Trébry

Langouhedre

Rance

Moncontour

Trédaniel

Yvignac

Plœuc-
sur-Lié

Notre-Dame
du Haut

le Gouray

Broons

D766

Lié

Abbaye de
Boquen

A   B   C

46

2

1

*Mock-Gothic villas overlook the harbour at Dinard. Close proximity to the Gulf Stream
ensures mild average temperatures and a profusion of palm trees*

Jolleuville
Sartilly D973
Champeaux
MANCHE
Pointe du Grouin
Baie   du
la Guimorais
theneuf   Cancale
Genêts
Mont-St-Michel
mé
van-
er   St-Benoît-
des-Ondes
sagère   le Vivier-
sur-Mer   Cherrueix
la Gouesnière   St-Marcan   Beauvoir
**Notre-Dame
de l'Espérance**   St-Georges-
de-Grehaigne
uliad   ■ **Mont-Dol**   N176-E401   Pontorson
**Dol-de-
Bretagne**
ert   **Menhir de
Champ Dolent**
Baguer-
Morvan   Epiniac   la Boussac
idifien
Rancel   D155   Trans
le Tronchet   Bonnemain
St-Pierre-   Lanhélin   **ILLE - ET -**
de-Plesguen   Cuguen   Antrain
Bazouges-
la-Pérouse
Trémeheuc   Tremblay
Combourg
■ **Château de la
Bourbansais**   **VILAINE**
Lanrigan
N137   St-Rémy-
du-Plain
Québriac   0   10   20 km
0   5   10 miles
Tinteniac **D**   **E**

47

THE EMERALD COAST Grassy clifftops and lush fields, not water, give this northern stretch of coast its poetic name. Sometimes though, even the sea takes on a luminous greenish hue, more often jade or turquoise than emerald. Whatever its shades, the Emerald Coast is undeniably picturesque, its jagged edges lunging into the Channel in a series of rocky headlands, deeply cut by sandy bays and river estuaries, and peppered with islets. The best views are from the sea, so if you have a fine, calm day to spare take a boat excursion from one of the larger resorts. The main coastal route runs some way inland, and to see the best bits of scenery you must take detours. The roads around Cap Fréhel and Pointe du Grouin lead to the most spectacular viewpoints. Inland, the countryside is tamer: mostly pasture, orchards and stands of maize.

DUTCH LANDSCAPES The Emerald Coast proper begins at the Pointe du Grouin just north of Cancale, and stretches west to the bay of St.-Brieuc. The eastern section of Ille-et-Vilaine, bordering on Normandy, is completely different. It is a low-lying landscape of salt marshes, mud flats and great wide skies, reminiscent of the Netherlands. Once, the brackish pastures around the bay of Mont-St.-Michel lay beneath the waves, but are now reclaimed polders. Ivy-hung poplars and willows line the watercourses, leading the eye towards straight horizons pierced by church towers and occasional windmills. The River Couesnon forms the boundary between Breton and Norman

The Emerald Coast

THE BRETON CLIMATE
If you have ever
experienced Brittany in a
westerly gale you will never
forget it. Plage de la
Torche or Pointe du Raz in
a Force 10 is a sight to
behold. In October 1987,
hurricane gusts ripped up
the old forest of Huelgoat
in a few minutes. Yet the
Breton climate is also
surprisingly mild. Softened
by the Gulf Stream, its
winter temperatures are
similar to those on the
Côte d'Azur, while the sea
temperatures are only a
fraction lower than those
of the Mediterranean.
Even more startling, the
annual rainfall in Dinard
(698mm/28in) is actually
lower than in Nice
(868mm/34in).

territory, and the historic vagaries of its now-canalized course have transferred one of France's most magnetic places of interest to Normandy, not Brittany. At least once in a lifetime, though, every visitor to France should make the pilgrimage to the sea-moated abbey of Mont-St.-Michel, and St.-Malo is the nearest entry port.

PLACES TO VISIT St.-Malo itself is a major attraction. Now faithfully restored after wartime damage, it is one of France's largest ports, and it deserves at least half a day's exploration. Other highlights lie within easy reach: the gorgeous old town of Dinan at the head of the Rance estuary, and the scenic headlands of Grouin and Cap Fréhel, an easy drive (or better still, boat trip) away. Inland, the historic towns of Lamballe, Dol-de-Bretagne and Corseul are worth a passing glance, if not a pilgrimage. This easterly section of Brittany (Haute Bretagne) is less overtly regional than the far west. Breton is rarely spoken here, but you may occasionally hear a Breton hurdy-gurdy played by a folk group in St.-Malo, and there are music festivals in Dinan and St.-Briac-sur-Mer.

Apart from a few notable exceptions (Mont-St.-Michel, Fort la Latte and the medieval part of Dinan), historic buildings are thin on the ground, and museums generally

A boat trip on the Rance estuary (above) takes in the delightful old town of Dinan
Le Val André (opposite)

unremarkable. But the area has several unusual sights. For curiosity value, visit the sculpted rocks at Rothéneuf, Cancale's oyster museum, the Rance tidal power station and Lamballe's National Stud. Besides coastal boat trips, consider an excursion up the Rance valley to Dinan. If you're feeling wealthy, a spin round Mont-St.-Michel in a light aircraft is an unforgettable experience.

SPLENDID SEAFOOD For *fruits de mer* addicts, the north-east Breton coast is superb. Cancale is the place to acquire a taste for oysters, available even in the months without an 'R'. Erquy is best for scallops, while mussels are harvested in vast quantities at le Vivier-sur-Mer and St.-Jacut-de-la-Mer, where they cluster prolifically like some strange maritime grape on thousands of dark wooden posts in the shallow seas. You can take a ride on high-axled tractor trains from Cherrueix or le Vivier-sur-Mer to visit the mussel and oyster beds. Today's fishing fleets are smaller than before, and mostly venture only into local waters, but St.-Malo has kept its deep-sea cod-fishing industry alive by introducing the latest in refrigeration technology to its trawlers.

SEASIDE ACTIVITIES The Emerald Coast has always been popular for its superb range of beaches. This part of Brittany is generally more sheltered from Atlantic gales than the western extremities of Finistère, but the mild climate is unpredictable and can be wet at any time of year. North Brittany is a place to bring bats and balls, buckets and spades, and watersports, riding and tennis are on offer everywhere. For an unusual spectator sport, head for Mont-St.-Michel bay on a windy day, where sand-yachting is an exciting craze in Cherrueix or St.-Benoît-des-Ondes. The best resorts for families are the more established places with safe beaches and plenty to do: Dinard, St.-Cast-le-Guildo, or le Val André. Erquy is a pleasant quieter choice, still with many of its original stone cottages; modern holiday homes have replaced these in many resorts. In July and August resort facilities are stretched to maximum capacity by a massive influx of French families, and every *gîte* is full.

Erquy combines seaside charm with a thriving scallop industry

49

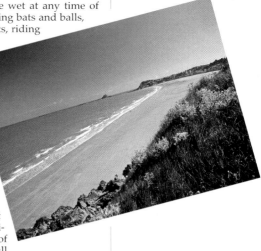

THE OYSTER MUSEUM
La Ferme Marine is an oyster farm on the edge of Cancale where you can learn about the evolution of oyster-breeding techniques and the life and work of an oyster breeder. After a film show, visitors are shown the beds where the oysters are raised and the workshop where grading and packing take place. You can buy and taste the oysters. There is also a display of 1,500 seashells (tel: 02 99 89 69 99. *Guided tours* Jun–Sep daily 11, 3, and 5 in French; 2 in English; low season Mon–Fri at 3. *Admission moderate*).

A brightly coloured flat-bottomed boat, used by oyster farmers

LA CANCALAISE
This loving re-creation of one of Brittany's most beautiful sailing craft now takes tourists on cruises from Cancale. Once a year, in a colourful pageant called La Caravanne, the black-hulled *bisquines* used to set off from the port to drag nets along the seabed in search of wild oysters. Commercial oyster-farming has since made them obsolete. *La Cancalaise* is the last of the *bisquines*, a recently restored 45-tonner which takes up to 25 passengers at a time. Contact the Association Bisquine Cancalaise, La Halle à Marée, Port de la Houle; tel 02 99 89 77 87; www.lacancalaise.com.

▶▶ **Cancale**   *47D2*

After the muddy salt flats of Mont-St.-Michel bay, Cancale provides the first real taste of Brittany's coastal drama, with grandstand views from its cliffs and headlands. Cancale is one of France's foremost producers of oysters, and they are sold in prodigious quantities at seafood stalls or are more expensive at a string of vibrant restaurants along the seafront. The muddy beaches are covered with shallow concrete beds or *parcs* where the oysters pass through their final stages of development.

Cancale is a split-level town, the main settlement separated from the picturesque port of la Houle by a long, steep, cobbled street. In the upper town the church belfry offers panoramic views. La Ferme Marine is Cancale's most compelling attraction (see panel). Models of old *bisquines* are displayed in the Musée des Arts et Traditions Populaires in Cancale's old St.-Méen church (tel: 02 99 89 71 26; *open* Jul–Aug Tue–Sun 10–6.30; Jun and Sep Fri–Sun pm; *closed* lunchtime. *Admission moderate*).

▶ **Corseul**   *46C1*

This small town northwest of Dinan is interesting for its Gallo-Roman remains. Corseul was the capital of the Armorican tribe of the Coriosolites, mentioned in Caesar's *Commentaries on the Gallic War*. Excavations have revealed the former town of Fanum Martis, and the vestiges of a Roman villa near the modern town. Finds from the sites are displayed in a little **museum**▶ (*Open* Jul–Aug Mon–Sat 9–12, 2–5; *closed* Sat pm off-season. *Admission inexpensive*), housed in the town hall and in the Jardin des Antiques outside. Roman sandals, jewellery and figurines can be seen. About 1.5km (1mile) from the town on the Dinan road (D794), in fields up a rough track, is the Temple of Mars (also known as the Temple de Haut-Bécherel), the half-shell of an octagonal tower dating from the reign of Augustus (freely accessible).

Oysters are cultivated in many places around Brittany's coast, and few restaurants fail to offer a plate or two. You may not find common or garden huîtres *on the menu but* creuses *(large hollow oysters of the type known as Portuguese or Pacific),* Bélons *(flat oysters, the real natives of the Brittany coast), and* pieds de cheval *(the biggest and most expensive).*

Pearls of great price The mystique of the oyster stretches back a long way. Romans gorged on them at their monstrous banquets and wagonloads were transported daily to the court of Louis XIV at Versailles. But they were not only food for the rich; once oysters were plentiful enough on the Breton coast to form the staple diet for fishermen's families. By the 18th century they were much prized, gathered in vast quantities, and becoming scarce. Today, oysters are farmed like any other crop. Their high price is justified by the fact that they take four or five years to reach maturity.

How to eat them Oysters should always be eaten on the day of purchase. If you buy them from a stall, make sure the shells are tightly closed, or close when tapped, to show they are alive. Scrub well in cold running water, then insert a strong, pointed knife into the hinged end of the shell. Twist the blade to open the oyster and then lever along the upper shell. The oyster dies when its anchoring muscle is cut, but its nervous system may still retract slightly on contact with lemon juice. In a restaurant, the shells will usually be opened already.

   The oysters should be creamy and fresh-smelling, sitting in a puddle of clear, salty fluid. You can either tip and swallow them directly from the shell or extract them with a fork. It may take a while to acquire the taste if you are not already an aficionado. Indeed, a good many folk go through life wondering what all the fuss is about.

OYSTER-FARMING
Earlier this century disease virtually wiped out the natural oyster stocks in the waters around Cancale, and now the young oysters (known as spat) are brought in from southern Brittany, where they are raised in the Bélon river and around Auray. The spat are placed in shallow rectangular beds, visible at low tide, where they develop in sacks of plastic mesh, undergoing a final purification process before being harvested. Farmers head out across the mud in tractors at the lowest tides every fortnight to tend the more distant beds.

AN 'R' IN THE MONTH
The belief that oysters are not fit to eat during the summer months stems from their breeding cycle, which lasts from May to August. After fertilization, the female oyster takes on a milky appearance, and as the spat (larvae) develop it goes dark. The oysters look unusual at this stage, but are not harmful to eat; the varieties of oyster produced in Brittany are edible all year. That said, there is a greater risk of seafood poisoning in the summer, when ambient temperatures are higher.

51

Thousands of oysters go through their final stages of development on the beaches of Cancale

►►► Dinan

46C1

Wherever else you go in Brittany, try not to miss Dinan, one of the best-preserved towns in the region and an ideal sightseeing base for a day or two. Inevitably its attractions do not pass unnoticed and it can get very crowded in high season. The town stands high above the Rance estuary and is linked by regular summer boat trips to Dinard and St.-Malo, though tidal conditions can make such excursions time-consuming (Eméraude Lines; tel: 02 96 39 18 04; you can take a boat one way and come back either by rail or by bus).

The keep of 14th-century Dinan castle

Medieval Dinan grew rich initially on its riverine trade, and later on the proceeds of wool and cloth. The town is notable for its associations with the Breton warrior, Bertrand Du Guesclin (see pages 34–35), whose heart is buried in the church of St.-Sauveur. Every second July the Fête des Remparts celebrates the town's vibrant past. Just outside the town, the abbey ruins of **Léhon** are worth a look (tel: 02 96 87 40 40; *open* Jul–Aug daily 3–6).

52

Arcaded buildings line the streets of Dinan's old town

Walk

The old town of Dinan

See map opposite.

Dinan has few obligatory tourist sights, but the cobbled old quarter is full of picturesque lopsided half-timbering. Ramparts encircle the old town, and a section is accessible via pleasant landscaped walkways. Allow half a day.

Start from the **castle**▶ guarding the southern side of the town, where a local history museum now occupies the keep. Follow the main rue du Château round the walls, picking up the **promenade de la Duchesse Anne**▶ for splendid views over the Rance and viaduct. Beyond the orderly flowerbeds of the Jardin Anglais lies the church of **St.-Sauveur**▶, bizarrely diverse in its architecture, combining Gothic and Romanesque styles. The present slated steeple dates from the 18th century. Head back into town through the quaint old **Place des Merciers**▶. The **Tour de l'Horloge (clock tower)** on rue de l'Horloge has good views and deafens passers-by hourly with the memorial bell, a present from the Duchess Anne. Note the **Maison du Gisant** nearby, where a headless stone statue lies, and the pretty **Hôtel Kératry**▶.

Turning down rue Ste.-Claire, you reach a large, tree-lined square where the horseback figure of the 14th-century military leader **Du Guesclin** surveys parked cars. This was the scene of his famous duel with Thomas of Canterbury, the English truce-breaker, at the siege of Dinan.

The square, a fairground in the Middle Ages, now has a weekly market (no parking Thu).

Weave back through **rue de la Cordonnerie** and up into the rue de la Lainerie, where the **Ancien Couvent des Cordeliers** (a Franciscan monastery, now used as a school) gives a fine view of the Gothic east end of the church of **St.-Malo**. Follow the ramparts along the **promenade des Grands Fossés**▶, enter the town via the **Porte St.-Malo** and walk down the rue de l'Ecole, then turn down the steep **rue du Jerzual** towards the **port**. Several charming old buildings, some converted into art and craft studios, can be seen on the way down.

At the quayside, cafés and restaurants overlook a nautical scene, and there is a glorious view of the town from the other side of the bridge. The charming **Maison d'Artiste de la Grande Vigne** was home to the painter Yvonne Jean-Haffen (1895–1993) (*Open* Jul–Aug daily 10–6.30; Jun, Sep 2–6.30. *Admission inexpensive*). A tourist train saves the walk back up, bumping over cobbles to reach the tourist office (summer only).

A converted tidal mill

Drive

The Rance valley

See map on pages 46–47.

Dinard, Dinan and St.-Malo form three compelling focal points on a narrow triangle of splendid estuary scenery. Allow the best part of a day for this 90km (55 miles) drive.

The Rance estuary is a classic example of one of Brittany's 'drowned valleys' (see page 111). The state of the tides makes an enormous difference to the estuary's appearance, and so varied are the Rance's tides that their forces have been harnessed for the world's first tidal power station. Typical scenery on this route consists of lake-like expanses of calm, glittering water flanked by fertile banks of woodland and apple orchards. Sheltered inlets provide mooring points for small craft. Boatyards, tidal mills, châteaux, churches and the elegant houses of wealthy corsairs can be glimpsed among the trees.

Starting from St.-Malo, head south via St.-Servan-sur-Mer, hugging minor roads close to the waterside rather than taking the main N137 where possible. Good vantage points include **la Passagère, St.-Suliac▶** (a tidal mill and an ancient watch-tower) and **Pont St.-Hubert** (a new suspension bridge across the river). At **Pleudihen-sur-Rance** the **Musée de la Pomme et du Cidre (Apple and Cider Museum)▶** offers visitors a glass of the potent local product.

Mordreuc supplements its fine river views with a ruined castle, while **Lanvallay▶** has tantalizing views of the old town of Dinan. On the west side, detour to **Taden** where waterfowl, fish and campers congregate. The lock to the north (**Ecluse du Chatelier**) regulates the Dinan basin, another tranquil point for boat-watching. The menhir of **La Tremblay** can be tracked down near St.-Samson-sur-Rance, leaning at a drunken angle. Tiny lanes potter northwards past the churches of **Plouër-sur-Rance** (carved tombs) and **la Richardais** (modern glass and frescoes). Ahead is the vast concrete barrage of the tidal power station (**Usine Marémotrice▶▶**), which can be visited from the Dinard side (see page 62).

Cider-making is a traditional industry around the Rance valley

▶▶ Dinard   46C2

'Pearl of the Emerald Coast' and 'Nice of the North' trumpets the tourist literature about this sophisticated resort, modelled on the ritzy watering holes of the Riviera. It has expanded massively from being a simple fishing port in the mid-19th century, when a wealthy American named Coppinger built a palatial villa on the cliffs. Other rich British and American visitors followed his example, and soon the seafront was studded with mock-Gothic and Belle Epoque architecture.

Many more holiday houses and apartments have appeared since the turn of the 20th century, and ultra-modern resort facilities have also been added. The attractions of Dinard's setting are instantly apparent. A natural amphitheatre of wooded heights overlooks three superb sandy beaches, with stunning views of St.-Malo and the roadsteads of the Rance estuary. Dinard, washed by the tempering effects of the Gulf Stream, emulates the sunny south with its equable climate, and subtropical vegetation flourishes: mimosa, camellias, eucalyptus and palms. Some of the world's highest tides attract keen yachters, and smart races and regattas are an important aspect of the social calendar, along with tennis, bridge and afternoon tea.

Dinard today is still expensive, but less of a foreign playground. French families now throng the summer beaches, and volleyball and *boules* replace the croquet once played on the sands, along with children's clubs and *moules frites*.

British and American connections, however, remain strong, especially at Dinard's prestigious sailing and golf clubs. In early October an annual festival of British cinema attracts the crowds. Behind the Plage de l'Écluse stands a statue of Alfred Hitchcock. *The Birds* was partly filmed on location in Dinard in 1963.

When the water is too chilly for sea-bathing, an Olympic-sized heated sea-water pool is the next best thing. At night the casino is the star attraction, but during the day Dinard concentrates on its beach life, ringing the changes with boat excursions along the Fréhel coast or up the Rance. St.-Malo is an easy step across the barrage bridge or by shuttle ferry.

PROMENADE DU CLAIR DE LUNE
The 'Moonlight Promenade is a public footpath running from the Plage du Prieuré to the Pointe du Moulinet, past an enchanting scene of rocky headlands smoth-ered in exotic vegetation. On summer evenings the pathway and adjacent gardens are bathed in colourful lighting and piped music.

55

The Plage de l'Écluse, Dinard's main beach, makes for a delightful stroll

Emerald-topped cliffs at Cap Fréhel

56

ST. MICHAEL'S FOOT
One of many legends about Mont-Dol declares it to be the site of the apocalyptic struggle between Satan and the Archangel Michael. At the summit of the hill, various indeterminate marks in the rocks have been interpreted as the Devil's claw and St. Michael's footprint, left as he leapt to Mont-St.-Michel after his victory. You need plenty of imagination to reconstruct these.

View from Mont-Dol

▶▶ Dol-de-Bretagne 47D2

The 'Capital of the Marshes' now stands 8km (5 miles) inland, but centuries ago it was an island in the sea. In AD709 a great tidal wave engulfed the low-lying land around the bay of Mont-St.-Michel, leaving Dol stranded on its clifftop site above the waves. Eventually the waters retreated behind brackish salt marshes, which were gradually reclaimed from the sea. Today the countryside consists of maize fields and pastureland, lined with poplar and willow and pierced with church spires. The salty fields provide grazing for *pré salé* lambs.

Dol was founded by St. Samson in AD548, and was for many years an important ecclesiastical focus. Today it has no bishop, but its granite **cathedral▶** still presides gloomily over the surrounding landscape. Construction of this massive building (*Open* daily 9–12, 2–6. Free guided tours in summer) took several centuries, and one of its towers is incomplete. One of its finest features is the carving on the great south door (see photo opposite); inside the vast nave is surmounted by splendid Gothic vaulting. A former school beside the cathedral houses an ambitious exhibition on medieval cathedrals called **Cathédraloscope▶▶** (tel: 02 99 48 35 30; *open* Easter–Oct daily 10–7. *Admission moderate.* English translation available). Behind the cathedral, several enjoyable streets contain quaint old houses sprouting unusual features at every turn: a granite shop bench outside one, pillars on another. Views from the public gardens, the Promenade des Douves, stretch over the marshes to Mont-Dol.

Mont-Dol▶ is a strange, flat-topped granite mound 2km (1 mile) north of the town. Its modest 65m (210ft) height takes on an awesome significance in this low-lying landscape, and views from the summit are extensive. From prehistoric times onwards it has attracted attention, and the site is dotted with holy wells and signs of earlier habitation. Pilgrims pay homage at the little chapel of Notre-Dame de l'Espérance, but most visitors today make more use of the small bar-restaurant near the disused windmill. You can walk or drive up the hill from the pretty huddled village of Mont-Dol, where the old **church** contains several ancient frescoes.

► Erquy 46B2

This agreeable fishing port, famed for its scallops, retains more of its original character than some of the Emerald Coast's resorts, and has a number of gorgeous beaches in exquisite settings; head for Caroual to the southwest or Cap d'Erquy to the northwest, where silver or grey-pink coves nestle among pine woods and bracken. At low tide you can reach the chapel-crowned islet of St.-Michel. Inland, to the south of the main D786, lies the **Château de Bienassis**, a late-medieval edifice rebuilt in the 17th century and furnished in Louis XIV and Breton Renaissance styles (tel: 02 96 72 22 03; *open* mid-Jun to mid-Sep daily 10.30–12.30, 2–6.30, Sun pm only. *Admission moderate*).

►►► Fréhel, Cap 46B3

This renowned beauty spot is one of the Emerald Coast's most dramatic promontories, and shouldn't be missed. Gnarled grey cliffs of schist and sandstone streaked with red porphyry rise to a grand height of 70m (230ft) above a sea of jade. The most impressive views of this section of coast are from the sea, and excursion boats ply regularly from St.-Malo and Dinard during the summer.

Alternatively, you can drive to the cape along the tourist route and park by the square-towered lighthouse (*Open* most days in summer on request. *Admission free*). Views extend to Bréhat, St.-Malo and the Channel Islands on clear days. Seabirds crowd on the fissured Fauconnière rocks (a nature reserve) the west of the lighthouse, while human perches are provided at the Restaurant de la Fauconnière (see page 278), with its spectacular cliff views. Walks around the cape are exceptionally beautiful, but do not expect to have the scenery all to yourself in the high season.

An old mill at Dol

57

MENHIR DE CHAMP DOLENT
Just southeast of Dol-de-Bretagne, off the D795, is a standing stone about 9m (30ft) high, stuck incongruously in a maize field. This menhir is alleged to have fallen from heaven to divide the armies of two warring brothers (Champ Dolent means 'Field of Sorrow'). It is said to be gradually sinking into the ground, a couple of centimetres (about an inch) every century, and when it vanishes the world will end. The stone is freely accessible from the road, and can even be admired from a picnic table, though it has no markings or particular features of interest.

South porch detail from Dol cathedral

A ruined tower at the Château de la Hunaudaye

THE NATIONAL STUD
The most interesting sight in Lamballe is the Haras National, France's second largest stud. The dignified stable-blocks stretching around multiple courtyards once accommodated up to 400 horses, including powerful Breton draught horses. Today about 70 stallions and 20 riding horses are kept here. Summer guided tours (some in English) take visitors through the stables, carriage house, harness rooms and farriery. There's a riding school inside. Many equine events are held, including summer horse shows, and carriage rides on Thursdays. *Open* for guided tours daily Jul–Aug; Wed and weekends off-season; closed Nov–Jan. *Admission moderate*; www.haraspatrimonie.com

► **Jugon-les-Lacs**   46B1

The original houses clustered around the unusual saddle-backed 13th-century church in this little town are passably venerable (one of the oldest is the **Maison Sevoy** of 1634). Most of Jugon-les-Lacs' buildings are, however, much more recent, as the resort cashes in, tastefully enough, on its artificial lakeside setting. Grey-white holiday homes stretch towards the dammed twin rivers, and there are plenty of watersport facilities.

Several sights just outside the town add to its attractions as a base. The Cistercian **Abbaye de Boquen** lies in ruins about 15km (9 miles) southwest, and the **Ferme d'Antan** in St.-Ésprit-des-Bois has a reconstruction of bygone Breton rural life. The most striking excursion is to the **Château de la Hunaudaye►** (tel: 02 96 34 82 10 for guided tours and show times. *Admission moderate*), 9km (5.5 miles) northwards in deep forests. It dates from the 12th century, was enlarged over several centuries, and battered into its present ruins during the Revolution. The monument is state-owned and its unpillaged parts are impressively preserved, including the Tour de la Glacière, Renaissance manor house and 15th-century keep. In high season a local drama group regularly enacts humorous stories of medieval folk.

►► **Lamballe**   46B1

A sizeable town these days, Lamballe has numerous industries related to its role as an agricultural centre, including animal foodstuffs and leather processing. It also hosts important cattle markets for the Penthièvre region. The most interesting part of Lamballe's old town is around the main square, Place du Martray, where several picturesque old houses can be seen. The best of these buildings is the half-timbered **Maison du Bourreau►** (Hangman's House), which contains an obliging tourist office and two good little **museums** (*Open* Jun–Sep, Mon–Sat; reduced hours off-season. *Admission moderate*). One recounts the town's local history in costumes and pottery, while the other displays the lively charcoal drawings, watercolours and ceramics of the artist Mathurin Méheut, who was born here in 1882.

Churches include **St.-Jean**, containing a 17th-century altarpiece and organ; **St.-Martin**, a priory with a strange little canopied porch; and the fortified collegiate church of **Notre-Dame►** at the top of the town, with its finely carved doorways and splendid rood screen.

► **Lancieux**   46C2

This small resort at the bridging point of the Frémur marks the easterly end of the Côtes-d'Armor coast and was originally a religious settlement founded by a British monk, St. Sieuc. It is renowned for its excellent championship golf course (the second oldest in France) and a striking 18th-century bell tower, which is the last remnant of the town's original church. Like most of the resorts along this coast, Lancieux has lovely sandy beaches, the best of these being the Plage St.-Sieu.

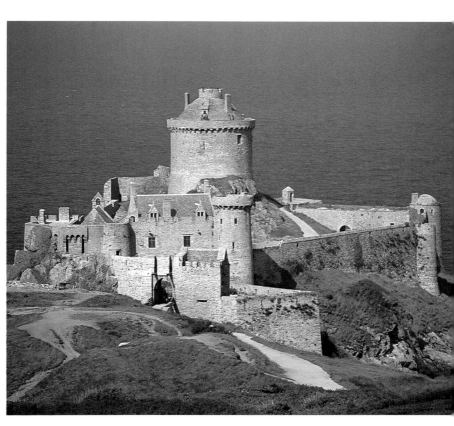

►► La Latte, Fort ⠀⠀⠀⠀⠀⠀46B2

www.castlelalatte.com

Open: Jul–Aug daily 10–7; off-season 10–12.30, 2–6; Oct–Apr Sat–Sun pm only; guided tours. Admission moderate

So photogenic is this coastal fortress that it was used as the set for the film *The Vikings* in 1957. It perches on a rocky promontory guarding the western entrance to the Baie de la Frênaye, just east of Cap Fréhel. Drawbridges cross two natural fissures in the rock, which form a sea moat at high tide. The crenellated castle dates back to the 14th century, but owes most of its present appearance to Louis XIV's military architect, Vauban (see page 176), who strengthened and remodelled it in the 17th century. During its history the castle has played host to medieval pirates, English spies during the French Revolution, White Russians, and the Old Pretender, James Stuart (son of England's James II, deposed by William of Orange).

Fort la Latte is now privately owned and still inhabited. One of its most interesting features is a kiln where cannonballs were heated to set fire to enemy wooden ships. There are panoramic views from the parapets and towers, and at the top of the gated track from the parking area is a small menhir known as Gargantua's Finger.

Romantic Fort la Latte (above) Cap Fréhel (below), home for thousands of seabirds, is a magnet to ornithologists

►►► Mont-St.-Michel ⠀⠀⠀⠀⠀47E2

See pages 60–61.

Rising from swirling mud flats, this granite island attracts more visitors than any other provincial sight in France. Technically it lies across the border in Normandy, but don't miss it if you are in the area.

THE MARVEL

'Climbing the steep narrow street, I entered the most wonderful Gothic building ever made for God on this earth, a building as vast as a town, full of low rooms under oppressive ceilings and lofty galleries supported by frail pillars. I entered that gigantic granite jewel, which is as delicate as a piece of lacework, thronged with towers and slender belfries which thrust into the blue sky of day and the black sky of night, their strange heads bristling with chimeras, devils, fantastic beasts, and monstrous flowers, and which are linked together by carved arches of intricate design.'
—Guy de Maupassant

TIPHAINE'S HOUSE

Behind the parish church near the foot of the Mount stands a quaint old house built by the Breton warrior Du Guesclin (see pages 34–35) for his scholarly wife, Tiphaine de Raguenel, in 1365. Du Guesclin, who commanded the garrison of the Mount during this period, left his wife studying astronomy and philosophy while he engaged in more active pursuits in the Spanish wars. Today the house is a small museum furnished in local style. There are three other little museums on the Mount; the Archéoscope gives you an archangelic multimedia tour guided by St. Michael, the Musée Maritime explains the ecosystem of the bay, and the Musée Historique has a collection of waxworks.

How long Mont-St.-Michel will remain an island is uncertain. The bay is gradually silting up, particularly since the creation of the causeway connecting Mont-St.-Michel with the mainland, which prevents tidal movements scouring away the sands. There are, however, plans to replace the causeway with a bridge (see panel). The sight of the advancing tide is still remarkable, even if it is less swift than galloping horses (a common claim). High tides can still flood the parking area, while at low tide over 10km (6 miles) of sand are exposed, and you can walk right round the Mount.

Before the causeway was built, all pilgrims had to walk across the sands at low tide, many drowning on the way. A scene on the Bayeux Tapestry shows King Harold charitably rescuing some stranded Normans from quicksand.

Holy place The site has attracted attention as a holy place and a strategic vantage point for many centuries. Hermits arrived in about AD500, and in AD708 the Bishop of Avranches experienced a vision in which the Archangel Michael told him to build a church on the rock. The Normans took the project further, fetching stone from the Iles de Chausey in the bay, cutting it into blocks and hoisting it up the perilous slopes. Later generations continued to build up and around the Mount until the 19th century. Sections collapsed several times, and had to be rebuilt. Today the structures seem as delicately poised as a house of cards, some cantilevered over thin air.

The base of the Mount is occupied by a village, and a good many souvenir shops and fast-food outlets, which can be offputting. The commercialization of the Mount is not a recent phenomenon; medieval pilgrims would have been plagued by beggars, touts, pickpockets and charlatans as they ascended. Once beyond the Grande-Rue the crowds immediately thin out and the atmosphere becomes noticeably more peaceful. Flights of steps lead everywhere and hence access is not easy for visitors with disabilities.

An architectural triumph The abbey church is a glorious blend of Romanesque and Gothic architecture. St. Michael brandishes his golden sword from the highest pinnacle. The Gothic structures on the north side of the

Mount, called la Merveille (the Marvel), house the domestic and guest quarters, and date from the 13th century. The buildings are regarded as some of the best examples of Gothic religious architecture in France. You pass through the Guests' Hall, the Knights' Hall and the Refectory (lit by mysterious invisible windows) to the cloisters balanced on the top floor, slim columns decorated with beasts and figures.

Walks around the ramparts and gardens give marvellous views, and also a better idea of this fantastically complex structure.

TURNING THE TIDE
Ambitious plans are underway to replace the existing causeway with an unobtrusively designed bridge. Eventually, visitors will be able to walk across, or take a high-tech, eco-friendly shuttle rail link from the mainland. This will remove the unsightly parking areas and make it unnecessary to carry out the present costly dredging process. The project will be vastly expensive, but will allow the tides (the largest in Europe) to sweep unchecked around the Mount and restore its magical island status.

DETAILS
Tel: 02 33 89 80 00; www.monum.fr. Free access to Mount (parking expensive). Abbey: *Open* May–Aug daily 9–6; Sep–Apr 9.30–5. *Admission expensive* (includes choice of self-guided, escorted, or audio-tour). Separate or combined tickets available for all four museums.

Visitors (left) besiege the lower town in summer

HARNESSING THE MOON
The idea of using the tides to generate power is not new. Even in the 12th century monks were experimenting on a small scale, using the force of the ebb tides to turn mill wheels on the Rance. You can see one of these primitive tidal mills at St.-Suliac, on the east bank. Today's massive barrage across the whole estuary would no doubt have astonished and fascinated those early monastic engineers.

▶▶ Rance, Usine Marémotrice de la (Rance Tidal Power Scheme)   46C2

Open: Tue–Sun pm, tel: 02 99 16 37 14.
Admission free (ID required)

A huge concrete barrage blocks the mouth of the Rance, creating a large reservoir upstream and is used as a bridge by the St.-Malo–Dinard road. From parking areas at either end, you can walk across the dam on footpaths and watch the sinewy currents arc through the sluicegates to the generators housed in a vast tunnel within the barrage. A film (in English) at the visitor centre explains how it works.

The dam was opened in 1967, and spans 750m (2,475ft), curbing a reservoir of 22sq km (7sq miles). A lock enables boats to pass through. Around 600 million kWh of electricity are produced by 24 generators each year, using both ebb and flow tides. It is slightly disappointing to learn that this massively imaginative and costly project generates only about 3 per cent of Brittany's total electricity needs, and although it sounds environmentally friendly its effects on local wildlife are significant. Conservationists are concerned about the habitat loss of vast numbers of wading birds.

▶ Sables-d'Or-les-Pins   46B2

For once, the tourist-brochure name does not deceive. The setting of golden sands and pines is truly breathtaking, though the resort itself (and even its glorious beach) is essentially artificial. The resort was constructed as a commercial enterprise during the late 19th century, which at one period lost an immense amount of money and was abruptly terminated. Luxury villas and hotels now stand in a curiously incomplete main street, supplemented by golf and watersports facilities. Swimming on some local beaches, including the beautiful Pléhérel-Plage to the northeast, can be dangerous because of the currents that swirl unpredictably around the sandbanks.

The ancient village of **Plurien** at the resort's southern end adds some historic weight, with a very early Knights Templar church and the remains of a Gallo-Roman villa.

▶ St.-Briac-sur-Mer   46C2

St.-Briac stands on the Ille-et-Vilaine side of the Frémur estuary, whose panoramic cliff road (the Balcon d'Émeraude) and long bridge overlook amazing views. Not much happens here except the Fête des Mouettes in mid-August, when Breton bagpipes and folk-dancing take over the resort. However, migrant birds seem to like the town (barnacle geese and ducks drop in each year) and a wave of holidaymakers takes advantage of its south-facing sandy beaches with islet views. The harbour area still has a core of pretty old streets and alleyways.

▶ St.-Brieuc   46A2

Too large and city-like for comfort, its road systems complicated by deep river valleys, St.-Brieuc is barely worth braving for casual sightseeing. However, it is a good shopping town, and you can pick up picnic provisions in its market. The cathedral of **St.-Étienne▶** is the town's most imposing building, a massive castle-like structure with fortified towers. The old streets around the cathedral are moderately picturesque.

Windmills were once a common sight along Brittany's north coast

62

▶▶ St.-Cast-le-Guildo
46C2

The complex geography of this resort takes some fathoming. It consists of several separate districts. Le Bourg is the administrative centre with a modern church, l'Isle is the port, les Mielles is a resort area of hotels and shops, and la Garde is a wooded residential sector. Over half a dozen good beaches lie around the promontory, with attractive cliffs at Pointe de St.-Cast and Pointe de la Garde. The fishing port specializes in scallops and clams, but self-catering developments and facilities for holiday activities show where this town's priorities lie. Several monuments stand on the cliffs around St.-Cast, such as the one dedicated to Free French *evadés* (escaped prisoners) of World War II, and another commemorates the Battle of St.-Cast.

Le Guildo, to the southeast of the resort, has a ruined fortress, which was dismantled on Cardinal Richelieu's orders, and the strange **Pierres Sonnantes** (stones that make a metallic sound when they are banged together). Nearby, the beach of Pen Guen is one of the most popular on the peninsula.

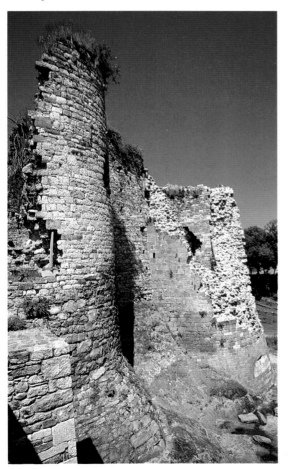

The fortress at St.-Cast-le-Guildo guarded the Arguenon estuary. It was one of many in Brittany partly demolished at Richelieu's behest to discourage insurrection

63

THE FLOUR AND THE GLORY

The monument showing a greyhound trampling a leopard in St.-Cast-le-Guildo's rue de la Colonne commemorates a French victory over a British attack on St.-Malo in 1758 (a reprisal for corsair plundering which constantly harassed British shipping). The Duke of Aiguillon, Governor of Brittany, directed operations from a windmill as British troops returned to their warships anchored in the bay of St.-Cast. One of the Duke's political enemies, La Chalotais (Procurator of the Rennes Parliament), on hearing that the Duke had 'covered himself with glory', acidly remarked, 'Yes, and with flour as well, I suppose!'

Detail, St.-Lunaire church

**JEANNE JUGAN
(1792–1879)**
Born into a fisherman's family in Cancale, Jeanne went into service in St.-Servan after her father was lost at sea. Her mistress left her a legacy with which she set up a refuge for impoverished old people, feeding and clothing them by daily begging. Several saintly women joined her and formed The Little Sisters of the Poor, now scattered all over the world in some 300 communities.

ISLAND STROLLS
Several tiny islands lie just off St.-Malo's shore, accessible from the town beaches at low tide. The Île du Grand-Bé is the burial place of the writer François-René de Chateaubriand (1768–1848), marked by a plain granite slab surmounted by a cross facing the ocean. Fort-National, on another island, was built by Vauban in 1689. Guided tours (tel: 02 99 85 34 33. *Open* Jun–Sep at low tide) include the dungeon and ramparts, from where there is a fine view of St.-Malo.

Another of Brittany's multifarious calvaries; this touchingly naïve version can be seen at St.-Lunaire

▶ **St.-Jacut-de-la-Mer**   *46C2*

This narrow peninsula rears cobra-like into the bay of St.-Cast, changing shape phenomenally as the tides ebb and flow. At low tide you can walk to Île des Ebihens (Ebihens Island), crowned by a tower; at high water it looks far out at sea (there is a good view of the island from the cliff at Pointe du Chevet).

Since the advent of tourism the resort has become much better known, but in earlier times the Jaguens were an isolated community who even had their own Breton dialect. The monks who first colonized the coast did their bit for regional harmony by building a causeway and joining St.-Jacut, once a tidal island, to the mainland. The older part of the village has jettied gables and considerable character. Mackerel fishing takes place from the small port, and at low tide hundreds of *bouchots* (mussel posts) emerge from the waterline in the bay of Arguenon on the west side of the peninsula. Shrimping among the rockpools at low tide is popular with locals. St.-Jacut has about a dozen beaches scattered around its long shoreline, though the sand here is interspersed with mud.

▶▶ **St.-Lunaire**   *46C2*

This resort is now virtually an enclave of Dinard. Out of season it may seem dull, its elegant holiday villas carefully shuttered, but in July and August, when it is colonized by a lively group of Parisian families, it is full of *joie de vivre*. The two main beaches are separated by a scenic promontory, the Pointe du Décollé. At the seaward end a natural rock arch called the Saut du Chat (Cat's Leap) spans a cave hollowed by the waves (Grotte des Sirènes), spectacular in rough weather. The 11th-century church in the old part of the village contains the tomb of St. Lunaire, resting on an even more ancient sarcophagus. His statue, and those on other tombs in the church, are curiously flattened as though their subjects have been crushed by a steamroller.

▶▶▶ St.-Malo
46C2

The modern pleasure-boat marina at St.-Malo

The most attractive of any of the Channel ports, St-Malo has more visitors than anywhere else in Brittany, and though many do no more than race in and out of the ferry terminal it is well worth a day of anyone's time to explore. If you can find accommodation (book ahead in summer) it makes an enjoyable and animated base, with good hotels and restaurants, plenty to see and do, boat trips galore and sandy beaches nearby.

Spirit of independence The town is named after a Welsh monk, St. Maclow, who settled in Aleth (now St.-Servan) in the 6th century and founded a religious community. Local people retreated to what is now the walled citadel (then an island) to escape the Norsemen. Later, in more peaceful times, a causeway was built to connect the island to the mainland. The development of the harbour encouraged a strong seafaring tradition, and St.-Malo built up a thriving trade with Spain and the Americas. During the 16th century it was an independent republic (one of the town's more truculent mottoes is 'I am neither French nor Breton, but a citizen of St.-Malo'), and few towns of its size have produced so many noteworthy inhabitants: explorers, writers, scientists and corsairs. The mansions of the corsairs sprang up all over town in their heyday (see page 68).

World War II St.-Malo was occupied by the Germans and then heavily bombed by the Allies in August 1944, when much of the town was destroyed. After the war it was painstakingly rebuilt. Some find St.-Malo's granite architecture austere, or complain that it is 'fake'. A glance at Brest, Lorient or St.-Nazaire (also badly damaged in the war but rebuilt with brutal modernity) may put things in perspective.

THE DISCOVERY OF CANADA Jacques Cartier, already in middle age, set sail across the Atlantic in 1534 in search of the fabled Northwest Passage. His first voyage took him to Newfoundland; two years later he sailed up the St. Lawrence and, believing he had reached Asia, asked the native Indians where he was. They told him the name of their local village (Canada) and so the name of this vast new territory was established.

65

Rampart walkways

The Emerald Coast

LES ROCHERS SCULPTÉS

A retired, partly paralyzed priest, Abbé Fouré, spent over 25 years at the end of the 19th century creating a Disneylike wonderworld of more than 300 monsters and grotesque figures, all carved out of rock. The effort involved in this labour of love is mind-boggling, though the results would perhaps interest a psychiatrist more than an art historian. Over time the elements have blunted the outlines of the sculpted rocks, and at some point they will be completely eroded away. The windswept setting above a sapphire sea is remarkable (tel: 02 99 56 23 95; *open* Easter–Sep daily 10–7; *closed* lunchtime in off-season. *Admission inexpensive*).

Les Rochers Sculptés, at Rothéneuf, were carved in the 19th century

Points of interest St.-Malo's main area of interest for visitors is *intra muros* ('within the walls'), but there are things to see further afield. One attraction is the costly **Grand Aquarium►►**, signposted off the Rennes exit road (tel: 02 99 21 19 00; www.aquarium-st-malo.com; *open* Jul–Aug 9.30–10; reduced hours off-season. *Admission expensive*). The circular shark-tank is particularly impressive. St.-Servan's **Aleth Corniche►►** (a headland footpath) is a splendid walk at sunset, and the **Tour Solidor►** contains an interesting museum recounting the voyages of Cape Horn sailors (*Open* Apr–Sep daily 10–6. *Closed* lunchtime, Nov–Mar Mon, and hols. *Admission moderate*).

Paramé has two fine beaches and a hydrotherapy centre. Both resorts have good hotels and are quieter than those *intra muros*.

Rothéneuf was the birthplace of Jacques Cartier, discoverer of Canada. Cartier's home, restored as a museum, was the delightful 15th-century **Manoir de Limoëlou►** on the edge of the village. It is furnished to period specifications, with charts and mementoes of Cartier's voyages and an audiovisual show (*Open* Jul–Aug daily 10–11.30, 2.30–6; low season Mon–Sat; guided tours at 10 and 3. *Admission moderate*. www.musee-jacques-cartier.com).

The second of Rothéneuf's attractions is the **Rochers Sculptés►**, a bizarre collection of cliffside rock carvings (see panel).

View of the port

Walk

St.-Malo *intra muros*

See map opposite.

The old walled citadel on its apron of sand (now firmly attached to the mainland) is a marvellous place for a stroll, best at high tide. Leave your car outside the ramparts and allow half a day, including museums.

Gates pierce the walls on all sides and the ramparts are freely accessible at several points, but the best place to start is **Porte St.-Vincent▶**. From here you can make a complete circuit of the ramparts for a magnificent overview of St.-Malo and its setting. Unlike the rest of the town, the walls are genuinely old, having survived even modern warfare virtually intact. Information panels point out features of interest, and statues of corsairs scan the horizon. On the seaward side you see the harbour, marina, town beaches, several fortified islands and a stretch of the Emerald Coast.

A restored tower of St.-Malo's 15th-century castle

Inwards is a dignified townscape of 18th-century houses, tall chimneys and dormers.

A well-signed historical trail leads through the old town, starting at the place Chateaubriand. Descend at Porte St.-Thomas where there is a small tropical **aquarium▶**, then head for the cathedral of **St.-Vincent▶** at the heart of the old town. Its main features are bright modern glass and the plain tomb of Jacques Cartier. Thread through the narrow old town streets past the Chapelle St.-Sauveur (making a detour through the Porte du Dinan for views of the harbour and the rocky Aleth promontory), towards the castle, where the **Musée d'Histoire de la Ville▶▶** has good sections on St.-Malo's seafaring past and its famous people.

The privateers of St.-Malo harassed European shipping well into the 19th century with full government approval. The most famous of them became great local heroes.

CORSAIR RULES

Captured ships were taken back to France with their crew, whereupon their cargo or valuables would be sold and distributed. Ten per cent went to the king, two-thirds to the ship-owner or *armateur*, and the rest to the corsairs. How many ships were boarded illegally and simply scuttled at sea to avoid sharing the spoils is anyone's guess. St.-Malo's town museum has a good section on the corsairs, including a sort of pirate's handbook, setting out the regulations.

PORCON DE LA BARDINAIS

Ironically in this town of privateers, the chosen career of Porcon de la Bardinais was to defend St.-Malo's merchant ships from enemy corsairs, particularly the Barbary pirates, in the reign of Louis XIV. Captured in one skirmish and brought before the Dey of Algiers, la Bardinais struck a deal that he would try to negoti-ate a peace treaty with the king of France but would return to captivity if the pro-posal was rejected. It was, and Porcon honourably kept his promise to return to Algiers, whereupon he was strapped to a cannon muzzle and blown to bits.

Licensed to swashbuckle The corsairs were 'gentlemen pirates', sometimes of good family and high military or naval rank. The Crown awarded them 'letters of marque' signed by the king, which empowered them to seize merchant or warships of hostile countries; in practice, any that refused to stop and disclose their identity. The beautiful mansions in and around St.-Malo give some idea of how profitable a business this was. Foreign governments were infuriated by their shipping losses, and the English, who sailed the high seas more than most, attempted several unsuccessful reprisal raids on Breton shores.

René Duguay-Trouin (1673–1736) Destined for the priesthood but led astray by a dissolute tutor, Duguay-Trouin went to sea early and showed great leadership qualities, becoming a commander at 24. During his short career at sea he captured more than 300 vessels, including 85 English ships. At one point he was taken prisoner and held in Plymouth for a year, but made his escape in a longboat, disguised as a Swedish skipper. He was given a peerage at 32, and in 1711 he seized Rio de Janeiro from the Portuguese. This was his greatest adventure, but he returned in poor health and retired from seafaring soon afterwards.

Robert Surcouf (1773–1827) Surcouf came from a wealthy ship-owning family who hoped he would enter the Church. It quickly became apparent he had no such vocation, and he was sent to sea at 14. A commander at 20, Surcouf specialized in the rich pickings of the Indian Ocean. He undertook several daring raids on heavily armed British ships, capturing HMS *Triton* and an East Indiaman, the *Kent*, in 1800. He also retired early, at 36, to become an *armateur* (shipbuilder) in St.-Malo, where he died, fantastically wealthy, at the age of 54.

Robert Surcouf spies booty from the ramparts of St.-Malo

▶▶ Le Val André   46A2

Founded in 1880 as a slightly less exclusive answer to
smart Dinard, farther east (see page 55), le Val André has
a similar period feel. Large bow-fronted Victorian villas
line the long, traffic-free promenade between two
wooded headlands, interspersed with 1930s developments. The resort was built by the architect Charles
Cotard, a colleague of Ferdinand de Lesseps, the French
diplomat responsible for building the Suez Canal. The
reason for the choice of site is immediately obvious, as le
Val André boasts one of the finest beaches in Brittany. At
low tide a vast expanse of gleaming sand is exposed,
freshly polished by the waves.

   The older port of Dahouët, a popular sailing centre, lies
to the southwest, offering boat trips to the Île de Bréhat
(see pages 76–77). Inland, the original village of Pléneuf-
Val André has shops and a Tuesday market, plus other
attractions of a seaside resort such as tennis courts, golf, a
concert hall and casino. Coastal walks or drives to Pointe
de Pléneuf or Pointe de la Guette have panoramic views
over the Baie de St.-Brieuc and the seabird sanctuary of Île
du Verdelet.

▶ Le Vivier-sur-Mer   47D2

Several centuries ago le Vivier was a significant trading
port, the main sea outlet for the Pays de Dol region. Now
all extensive seafaring has dwindled and le Vivier concentrates on shorebased enterprises.
At low tide the waters of Mont-St.-
Michel bay retreat behind mud flats,
leaving small boats stranded in the
trickling channels.

   Mytiliculture (mussel farming) is big
business in le Vivier, which is responsible for about 25 percent of France's
total production (about 10,000 tonnes
annually). The local *moules* are much
prized for their flavour and succu-
lence, a result of the rich plankton in
the shallow seas around the bay.

   A film show and exhibition at the
Maison de la Baie by the port explain
this unusual industry (tel: 02 99 48 84
38; *open* all year. *Admission inexpensive*). Sand-yachting, riding and
bicycling are popular local pastimes.

*The tide retreats at le
Val André*

MUSSEL-HUNTING
Out to sea, the tops of a
myriad dark wooden poles
are visible above the
waterline. These are *bouchots*, which are used for
mussel cultivation.
Millions of seed mussels
attach themselves in
heavy clusters to ropes
wound round the posts,
where they grow until they
are harvested between
June and March each
year. At le Vivier-sur-Mer
and Cherreuix little tractor-
trains trundle over the
muddy sand for tours
round the bay.

*Time ashore for one of
Dahouët's fishermen*

The Pink Granite Coast

Looking out towards Château de Costaérès on its rocky island in Ploumanac'h bay

Sillon
de Talbert

Île de Bréhat

Hir

Pleubian

éry

oche Jaune Loguivy Pointe de l'Arcouest

Ploubazlanec Porz-Even

Lézardrieux Paimpol

er

Abbaye de
Beauport

Plourivo Plouézec

Château de
la Roche Jagu Pointe de Minard

Pontrieux Lanloup Bréhec

Plage Bonaparte Baie de

Port-Moguer St-Brieuc

St-Clet Kermaria-
an-Iskuit Plouha

D786

Lanvollon St-Quay-Portrieux

noroc'h Pléguien Étables-sur-Mer

Goudelin Notre-Dame
de la Cour Lantic

Pabu Binic

St-Jean- Parc Zoologique

Guingamp Kerdaniel Pointe de Pordic

Trégoméur Pordic les Rosaires

agoat Châtelaudren

R M O R N12-E50 Plérin

Gouët ST-BRIEUC

D Plerneuf E

THE PINK GRANITE COAST Brittany's northerly peninsulas face the sea in a welter of coastal drama. Their ragged
promontories, deeply cut by river valleys, offer a great
variety of brooding cliffs, expansive beaches, islands and
coves. Most striking, however, is the richly coloured rock
that gives the region its name, lying mainly between
Paimpol and Trébeurden. These russet outcrops of
granite are quite extraordinary, not merely in hue but
also for the strange forms they assume. Not surprisingly,
these often acquire fanciful names, such as the Turtles,
the Pancakes and Napoleon's Hat. Ploumanac'h and
Trégastel-Plage are the places that show this strange rock
garden at its most spectacular, especially at sunset.
When quarried and polished for building purposes the
granite sparkles with diamond precision, and its attractive colour makes it popular for Parisian shopfronts and
luxury bathrooms.

LONELY SHORES This chapter covers not only the Pink
Granite Coast but also the adjoining stretches between
St. Brieuc and Paimpol, plus Lannion and Morlaix. Both
are equally impressive in their way. The eastern section
on St.-Brieuc Bay, with its sweeping grey cliffs and sheltered beaches, is sometimes called the Goëlo coast, after
the local landowning family who built Beauport abbey.
The Circuit des Falaises (see page 86) is worth exploring,
not just for the brooding cliff scenery but for its historic
associations as a Resistance headquarters in World
War II, as some of Brittany's most exciting escape stories

The Pink Granite Coast

The Pink Granite Coast

Right: The curious bent spire of St.-Gonéry chapel on the Plougrescant peninsula crowns a 10th-century building that contains reliquaries, frescoes and lively woodcarvings

UPPER AND LOWER BRITTANY

This chapter spans the divide between French-speaking Haute (Upper) and Breton-speaking Basse (Lower) Brittany. It may seem illogical to refer to west Brittany as 'Lower Brittany' and east Brittany as 'Upper Brittany' but this tradition stems back to Celtic times. Celts regarded the rising sun as the focal point of their world, and orientated their compass on it. So the east was the equivalent of our modern north and the west the south. Basse Bretagne has more vibrant regional traditions and is divided into four districts based on ancient bishoprics: Trégor (Tréguier), Léon (St.-Pol-de-Léon), Cornouaille (Quimper) and Vannetais (Vannes).

The restored 15th-century château of la Roche Jagu

are set on these lonely shores. The coast between Lannion and Morlaix straddles the Finistère border and is known as the Armorique Corniche. Only patchily pink, it makes a delightful drive for its pretty fishing ports and its glorious beaches (see pages 82–83).

The charms of the Pink Granite Coast make it one of the area's most popular holiday regions, and facilities are predictably extensive in the larger resorts of Perros-Guirec or St.-Quay-Portrieux. Nowhere, however, feels overpoweringly urban, and as there are no major ferry ports along this coast, holiday traffic is more evenly distributed. Off the beaten track, especially if you are willing to walk, you can have whole beaches entirely to yourself.

MARITIME TRADITIONS The inhabitants of the Pink Granite Coast have always gazed seawards for their livelihoods, trawling the rich cod-fishing waters of Iceland and Newfoundland and manning the French navy. Some were wreckers who lived on plunder, luring ships on to their deadly reefs with lanterns slung on cattle horns. Others pillaged neighbouring national merchant fleets as corsairs (see page 68). Even the region's historic inland towns, Tréguier and Lannion, stand on tidal estuaries and feel unmistakably briny.

The Breton character becomes more pronounced as the French border recedes, and from the Goëlo coast westwards, Celtic place-names appear more frequently, often with the prefixes *Tre, Pen, Ker, Plou* or *Lan*. Many of these settlements were originally founded by monks from Britain or Ireland fleeing the Norsemen in the Dark Ages. Annual events also indicate a sense of regional tradition, with the rituals of the festivals in Tréguier and Paimpol dating back centuries.

EXPLORING This northern extremity is surprisingly mild, and the sheltered Île de Bréhat is a lush paradise of subtropical flowers and pink granite reefs. Even the worst sailor won't have time to feel seasick on this 10-minute hop. Equally enjoyable for bird-lovers is a spring jaunt around les Sept Îles off Perros-Guirec when the gannets and puffins are nesting. Take binoculars and a camera.

Even though most visitors favour the seaside, the hinterland is worth exploring too. Off the busy N12, two places repay a detour: The lively market centre of Guingamp with its mysterious Black Virgin, and the countryside around Belle-Isle-en-Terre where the land peaks at Menez-Bré.

Church architecture (Runan, Kermaria, Tréguier, Lannion, St.-Jean-du-Doigt) and interesting châteaux (la Roche Jagu, Rosanbo, Tonquédec and Kergrist) are in plentiful supply. Prehistoric sights don't match the megaliths around Carnac, but if your tour is confined to northern Brittany, see the Barnenez cairn near Morlaix and one or two of the dolmens around Trébeurden. The towns with the most character and best-preserved old quarters are Tréguier, Paimpol and Lannion, while the prettiest villages include Binic, Port-Blanc, Locquirec and le Diben. The best wet-weather venue by far is the futuristic Musée des Telecoms at Pleumeur-Bodou. Spare half a day there, especially if you have children on board (see pages 84–85).

The rocky shoreline at Trégastel is one of the most scenic stretches of the Pink Granite Coast

DEATH'S GENTLEMEN GO BY...
In superstitious Trégor, near Pleumeur-Bodou, the Breton bogeyman, Ankou, was feared greatly by all the country people. Even in the early 20th century, local smugglers took advantage of people's strong beliefs to gain unhindered passage through the villages on dark nights. They loaded their contraband onto a cart with rag-wrapped wheels to reduce the noise. Then one of their number would dress up in a white sheet and brandish a scythe to frighten away any prying eyes.

The chapel of St.-Hervé surveys a vast sweep of countryside from the summit of Menez-Bré

AN OLD-FASHIONED MILLIONAIRE
Marie Le Manac'h was a miller's daughter born in Belle-Isle-en-Terre. On a visit to Paris she had the good fortune to meet an extremely wealthy English aristocrat, who was so bowled over by her charms that he asked her to marry him. When she was left affluently widowed, Lady Mond returned to spend her remaining days in a château on the outskirts of Belle-Isle. She is buried with her husband in a fine marble monument in the ossuary of the Chapelle de Locmaria.

▶ **Beauport, Abbaye de**   71D2

www.abbaye-beauport.com
Open: mid-Jun to mid-Sep daily 10–7, artistic events;
late-Sep to early Jun 10–12, 2–5. Admission moderate
Serious restoration work (scheduled for completion in 2009) is in progress on the abbey, which once held sway over 13 parishes. The abbey ruins lie just southeast of Paimpol, in a verdant setting overlooking the sea. Founded in 1202 by an order of la Lucerne monks called Premonstratensians, it was once a significant halt along a medieval pilgrim route to the shrine of St. James at Santiago de Compostela in Spain. Its gates were left open as a sign of hospitality. In later centuries the abbey fell into decline, and was sold in 1790 after the last monks left.
Visitors are shown the vestiges of the 13th–14th-century church, cloisters and a Gothic Norman chapter house. More intact sections are the Romanesque refectory, with a cellar below resting on great granite pillars, and the visitors' hostel, where a rare double-decker Breton box bed stands, big enough for a whole family. Concerts and cultural events take place throughout the year.

▶ **Belle-Isle-en-Terre**   70C1

A brief detour off the N12 leads to this pleasant grey-stone town, swathed in woodland where two rivers meet. There isn't much to see in the town itself but it livens up greatly on the third Sunday in July when a *pardon* is held, followed by a more secular festival featuring Breton wrestling (see page 24).
Several places of interest lie close at hand. The chapel of **Locmaria**▶ is just north of town, worth seeing for its 16th-century rood screen bearing polychrome statues of the Apostles. The marble tomb of Lady Mond conceals a tale of rags to riches (see panel). The church of **Loc-Envel**▶

(4km / 2 miles south) also has a beautiful rood screen and many carved and painted beams. A little farther away (9km / 5.5 miles southeast) is **Gurunhuel**, where the calvary depicts an unusual scene of souls leaving the bodies of the two robbers crucified with Christ: One is received by an angel, the other by a demon.

The hill of **Menez-Bré▶** is another popular destination from Belle-Isle (9km / 5.5 miles northeast off the D116 Guingamp road). At 302m (990ft) above sea level, this pudding-basin hill of gorse and grass is the highest point in northern Brittany. A brief yet steep ascent from the Trégorrois plateau rewards you with views of a valley-etched landscape, fringed by the distant sea and the foothills of the Monts d'Arrée. There's a viewing table, and the tiny chapel of St.-Hervé provides a closer focal point (see panel).

▶ Binic   71E1

This resort is by-passed by the main coastal road and overshadowed by St.-Quay-Portrieux to the north. Many visitors, therefore, miss the chance to discover this attractive low-key holiday base on the bay of St.-Brieuc. Its grey stone and slate houses by the port once housed a sizeable deep-sea fishing community, whose intrepid seafarers used to leave their homes each April for six-month stints fishing in the waters of Newfoundland or Iceland. A little museum charts their history. Now its fleet stays fairly close inshore, and the town supplements its tourist revenue with the sale of mud from the River Ic for fertilizer.

Penthièvre Pier is a good vantage point for Binic's beach. A scenic coastal footpath leads to the Pointe de Pordic and the splendid 3km (2 mile) beach of les Rosaires to the south. Inland, the **Zoo de Trégomeur**, a 12ha (30-acre) wildlife park (tel: 02 96 79 01 07; *closed* for renovation, due to open in April 2006, check opening times after this date. *Admission moderate*), and the pretty 15th-century chapel of Notre-Dame de la Cour at **Lantic** (stained glass and granite statuary) make a good day out.

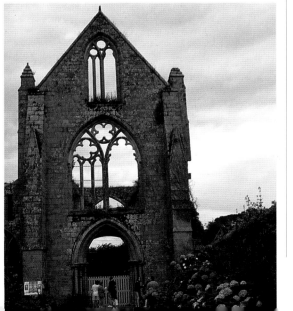

ST. HERVÉ

St. Hervé is one of those mysterious Breton saints about whom many legends have grown. He cured mental disorders and irrational fears, and in local churches is often represented being led by a wolf. This was his guide, for St. Hervé was born blind. When his mother was pregnant she prayed that her child would never witness the world's cruelty and dishonesty, and her prayers were answered all too well. Hervé's blindness, though, gave him the power to see into men's souls, and he was credited with great intuition. He became a celebrated poet, a monk, and, some say, a horse-thief.

75

Flower-decked shopfronts at Belle-Isle-en-Terre

The Gothic shell of Beauport abbey's medieval church stands open to the elements

DUCKING THE STORMS
Bréhat's low-lying topo-
graphy gives its residents
and visitors an additional
advantage. Atlantic rain-
clouds frequently pass
right over the island,
leaving it dry and sunny.

NEW-FOUND LANDS
According to Bréhat
legend, Columbus used
the same route as the
island's fishermen when
he was on his way to the
New World. A Breton
sailor told him of the
Bréhat route to the
Newfoundland cod
fisheries some eight or
nine years before his first
voyage in 1492. Could
Bréhat sailors have been
the first Europeans to
reach America?

▶▶▶ Bréhat, Île de   71D3

Pointe de l'Arcouest, just north of Paimpol, is the closest
point of access for this idyllic island. The Île de Bréhat lies
about 2km (1 mile) offshore, enticingly visible from the
mainland as a low-lying wooded paradise encircled by a
bracelet of pink granite reefs and islets. There is little to
see or do on Bréhat, but the look of the place is hard to
resist, and many eminent writers and painters have been
enchanted by it. Now Bréhat's permanent population
stands at under 400, which swells to about ten times that
number each summer, when its three hotels are often fully
booked. A pleasant alternative is its wooded campsite. All
year round, Les Vedettes de Bréhat shuttle back and forth
on 10-minute hops, hourly in summer. You can also reach
the island from Erquy, Binic and St.-Quay-Portrieux.

Bréhat is effectively two islands balancing together and
now firmly anchored by one of Vauban's useful bridges.
No cars are allowed, but a few tractors are used by the
locals and bicycles are available for rent. You can walk
from one end of Bréhat to the other in under an hour, and
waymarked paths lead all over the island.

A turbulent past Despite Bréhat's apparent peacefulness,
it has witnessed some grim episodes, notably at the hands
of English raiders who blew up its castle and massacred
the local population at Crec'h ar Pot mill in 1409. Another
mill, Crec'h Tarec, was an execution site during the 16th-
century Wars of Religion.

Like most islanders, many of Bréhat's inhabitants chose a seafaring life. Its fishermen ventured great distances, and many became privateers in the 18th and 19th centuries. During World War II Bréhat remained under German occupation until 4 August, 1944.

Island paradise Today ferries dock at Port Clos on the southern island, where passengers disembark to explore an orderly subtropical jungle of hydrangeas, honeysuckle, mimosa, figs and geraniums, half-concealing elegant luxury villas in spacious gardens. Beaches of pink shingle stud the scalloped coastline, and some of the reefs are accessible at low tide. The northerly island is bleaker, with wilder beaches and a desolate coastline. Head here for quiet picnics; alternatively, try the pine-clad slopes of the Bois de la Citadelle at the southwest tip of the island. A glass-making studio is housed in the old fort.

Bréhat has only one main village, **le Bourg,** where houses are grouped around a square surrounded by plane-trees and overlooked by the pink-granite bell tower of the church. The island's tourist office is also here. Other sights include the chapel of St.-Michel, where just 39 steps lead to a grandstand island view, and the Croix de Maudez, an 18th-century calvary commemorating a Celtic monk. La Corderie, surrounded by palatial Parisian holiday homes, is a magnificent rounded bay, Bréhat's main anchorage for pleasure craft. There is an interesting tidal mill at le Birlot (*Open* occasionally at weekends). At the island's northern tip is Paon lighthouse, which commands marvellous coastal views amid a profusion of wild flowers and seabirds. Inland, Rosédo lighthouse dates from 1862.

77

Île de Brehat (above and below)

WOLF-SCARING
A few weeks after Guingamp's annual *pardon* in July, the town lays on more festivities. The Festival de la Danse Bretonne in mid-August helps to keep local traditions thriving, with Breton music and dancing. A special shepherds' dance is performed, accompanied not by music but by stamping feet, allegedly to frighten wolves away.

The Black Virgin at Guingamp (right)
Wooden caryatids adorn some of the old houses in Lannion (below)

78

▶ Guingamp   71D1

This large, busy town lies on the main N12, some 30km (20 miles) inland. Its modern industrial outskirts do not entice, but if you are passing by, the dignified, well-kept old centre is well worth a visit. Once Guingamp was a Roman way-station, and it was heavily fortified during the Middle Ages when it grew wealthy on the cloth trade (some say Guingamp is a corruption of the word *guingan*, or 'gingham', allegedly first made here). It has continued to prosper, and has expanded greatly with engineering works and food-processing factories. It is also an agricultural centre with a good market which is held on Friday. The town is famed throughout France for its very successful football team. Local enthusiasm for the beautiful game is such that Guingamp's Roudourou stadium is capable of holding twice the entire population of the town. If you have no objection to staying in towns, Guingamp makes a comfortable and strategic excursion base for some attractive parts of the *argoat* (inland Brittany), particularly the wooded Trieux valley and the lonely calvary villages to the south.

Little remains of Guingamp's fortifications except a couple of sections of ramparts and a ruined castle with weighty drum towers. Its main sight is the 14th-century church of **Notre-Dame-de-Bon-Secours▶** on the pedestrianized main street. One of its twin Gothic towers collapsed in the 16th century and was replaced by a Renaissance version. Inside and out, the basilica is full of interest, with a fine doorway at the west end, graceful pillars and buttresses in the chancel. However, the bit not to miss is the separate chapel on rue Notre-Dame, which houses Guingamp's revered **Black Virgin▶**, another of those dark images allegedly brought back from the crusades. A July *pardon* celebrates the Virgin, with bonfires lit in the Place du Centre, a seemly square of cafés and half-timbered houses. The square's most striking feature is a lovely Renaissance **fountain▶** of lead and stone, adorned with winged griffins and spouting nymphs.

▶ Lannion   70C2

The second-largest town in the Côtes-d'Armor and the administrative centre of the Trégor region, Lannion stands at the head of the Léguer estuary. The hilly old port spreads both sides of the river, bordered by long quays and wooded towpaths which high tides often submerge. Fishing boats, some abandoned in the mud, line the waterfront, and the huge monastery of St. Anne is a prominent landmark. In the old town, beautiful 15th- and 16th-century houses form a stately picture in the cobbled Place du Général Leclerc and along the streets near the sundialed church of St.-Jean-du-Baly. Some of these houses are corbelled and turreted, while others are carved with caryatids, dragons, and impish faces.

Lannion's most interesting building occupies a wide vantage point at the top of the town, reached by climbing up a long flight of steep steps. The church of **Brélévenez**▶ dates from the 12th century, when it was founded by the Knights Templar. Remodelled in the 15th century, it is alive with curious features: a stoup just inside the main entrance, used for measuring tithe wheat; a Romanesque crypt eerily half visible beneath the chancel, and an intricate apse festooned with carved capitals and pillars. If you can't manage the 142 steps to the church, it can be reached by a rather circuitous trek through backroads; the helpful tourist office by the waterfront can provide a map.

Lannion makes an excellent excursion base (though traffic congestion is a problem in summer) and is also an attractive shopping centre for lace, antiques and crafts. There is an especially lively atmosphere on Thursdays, when a market is held in the main square, and during the Shrovetide carnival, but at any time the town feels pleasantly animated. The pulse of the local region can be felt here, and many roads meet at Lannion.

The elaborately carved doorway of Notre-Dame-de-Bon-Secours, Guingamp

CHATEAU DE ROSANBO
At Lanvellec, not far southwest of Lannion, stands this château, built on a former castle-topped rock over the River Rosanbo. The existing buildings date from various periods from the 14th to the 19th centuries, and the interior is richly furnished with tapestries, silverware and books (the library once belonged to Louis XIV's finance minister). Terraced grounds inspired by Le Nôtre, the famous French landscape gardener, surround the château (tel: 02 96 35 18 77; *open* Apr–Jun and Sep daily 2–5; Jul–Aug 11–6; Oct, Sun 2–5; guided tours. *Admission: moderate*).

79

Picturesque houses, slate-hung or timber-framed, stand on Lannion's main square

Drive

The woodland setting of Tonquédec castle

Inland from Lannion

See map on pages 70–71.

Though most people head for the spectacular coastline of Trégor, its wooded river valleys can be equally appealing, and the River Léguer is no exception. A few detours are essential on this 45km (28 miles) drive to see the points of interest. Allow half a day.

Heading south from Lannion along the D11, turn off past Ploubezre for the **Chapelle de Kerfons▶**, built during the 15th and 16th centuries. The chapel's outstanding feature is a rood screen with carved panels of the Apostles. Farther south is the ruined **Château de Tonquédec▶**. It was demolished at the behest of Cardinal Richelieu to prevent insurrection, but a couple of towers and some of the curtain walls are still intact.

From yet another side-turning on the left side of the road is the **Château de Kergrist▶**, intact and still inhabited.

This fine manor house is partly Gothic, partly neoclassical. The gardens differ in style, passing from formal parterres to naturalistic landscaping and woodland (*Open* Gardens: Jul–Sep daily 11–6.30; Apr–Oct 2–6. Château: guided tours pm only. *Admission expensive*).

Continuing south along the D11, turn left for **les Sept Saints▶**, south of le Run. This 18th-century chapel is built on top of a dolmen, accessible from a door in the south transept. A curious legend is associated with the chapel, which is dedicated to the Seven Sleepers (or Saints) of Ephesus, a group of Christians who were walled up by Emperor Decius in a cave in the 3rd century for refusing to renounce their faith. They awoke miraculously 200 years later and were released. The Seven Sleepers are mentioned in the Koran, and a pilgrimage to the chapel is organized each summer as a gesture of Christian–Muslim friendship.

Head back northwards up the D31. At Buhulien turn left for the ruins of the **Château de Coatfrec▶**, dating from the 16th century. The remains of a tower and parts of the domestic wings lurk beneath an ivy coat.

►► Paimpol

71D2

Sheltered in a deep cove at the north end of the bay of St.-Brieuc, Paimpol is an attractive, bustling port packed with pleasure craft and chandlery. It doesn't have any good beaches but its pleasant, workaday atmosphere attracts plenty of visitors who prefer its more authentic charms to those of purpose-built holiday resorts. The town's two harbour basins are modern and practical rather than aglow with nautical character, but the surrounding buildings are harmoniously shuttered and dormered. The Repaire de Kerroc'h (now a hotel, see page 269) was built by a former corsair.

There are more delightful old houses scattered throughout the cobbled town centre, especially around the Place du Martray, where a weekly market (Tuesday) displays the pick of fresh local produce, such as oysters, garlic, carrots and lettuces. Paimpol also has a wholesale market

Modern sculpture (above) and models of sailing ships (left) are some of the objects on display at Paimpol's Maritime Museum

81

which is held behind the station every day. Once Paimpol was an important deep-sea fishing port whose menfolk set sail en masse for the rich cod-fishing waters off the coast of Iceland. In the heyday of the trade, at the beginning of the 20th century, more than a hundred vessels worked from the port. The last boats sailed in 1935, and since then Paimpol has turned to inshore fishing and the less arduous cultivation of oysters in the nearby Trieux estuary. If you wander through the old town, you may spy a beautiful old chemist's shopfront advertising 'directly imported' cod liver oil.

Paimpol's **Musée de la Mer (Maritime Museum)►** (tel: 02 96 22 02 19; *open* mid-Jun to Aug daily 10.30–12.30, 2–6.30; Apr–May, Sep 2–6. *Admission moderate*), on rue de Labenne, contains memories of dangerous voyages, with navigational equipment, charts and models. Near the quayside is another small museum of regional costume (*Open* Jul–Aug daily 10.30–12.30, 2.30–6. *Admission inexpensive*). A statue in town commemorates Breton songwriter Théodore Botrel (see panel, page 162).

PIERRE LOTI
The author Pierre Loti (1850–1923), who lived in Paimpol's Place du Martray, set one of his novels here, *Pêcheur d'Islande* (Fisherman of Iceland), a classic sea-faring story made into a silent film in 1924. Loti (whose real name was Louis-Marie Julien Viaud) worked at sea himself for over 40 years, eventually becoming a captain.

EXCURSIONS FROM PAIMPOL
Take the scenic road to Pointe de l'Arcouest, where boats leave for the Île de Bréhat (see pages 76–77). On the way, detour down a side-road to the hamlets of Perros-Hamon and Porz-Even. The little chapel of 1770 at Perros-Hamon lists the names of those lost at sea, and the Widow's Cross marks the spot where the women of Paimpol would stand gazing out to sea in the hope of seeing sails. Southeast lie Pointe de Guilben, the Abbaye de Beauport (see page 74) and the Circuit des Falaises (see page 86).

Craft moored at Paimpol

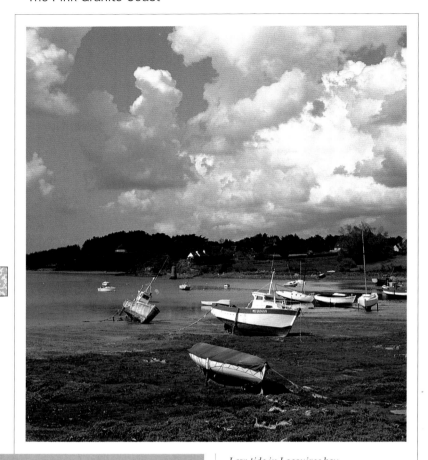

Low tide in Locquirec bay

Drive

The Armorique Corniche

See map on pages 70–71.

This 70km (42 miles) drive straddles the coastal borderlands of Finistère and the Côtes-d'Armor, through a varied landscape of vast sandy beaches, rocky headlands, and pretty fishing ports. The coast is jagged and there is no obvious main road, so just follow the lanes closest to the sea. Allow half a day.

If you have time, detour westwards from Lannion via the Léguer estuary, best at high tide. The coastal scenery is beautiful, and several small churches are worth inspecting. The 15th-century church at **Loguivy-les-Lannion** has a wooden altarpiece depicting the Adoration, with shepherds in local costume playing Breton instruments. The chapel at **le Yaudet** contains a carved panel of the Virgin and the Trinity. Farther south, **Trédrez** once had as its rector the redoubtable St. Yves, patron saint of lawyers (see page 21). Notice the angels and strange beasts carved on the ends of the beams. Inland, **Ploumilliau**'s 17th-century church contains more carved and painted panels and an unnerving sculpture of Ankou, the grim reaper, ready with scythe and spade to gather in his human crop.

The Corniche proper starts at **St.-Michel-en-Grève►**, a small resort with a pretty seafront church. It is surprisingly low key considering that it stands on one of Brittany's star beaches, a magnificent 4km (2-mile) crescent of perfectly golden sand that stretches 2km (1 mile) out to sea at low tide. Sand-yachting and other sports activities take advantage of the beach. Behind, a rocky knoll called the Grand Rocher is 80m (262ft) high, and is worth the climb for panoramic views. Farther along, **St.-Efflam** has a chapel with a domed fountain dedicated to the local hermit saint who lived at nearby Plestin in AD470, vanquishing dragons and doing good works.

Locquirec►, a popular resort and fishing port, occupies a scenic headland where affluent villas take advantage of the views. The church was built by the Knights of St. John and has a Renaissance bell tower. Westwards lies a series of glorious beaches, visible from the high viewing points beside the coastal road at Marc'h Sammet (good picnic spots on a clear day). **St.-Jean-du-Doigt►►** has one of the most interesting parish closes in the area (see pages 136–137), with a triumphal arch and a beautiful Renaissance fountain. The parish gets its name from its celebrated relic, the first joint of John the Baptist's index finger, which was brought here in the 15th century. The sacred finger was dipped in water and the water was then used to anoint the eyes of those afflicted with an infection. Duchesse Anne was cured of an eye complaint in this way and in gratitude she donated funds to complete the church in its present style. Ask for permission to see the finger, and the church's other treasures.

Westwards, **Plougasnou** and a series of pretty fishing ports (**le Diben, Térénez**) have superb driving past deep sandy bays, shellfish farms and rocky headlands. One of the best vantage points is **Pointe de Primel►**, accessible only on foot from the resort of Primel-Trégastel.

The last worthwhile sight before Morlaix lies well down the estuary, amid artichoke fields and swathes of gorse. The **Cairn de Barnenez►►** is one of the best prehistoric sights in northern Brittany. A huge mound of terraced brown granite nearly 80m (262ft) long and about 8m (23ft) high conceals two separate mounds of different stone, one predating the other (4400BC) by about 200 years. Eleven separate south-facing burial chambers overlook the estuary; most are blocked off for safety reasons but you can peep inside a couple. There are no carvings or interesting bits of tomb to see, and the few finds are on display at the visitor centre or in local museums (tel: 02 98 67 24 73; *open* Jun–Aug daily 10–6.30; Sep–May Tue–Sun 10–12.30, 2–5.30; guided tours; leaflets in English. *Admission moderate*).

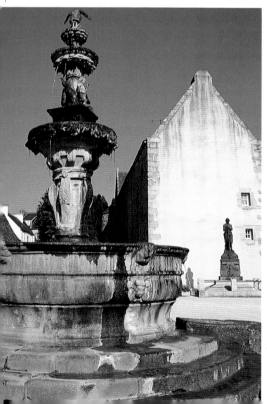

St.-Jean-du-Doigt's churchyard fountain depicts the baptism of Christ

83

Yacht masts jostle for space in Perros-Guirec's popular marina

ST. GUIREC
This Celtic monk arrived from Welsh shores in the 6th century and settled in a hermitage on the spectacular Pink Granite Coast. St. Guirec's talents spanned a wide range. He was variously associated with the cure of retarded children, abscesses and fiery tempers. Despite his celibate status he also acted as something of a marriage guidance counsellor, and would patiently listen to the hopes and fears of young women nearing their wedding day. Until the original wooden statue of St. Guirec in the oratory at Plage St.-Guirec was replaced with a more durable granite version, girls hoping to find a husband would stick a pin in his nose.

▶▶ **Perros-Guirec**   *70C2*

This is the largest resort on the Pink Granite Coast, and for a traditional family beach holiday there are few places to beat it. Well equipped, and spacious enough to disperse the summer crowds, it attracts older visitors as well. Two superb beaches lie to the northwest; southwards, a serpentine corniche road meanders past a gritty foreshore to the busy marina. On this side of town a small waxwork museum (tel: 02 96 91 23 45; *open* Jun–Aug daily 9.30–6.30; Apr–May, Sep 10–12.15, 2–6. *Admission inexpensive*) chronicles a century of turbulent local history from the Revolution onwards, while a casino, congress centre and thalassotherapy centre occupy the attractive seafront at Trestraou beach. A short footpath leads to the rocky tip of the promontory, Pointe du Château, from where a panoramic view of the coast can be seen. The semaphore signal station to the west provides another vantage point.

The unusual church of **St.-Jacques▶** in the middle of town is worth seeking out. Huge trefoil motifs decorate the porch, surmounted by a spiky bell tower like a German helmet. Inside, carved capitals crown its Romanesque pillars, and there is a Gothic nave. One of the best walks from Perros-Guirec leads along the old watchpath to Ploumanac'h (see page 87). Boat trips to the bird sanctuary at les Sept Îles (see page 90) are another popular excursion.

▶▶ **Pleumeur-Bodou**   *70B2*

The heathlands around this small village, northwest of Lannion, have one unmistakable landmark: a giant white puffball structure surrounded by banks of satellite dishes, called the Radôme. This futuristic scene marks the site of France's telecommunications research organization, the Centre National d'Études des Télécommunications (CNET), whose proudest moment came in 1962 when it received the first signals from the American satellite *Telstar*. No longer used for research, the site is now a large combined tourist attraction called **Cosmopolis**. Since 1991 the fascinating **Musée des Telecoms▶▶** (tel: 02 96 46 63

Detail from Notre-Dame-de-la-Clarté chapel, near Perros-Guirec

80; www.leradome.com; *open* Feb–Dec, variable hours. *Admission expensive*) has attracted visitors with its lively interactive displays charting the progress of message-relaying from the earliest semaphore systems to state-of-the-art modern technology. The highlight of a visit is a Radôme (radar dome) show, when you enter the huge dome for a high-tech account (in French) of satellite communication.

Also within the complex is the **Planetarium▶**, which supplements its starlit presentations with more down-to-earth details about Brittany today, these being relayed across a 67m (220ft) auditorium. Show times are found posted outside (or tel: 02 96 15 80 30; www.planetarium-bretagne.fr; combined ticket available).

Just opposite the Planetarium, **Le Village de Meem le Gaulois** conjures up a Romano-Gaulish settlement with modern African elements. Proceeds go to a charity for Third World education (tel: 02 96 91 83 95; *open* Jul–Aug 10.30–7; Easter–Sep Sun–Fri 2–6. *Admission moderate*).

THE RADÔME
The huge white globe at Pleumeur-Bodou measures more than 200m (650ft) in circumference and could shelter the Arc de Triomphe easily, yet its Dacron casing is only 2mm (0.8in) thick. To resist storms and high winds the air pressure inside is increased. The *Telstar* transmission was the first live television broadcast to be relayed across the Atlantic, from Andover in Maine just after midnight on 11 July, 1962.

The Radôme and visitor centre at Pleumeur-Bodou

The Pink Granite Coast

THE HOUSE IN THE ROCKS

A popular spot for coach stops on the Plougrescant peninsula is Castel-Meur, where a tiny stone cottage buttressed between huge lumps of granite stands isolated by the sea. The Kerguezec family first built their remarkable house in the 1860s, and descendants still live there today. So picturesque is the setting that the house was used in a tourism campaign several years ago. It is now a postcard cliché of Breton charm, so popular that leaflets beg you to respect the owners' privacy.

The scenic coastline of the Plougrescant peninsula

DANCING WITH DEATH

Inland from Plouha, the stone chapel of Kermaria-an-Iskuit (the House of Mary who Cures) makes a fascinating detour. The key keeper lives up a small track opposite the church. Inside, vivid frescoes illustrate the frailty of all mortal things in a *danse macabre*. In one section three noblemen out hunting encounter three dead men in a cemetery who assure them:

'Nous avons bien esté en chance
Autrefoys, comme estes à présent
Mais vous viendrez à nostre dance
Comme nous sommes maintenant.'

('We were like you once, but you will join our dance one day.')

Some say that St.-Saens' *Danse Macabre* was inspired by these paintings. The rest of the chapel has many oddities and is thoroughly memorable.

▶▶ Plougrescant, Presqu'île de 70C3

This ragged peninsula makes a fine excursion from either Tréguier or Perros-Guirec and can easily be tackled in half a day. Minor roads close to the shoreline can be confusing to follow, but the *route touristique* called the Circuit de la Côte des Ajoncs is some help. As the name suggests (*ajoncs* means 'gorse'), gorse makes a bright splash on local heathland throughout the summer.

Starting from Perros-Guirec, the drive through Louannec (where St. Yves was once rector) is fairly dull until after Trestel. **Port-Blanc▶**, a delightful fishing village resort, is the first bright spot. Stone villas gaze out over a mass of craggy islets, some of which have been commandeered for celebrity holiday homes. The chapel of **Notre-Dame▶** stands on a grassy hill, its roof sweeping almost to the ground and with a typical stepped wall belfry at one end. Inside, St. Yves adjudicates between a rich man and a poor man.

Brittany's most northerly peninsula, tipped by the **Pointe du Château▶▶**, is a magnificent sight at sunset. Nearby, signed paths lead to **le Gouffre▶**, a chasm

between rocks where the sea boils. Don't miss the pretty house at Castel-Meur (see panel). Round the headland, **St.-Gonéry▶** has a fascinating church with a stumpy spire of lead, bent out of true as though knocked by some giant bird (see page 72). Ask for the key at the shop opposite.

Finally, detour to **la Roche Jaune** on the Jaudy estuary, which is famed for its oysters.

▶▶ Plouha 71E1

Plouha itself is of no great interest, but from here it is possible to explore the dramatic slice of coastline south of Paimpol. Tourist authorities have devised a signposted route called the **Circuit des Falaises**. Highlights are the **Pointe de Minard▶▶** and the huddled port of **Bréhec**. For history buffs, though, the best destination lies just north of Plouha at **Plage Bonaparte▶▶**, which was the scene of a daring series of escapes during World War II (see page 43).

▶▶ Ploumanac'h 70C2

This smaller offshoot of Perros-Guirec is one of the most striking places in which to see the Pink Granite scenery. The resort is popular with young families, its pretty beach backed by a cluster of cheerful cafés, shops and restaurants. Fishing trips and excursions to the bird sanctuary at les Sept Îles leave from the bustling port to the south. The Château de Costaérès, just offshore, is where the author Heinryk Sienkiewicz, wrote the last pages of *Quo Vadis?*

Walk

Granite formations at Ploumanac'h

Le Sentier des Douaniers

The 6km (3.5 miles) coastguard's watchpath by the seashore from Perros-Guirec leads past an astonishing wilderness of rose-tinted boulders weathered into curious shapes. The walk is much more attractive than the road route, which is mostly built up. Allow about 90 minutes each way.

From Perros-Guirec the path begins at Plage de Trestraou, hugging the shore beneath the cliffs. At first it is unspectacular, with views of les Sept Îles and claw-like headlands.

At Pors Rolland the rocks change gear, transmogrifying into weird forms strewn chaotically over the seafront like unclaimed suitcases. The most peculiar of all are in Les Landes de Ploumanac'h, an orderly conservation zone where each formation is given some fanciful name, for example, the Tortoise and the Armchair. The neat, polished number-posts of pink granite scattered around show the different qualities of this stone when artificially cut instead of eroded naturally. One of the largest and most remarkable rock formations is called the **Château du Diable►** (Devil's Castle). A pink lighthouse guards the headland.

You can follow the rocks round to Plage St.-Guirec, where an oratory and a statue mark the local patron saint. At the research unit housed in the Maison du Littoral on the edge of the park, there is a permanent exhibition on local geology and natural history (*Open* Jun to mid-Sep, daily 10–1, 2–6; Tue–Sun pm low season. *Admission free*).

A flower growing near Perros Guirec

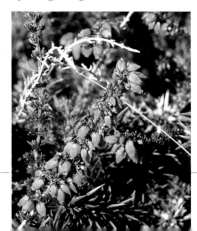

Walking is Brittany's most popular recreational activity, and with over 5,000km (3,000 miles) of waymarked routes there is no shortage of choice: along canal towpaths (chemins de halage), coastguard tracks (sentiers des douaniers) or open countryside (sentiers de pays).

THE TRO BREIZ

The cathedrals of the Seven Founding Saints were the subject of a great medieval pilgrimage called the Tro Breiz, which had to be completed in under a month. Those who didn't do it in their lifetime had to undertake it after death (at the rate of a coffin's length every seven years) before they could rest in peace. The tradition ended during the 16th-century Wars of Religion, but today's tourist-pilgrims can still follow the route.

Feet (or wings) are the only way to reach the summit of Roc'h Trévézel

USEFUL ADDRESSES

• Fédération Française de la Randonnée Pédestre, 14 rue Riquet, 75019 Paris (tel: 01 44 89 93 90; www.ffrp.asso.fr)
• Randobreizh, 1 rue Raoul Ponchon, 35068 Rennes Cedex (tel: 02 99 27 03 20; www.randobr-eizh.com)
Detailed Topoguides cover the GR routes, available in English from good special-ist bookshops in the UK.

Themed walking Any tourist office can present you with many suggestions for local walks. More than 20 of France's Grandes Randonnées (long-distance footpaths) pass through Brittany, marked with distinctive red-and-white trail signs. One of the longest and best-known of these is the GR34, hugging the Breton coastline for more than 2,000km (1,243 miles) from Mont-St-Michel to the

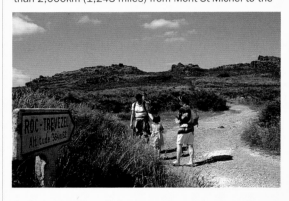

Golfe du Morbihan. These long routes are supplemented by a host of shorter ones, some circular, some linking particular themes.

Retrace the footsteps of medieval pilgrims on the Tro Breiz, an 800km (500 mile) trek around all the cathedrals and shrines of Brittany's seven founding saints (see panel). At one time all Bretons hoping for a place in heaven attempted this walk, a tall order in the days when signposts, campsites and rest huts were less readily available.

Undemanding terrain Compared with some regions of France, Brittany has little true wilderness and no signifi-cant mountains, so its scenery scarcely matches Alpine or Pyrenean heights. On the other hand, most of it is accessible to any walker of moderate fitness. All you need is sensible footwear (trainers are fine for lighter routes in the summer), a good map (the IGN 1:50,000 series is excellent for walking), and preferably a compass. Be prepared for changeable weather with light waterproofs, a warm sweater and a sun hat, and take along something to drink and some emergency rations. As in all areas that are intensively farmed, not all footpaths across agricultural land are readily accessible or clearly marked.

If you are at all interested in birds, don't forget to pack your binoculars. Brittany's location on the western seaboard makes it the first landfall for a wide variety of migrant birds. Inland, the region's diverse habitats offer sanctuary to many unusual species.

Coastal reserves Two of the most important island reserves in Brittany are les Sept Îles off Perros-Guirec (see page 90), where gannets and puffins breed at the southerly limit of their range, and the Île des Landes near Cancale. There is no public access to either of these sanctuaries, so you can see the birds only with fieldglasses from a boat. Koh Castell near Sauzon on Belle-Île (see pages 180–181) is also a good place to watch seabirds, and Île Grande, near Trégastel, has an ornithology centre where sick birds are treated. The Goulien reserve on Cap Sizun (see page 173) is open to visitors from March to August, and the Maison de la Baie d'Audierne on the Penmarc'h peninsula (see page 158), with a 600ha (1,500 acre) reserve of pools, marshland and sand dunes, has good information for bird-watchers at the visitor centre (*Open* Jul–Aug, 11–7; 2–6 low season).

The best times to visit reserves are spring and summer, when nesting birds can be seen, although autumn can be an exciting time for migrating species. In winter the Golfe du Morbihan (see page 193) is home to the largest concentration of seabirds and wildfowl on the French Atlantic coast.

Inland bird-watching One of the most interesting bird-watching centres inland is the strange peat marsh called la Grande Brière (see pages 232–233), where coastal species mingle with purple herons, bitterns and rare songbirds. Watch them at the Parc Animalier near Rozé. The lonelier uplands of the Monts d'Arrée (see pages 120–121) are home to birds of prey and moorland species. Ospreys even cruise in occasionally. Wooded valleys encourage woodpeckers, owls, warblers and nightingales.

However, as in many parts of Europe, modern agricultural practices and urban development, along with the indiscriminate shooting of migrant birds around the Mediterranean, have severely reduced bird populations.

Razorbills (below) near the Île Grande, near Trégastel. The island is one of Brittany's foremost bird sanctuaries

The Pink Granite Coast

90

Neat grey and white houses at Trébeurden provide holiday homes in the summer

▶ St.-Quay-Portrieux 71E1

As was the case with several of the ports along the Goëlo coast, St.-Quay once dispatched its menfolk to fish for cod off Newfoundland. Today it has replaced its cod-fishing revenue with scallops, lobsters, mackerel and plaice

FLOATING STONES
Despite its modern facilities, St.-Quay-Portrieux has a historic pedigree. Its founder was yet another of those Irish monks fleeing from raiding Norsemen. St. Ké (or Quay) arrived sometime in the 5th century in a boat laden with stone troughs, used as ballast to steady his craft. Some legends even associate this saint with Sir Kay of King Arthur's court.

Le Père Eternel has an excellent vantage point of Trégastel from the rocks by the aquarium

caught more locally. Most important nowadays, however, is tourism. St.-Quay has boomed as an all-purpose resort with a massive new harbour built in 1990 and continues to expand in all directions. To some extent it has outbuilt its natural charms and is not the prettiest or most peaceful place to stay. Its leisure activities, though, are admirable, and it even has some semblance of nightlife with a casino, disco, bars and cafés.

St.-Quay has five good beaches to accommodate its crowds, with Mickey Clubs (supervised entertainment for young children) and lifeguards, while an outdoor swimming pool provides calmer waters. Sea-angling trips and cruises to the Ile de Bréhat (see pages 76–77) are available, while the Chemin de Ronde footpath is also popular.

▶ Les Sept Îles 70B3

The seven scraps of land visible from the coast around Perros-Guirec form one of Brittany's most important bird sanctuaries. Half-day boat trips during the spring nesting season offer views of many types of gull, plus oyster-catchers, guillemots, razorbills, cormorants and kittiwakes. Rarer species include petrels and auks, while one island, Rouzic, is noted for a large breeding colony of gannets.

Regular seasonal cruises from Ploumanac'h and Perros-Guirec sail all round the islands, but not all allow time to land. Landings are permitted at only one island, Île aux Moines, which was once home to a colony of Franciscan friars. An hour's sojourn there allows enough time for a look at the ruined fortress and an old gunpowder factory, and even a scramble up the lighthouse's 83 steps for a glance back at the mainland coast. The islands were once a base for English marauders, hence the fortifications.

▶ **Trébeurden**   70B2

Approached from the west, this is the first village on the Pink Granite Coast proper, and the local rocks suddenly take on a magical hue. Trébeurden is a popular but low-key family resort with facilities for watersports and several good beaches split by rocky piers. Off shore, views of granite reefs and tidal islets add great charm to the setting, though the seafront development is fairly dull. Le Castel and Pointe de Bihit make good viewpoints.

Île Milliau and Île Molène (small islands near by) are *sites naturels protégés* (protected areas) with interesting flora and fauna, and guided walks are available. The marshland behind the resort (Marais du Quellen) is also a paradise for nature-lovers, and provides a grazing patch for a group of Camargue horses.

▶▶ **Trégastel**   70B2

The community of Trégastel is split into two sections: *bourg* (town) and *plage* (beach). The resort is obviously the place most visitors head for: a continuation of the scenic rock formations of Ploumanac'h (see pages 86 and 87). Although the beaches are good here the sand is rather coarse. Plage de Coz-Porz is the central beach, with plenty of things to do (children's clubs, watersports and a large indoor sports complex, the Forum). Beneath one of the more dramatic rock clusters a series of caves has been turned into an **aquarium**▶ of local and Mediterranean species (tel: 02 96 23 48 58; *open* Apr–Sep daily 10–12, 2–6; Jul–Aug, 10–7, Oct 2–5. *Admission moderate*). The caves were once used as a church.

More intriguing shapes and islets lie near the Île Renote, and the Grève Blanche to the south. Inland, the 12th-century church in the older Trégastel *bourg* houses the grave of the writer Charles le Goffic. Several megaliths lie scattered in the area: A menhir topped by a cross can be found on the coast road south and there is a dolmen at Kerguntuil. The Île Grande, 6km (4 miles) south, is linked to the mainland by a narrow bridge, and has an ornithology centre and an *allée couverte* (gallery grave).

OUR LADY OF HOPE
To the south of St.-Quay-Portrieux, quieter Étables-sur-Mer is a place of established villas and clifftop views. The chapel of Notre-Dame-de-l'Espérance, built after a devastating cholera out-break in 1850, has an interior bright with blue stained glass, paintings and tapestry.

91

Trégastel harbour

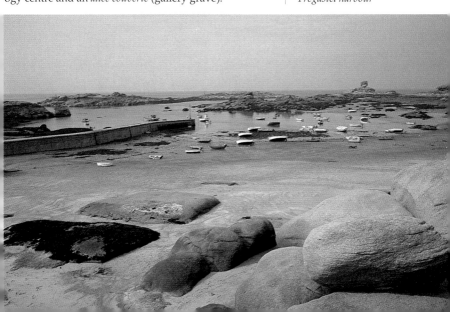

The Pink Granite Coast

ERNEST RENAN (1823–1892)
The 19th-century writer and philosopher spent the first 15 years of his life in an old house near Tréguier's cathedral, now a museum to his memory (tel: 02 96 92 45 63; *open* Jul–Aug daily 10–12, 2–6; Apr–Jun and Sep Wed–Sat 10–12, 2–6, Sun 2–6. *Admission moderate*). One room contains his school desk. Renan began to train for the priesthood but lost his vocation and became a free-thinking rationalist, questioning traditional religious views in the light of contemporary scientific discoveries. He appalled the Catholic Church by suggesting in his *Life of Jesus* that Christ, though utterly remarkable, was no more than human. Strong objections were lodged when a memorial statue was erected in the town's main square, but there it remains: The philosopher sits hunched in a chair, lost in thought.

The cloisters of Tréguier cathedral, with the bishop's palace behind

▶▶▶ Tréguier   70C2

Now usurped by Lannion as the capital of Trégor, this historic town remains one of the most appealing in the whole region. It occupies a hilly site over the Jaudy estuary, where a sheltered inlet provides safe anchorage for many yachts and the occasional cargo vessel.

A couple of tall gateway towers are all that remain of the town's old fortifications. Tréguier's medieval status as a place of art and learning, however, is still echoed in the bookshops and craft galleries that crowd its picturesque half-timbered buildings. The town was founded by a Welsh monk, St. Tugdual (or Tudwal), in the 6th century, became an independent diocese 300 years later, and by the 13th century was a place of great significance. This was largely due to the widespread fame of a later saint, Yves, patron saint of lawyers (see page 21), who was then resident in the town.

Tréguier's cathedral, built of pink granite, is its most impressive building—a candidate, indeed, for the prize among any in Brittany. Its piecemeal construction in a variety of styles over several centuries has achieved a pleasing harmony. Most of it is Gothic, though one of its three towers, over the transept, is Romanesque. The great spire at its west end is a masterpiece of the Decorated period, fretted into multi-patterned holes like the shapes from a child's stencil box, to reduce wind resistance. Inside, there is much to enjoy: vaulting, Renaissance choirstalls, stained glass glowing from nearly 70 windows, and 15th-century cloisters, where recumbent statues lie in an ambulatory of Flamboyant arches on delicate columns. Its most striking feature is the tomb of St. Yves, romantically marbled in the 19th century after mindless desecration of the original grave during the Revolution. Votive candles and plaques of thanks stand by his effigy, placed there by generations of grateful lawyers. On the third Sunday in May, the anniversary of Yves' death, a *pardon* is held in Tréguier, when the saint's reliquary is wheeled out of the Treasury and carried along the streets to his birthplace down the road at Minihy-Tréguier.

Outside the cathedral lies Place du Martray, a wide square surrounded by lovely old houses, some turned into restaurants and shops. Near the tourist office is Renaud's war memorial, a sculpted woman in Breton dress grieving for lost menfolk.

▶ **Trieux Estuary**   *71D2*

This is best seen by boat (summer day trips from Bréhat and Pointe de l'Arcouest), and it is a popular destination for pleasure-sailors, although sandbanks and rapid currents require cautious navigation. The railway line from Paimpol to Pontrieux hugs the banks closely, as does the GR34 footpath. At the river mouth, **Loguivy** is one of Brittany's prettiest fishing ports, where lobsters are a delicacy. Lenin chose it as a holiday base in 1902, though not for its beaches: it has none. Farther upstream, **Lézardrieux**'s suspension bridge gives good views of oysterbeds and tiny coves, and the local church has an elegant gabled belfry typical of the region.

Some of the boat excursions allow time to visit **Château de la Roche Jagu** on the west bank (*Open* Jul–Aug daily 10–7, Feb–Oct 10.30–12.30, 2–6. *Admission moderate*). One of the region's most imposing castles, now state-owned, it was restored to its former glory in 1968. On its wooded eyrie over the Trieux, the castle's 15th-century shell conceals a Renaissance interior of huge fireplaces and fine ceilings. The château is an imposing venue for summer events, including a jazz festival in August.

Pontrieux commands the original bridging point over the Trieux river, and is a pleasant old port of lovely wood and stone buildings. Once Pontrieux kitted out vessels for the Icelandic fishing runs; now it deals in shipping *maërl*, a kind of mud used to improve agricultural land.

A quiet corner of Tréguier's old town

PRESQU'ÎLE SAUVAGE
The most striking feature of the Wild Peninsula is a strange 2km (1 mile) long spit of sand and pebbles trailing northeastwards into the ocean, called the **Sillon de Talbert**.

At Runan is a richly ornate 14th-century church associated with both Templar and Hospitaller knights, containing painted vaults, sculpted altar scenes of the Virgin's life, and a lovely east window.

THE USES OF SEAWEED
The seaweed that collects on this remote coast is gathered and then processed inland at Pleubian in a research station called the Centre d'Études et de Valorisation des Algues (CEVA) (tel: 02 96 22 89 16; *open* for guided tours Jul–Aug Wed–Fri at 10.30 and 4, Sun at 3. *Admission moderate*).

Smooth granite boulders and soft sand at one of Brignogan-Plages' attractive cove beaches.
Several good walks can be taken across the nearby dunes

NORTH FINISTÈRE Most territorial extremities have a romantic fascination, and Brittany's Finistère is no exception. In terms of landscape, however, this tempestuous coast is disappointingly mundane. There are few breathtaking highlights to compare with the jagged, snarling headlands farther south or the gorgeous rock and cliff scenery to the east. To enjoy this northern section of Basse Bretagne you must learn to love muddy estuaries, thrive on exposed beaches and appreciate the symmetry of an immaculately tended cabbage field.

In Latin the region's name signified the end of the known world (*finis terrae*). The Celtic Bretons knew the westerly outpost as *Penn-ar-Bed*, 'the beginning of the land'—perhaps a more optimistic way of looking at it. Today the administrative *département* of Finistère covers the whole of western Brittany, and North Finistère is the section between Morlaix and Brest harbour, the old Pays de Léon, once a bishopric based on St.-Pol-de-Léon.

REGIONAL COLOUR Finistère is the most Breton of Brittany's regions, deeply imbued with ancient customs and Celtic beliefs. It is the area where you are most likely to hear Breton spoken, and even (though rarely these days) see costumes and *coiffes* worn as everyday garb. Intense religious fervour is mixed with the most farfetched superstitions; it's a land of priests and a land of pagans, as medieval visitors remarked. Even today, strict morality and pious observance of church services are upheld in the more rural districts. If you happen to visit

North Finistère

Typical half-timbering and granite on a north Breton house

THALASSOTHERAPY

Many Bretons have perished in the sea, but others testify to its healing powers. Brittany is France's most ardent exponent of sea-water health cures. Sea-bathing first became popular in Louis-Philippe's reign (1830–1848), and the first coastal spa was set up in Roscoff by Louis Bagot. Now thalassotherapy centres have sprung up in about a dozen resorts. Here you can bask in sea-water whirlpools, be massaged with high-pressure jets, or smeared with seaweed creams in the interests of health, beauty or sheer hedonism. Physiotherapy sessions aim to relieve all manner of aches and pains, including rheumatism and arthritis.

Finistère in early September, be sure to make for the little pilgrimage village of le Folgoët, where one of Brittany's most vivid and evocative *pardons* is held.

HISTORIC LANDMARKS In the 16th and 17th centuries North Finistère grew rich from the grain trade, often exporting it to England and the Low Countries. A large share of the proceeds inevitably went to the local churches, and today the flattish countryside is punctuated with tall and splendid bell towers, pierced with holes to reduce wind resistance. Some of the best of these are at Berven, Bodilis, Goulven and Lampaul-Ploudalmézeau, and the mightiest of all is in St.-Pol-de-Léon.

Other signs of prosperity lie in Léon's castles and manor-houses, many of which are frustratingly tucked away down long drives or camouflaged in thickets of woodland. An exception is the Château de Kerjean, south of Plouescat, worth a visit for both the building and its contents. Coastal landmarks include a stately palisade of lighthouses warning shipping off the treacherous reefs. The Phare de l'Île Vierge, near Plouguerneau, is the tallest in France, and on the Île d'Ouessant, site of the powerful Phare de Creac'h, there is even a museum about lighthouses.

THE MODERN ECONOMIC SCENE For centuries Finistère's geographical remoteness was a serious handicap. Hampered by poor communications and bad roads, its people looked elsewhere than central France for trading partners. Modern Finistère is now linked by fast expressway and TGV connections to its hinterland, but newly equipped refrigerated container lorries still roll on and off the ferries at Roscoff, laden with early vegetables and prime seafood. There are no large resorts, but revenue from tourism is important to the region, trickling into the system from a multiplicity of seaside *gîtes*, villas and campsites. Today the agricultural scene is counterbalanced by the large industrial city of Brest, an important naval base, which since the late 1980s has been a target of large-scale government investment.

TOURING SUGGESTIONS The historic towns of Landerneau (covered in the Armorique section) and Morlaix have much more visual appeal than Brest. None the less, the roadsteads of Brest harbour make a pleasant day out, and the region's best wet-weather destination by far is Brest's impressive Océanopolis. The attractive little ferry port of Roscoff could happily make a base for a night or two, but book accommodation ahead if you intend to visit in high season.

If the region fails to charm, you can easily skate round selectively in a day or two and move on. Don't dismiss it too quickly though; its peace and small-scale sights may grow on you. Truly glorious beaches take some searching out but they do exist and a stay in the small resorts of Carantec, le Conquet or Brignogan-Plages can be delightful. Many visitors enjoy the *abers* country on the west coast (Welsh-speakers will recognize the Celtic word for a tidal estuary). In fine weather, one excursion is definitely worthwhile: the choppy boat ride to the Ile d'Ouessant off the west coast. This forms part of the Armorique Regional Nature Park, but as it is reached either from le Conquet (about an hour) or Brest (two hours) in North Finistère it is covered in this chapter.

A detail from one of old Morlaix's quaint houses

97

ÎLE DE BATZ

If you stay in Roscoff for any length of time, be sure to take a trip to the little Île de Batz, a 15-minute boat ride off shore across a treacherous tidal race. Its thousand or so inhabitants subsist on fishing, seaweed-processing, and vegetable cultivation. Increasingly, Batz is a tourist destination, popular for sailing, with sandy beaches and several simple hotels and *crêperies*. At only 4km (2.5 miles) long, it is easily walked in less than three hours. Attractions include the **Jardin Georges Delaselle**, containing some 1,700 exotic species (tel: 02 98 61 75 65; *open* Apr–Sep pm; *closed* Tue low season; Oct weekends only. *Admission moderate*). The lighthouse can be visited (200 steps).

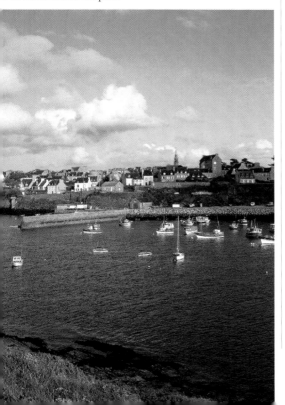

Small fishing boats and pleasure craft moored in the harbour below the houses clustered around the port of le Conquet

BOTANIC GARDENS
Not far inland from the Océanopolis lies the Conservatoire Botanique National de Brest, a fine 22ha (54-acre) botanic garden containing rare and endangered species. The project was set up under the auspices of the Armorique Regional Nature Park and carries out much important research ((tel:02 98 02 46 00); *open daily 9–6, 9–8 in summer. Admission free to park and visitor centre. Hothouses: small charge*). An exhibition pavilion outlines the ecological challenges to plants in the modern world.

Brest is still a bustling naval, commercial and leisure-sailing port

►► Brest   94C1

History It is hard to imagine that the uncompromising modern architecture of Brest conceals anything historic, but in fact the city dates back to Roman times: A military camp was established here in the 3rd century. Brest expanded in the 13th century when its strategic importance began to take on international significance. The English (invited in to protect the city for Jean de Montfort during the War of Succession) outstayed their welcome for over half a century from 1341, eager to have a toehold in such a useful harbour.

The roadstead (Rade de Brest) is colossal by any measure, over 150sq km (60sq miles) of water between 15m (50ft) and 20m (65ft) deep, and, as such, it has determined the fate of the city, for good or ill, since the Middle Ages. The deep-water harbour was valued for its defensive rather than its trading purposes, and so Brest became a naval base, denied the chance to accrue the merchant wealth of Nantes or St.-Malo. The naval dockyards were established by Cardinal Richelieu, and those other *ancien régime* strategists Colbert and Vauban also made their mark.

During the German Occupation, Brest became a U-boat base, and thus a target for some of the most ferocious and sustained Allied bombing missions of World War II, 'a storm of iron, steel and blood', as the poet Jacques Prévert put it. More than 165 air raids hit the city in an attempt to prevent German submarines attacking transatlantic convoys. Eventually General Patton's laconic order, 'Take Brest', resulted in a bitter 43-day siege, ending in hand-to-hand fighting. Before they left, the Germans blew up the docks and as much of the naval installations as they could, and by 1944 Brest was devastated.

What to see Vast sums of post-war finance have restored the city in a modern, blockish style of spacious boulevards and bleak, tidy plazas: efficient, perhaps, but

99

Once a garrison and prison, Brest castle now houses a museum and the offices of the harbour authorities

scarcely enticing. There is little of the central area worth braving, but anyone who loves ports will want to see the dockyards. You get a good vantage point of the Rade de Brest from the **castle**, which was spared by the bombs. Inside is the **Musée de la Marine▶** (tel: 02 98 22 12 39; *open* Apr–Sep 10–6.30; Oct–Mar Wed–Mon 10–12, 2–6. *Admission moderate*), not an exceptional maritime museum but it does contain a few intriguing objects, such as a curious manned torpedo from World War II and a 10m (33ft) wooden boat in which 40 Vietnamese refugees escaped across the South China Sea. Nearby is the massive Pont de Recouvrance (Europe's largest lift-bridge) and, opposite, the Tour Tanguy, a 15th-century tower housing another small museum of old Brest. Best of the city's museums, however, is the **Musée des Beaux-Arts (Fine Arts Museum)▶▶**, worth finding for its collection of Pont-Aven School paintings (*Open* Wed–Sat, Mon, 10–12, 2–6, Sun pm. *Admission moderate; free on Sun*). Look out for Kneipp's *trompe l'oeil* cow with real horns emerging from the canvas.

One of Brest's few interesting buildings is the modern church of **St.-Louis▶**, an angular, sharp-edged structure topped by a shallow cupola. Inside, all is space and garish light from its splinter-glass windows.

Best by far in Brest, though, is the **Océanopolis▶▶▶** (*Open* Apr–Aug daily 9–6; low season 10–5, *closed* Mon. *Admission expensive*), on the east side of the port. This is far more than just an aquarium, rather a massive research centre and exhibition of sealife in all its aspects: ocean currents, algae and seaweed, marine pollution, as well as huge tanks of fish and sea mammals. Three pavilions house temperate, tropical and polar marine life. Labelling is high-tech and in several languages, and there are lots of hands-on activities to entertain children of the video and computer era. There's plenty here for at least half a day.

LA BELLE CORDELIERE
In August 1513 an English fleet was sent by Henry VIII to attack Brest. When it hove into sight of harbour, guests of honour celebrating the Feast of St. Lawrence aboard one of Brittany's warships, *La Belle Cordelière*, found their party rudely interrupted by a full-scale alert. The captain, Hervé de Portmuguer, weighed anchor immediately, still with his civilian crew aboard in ceremonial regalia. The Breton fleet commander retreated in panic, but Portmuguer bravely tackled the English flagship to buy time. Both ships caught fire and exploded. All 300 guests perished, exhorted by their captain to 'celebrate the Day of St. Lawrence, who died by fire'.

CROSSING THE STONES
The Men-Marz menhir just outside Brignogan-Plages is a good example of a Christianized megalith. Many standing stones were topped with crosses in Celtic times, as a painless way of making the transition from the old religion to the new. The crosses quelled, but did not entirely subdue the pagan beliefs, some of which linger on even today in superstitions and festivals.

THE ARTICHOKE DRIVE
If you approach Carantec from the Morlaix direction, take the minor D73 road which hugs the estuary. It is a marvellous drive at high tide, past fishing villages and artichoke fields. During September the crops are just getting to their best, a glaucous expanse of tightly furled, spiky buds on tall, robust stems.

The Château du Taureau was a state prison during the reign of Louis XIV

▶ Brignogan-Plages   95D2

Though not particularly pink in colour, Brignogan-Plages echoes the coastal drama of the Pink Granite coast farther east. Its eight linked beaches are strewn with massive, curiously shaped boulders, some of which dwarf the small grey and white houses scattered unobtrusively around the shallow, curving bay. This is an immensely appealing stretch of seaside, ideal for beachcombing in rockpools, building sandcastles or sheltered sunbathing in private coves. Beyond beach activities there isn't much to do here, apart from visiting the quaint little Chapelle Pol stuck on a boulder with a toytown watchtower, or admiring the tall Men-Marz menhir, depaganized by a cross (see panel). The Castel Régis hotel is an ideal place to relax (see page 270).

To the southeast of the resort, the magnificent belfry of **Goulven**▶▶ makes a splendid landmark. The church, which dates from the 15th and 16th centuries, also has fine doorways, carved stoups and an ornate altar depicting the miracles of St. Goulven.

▶ Carantec   95E2

This pleasing little resort occupies a spiky headland jutting into the bay of Morlaix. Sheltered from Atlantic storms by the Roscoff headland, Carantec is an unusually green and lush place, with pines flourishing on the promontories and hydrangeas blooming in large gardens. Its range of clean beaches and its attractive hilly setting make it a fashionable, even slightly exclusive, destination, popular with writers, painters and other celebrities. It has good facilities for holidaymakers including an excellent campsite, but despite this it still feels quite unspoiled.

The best beaches are the Grève Blanche, Porspol and the main town beach, Grève du Kélenn. Coastal cliff paths lead to numerous secluded coves. One of the best vantage points is Penn-al-Lann, one of Carantec's antler-like prongs overlooking the island fortress of the Château du Taureau, which was built to guard Morlaix from the marauding English. Another viewpoint is the rocky throne called the Chaise du Curé (Priest's Chair), with panoramas of a wide sweep of Morlaix bay.

Carantec's other coastal protuberance is a 1.5km (1 mile) tidal causeway leading to the Île Callot, a popular fishing haunt accessible at low tide on foot. On the island is the chapel of Notre-Dame, the scene of an August *pardon* venerating the 16th-century statue inside, followed by a Blessing of the Sea ceremony. *Pardons* are also held in Carantec itself, where the village's parish church has two valuable processional crosses. A small maritime museum expounds Carantec's briny background, with displays on oyster-farming, seabirds and corsairs.

▶▶ Le Conquet 94B1

Set on the far west coast, this ancient fishing port is the most attractive holiday base for miles around. Trips to the islands of Ouessant and Molène make an interesting diversion, though local facilities for beach sports are good. Motorboat trips on the Aquafaune, with its underwater viewing chamber, give a glimpse of the rich marine life around the Molène archipelago (Cruises Feb–Oct; tel 02 98 89 14 13). The early church is illuminated by a striking mix of 16th-century and sophisticated modern stained glass. A typical Breton representation of Christ, seated and bound, can be seen above the main porch, where 15th-century statues of the Apostles shelter from the elements. Old stone houses line the hilly streets down to the port, some of which have exterior staircases. A very modern hotel on the cliffs, La Pointe Ste.-Barbe, is the only out of character touch, and even this is low-rise enough to blend in at a distance (it is also a useful place to stay).

Attractive craft shops, galleries and simple eating places can be found in the central streets. In the harbour, lobster- and crab-pots lie piled up by the quaysides. At certain high tides the harbour parking area may flood, so check before you set off for the islands.

Le Conquet is best appreciated from the opposite bank of the estuary

WHITE SANDS
One of Finistère's loveliest beaches is the Anse des Blancs-Sablons, 2km (1 mile) north of le Conquet, a *site naturel protégé* (protected natural site). It's about a 20-minute walk from the harbour via a footbridge. By car it's a longer detour; the road ducks some way inland past marshy pools and grassy dunes. You can walk out on the long nose of the Pointe de Kermorvan past a ruined blockhouse to the lighthouse, with panoramic coastal views. An attractive campsite lies behind the beach.

Left: Carantec's hotels and restaurants take advantage of the coastal panorama

▶ Le Folgoët   95D2

The outstanding feature of this small rural community is its massive church, the focus in early September of one of Brittany's largest *pardons* (see opposite). The name means 'Fool's Wood', which refers to the miraculous legend of Salaün (Solomon). Despite his wise name, Salaün was what would have been called the village idiot in crueller times. He lived in woods on the site of the church during the 14th century and could speak only a few words—the Breton for 'Hail, Lady Virgin Mary', which he repeated over and over to himself. He begged for food and drank water at a local spring (now tamed into a fountain by the east wall of the church). When Salaün died in 1358, a white lily sprang from his grave bearing the Latin inscription '*Ave Maria*' in gold letters, and it was widely presumed that he was a saint. News of the miracle soon spread, and Duke Jean IV built a commemorative chapel on the holy site.

Later, the irrepressible Duchess Anne (then Queen of France) made a pilgrimage to le Folgoët to give thanks for her husband's recovery from a serious illness. She financed a massive refurbishment of the church, a splendid affair with one of Finistère's finest bell towers, Kersanton altars like stone sideboards, and a magnificently knobbly rood screen, most unusually worked in solid granite.

The church was damaged during the Revolution, and would have been demolished had it not been for the goodwill of a dozen farmers who clubbed together to restore it. Today the huge basilica towers over a sprinkling of modest houses and pilgrim hostels clustered around an enormous green. A small museum of ecclesiastical statuary and Breton furniture is housed in one of the historic inns (*Open* mid-Jun to mid-Sep Mon–Sat 10.30–12.30, 2.30–6.30. *Admission inexpensive*).

The 15th-century rood screen of le Folgoët's basilica is one of Brittany's finest examples of Kersanton stone-carving

MIXED BLESSINGS
Devotional practices at le Folgoët are taken to unusual lengths. Besides the *Grand Pardon* in early September, it holds another religious ceremony in the last week of July. The *pardon* of St. Christopher involves a blessing of motorcars, which raises eyebrows among some traditionalists.

Modern pilgrims continue the tradition of paying homage at Salaün's holy well, which springs from beneath the altar on the east side of le Folgoët's church

Le Folgoët's **pardon** *is one of the largest and most colourful of the Breton festivals. It is held on the first Sunday in September (or on 8 September if the first day of the month falls on a Sunday).*

Celebrations begin on the preceding evening, with all-night vigils and hourly masses in the church. On the Sunday morning villagers and pilgrims begin to arrive for the grand Mass, held at 10.30am. The church is full of votive candles and flowers, while outside, souvenir stalls occupy the huge village green. After the service the local cafés and bars fill up, as pilgrims prepare themselves for a long day. Eventually, the church elders file out across

the green, incongruously bearing crosses past the toffee-stalls and balloon-sellers to a small granite oratory chapel on the opposite side. Another service begins, featuring lengthy sermons and prayers interspersed with stirring Breton hymns. Many canny parishioners bring their own little folding stools or picnic chairs.

After this long service, the crowd disperses for lunch, older villagers speaking Breton as they wander back up the hill from the church. Is it all over? Far from it. At 2.30pm an even bigger crowd assembles for a massive procession of colourful banners and floats, and everyone is decked out in beautiful Breton costumes: women in black dresses with embroidered aprons and lace *coiffes*, men in wide-brimmed felt hats and bright waistcoats. Camera shutters snap again and again as the banners pass, to the accompaniment of a haunting Breton hymn tune repeated many times. Last to arrive is the Black Virgin, a 15th-century statue of Our Lady of Folgoët on her gorgeous dais. Crowd control in this small community is undertaken by one relaxed gendarme and a couple of volunteer Red Cross stretcher-bearers.

In the evening the mood lightens even further, with dancing to Breton music and plenty to eat and drink. For an interesting memory of the *pardon*, buy a recording of the local hymns.

TROLLOPE AT THE *PARDON*

In medieval times the processions swarmed with beggars seeking alms and sick people hoping for cures. Early visitors to Brittany were repulsed at the sight of such poverty and suffering, and reacted as many Western travellers to India do today. 'Let [the reader] combine every image that his imagination can conceive of hideous deformity and frightful mutilation; of loathsome filth, and squalid, vermin-breeding corruption; of festering wounds, and leprous, putrefying sores…and when he has done this… I feel convinced that he will have but an imperfect idea of what met my eyes at St.-Jean-du-Doigt.'
—*A Summer in Brittany*, Thomas Adolphus Trollope (1839)

103

All generations help to carry the banners at le Folgoët's Grand Pardon *(above left and below)*

SLEEPING LIKE THE DEAD

If you visit any Breton folk museums, you will certainly see wooden 'box beds', enclosed by sliding panelled doors or curtains, which were used until this century in many rural homes. There is a fine example in the Château de Kerjean. One thing that strikes you immediately is how very short they are and surely not large enough to lie down in comfortably, even allowing for the Breton of less well-nourished times. This is because many Bretons believed that if they lay down like the dead they would never wake again, so they slept propped upright on piles of pillows.

The rood screen at Lambader, south east of the Château de Kerjean

THE VIRTUOUS FRANÇOISE

One of the rooms in the Château de Kerjean is alleged to be where Françoise de Quelen, a 16th-century lady of the manor, locked up three young noblemen. Her husband, who had left his wife behind at the château while he served at court, accepted a wager with these three men that one of them would manage to seduce her. But Françoise locked them up and set them to work for their supper; if they didn't work hard enough, they didn't get any food. They were only released from their drudgery when the lord of the manor returned. What his wife said to him about his ungentlemanly wager unfortunately goes unrecorded.

►► Kerjean, Château de 95D2

Tel: 02 98 69 93 69
Open: Jun–Sep Wed–Mon 10–6 (Jul–Aug, 10–7); Apr–May, Oct Wed–Mon pm; Nov–Mar Wed Sun pm.
Admission moderate.

Well signposted off the D30 between Plouescat and Landivisiau, this impressive fortified manor house makes an enjoyable excursion inland. It dates from the 16th century, when Louis Barbier inherited his uncle's wealth and decided to build a château to rival that of the Barbier family's resented overlords at nearby Lanhouarneau. The

resulting building was indeed a fine house, stoutly fortified by a high rampart and wide moat, and fashionably furnished. In 1710 the house was badly damaged by fire, and suffered again during the Terror when the last widowed incumbent of Kerjean was guillotined. In 1911 it passed into State ownership and has since been thoroughly restored, with appropriate imported furnishings. Visitors are welcomed with an audio-visual presentation and there are regular exhibitions and events, including summer concerts and *son-et-lumière* shows.

The château is set in 20ha (50 acres) of parkland. A drive sweeps past a dovecote with 1,200 nesting holes (all, alas, devoid of doves) to the drawbridge entrance where jackdaws caw. Nearby is a gallows tree, from which the lord of the manor usd to dispatch local miscreants.

Inside the main courtyard, look out for a lovely Renaissance well with Corinthian columns, and the *lunettes* (half-moon-shaped finials) on the roof dormers, which is a mark of the local builder. The castle interior contains a museum of Breton furniture, which is set out as it would have been in the original rooms—box beds, linen presses, grain chests and sideboards—solid, weighty pieces carved with the typical wheel or medallion patterns of the region. You can also visit the vast, high-ceilinged kitchen, cellars reached by steep steps, and a chapel with carved vaulting.

Attractions nearby Near Kerjean lies a cluster of interesting churches, worth tracking down if you are touring the area. **Berven►**, to the northeast, has a splendid lanterned belfry and one of Finistère's best examples of a triumphal arch in its close. The interior is just as impressive, with an ornately worked chancel screen and carved shutters in the side-chapel niches which open to reveal statues. **Lambader**, to the southeast, contains a lovely rood screen. **Bodilis▶**, due south, is ablaze with carved beams and a starry blue roof, enough to keep you amused through even the dullest of sermons, though you could end up with a crick in your neck. **St.-Servais**, close by, has another impressively balustraded belfry. This village was the home of a local artist, Yan Dargent (1824–1899), and a small museum here is dedicated to his works (tel: 02 98 68 15 21; *open* Jul–Sep Fri–Wed pm). His most famous painting now hangs in the Musée des Beaux-Arts at Quimper (see page 169). *Les Lavandières de la Nuit* is a highly romanticized canvas depicting the ghostly legend of unfortunate women condemned to return to earth after death to wash their linen eternally on a lonely moor because their loved ones failed to pray for their souls.

▶ Lesneven
95D2

There is nothing particularly compelling about this cattle-market town and local administrative centre, but if you are passing through (it lies very close to le Folgoët and could make a convenient base for a night), note its fine main square, where there is a distinguished statue of General Le Flô, apparently remembering his stint as France's War Minister in 1871, during the troubled days of Bismarck's expansion of Prussia.

A few venerable 17th- and 18th-century buildings remain in the town centre. Just outside, on the Ploudaniel road, a German cemetery starkly evokes memories of later Teutonic incursions. A 17th-century Ursuline convent just off the main square houses the Musée du Léon, a local history collection whose prize possession is a charter signed by Louis XIV (*Open* 2–6, except Tue and Fri).

PAGAN COUNTRY
Lesneven looks a peaceful and civilized little town today, and it is hard to imagine its lawless ancestry as the head-quarters of Ar Paganitz (Pagan Country), as Irish visitors in the Middle Ages called the wild northerly parishes around Brignogan-Plages. The locals had a reputation as wreckers, who lured ships on to the reefs and swam out to capsized vessels to bite the ring fingers off drowning women. No doubt some of these tales were apocryphal, but the salvage of wrecked ships certainly made a signifi-cant contribution to the local economy. Govern-ment attempts to prevent this type of privateering were bitterly resisted.

105

The Château de Kerjean makes an imposing statement amid regal parkland

THE BITERS BIT
When corsairs sacked Bristol in 1522, Henry VIII sent a fleet of 60 warships to teach Morlaix a lesson. Many of the inhabitants were away at a festival in Guingamp, so the English raiders met little resistance as they ransacked the town. Unfortunately, they discovered Morlaix's well-stocked wine cellars and, having made free with them, staggered away to the nearby woods to sleep off their hangovers. They were thus easily dispatched by the returning townsfolk. Morlaix adopted as its crest an English leopard fighting a French lion, with the motto (a play on the town's name): *S'ils te mordent, mords-les!* ('If they bite you, bite them back!')

▶▶ Morlaix   95E2

This fine old town grew up at the head of a large estuary, becoming a strategic bridging point and an important inland port. Once it was Brittany's third city, prospering from fishing, linen, paper, shipbuilding—and piracy. Like St.-Malo, Morlaix was a corsair town (see page 68), and the losses of English ships provoked reprisals, notably in 1522. In more peaceful times Morlaix traded extensively with England and the Low Countries, developing strong links through illegal tobacco and, more recently, beer. A couple

of French enthusiasts who had tasted real ale in Wales set up the Coreff brewery here in 1985, but it has now relocated to Carhaix-Plouguer.

Though the town suffered some war damage, enough of its historic quarter remains to captivate visitors. It is the most appealing large town in North Finistère, with plenty to see and lots of good restaurants. Unfortunately, the hotels are rather lacking in charm, and Morlaix is best visited on a day trip rather than used as a base. Many visit its superior shopping malls to stock up with goods before heading for Roscoff, but there is far more to see than hypermarkets. It is surprisingly easy to find your way round Morlaix: its imposing railway viaduct bestrides it like a colossus, making an instant landmark, and the old town and port lie immediately at its feet, compact and walkable. To find your way out of town again, simply follow either bank of the river downstream, or follow the sign-posts to the expressway (N12).

Colourful houses in old Morlaix

Morlaix's 58m (190ft) high viaduct spans the Dossen valley

Walk

The old town of Morlaix

See map opposite.

Half a day should allow you to see most of the old town, with time to climb its steep hills and meander along quaint alleyways (known locally as *venelles*).

Start by the huge granite **viaduct▶▶**, where you should find a place to park in Place des Ôtages or by the quayside. Through the arches of the viaduct you can glimpse the canalized port crammed with pleasure craft and an occasional cargo boat.

Up the steps near the tourist office is the 15th-century church of **St.-Mélaine▶**. Outside, an old stone stoup is used as a flower tub. The dim interior is lit by brilliant modern stained glass. Up the steps behind the church a steep path leads to the first level of the viaduct, which you can walk across for excellent views of the town. More steps and alleys at the other side take you down to Place Cornic, or on to hilly walks.

Back behind St.-Mélaine again, take rue Ange-de-Guernisac, lined with typical corbelled and half-timbered houses. Join the Grande-Rue near Place des Viarmes, where there are many more lovely houses including the restored **Maison à Pondalez▶▶** now part of Morlaix's museum (*Open* Jul–Aug daily 10–12.30, 2–6.30; Wed–Mon low season; closed Sun in winter. *Admission moderate,* combined with Musée de Morlaix, below). Another is the 16th-century **Maison de la Reine Anne▶▶** (rue du Mur; tel: 02 98 88 23 26; *open* Jul–Aug Mon–Sat 11– 6.30; reduced hours low season. *Admission inexpensive*), a quaintly carved three-floor 'lantern house'. A decorated newel post, carved from a single tree trunk, supports a spiral staircase rising to a skylight. The Duchess Anne stayed here in 1505, when the town presented her with a live ermine in a diamond collar.

Follow rue du Mur to the church of **St.-Mathieu▶** with its square tower. Inside is a 14th-century hinged statue of the Virgin, which opens up to reveal the Trinity. The old church on Place des Jacobins houses another section of the **Musée de Morlaix▶▶▶** (*open* as Maison à Pondalez, above).

ISLAND TRADITIONS

The local costumes are not often worn today, though you can see examples in the folk museum. Women used to wear a black outfit with an unusual headdress. They played an important role in social and domestic life (husbands were often away at sea) and even proposed marriage.

Sheep-farming is one of Ouessant's mainstays, and sheep are allowed to roam freely over the unfenced island. Their ears are tagged, each family using a different pattern, so that they can be recognized when they are rounded up. Star-shaped shelters can be seen (for example, near Pointe de Pern) to protect the sheep from the wind.

▶▶ Ouessant, Île d'   94A2

Anglicized as Ushant, this bare, windswept island lies 20km (12 miles) due west of the Rocher du Crapaud on Finistère's west coast. These are some of the most dangerous waters off the French coast, with lethal reefs and the swiftest currents in Europe. Despite the sterner aspects of the island in bad weather, Ouessant is a popular excursion from North Finistère. The quickest sea crossing is from le Conquet, where ferries race across in about an hour. There are also boat services from Brest, or you can take a 15-minute hop in one of Finist'Air's light planes from Brest airport in summer. Although winter storms can be spectacular the climate is mild, with the highest winter mean temperatures in France.

In 1988 this archipelago was designated, somewhat pompously, a *réserve de la biosphère*, forming part of the Parc Naturel Régional d'Armorique. Ouessant itself is about 7km (4 miles) by 4km (2.5 miles), shaped like a clawed crustacean. Ferry passengers arrive at the Baie du Stiff, where a modern lighthouse guards the east side of the island. Next to it is the original structure, built by Vauban (see panel, page 176), and this can be visited and climbed at certain times of day. Ouessant is rather too large to explore on foot, and the best way to travel about is

to rent a bicycle at the quayside. Be sure to get one with gears, as the island may look pancake flat from a distance but when you are cycling against strong winds you'll soon find that there are some gradients. Minibus or taxi tours are available if bicycling doesn't appeal.

Time-capsule Ouessant is a fascinating repository of a way of life now fast disappearing in Brittany. Its thousand or so inhabitants now turn to tourism and the scientific cultivation of seaweed rather than to traditional livelihoods like seafaring and farming. Fishing activity has always been limited because there is no good harbour, but many islanders join the French naval services, leaving their

A ferry bound for the Oussant archipelago waits for passengers in the port of le Conquet

PROËLLA CROSSES

The Ouessant custom of mourning the dead lost at sea was observed until only about 40 years ago. Whenever the report of a shipwreck or drowning arrived, sometimes after months of anxious waiting, the island officials would first inform a male relative. He would then break the dreaded news to the mother or widow with the words '*Il y a Proëlla chez toi ce soir*' ('There will be a Proëlla in your house tonight'). A Proëlla, or small wax cross, was placed in the window of the bereaved family's house for the night preceding the funeral, when all the family and friends would keep vigil. After the funeral the crosses were placed in the cemetery mausoleum.

109

womenfolk behind to tend fields and raise stock: Ouessant society is still largely matriarchal. Today, most of the land is uncultivated heath, criss-crossed by sheep tracks where a few flocks roam at will. Lampaul is the main village, where you will find cafés, small hotels and a tourist office.

The best way to find out about Ouessant's background is to visit the charming little ***écomusée***► ► (tel: 02 98 48 86 37; *open* Apr–Sep daily 10.30–6.30; low season Tue–Sun pm. *Admission inexpensive*) at Niou Uhella, where two tiny cottages provide space for exhibits of costumes, tools and utensils, as well as furniture made from the timbers of shipwrecks. A section upstairs shows the island way of death: Ankou was a frequent visitor to these seafaring families. One of the cottages is furnished as a 19th-century home, everything as neat and compact as on board ship, and painted bright blue. (The stone houses on the island nearly all have blue shutters and doors; blue being the colour of the Virgin Mary, who protects them from harm.)

The other place to visit on Ouessant is the **Phare de Creac'h**► ► set on the west side of the island. The lighthouse itself is not open to the public, but the adjacent museum makes a fascinating introduction to the 50 or so coastal warning systems in Brittany. Find out what a 6,000-watt lightbulb looks like amid the whirling prismatic beams. Labelling is in French only (*Open* as for Ecomusée, plus some summer eves. *Admission moderate*).

SHIPWRECK

Ouessant and its smaller neighbour, Molène, frequently lie blanketed in thick sea fogs. Despite all the lighthouses that lie around the rocks, terrible disasters periodically occur. In 1896 the *Drummond Castle* foundered here with the loss of 248 lives. An old rhyme starkly declares the dangers of Brittany's westerly islands for shipping: '*Qui voit Molène, voit sa peine; Qui voit Ouessant, voit son sang; Qui voit Sein, voit sa fin.*' (Meaning roughly: 'If you see Molène, you've got problems; if you see Ouessant, you're in bad trouble; if you see Sein, your end is near!')

RUDE GRANITE
In 1987 the town council of Plouescat decided that it could no longer tolerate the existence of a suggestively shaped rock on one of the local beaches. One dark night they blew it up, only to find local artists retaliating against this piece of municipal vandalism by creating even more disturbingly phallic sculptures, which now lie scattered around some of the lonelier shores.

LE GROUANEC
The church and parish close of le Grouanec, about 4km (2.5 miles) southeast of Plouguerneau, have been restored to reveal a set of typically Breton features: fountain, ossuary, cloisters and gargoyles. The church contains stained glass by the modern master, Max Ingrand, and charmingly carved beams in the south aisle.

A rocky stretch of the Côte des Abers, near Plouguerneau

▶ **Plouescat**   95D2

The most interesting thing about this little town is its magnificent 17th-century covered market building, a forest of oak timbers under a slate roof. It is still a market and a good place to buy provisions. A strange seahorse statue stands next to the church opposite the market.

There are lots of quiet beaches near Plouescat, huge expanses of sand dunes and rocks at low tide, and it's a popular place to camp. Inland, the countryside around the town is sprinkled with châteaux, some fortified, others more like the pleasure palaces of the Loire. Among the best of these are the Renaissance **Manoir de Traonjoly** (7.5km/4.5 miles northeast), the 15th-century **Château de Kérouzéré** (4km/2.5 miles east), the elegant 16th-century **Château de Maillé** (4km/2.5 miles south) up a beech and chestnut drive, and the **Château de Kergornadeac'h** (7km/4 miles south), one of the last fortified houses built in France (1630), with false machicolations and tall chimneys. Not all these are open to the public, but you can get a good idea of their architecture from outside. Greatest of all is the **Château de Kerjean** (see page 104), run by the state and easily accessible to visitors.

▶ **Plouguerneau**   94C2

Many holiday homes now expand this village into dull suburbia, threaded by a web of confusing lanes. The reason for the development becomes clear once you reach its coastal attractions—a series of sheltered coves of very fine sand. The village was originally built on an ancient Gallo-Roman camp called Tolente, sacked by the Vikings in AD875. Some way inland, the old village church contains a collection of wooden statues placed there by thankful parishioners who had escaped the plague. The **Écomusée** here has an exhibition on the local trade of seaweed gathering (tel: 02 98 37 13 35; *open* Jul–Aug Wed–Mon 2–6; Jun, Sep Sat–Sun 2.30–5. *Admission inexpensive*). On an island just off the Plouguerneau headland stands France's tallest lighthouse, the Phare de l'Île Vierge, 82.5m (274ft) high. Trips from Lilia beach take visitors to see it at closer quarters.

Finistère's dramatic coast

Drive

Around the *abers*

See map on pages 94–95.

A pleasant and varied 70km (42 miles) drive past beaches, fortresses, lighthouses, dunes, reefs and wide valleys. Take a picnic; peaceful views are more plentiful than restaurants. Stick to minor lanes near to the sea and allow half a day.

An *aber* (the Celtic word for estuary) is formed when sea levels rise to flood the steep shoulders of a former river valley and its tributaries, resulting in wide fjord-like inlets that are often navigable far inland. Unlike the great tidal estuaries of the Rance or the Dossen on the north coast, the western *abers* are shallow and full of silt. They lack the lush woodlands of those in southern Brittany but the views are broader, with sheets of water mirroring the surrounding heathery moorland. The *abers* are more picturesque at high tide, while the offshore reefs are dramatic at low water.

Start near **Plouguerneau**, detouring around the ragged headlands past sheltered coves and France's tallest lighthouse, the Phare de l'Île Vierge. Wind upstream along the Aber Wrac'h, the most scenic *aber*, to cross at Pellan. This is particularly beautiful at sunset. Now head back to **l'Aber Wrac'h,** a pretty sailing port and resort. Footpaths through the Ste.-Marguerite dunes give views of drying seaweed (processed for fertilizer), the islet-strewn Aber Wrac'h estuary and the Rochers de Portsall where the *Amoco Cadiz* foundered in 1978. South of Aber Benoît, detour coastwards through **Lampaul-Ploudalmézeau**, memorable for its lantern belfry. Between **Château de Trémazan** and **Porspoder** is the most dramatic stretch of coastal scenery. L'Aber Ildut is the official boundary between Channel and Atlantic, where the Rocher du Crapaud (Toad Rock) gazes towards Ouessant. Southwards, the Pointe de Corsen is France's true Finistère, the most westerly mainland finger, ending in a tame 50m (164ft) cliff. Head south via **le Conquet** (see page 101) to Pointe de St.-Mathieu (see page 114).

A catamaran near Aber Wrac'h

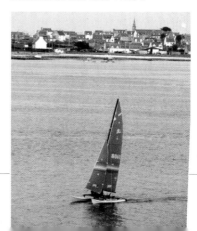

ONION JOHNNIES
A street in Roscoff, rue des Johnnies, commemorates these colourful characters, once a familiar sight the length and breadth of the UK as they wheeled bicycles engulfed with strings of Breton onions. Henri Ollivier began the trade in 1828 and it lasted until about 1930, a popular way for Breton farmers to offload their perishable produce at a time when communications with the rest of France were hampered by poor road and rail links. A small exhibition in the chapel by the tourist office traces their story (*Open* mid-Jun to mid-Sep Wed–Mon 10–12, 3–6. *Admission inexpensive*).

*One of the corsairs' houses (above right) near the church in Roscoff
The belfry of Roscoff's Notre-Dame-de-Kroaz-Batz (below right)*

ST. PAUL AND THE DRAGON
The 19th-century village church on Île de Batz (a 15-minute boat ride from Roscoff; see panel on page 97) contains the statue of St. Paul the Aurelian, who died on the island in AD573. St. Paul is associated with a dragon legend. This 'laidly worm' was alleged to be terrorizing the island when St. Paul arrived. He wrapped his stole around its neck and cast it into a pit called the Trou du Serpent (Monster's Hole), which is marked by an offshore rock near the lighthouse. The stole (now proved to be an 8th-century oriental textile) is kept in the north transept of the church.

►► **Roscoff** 95E3

This town is certainly worth more than the blinkered glimpse many ferry passengers award it, and it is no hardship to spend a first or last night here (book accommodation ahead in season). The deep-water ferry terminal east of the town leaves the old fishing harbour unspoiled. The old town, little more than a single street, runs along the back of the bay, where several concrete jetties erupt from the shore.

Roscoff is really a multipurpose town. Besides being a popular seaside resort specializing in thalassotherapy, it is one of France's main shellfish ports and a great centre for vegetable export. Roscoff's traditional beret-clad 'Onion Johnnies' (see panel) have been replaced by the huge container juggernauts that whizz artichokes and cauliflowers across the Channel today.

Sights to catch in town include the splendid church of **Notre-Dame-de-Kroaz-Batz►►**, with one of the finest of Finistère's belfries. A sundial warns you to *Craignez la dernière* ('fear the end'). The exterior is carved with galleons and cannon, signs of its corsair patronage, and around the church are the lovely 16th- and 17th-century houses of rich privateers. The **Jardin Exotique►►** contains 3,000 species of plants from the southern hemisphere.

Roscoff's small **aquarium►** near the church, part of an oceanological research centre, has many kinds of local fish. **Thalado►**, a discovery centre on seaweed, reveals the wide-ranging uses of this important local product (*Open* Mon–Sat 9–12, 2–7. *Admission free*; guided walks (fee charged) and talks arranged). On the other side of the harbour, almost at the top of Pointe de Bloscon, is the tiny white Chapelle Ste.-Barbe (St. Barbe was entrusted with the task of protecting Roscoff from pirates and enemies of the Church). From here there are fine views of the town, the harbour, Île de Batz and Pointe de Primel. From a glass viewing gallery, visitors can watch what's happening at Roscoff's lively *criée*. A visit to the Île de Batz is one of Roscoff's most popular excursions (see panel page 97).

The story of Brittany Ferries, which grew from a converted tank-landing craft into a fleet of roll-on, roll-off ships carrying passengers and freight, is a lesson in daring in the great Breton seafaring tradition.

Breton trading links with the UK are ages old, but when Brittany joined with France in 1532 these links were suppressed. Until the early 1980s, roads and railway links between Brittany and the rest of France were poor, and the problem of finding alternative markets ready to accept Brittany's perishable vegetables became acute. During the 1950s and '60s Breton farmers became increasingly dissatisfied about the lack of government support. Alexis Gourvennec was, at only 24, a leading militant light in his local farming cooperative, which sought to achieve the best possible prices for farmers. For several years they tried unsuccessfully to persuade existing shippers to carry Breton produce to new markets in the UK. Eventually, Gourvennec took the daring initiative of setting up an independent shipping line, the first French-owned cross-Channel operator, and the first scheduled link between Brittany and the UK.

In January 1973 a converted tank-landing craft, laden with freight vehicles, made its first sailing from the deep-water port of Roscoff to Plymouth. It was quickly dubbed 'The Cauliflower Run'. Within a year, the demand for passenger facilities grew, and the company felt confident enough to build a ro-ro ('roll-on, roll-off') ship to carry both passengers and freight vehicles. This first ship was named the *Penn-ar-Bed*, the Breton name for Finistère.

Since those early beginnings Brittany Ferries has proved a runaway success story. Today it is the principal operator on the western Channel, running services from Ireland, Normandy and Spain, as well as Brittany. Besides transporting passengers across the waves it has blossomed into a fully fledged holiday company, offering the largest number of self-catering *gîtes* and motoring holidays of any operator in France or Spain.

Brittany Ferries has grown from just one boat into a huge company over 35 years

114

ST. POL'S BELL

In the great cathedral of St.-Pol-de-Léon are the relics of the founding saint, Paul the Aurelian, and his famous bell. When St. Pol (Paul) had successfully evangelized the immediate area he planned to take God's word further afield. To help him in his mission he asked Duke Mark for a single item, one of the seven bells used as dinner gongs at the duke's castle, but this request was refused. Soon afterwards a fisherman came to St. Pol saying he had caught a huge fish with a bell in its mouth. 'What Mark refused, God has provided,' said the saint.

Twin lighthouses and an abbey guard the rocks of Pointe de St.-Mathieu

▶ St.-Mathieu, Pointe de   94B1

'There, the two old enemies are face to face—the land and the sea, humankind and nature', wrote Michelet in his 19th-century *Tableau de la France*. On this dramatic spot a Benedictine monastery was founded in the 6th century, allegedly where St. Matthew's relics were brought from Ethiopia. A great storm blew up and the sailors feared shipwreck, but when they held up the apostle's head the waves subsided and the boat sailed safely ashore.

Today the roofless abbey church stands gauntly on the windswept headland, with a small exhibition inside (tel: 01 98 89 10 52; *open* Jul–Aug Mon–Sat 10.30–12.30, 2–7, Sun pm. *Admission inexpensive*). A red and white lighthouse erupts from the grounds. A newer lighthouse nearby is open to visitors in summer, and 163 steps lead to superb views of the Crozon peninsula and the Ouessant archipelago. Down on the dark rocks below the abbey, a memorial pays tribute to French sailors killed in the Great War. The smart, modernized hotel-restaurant overlooking the abbey, L'Hostellerie de la Pointe de St.-Mathieu, has an excellent reputation for seafood (see page 271).

▶▶ St.-Pol-de-Léon   95E2

During the Middle Ages St.-Pol was the religious centre of North Finistère, a bishopric founded by St. Paul (Pol) the Aurelian. It no longer has a bishop but the cathedral still stands, its crisp twin spires rivalled by the magnificent belfry of the nearby Chapelle du Kreisker, soaring 77m (255ft) above the town. These two remarkable Norman-style churches apart, St.-Pol is best known as an agricultural centre of the immensely fertile Ceinture d'Orée (Golden Belt). All around the town early vegetables flourish, particularly artichokes, onions, potatoes and cauliflowers. Refrigerated lorries rumble along the nearby roads, rapidly moving the produce to appreciative destinations. Aside from its churches and a few pleasant old houses, St.-Pol is a working town that regards tourism as a secondary priority. It has few hotels or restaurants, and lacks the charm of Roscoff as a base. If you catch it on a Tuesday, which is market day, you will see it at its liveliest, doing what it does best.

The **Kreisker bell tower▶▶** is best seen from a distance, when its stately proportions can properly be admired. Despite the vaguely Germanic-sounding name (which is actually Breton and means, prosaically, the church in the town centre), its architecture was inspired by the church of St.-Pierre at Caen, which was destroyed during World War II. The spire is pierced with daisy-like shapes, as if by a pastry cutter, to reduce the windload. At its base, four smaller, perfectly balanced pinnacles rise from its balustraded balcony. You can climb the tower as far as this balcony for marvellous views (Jul–Aug only).

St.-Pol-de-Léon's churches offer a scenic backdrop for café visitors

The interior of the **cathedral**▶▶ is more interesting than that of the Kreisker (which is now used as a college chapel), but quite a shock after the ubiquitous granite of most Breton churches. A chilling nave of sallow Norman limestone soars above your head and within this lofty space of light and symmetry, fascinating details soon emerge. Over the high altar is a curious snowdrop object carved from palm wood, holding the Host. What looks like an old stone bath-tub (a Roman sarcophagus) serves as a stoup, and a little door below the right tower was used by lepers. Lovely old glass tinges the transept walls with warmer colours. The remains of St. Paul the Aurelian lie in a gilt reliquary, near a bell rung on *pardon* days to cure headaches and ear disorders.

The best of St.-Pol's old houses can be found in rue Général Leclerc, between the two churches. The Maison du Pilori, where convicts were once put on public display, has a beautiful Renaissance door. Look out for the escutcheoned Maison Prébendale behind the cathedral—it was a 16th-century canon's house. Champ de la Rive and the Rocher Ste.-Anne give good views over the bay.

THE KREISKER LEGEND
A dressmaker was working on the day of the Feast of the Virgin when she suffered a paralytic stroke. Healed by St. Kireg after she prayed to him, she gave up her house as a chapel to the Blessed Virgin. This was sacked by the English in 1375, but was soon rebuilt. A second misfortune befell the building when its roof was damaged by lightning in 1628. The final spire dates from 1668, and has been copied (with variations) all over North Finistère.

Well-kept old buildings in St.-Pol-de-Léon

Armorique

A casualty of the declining fishing industry at Camaret-sur-Mer, which specializes in catching sea crayfish

ARMORIQUE The Parc Naturel Régional d'Armorique, to give it its full title, is a slightly odd concept. It is one of more than 40 regional nature parks in France and was set up in 1969. Geographically confusing, it penetrates waveringly deep into Brittany's *argoat*, or forested heartland, and equally far into the Atlantic to encompass the reef-strewn archipelagos of Ouessant and Sein (both of which are covered in other chapters of this book, see pages 108–109 and 172 respectively). Brittany's highest mountains, the Monts d'Arrée, the lovely Aulne estuary, and some of its best coastal scenery (the Crozon peninsula) are also included within the park boundaries. Its 112,000ha (270,000 acres), therefore, represent many typical Breton landscapes. Half as much again of the area consists of islands and open sea, featuring over 300 maritime bird species as well as seals and dolphins.

France's regional parks are administered by locally elected delegates whose duties are laid down by charter. The parks' function is broadly similar to that of the national parks in that they are conservation areas designed to protect sites of natural and historic interest from inappropriate development or exploitation. But Armorique is not simply a nature reserve; it is an entire ecosystem that includes, of course, its human inhabitants. Local residents are encouraged to continue traditional trades, crafts and pastimes, while little museums scattered throughout the region explain various aspects (current or bygone) of rural life. Breton culture is fostered through events and festivals. In practice, however, lack of funds curtails any very ambitious projects, and the region is therefore becoming ever more dependent upon tourism for its revenue.

▶▶▶ REGION HIGHLIGHTS

Crozon peninsula
page 124
Guimiliau *page 129*
Huelgoat
pages 130–131
Lampaul-Guimiliau
page 132
Monts d'Arrée
pages 120–121
Pleyben *page 135*
Parish closes
pages 136–137
St.-Thégonnec
pages 138–139

The beach at le Pouldu, on Finistère's sunny south coast

CLOG-SPEAK
At the beginning of the 20th century, State schools formally discouraged pupils from speaking Breton. A humiliating device called a *vache* (usually a wooden clog) was hung round the neck of any pupil heard talking in Breton, who would then become an object of ridicule. The only way he or she could get rid of the *vache* was to denounce another child, when it would be transferred. In this way many Bretons learned to despise the language they heard in their homes and treat it as a sign of *ruralité*, or uncivilized peasant upbringing. See Trégarvan's Musée de l'École Rurale for more on this (page 125).

Keen walkers, anglers, birdwatchers and cyclists will find plenty to do here, but facilities for the more sybaritic holidaymaker are limited; this is not the place to find gourmet restaurants or suave thalassotherapy centres. Most villages accustomed to visitors will have a *crêperie* or two, however, and increasingly *fermes-auberges* (farm guesthouses) are starting to cater for summer tourists by offering home cooking and regional produce. If you feel like splashing out on serious food, head for St.-Thégonnec's splendid *auberge* (see Hotels and Restaurants, page 271).

LANDSCAPES Unlike some areas of Brittany, the Armorique Park is not intensively cultivated (though some parts are afforested). Its landscapes are pleasantly, if unspectacularly, wild, with heather and gorse making ubiquitous ground-cover in unfarmed areas. Much of the countryside is hilly or undulating moorland, erupting in softly contoured pudding-basin domes or outcrops of toothy granite. The hill summits overlook a patchwork of gently hedged fields known as *bocage* country, plaited by a maze of rivers, lakes and streams.

The underpopulated Monts d'Arrée region has always been somewhat isolated, and in the past its inhabitants were regarded with a degree of suspicion. But the startling rock forms of Huelgoat, the dinosaur crests of Trévézel, and the lonely peat bog of Yeun Elez contribute to an unexpected variety of scenery.

There are no very large towns or resorts in the region; the largest settlements are country markets such as Landivisiau or Carhaix-Plouguer. Industrial intrusions are minimal apart from a little agri-business in the main centres. However, the nuclear power station at Brennilis (now decommissioned), in the heart of the Armorique Park, was a controversial project. Breton nationalists unwisely attacked it with a rocket launcher in 1975 (fortunately without success). Army manoeuvres in the Monts d'Arrée, and the submarine base on Île Longue, are similarly unpopular in some quarters.

PARISH CLOSES Apart from the scenery, coastline and *écomusées*, the main attractions for visitors to this region are the remarkable parish closes, elevated here to a unique and striking art (see pages 136–137). Most of the parish closes are clustered to the north of the region in the Elorn valley. Visitors often speed round them one after the other, clocking them off as if train-spotting, and inevitably cultural overload can soon result. Interesting churches, with or without closes, can be found throughout the area, and it is more enjoyable to intersperse them with other types of sightseeing than to try to squeeze too many of them into a single day.

If you do get hooked on this type of architecture there are more than 20 churches worth seeking out in this

region alone. At the very least, try to see the 'big three': St.-Thégonnec, Lampaul-Guimiliau and Guimiliau, all within a short drive of each other near Landivisiau. The parish closes reveal more about Breton culture than almost any other aspect of the region.

ECOMUSÉES
A useful leaflet available at local tourist offices lists over a dozen museums of the Parc Naturel Régional d'Armorique. Especially worthwhile are:
● Domaine de Menez-Meur (animal reserve, horse museum and hiking trails)
● Moulins de Kérouat (restored watermill complex and exhibition)
● Maison Cornec (traditional farmhouse and outbuildings)
● Maison des Minéraux (geology exhibition)
● Musée de l'Ecole Rurale (re-creation of an early 20th-century Breton school)
● Maison de la Rivière, de l'Eau et de la Pêche (economy of water and fishing)
● Maisons du Niou (life on the Île d'Ouessant)
● Musée des Phares et Balises (lighthouse and beacon museum)
● Musée des Champs (agricultural museum)
● Conservatoire Botanique National de Brest (rare and endangered plant species).

119

Enjoying the views from Roc'h Trévézel

Stone cottages at Lampaul-Guimiliau

Armorique

Young trout swim in the streams at Sizun's Maison de la Rivière

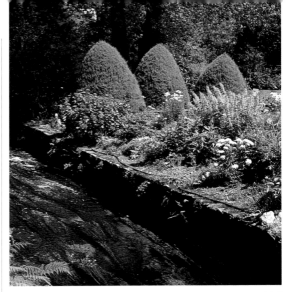

THE GATES OF HELL
Often shrouded in mists, the lonely and treacherous peat bog near Brennilis, known as Yeun Elez, is associated with many strange tales of witchcraft and exorcism. If a household was troubled by ghosts, the local priest would carry out a ritual in which the wandering spirit was driven into a black dog, which was then drowned in the bog. Ancient Celtic legends referred to it as the entrance to hell.

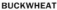

BUCKWHEAT
The classic Breton pancake is made with buckwheat flour. Buckwheat is not a cereal crop, but a plant allied to the sorrel family, with small white flowers. It grows in many parts of the world, particularly the Far and Middle East, hence its French name *sarrasin*, meaning 'saracen', from its discovery during the crusades. Buckwheat was grown extensively in Brittany several hundred years ago, but most of it is now imported.

▶▶ Arrée, Monts d'   117D2

These ancient heights once towered over 4,000m (13,000ft) tall. Now, worn down to mere stubs of granite and sandstone, they reach less than 400m (1,300ft). What they lack in altitude, though, they gain in antiquity, for these are some of the oldest rocks on earth. They are still the highest hills in Brittany, forming a desolate stretch of moorland covered with gorse and heather. The hills are either softly domed summits (*menez*) or saw-like, crested outcrops of quartz (*roc'h*) which make tremendous vantage points despite their modest height. Wildlife thrives: Deer, wild boar, otters and even beavers can be found in these remote haunts, while kestrels, curlews and buzzards hover overhead. Other signs of life often associated with wild places can also be detected, as France's armed forces play wargames here. On the mysterious swampy moor called Yeun Elez, a nuclear power station (now decommissioned) has been the focus of much regional controversy.

Besides the natural attractions of the Monts d'Arrée, there are several well-presented small museums in rural buildings that trace various aspects of local life. Visits to the fascinating parish closes (see pages 136–137), most of which lie just north of the main Arrée range, can easily be combined with a day's drive through the countryside. Places to stay or eat, however, are in short supply.

Heath and conifers cloak the crests of the Monts d'Arrée

Sizun's triumphal arch

Drive

The Monts d'Arrée

See map on pages 116–117.

This 100km (60-mile) drive incorporates a mix of natural landscapes, old villages, and sightseeing, including some parish closes. Allow a day if you want to see the sights and go for a walk as well.

Sizun▶▶ makes a pleasant base for this drive. The village is dominated by a tall church with elaborate panelled vaulting and decorated beams, while the surrounding parish close attracts most attention for its magnificent triumphal arch. Other attractions are the **Maison de la Rivière**▶ (a museum about waterways) in an old mill, and the **Maison du Lac**, an exhibition on river fishing in an annexe, near the Drennec Dam to the south (both are well signposted from the village).

Beyond the **Moulins de Kérouat**▶▶ (see page 132) the landscape becomes wilder and the hills higher. **Commana**▶ (see page 123) has another fine church and an *allée couverte* (gallery grave), at Mougau-Bian to the south. The **Roc'h Trévézel**▶▶ (384m/1,260ft) is one of the best viewpoints on a clear day, with views as far as Lannion bay. It takes about 15 minutes to scramble up the rocky crest. Head south down the D785 to the **Montagne St.-Michel**▶; this is slightly lower than Roc'h Trévézel (380m/1,247ft), and the summit can be reached by car. If you are feeling adventurous, try a detour eastwards across the spooky peat bog of Yeun Elez (see panel opposite). You can walk around the St.-Michel reservoir, but stick to the paths carefully as the marshland can be treacherous.

Brasparts has a notable parish close and a fine church (see page 137). The hamlet of **St.-Rivoal** contains one of the Armorique's most attractive *écomusées*, the **Maison Cornec**▶, a typical Arrée farmhouse restored to its 18th-century appearance. Note the outdoor stairs, protected by an awning. Out-houses can be explored in addition to the box-bedded, earthenfloor interior.

Wind westwards through the lanes, detouring north to **Menez-Meur** (see pages 134–135), a wildlife park and information centre. Beyond lies the **Forêt du Cranou**, extending over more than 600ha (1,000 acres), good for walks and picnics. Nearby **Pen-ar-Hoat** hill can be climbed for good views. The church at **Rumengol** dates from the 16th century. Two *pardons* in honour of Our Lady of Remedies are celebrated here annually. The two splendid altarpieces both date from 1686. The scattered parish of **Quimerc'h** still has the ruins of its church, which fell into disuse after inhabitants found it too remote.

121

The sheltered harbour of Camaret-sur-Mer

THE FIRST U-BOAT In 1801 Robert Fulton, an American engineer, tried to demonstrate his brilliant naval warfare invention. This was a submersible craft propelled by oars which could stay underwater for about six hours, during which time it could attach a timed explosive charge to enemy shipping. Fulton intended to use a British frigate at anchor off Camaret as target practice. Unfortunately for him, it weighed anchor at the critical moment and sailed serenely away, unaware that a five-man submarine crew was ploughing frantically beneath the waves to attack it. Disillusioned, Fulton returned to his native America. It was nearly a century before his revolutionary submarine concept was reattempted.

▶ **Camaret-sur-Mer**   *116A1*

This little lobster-fishing port occupies the most westerly tip of the Crozon peninsula, near some of its most dramatic coastal scenery. Once Camaret was a prosperous place, a popular haunt of artists and writers. Today tourism is increasing, but the fishing industry is severely depressed, and several boats lie rotting on the beach.

The crescent of buildings around the port is pleasantly unpretentious. A long natural bank of silt and pebbles called the Sillon protects the harbour and is the site of a tiny pilgrim chapel, **Notre-Dame-de-Rocamadour▶**, restored after fire damage in 1910. At the September *pardon*, a Blessing of the Sea ceremony is held here. The red-brick doll's house **fortress▶** at the far end of the Sillon was erected by the military engineer Vauban in 1689 (*Open* mid-Jun to mid-Sep daily 2–5. *Admission moderate*; combined ticket withthe Maison du Patrimoine Maritime by the tourist office).

Just west of the town stand 143 stumpy megaliths, the **Alignements de Lagatjar▶**, arranged in an indeterminate pattern. Nearby a memorial inside a clifftop German blockhouse commemorates the 45,000 Allied seamen who died during the Battle of the Atlantic in World War II (*Open* Apr-Oct. *Admission inexpensive*). The **Pointe de Pen-Hir▶ ▶** is the Crozon peninsula's best coastal viewpoint, a natural amphitheatre of 70m (230ft) high cliffs overlooking a scattering of rounded boulders in the sea known as the Tas de Pois (Heap of Peas). You can scramble down the cliff path to a grassy platform called the Chambre Verte (Green Room). Several beaches lie below the Camaret headland, but note that the Anse de Pen-Hat is unsafe for swimming.

▶ **Carhaix-Plouguer**   *117E1*

This former Roman encampment is still an important route-hub. Have a look at the **Maison du Sénéchal▶** (now the town's tourist office) in the main street. The exterior of this stone and wooden mansion fizzes with corbelling, slatehanging and strange carved figures. The town's large central church, with its square tower, is dedicated to St. Trémeur, who bears his head in his hands over the main entrance.

The **Coreff Brewery▶**, now relocated from Morlaix, stands on Place de la Gare. You can learn about this traditional Breton ale on a guided tour, and taste some with a good meal at the on-site brasserie (see page 280).

► **Châteaulin**   *116C1*

Steamers once made the journey up the Aulne estuary from the Rade de Brest. Today the serpentine river is tidal only as far as Port-Launay, and canalized through Châteaulin—a placid scene of water-meadows and steep wooded cliffs. In the spring the water churns with salmon and trout, making it one of Brittany's leading angling centres. A recently installed *passe à poissons* (fish ladder) lets you watch the fish as they head upstream to their spawning grounds. The riverside towpaths make good walks or bicycle tracks. The **Chapelle Notre-Dame►** (above the town on the north bank) has a triumphal arch and a 15th-century calvary.

Hidden in tiny lanes a couple of kilometres (1 mile) downstream, the 16th-century chapel at St-Sébastien houses several ornate altarpeices. The patron saint provides archery target practice above the triumphal gateway in the parish close, which unusually depicts a scene of the Last Judgement.

► **Commana**   *117D2*

This bleak village deep in the Monts d'Arrée is visited mainly for its church. Although the parish close lacks the impact of some in the region, it is worth seeing for its triumphal arch and an ossuary containing a small museum of sacred art. Inside the church, three elaborately carved and coloured **altarpieces►►** present a masterly array of baroque peasant art.

Just outside the village, in the hamlet of Mougau-Bian, is one of the region's finest prehistoric antiquities, an ***allée couverte►***, about 14m (45ft) long with five horizontal slabs supported on 28 upright stones. If you creep inside the monument you can just make out one or two faint carvings.

LA TOUR D'AUVERGNE
A statue in Carhaix-Plouguer's main square commemorates Théophile-Malo Corret (1743–1800), who was so keen to join the army that he presented false papers when he entered the king's service. He enjoyed a brilliant career and proved valiant and loyal, being wounded many times during the Napoleonic wars. Though ambitious as a youth, he was extraordinarily modest and consistently refused any promotion to a rank higher than captain. He was killed in action on the Rhine in 1800, but is still revered as a hero among French regiments.

123

The Chapelle de Notre-Dame, Châteaulin

Armorique

POINTE DES ESPAGNOLS
In 1594, 400 Spaniards occupied this headland for a period of over four years. They had been sent by Philip II in support of the Catholics, at war with the Protestant Henry IV. Elizabeth I of England eventually sent reinforcements to help dislodge the Spaniards, who were finally ousted after a six-week siege. This surprising piece of Anglo-French cooperation was a self-interested manoeuvre to prevent the Spaniards taking Brest harbour, which would have made an ideal base for a much-feared second Armada attack on England.

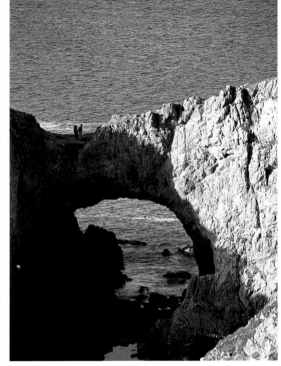

You can walk out to the rock arch at Crozon's Pointe de Dinan

Château de Dinan is one of the Crozon peninsula's most dramatic rock formations

▶▶▶ Crozon, Presqu'île de   *116B1*

The Crozon peninsula forms the foaming tongue of Finistère's mad-dog profile. As its regional park status indicates, it has some spectacular coastal cliff scenery, particularly at its westerly capes. The sea laps along large, quiet beaches and reed-filled creeks edged with sea holly.

There is little intensive farming and virtually no heavy industry. On the north side there are fine views of the Rade de Brest, glimpsed through wooded inlets. Many of the idyllic southern beaches are popular with campers, although those at the tip of the hammerhead can be chilly and dangerous, with shifting sands and currents. Apart from the isolated height of Menez-Hom, the countryside is no more than gently rolling. The best holiday bases are Morgat and Camaret, being good for boat trips, beaches, fishing and watersports. Hotels are mostly simple and seasonal.

Drive

The Crozon peninsula

See map on pages 116–117.

A varied 70km (42 miles) drive through quiet villages, bracing headlands, and gorgeous beaches to some of Finistère's most exciting coastal scenery. You can easily see most of Crozon in a day, with time for the beach, a clifftop walk or even a short boat trip. Sightseeing is limited, apart from three or four little museums. Camaret is the best lunch stop-off (cheap fish restaurants around the port) or take a picnic.

Le Faou (see pages 128–129) makes a good starting point. Southwest of the town, the road known as the Térénez Corniche (D791) gives lovely views over the Faou and Aulne estuaries and the Rade de Brest. The bridge at Térénez forms a panoramic entrance to the Crozon peninsula. At les Quatre Chemins, you can make detours: northwards to the ruined **Abbaye de Landévennec▶** (see page 133) or southwards to the small village of **Argol▶**, which has a cider museum and the **Maison des Vieux Métiers Vivants**, an exhibition on traditional crafts and trades. Its church has a fine parish close. Near **Trégarvan**, on the south bank of the Aulne, a former school has reopened as the **Musée de l'École Rurale▶**. Visitors are transported back to the

Reefs and quiet beaches

early 20th century, with slates, inkwells and old school photos. The museum is interesting (note the attempts to suppress the Breton language), but heavy on documents, for which no translation is provided.

Crozon, the peninsula's main town, has little to detain you except its church, where a remarkable altarpiece commemorates the defeat of a Roman legion. Take the minor road north to **le Fret**, a small, pretty ferry port with views of the Rade de Brest. Continue north towards the **Pointe des Espagnols▶▶** for spectacular views. Vauban fortifications guard the peninsula. To the east you can see the mysterious Île Longue, a nuclear submarine base. The east road through **Roscanvel** (there is striking modern stained glass in the church) is much lusher than the exposed western side of the headland. Follow the coast through **Camaret-sur-Mer▶** (see page 122) and the **Alignements de Lagatjar▶** to the **Pointe de Pen-Hir▶▶**, Crozon's most exciting viewpoint. Back at Crozon again, head south for **Morgat▶** (see page 135), or take the coast road to the Pointe de Dinan, where the rocky mass known as the **Château de Dinan▶▶** stands beyond a natural rock arch. Down past Morgat the road leads to the **Cap de la Chèvre▶**, where observation posts offer grand Atlantic views. Near St.-Hernot, call in at the **Maison des Minéraux▶**, a collection of geological specimens. On the return leg, detours off the D887 lead to lovely long beaches, such as **Pentrez-Plage▶▶**, or the viewpoint of **Menez-Hom▶** (see page 134).

As a French holiday region, Brittany runs the Côte d'Azur a close second. More than 1,000km (600 miles) of sand lie waiting for its visitors; far more than the Riviera offers and much less crowded, even at the height of summer.

SETTING THE TREND
Though sea-bathing was popular throughout the 19th century in the north coast resorts, it took longer to reach more isolated communities. Pierre-Jakez Hélias describes in his autobiography, *The Horse of Pride*, the astonishment the first seaside holidaymakers caused in the Penmarc'h peninsula: 'Little by little, on summer Sundays, we would see families of peasants coming to sit by the sea, first on the grassy clifftops, to watch the half-naked holidaymakers frolicking down below in their one-piece bathing costumes. Then in their turn they would go timidly down to the shore, first to wash their feet, the men first, the women behind.'

Sailing at Bénodet

The variety of coastal scenery in Brittany means that there is some sort of beach for everyone: idyllic sheltered coves or vast wild expanses of shingle; lively resort beaches equipped for any type of seaside sport; or remote hideaways for solitude. There are island beaches, estuary beaches, beaches strewn with fascinating rock formations, and beaches below awesome cliffs or panoramic headlands. At low tide a rockpool wonderland emerges from the waves, teeming with hundreds of mysterious crustaceans and seaweeds.

Clean beaches Scoured daily by boisterous Atlantic tides, Brittany's beaches are much cleaner and fresher than those around the soupy Mediterranean. Pollution is rarely a problem except near large centres of population, such as St.-Malo, Lorient or Vannes (notices warn against collecting shellfish on some beaches). Many resorts proudly display the EU mark of beach approval—the Blue Flag. If one of these is flying, the water should be cleaner than average. The strong tides bring their own problems, though. At low tide the sea may retreat behind a mournful wasteland of mud, while storms deposit huge quantities of seaweed along the strand.

Keeping warm Squally weather brings its own drama to the Breton coast. The Plage de la Torche (see panel, page 158) in an Atlantic gale is a spectacular sight. Endlessly changing cloudscapes and rainbows compensate for inclement weather, and no enervating *mistral* or *sirocco* winds disappoint, as they may do on the Mediterranean. Water temperatures, though, are a fraction lower on this coast (even in August they rarely rise above 17°C/63°F), and it may be too cold or rough for young children.
Exciting beach sports such as sand-yachting, windsurfing, waterskiing and kitesurfing provide entertainment for spectators as well as participators. Simpler pleasures like kite flying or *boules* require less organization and less expense. Many of the main resorts operate beach clubs (often known as Mickey Clubs in France) where young children are entertained and looked after for a daily charge.

Beach safety Some Breton beaches are extremely dangerous because of unpredictable currents or strong swell. Large resorts generally provide lifeguard supervision on at least one beach during the main holiday season, though this may not be constant. Many supervised beaches also operate the well-known flag safety system: red means don't swim; orange means that swimming is risky; and green means that swimming is considered safe.

A particular hazard on some of Finistère's west-facing beaches is *baïnes*, or large hollows enclosed by sandbanks. When the tide comes in the *baïnes* become invisible; bathers may fall into them, and soon find themselves out of their depth. Currents may sweep even strong swimmers far out to sea. Noticeboards warn of these on some coasts, and tourist offices provide cartoon leaflets in several languages explaining the dangers. Exposed beaches on the Crozon peninsula, Cap Sizun, Penmarc'h peninsula, and west coast of Quiberon and Belle-Ile can be especially hazardous.

Pick of Breton beaches These are recommended for scenery and interest as well as sand but not all are safe for swimming.
Emerald Coast Dinard; St.-Cast-le-Guildo; Sables d'Or-les Pins; Erquy; le Val André.
Pink Granite Coast Binic; Plage Bonaparte; Bréhat; Perros-Guirec; Ploumanac'h; Trégastel-Plage; St.-Michel-en-Grève; Locquirec; le Diben.
North Finistère Carantec; Plouescat; Brignogan-Plages; Plouguerneau; Trémazan; le Conquet.
Armorique Camaret-sur-Mer; Morgat; Trez-Bellec Plage; Pentrez-Plage.
Cornouaille Ste.-Anne-la-Palud; Baie des Trépassés; Penhors; Plage de la Torche; Bénodet; Beg-Meil; Raguenez-Plage; Port-Manec'h; Guidel-Plages.
Morbihan Quiberon; Carnac-Plage; Île aux Moines; Houat; Hoëdic; Belle-Île.
Loire-Atlantique Penestin; le Croisic; Batz-sur-Mer; la Baule; St.-Marc.

Canoe surfing at Cap Sizun

127

THE BAIE DES TRÉPASSÉS
The name translates ominously as the Bay of Souls because drowned shipwreck victims often washed ashore here (it is said their souls rise from the surf on All Souls Day). The bodies of dead Druid priests were ferried across this bay in pagan times to their final resting place on the Île de Sein.

Fun in the sand at Dinard

Medicinal plants, Abbaye de Daoulas

MARY, QUEEN OF SCOTS
Unconfirmed accounts declare one of the figures representing the Three Holy Women on Guimiliau's calvary (the one on the right) to be Mary, Queen of Scots in 16th-century court dress. She was executed in 1587, about the time the calvary was carved.

CATELL GOLLET
A couple of Brittany's most elaborate calvaries (Guimiliau and Plougastel-Daoulas) include horrific scenes of a young girl being torn apart by demons. This is not a biblical tale but a Breton morality story. Catell or Katell (Catherine) loved dancing and other sinful activities, not all of which she confessed to in church. In her fallen state she took a handsome lover and, like many another woman before and since, discovered all too late that he was the Devil in disguise. Her final damnation was to steal consecrated wafers for her lover at Mass, and her dreadful punishment is publicized on the calvaries as an 'awful warning' to all bad girls.

Gothic porch at Daoulas church

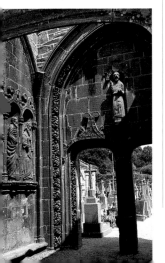

▶▶ Daoulas, Abbaye de   116C2

Tel: 02 98 25 84 39. Open: Mar–Nov 10–5; Jul –Aug 11–7 during exhibitions only; www.abbaye-daoulas.com. Admission moderate

Daoulas has been the site of an abbey since the 5th century, when the monks of St. Columba arrived. It fell into disuse after an attack by the Normans, but in the 12th century it was rebuilt by Augustinian monks. The abbey flourished for the next 600 years until it was badly damaged during the Revolution. It is now in the care of the local authority, and is imaginatively used as a cultural centre, the setting for summer events and exhibitions. The ruins can be visited at any time of the year and are one of Brittany's best examples of Romanesque architecture.

The ruins stand at the head of the Daoulas creek, which flows into the Rade de Brest. A small town of gold-stone houses huddles below the abbey, the best of which can be seen in the cobbled rue de l'Église. A belfried **porch▶▶** (the former south door), adorned with statues and animal carvings, now provides a triumphal entrance to the parish close. The **church▶▶** still has its original 12th-century west door. The tranquil abbey grounds nearby contain the remains of 12th-century **cloisters▶▶**, ornamented with foliage and geometric patterns. Only three sides still stand, surrounding a courtyard with a large decorated basin. A few exotic sheep graze in a nearby field and ducks paddle near a small fountain and oratory with quaint ancient statues, one showing St. Thélo riding a stag. To one side is a medieval **herb garden▶** containing several hundred species of medicinal plants, each neatly labelled: 'Sage—against gastric and intestinal infections, aches, and toothache', or 'Lemon balm—for the stomach, a sedative'. Excavations continue to unearth the old convent buildings and chapter house.

▶ Le Faou   116C1

There's not much to see in this little medieval port, but it is a place of great charm, particularly at high tide when the brimming estuary mirrors the domed church by the waterside. Once it was a significant timber port; today it has no riverine trade. In the main street 16th-century jettied houses, half-timbered and slate-hung, make a picturesque scene. Two hotel-restaurants on the main square make useful places to stay or eat. The covered market and pleasant streets containing traditional food shops are good places to buy supplies for a picnic.

Café scene in le Faou

▶▶▶ Guimiliau   *117D2*

This is one of Brittany's star parish closes (see pages 136–137), not to be missed unless you have special dispensation from church visiting. The calvary is one of the most complex and animated in the region, with over 200 carved figures from the famed masonic workshops of Landerneau depicting numerous scenes from the life of Christ. The whole assembly, attired in 16th-century dress, looks as theatrical as a Shakespearian play. The knobbly cross in the heart of this wonderful carousel shows the Virgin, St. Peter, St. John and St. Yves with Christ. The thieves, unusually, are absent. More intriguing than these scenes is the vignette of Catell Gollet (Catherine the Damned; see panel opposite).

A gargoyle grimaces from the church at le Faou

The church, too, is crammed with busy decoration. A beautifully carved south porch (the creation of Eve is shown on the left inner frieze, and a cat and dog chase each other round the outside) leads into a blaze of timber-panelled vaulting and exquisite woodwork. St. Cecilia and St. David play a duet on the organ loft, and the domed canopy over the font is superbly carved. The pulpit sports sibyls and cardinal virtues; the fine altarpieces represent St. Yves the lawyer between the rich man and the poor man, St. Hervé with his guiding wolf, and the headless St. Miliau. Allow plenty of time to take in all the detail.

AROUND HUELGOAT
A few local villages are of interest. Scrignac, northeast, is famed for its Breton wrestling champions (contests are still held in nearby Berrien) and its hunting museum, Maison de la Faune Sauvage et de la Chasse, in the old railway station. Brennilis has a lovely 15th-century church (daylight belfry and rich polychrome panels) and a dolmen. At Loqueffret you can visit another of the Armorique Park's little museums, the Maison du Recteur (Priest's House) and a richly decorated church. The next parish church, Lannédern, contains the relics of St. Edern, who is depicted on the calvary riding a stag. Beyond Roc'h Trévézel, a short detour northeast takes you to the ruined Cistercian remains of le Relecq abbey.

130

Mossy rocks in the forest of Huelgoat (above right)
The Grotte d'Artus (below)

▶▶ Huelgoat   117E2

The name means 'high wood' and, appropriately enough, Huelgoat is the main community of one of Brittany's last remaining forests. Until the 1980s the forest was a wondrous place of tangled vegetation, thick with moss and ferns. Then the hurricane of October 1987 smashed many of its ancient trees to matchwood in about a quarter of an

hour. Steadily, replacement trees are springing up above the chaos of uncleared lumber, but in places the woods resemble a fleet of wrecked sailing ships; all stricken masts amid a morass of driftwood and flotsam, now overgrown with brambles and gorse. Some fine old specimens remain, mostly of beech, oak and pine. Newer plantings are often glumly coniferous.

Huelgoat stands by the shores of a large lake, which together with its neighbouring hilly woodland makes it a popular summer resort and excursion centre for activity holidays. Sailing, fishing (carp and perch in the lake; trout in the river), horseback-riding, bicycling and walking are all catered for locally. The tourist office in the village can provide detailed maps of all the nearby paths, wider and more obvious since the great storm. Car parking areas and picnic sites around the 600ha (1,500 acre) forest make access possible at many points. The village itself is not particularly interesting, and has a certain mountain-resort dourness, particularly out of season. St. Yves stands in the parish church, flanked by the rich man and the poor man as usual (see page 21).

Woodland walks The main walks are well signposted from the village. Paths lead along the banks of the River Argent, which flows out of the lake, or along the canals dug in the 19th century when the silver and lead mines were worked. Signs of earlier habitation can be found on the hilltops above the valley floor. One strategic defensive site was used by Celtic peoples and became a Gallo-Roman camp after the arrival of Caesar's legions. A small exhibition in a mill, the **Moulin du Chaos▶**, highlights local life and history. Within about 100m (328ft) of the lakeshore road the name is transposed into Chaos du Moulin in a magical scene of mossy, tumbled boulders, where water-smoothed granite, now softened by vegetation, lines the river valley. A short distance on is the **Grotte du Diable (Devil's Cave)▶**, accessible down a steep iron ladder. A soldier fleeing the Chouans (see page 179) is alleged to have spent a night here, protecting himself with a pitchfork. When the locals saw his shadow by firelight they had an understandable fright.

In a natural forest amphitheatre nearby, occasional cultural events are staged in season. Across the stream, more curiosities include the **Roche Tremblante (Trembling Rock)▶**, a huge oblong stone that will apparently rock on its axis if you push it in the right place, and the **Ménage de la Vierge (Virgin's Kitchen)▶**, a cluster of rocks which a very creative imagination could conceivably convert into pots and pans. At this point the path diverges. The Allée Violette continues by the riverbank towards the road (D769), diverging again around the **Promenade du Fer à Cheval (Horseshoe Walk)** to **Le Gouffre (The Chasm)▶** where the River Argent disappears briefly into a swallow-hole (access via steep steps or a difficult path). The **Sentier des Amoureux (Lovers' Path)** leads uphill to join other paths past the **Grotte d'Artus (Artus' Cave)** and the **Mare aux Sangliers (Boar's Pool)**, to the **Camp d'Artus**, a Gallo-Roman camp consisting of an artificial mound surmounted by oval fortified enclosures and a lot of dead trees.

South of the River Argent lie **La Roche Cintrée**, a natural belvedere with views over the town, and **Mare aux Fées (Fairy's Pool)** and the old silver mines. The countryside around Huelgoat is a mixture of woodland and open moor, rising to the Monts d'Arrée.

There are lovely views of Huelgoat from across the lake

SKETCHERS AND SPORTSMEN
Thomas Adolphus Trollope (brother of the novelist Anthony) remarked on Huelgoat's advantages for 19th-century leisure travellers, whose pastimes usually included drawing and painting or hunting: 'For the first [sketchers], there is an infinite variety of combinations of rocks, wood, and water, with an abundant supply of picturesque figures of both sexes and all ages. For the second [hunters] there are partridges, and hares, and trout, in any quantity he pleases to kill, wolves frequently to be met with, stags sometimes, and boars occasionally.'
—*A Summer in Brittany* (1839)

The revived cornmills at Kérouat grind again—at least when visitors arrive (right and below)

132

ST. MILIAU
Several of the famous parish close churches in Finistère (notably Guimiliau, Lampaul-Guimiliau and Ploumilliau) depict the strange legend of St. Miliau, a 6th-century prince of Cornouaille whose jealous brother cut off his head during a quarrel over the succession. Miliau calmly picked up his severed head and let the blood spill over his brother, so proving his guilt for all time. A little boy with clogs and a Breton hat (Miliau's son) adds pathos to the scene. The blameless Miliau was canonized after the miracle and is now the patron saint of the Elorn valley parishes.

▶▶ Kérouat, Moulins de   117D2

Tel: 02 98 68 87 76. Open: Jul–Aug daily 11–7; Sep–Jun Mon–Fri 10–6, Sun pm. Admission moderate

An abandoned mill village near Sizun, consisting of about 15 buildings surrounded by farmland, has been attractively restored as an *écomusée* by the Armorique Park authorities, and is now much frequented by school-children and coach parties for its educational and entertainment value. The mills were built between the 17th and 20th centuries and once belonged to a mayor of Commana. The living quarters, with their bourgeois furnishings, are those of a well-to-do family. One of the watermills is in working order, and you can see the mill-stones turning on the gearing mechanism. Explanatory panels in the cottages and outbuildings outline the activities in barns, stables, a tannery and bread ovens.

▶▶▶ Lampaul-Guimiliau   117D2

Though it is usually listed as one of the great Breton parish closes (see pages 136–137), this church is more notable for its interior than its calvary, which is plain and damaged. Before you go in, however, notice the triumphal archway surmounted by triple crosses and the funerary chapel containing an elaborate altar and saintly statues. The stumpy tower of the church is the result of a lightning strike in 1809, and from the outside it is not impressive. Inside, however, marvels await.

The decorated rood beam that spans the nave bears a crucifix and statues of the Virgin and St. John, while other carvings include fishy dragons on choirstalls and wicked robber faces. A stone stoup dating from the 17th century shows two devils writhing in agony as they touch the holy water. Biblical and mythical scenes are enmeshed in a kaleidoscopic turmoil of high relief on the altarpieces. Annunciation, Passion, Resurrection and Martyrdom slowly emerge amid baroque columns and harvest festival swags. A more sober impression is left by Anthoine's emotive *Entombment* (1676) in a downstairs chapel.

▶ Landerneau   116C2

The one-time capital of Léon stands on the Elorn estuary, a pleasant mix of old and new. Its elegant shops (see panel), fine restaurants and well-kept accommodation give it a more cosmopolitan feel than most of the towns in this region, and it makes an excellent touring base for a night or two.

There are no specific sights within the town except its bridge. The 16th-century **Pont de Rohan▶▶** is one of the few left in Europe with houses built on it. Walk to the northeast side of the bridge for a good view of the stone and slate-hung buildings mirrored in the water.

The most interesting and picturesque parts of the old town lie on the west bank of the Elorn. A wander up the main street and the sidestreets off it reveals a number of traditional facades, turreted and ornamented with statues in niches. The Maison de Rohan at the east end of the old bridge has a fine sundial. The town's two historic churches are St.-Houardon, with a Renaissance domed tower, and St.-Thomas-de-Cantorbéry, with a three-tiered belfry and an adjacent ossuary.

▶▶ Landévennec, Abbaye de   *116C1*

Tel: 02 98 27 35 90. Open: Jul to mid-Sep 10–7; May–Jun, late Sep Sun–Fri 2–6; Oct–Apr Sun pm only. Admission moderate.
The main reason to visit this hook-nosed stretch of coast is to see the Romanesque ruins of an abbey originally founded by St. Guénolé in the 5th century. King Gradlon (see pages 18–19) is alleged to be buried here, and some of the abbey's remains show spiral or circular designs of very ancient origin. A museum of monastic history (with an audio-visual show) is housed in a nearby 17th-century convent building. A Benedictine community now occupies modern quarters in the village.

Landévennec's location (a *site naturel protégé*) at the mouth of the Aulne estuary is extremely pretty, and its sheltered climate cloaks it in a mass of Mediterranean vegetation and lush woodland.

SHOPPING IN LANDERNEAU
Landerneau is especially appealing on market day (Tuesday), when the main square is lively with stalls selling crêpes and farmhouse cheeses. If you are looking for souvenirs, try Comptoir des Produits Bretons on Quai de Cornouaille, where beautifully displayed Breton products include books, traditional music recordings, boat woodcarvings, cider, food and crafts (tel: 02 98 21 35 93; www.comptoir-produits-breton.com).

133

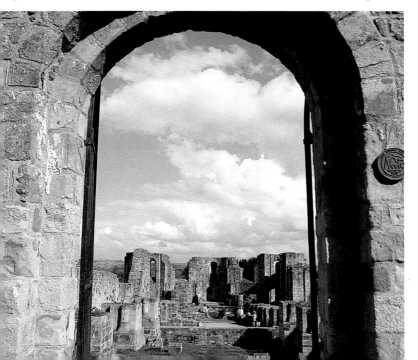

The ruins of the Abbaye de Landévennec enjoy a remarkable setting

ST. ANNE OF BRITTANY
The cult of St. Anne, mother of the Virgin Mary, is strong in central Finistère (see page 20), as the statues at Landivisiau indicate. St. Anne is sometimes represented in Breton art teaching Mary to read, or in a sort of alternative Trinity with Mary and the infant Jesus.

▶ Landivisiau   116C2

This sizeable cattlemarket town is scarcely riveting, but its mostly modern-Gothic church is worth a glance (outside at least) for a very large carved porch dating from the 16th century. If you can find a parking place outside, walk down a small side alley (rue St.-Thivisiau) to find the fountain of its patron saint, St. Thivisiau, decorated with granite panels in low relief. In a cemetery near the tourist office, the little ossuary chapel of Ste.-Anne is adorned with caryatids. Inside are a couple of quaint statues of St. Anne with the Virgin and St. Anne crushing a dragon.

▶ Menez-Hom   116C1

At only 330m (1,100ft) high, this gorse-covered peak hardly qualifies as a mountain, but its elevation above the surrounding countryside makes it a good vantage point. Cars line up at the summit for picnics on clear days in summer, while more energetic folk walk or cycle to the top. Menez-Hom is the final westerly hiccup of the Montagnes Noires, erupting suddenly from a lonely forested landscape. From the top the views extend over the whole of the Crozon and Plougastel peninsulas and Douarnenez bay, with the Noires and Arrée mountains inland. Although it is a peaceful place now, Menez-Hom

134

The sheltered harbour at Morgat is a popular sailing centre

was a key site in the German defence system during World War II, and was repeatedly strafed. A small chapel at the foot of the hill is dedicated to St. Mary.

CAP DE LA CHEVRE WALK
The coast south of Morgat consists of rocky heathland scattered with huddled hamlets of white cottages. It is an area of megaliths, with an unusual alignment formation near St.-Hernot called Ty ar C'Huré (Priest's House).

▶ Menez-Meur   116C2

Open: Jul–Aug daily 10–7; May–Jun, Sep 10–6; Oct–Apr Sun pm only. Admission moderate

At the heart of the Monts d'Arrée, the Domaine de Menez-Meur is a curious mixture of country wildlife park, exhibition and information centre. It covers about 520ha (1,285 acres) of rolling upland country, through which visitors can stroll along nature trails and past enclosures of local fauna such as wolves, Highland cattle and Swaledale sheep. A special exhibition is devoted to the sturdy Breton draught horse, and an adventure playground and bar-restaurant add to its family appeal.

▶ Morgat 116B1

More genteel than Camaret, the other main resort on the Crozon peninsula (see page 122), Morgat is a popular holiday spot, especially for water-based activities, and has an excellent curving sandy beach backed by pine trees. Tuna-fishing boats once set sail from its sheltered harbour; today most of the boats are private yachts or pleasure cruisers taking visitors round the rocky Cap de la Chèvre or to the caves beyond Beg-ar-Gador, remarkable for their vivid mineral colours. Largest of these is **la Grotte de l'Autel (Altar Cave)▶▶**, 80m (265ft) deep and 15m (50ft) high. Tall openings rise from the caves to the cliffs above, where saintly hermits used to rescue shipwrecked mariners. Other, smaller caves are accessible at low tide from local beaches.

In high season a ferry service plies between Morgat and Douarnenez. There are excellent cliff walks down the coast to Cap de la Chèvre (see panel opposite).

▶▶ Pleyben 117D1

As it is geographically separated from most of the parish closes, Pleyben is sometimes ignored, but it is one of the finest and largest, and is worth making a special detour for. The **calvary▶▶** was originally constructed in the 16th century, but parts of it date from later periods and it has an unmistakable neoclassical air about its solid pedestal and triumphal arches. The whole structure bustles with naïve, animated scenes from Christ's life; notice the weeping witnesses of Christ's Passion, and the pie ready for the Last Supper. The whole close is overshadowed by the massive twin-towered church of **St.-Germain▶▶**, whose interior boasts some splendid panelling, stained-glass windows, and decorated roof beams.

The town has a prosperous air and welcomes visitors with crêperies and souvenir shops. A local confectioner (Chantillot) invites you to watch biscuits and chocolates being made, and stalls on the main square sell honey and *chouchenn* (mead).

WASH HOUSES
Wash-troughs were once a feature of every village, a great source of social interaction and gossip among the womenfolk who undertook this backbreaking task. After soaking the hempen clothes in boiling water and ashes, they took them to the wash house and beat them with paddles. Pierre-Jakez Hélias describes the routine in *The Horse of Pride*: 'When the last piece had been washed, one of the women would strip off all her lower garments and step down into the trough, her skirts tucked up to her hips, to collect the laundry…More than one of them caught their deaths for having ventured into the cold water while in a sweat.' Laundry was washed only twice a year, in spring and autumn. There are good examples of wash houses at Landivisiau and Vannes.

135

Ankou at Landivisiau's chapel of Ste.-Anne (above left)
The calvary (below) at Pleyben

The idiosyncratic parish closes of Finistère are quite unique to the region, and one of Brittany's highest forms of art. The best of them are concentrated close to the Armorique Regional Park.

SCULPTURAL THEMES

If you become interested in Breton religious art you will soon spot recurring themes among the regional parish closes. The thieves crucified with Christ, for example, are often sculpted in contorted positions, with their arms and legs wrapped awkwardly around the bars. Christ is sometimes depicted blindfolded and seated with his hands tied in his lap. Many of the ancillary figures on calvaries wear not biblical robes but the elaborate 16th-century dress of the period when the churches were built.

136

Argol, on the Crozon peninsula, has an exceptional triumphal arch (1659) with a statue of King Gradlon on horseback

The phrase *enclos paroissial* (parish close) refers to the enclosed cemetery around a church. It is usually walled to keep animals out, but pierced with low stiles. The main entrance, through which funeral processions pass, is generally marked by an imposing gateway, often a neoclassical triumphal arch. Inside the close, the most striking feature is the calvary. Breton calvaries are more than mere crucifixes; they are vastly elaborate sculptures detailing many biblical scenes, but are sometimes secular. These naïve carvings were worked in granite, and most are now softened by time and weathering, and covered with lichen. In the days when many parishioners were illiterate, the stone carvings provided a vivid pictorial subtext to the Church's teachings. They also reinforced the association that was ever-present in Breton society between the living and the dead: the link between generations, and the hope of resurrection amid the despair of mortality.

The typical Breton close also includes an ossuary, or charnel house. Such was the pressure on these patches of hallowed ground in times of plague or famine that every five years or so old corpses were exhumed to make room for the new ones. The bones were then placed in the ossuary, and when that in turn was full all the bones were given a grand ritual burial in a common grave. Ossuaries look like small chapels, some with a skeletal Ankou outside to remind the living that their

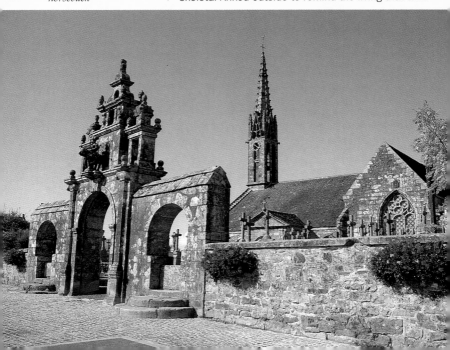

turn will come. Today very few still contain bones; instead they have been turned either into souvenir shops or treasury museums.

During the 16th and 17th centuries parts of Finistère grew rich on sea trade and linen, and parishes began to spend their newly acquired wealth on churches and calvaries. The most famous parish closes date from this period. Some villages became rivals, each anxious to have the biggest and best, and the most skilful masons and wood-carvers could set a high price for their work. Church interiors blossomed with baroque altarpieces and coloured statues, while beams and vaults sprouted carvings and paintings, particularly on the side beams (purlins) and on the rood, or glory, beams spanning the naves.

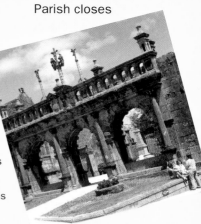

Pick of the parish closes
Brasparts St. Michael slays his dragon on the calvary; lovely baroque altarpiece with blue and gold barleysugar columns decorated with vines, snakes, and birds.
Guimiliau (see page 129) Vast, ornate calvary in 16th-century dress; Catell Gollet scene; altarpieces, porch, pulpit and domed baptistery.

Lampaul-Guimiliau (see page 132) The church interior is the place to look: glory beam, choirstalls, stoups and altarpieces glow with vivid detail; lovely Entombment sculpture.
Locmélar Less well-known but enjoyable; cross-barred calvary, altarpieces and banners, painted beams and ceiling.
La Martyre One of the oldest closes; ossuary, triumphal door, carved porch.
Pencran 16th-century ossuary, carved porch and balconied belfry.
Pleyben (see page 135) Elaborate, very large calvary; twin-towered church with carved beams and altarpieces.
Plougastel-Daoulas (see page 138) Large, elaborate calvary and plague cross; carvings of Catell Gollet.
La Roche-Maurice Classical ossuary with Ankou figure; twin-galleried belfry; splendid rood beam.
St.-Thégonnec (see pages 138–139) Triumphal arch; superb calvary; inside the church, magnificent pulpit and a life-size Holy Sepulchre sculpture.
Sizun Triumphal arch with coffin rest; ossuary; rich panelling and vaulting.

Others parish closes worth seeing Guéhenno, Lanrivain, Kergrist-Moëlou, St.-Jean-du-Doigt, Argol, St.-Herbot, Cléden-Poher, Lannédern, Brennilis, Pleyber-Christ, Bodilis, Berven.

CHARNEL HOUSES
Although hardly any ossuaries contain bones today, in former centuries the piled bones inside would have been clearly and horrifyingly visible. In some parish closes the skulls were kept in small boxes fixed to the ossuary walls. After 25 years or so they were taken out and added to the rest of the bones, which were recycled regularly to make room for fresh corpses.

Sizun's calvary (above)
St.-Thégonnec's calvary (left)
Detail, Pleyben calvary (below)

138

PLOUGASTEL-DAOULAS MUSEUM

The Musée du Patrimoine et de la Fraise, housed in a modern building near the church, provides an absorbing and well-presented introduction to the history of this insular community, which has developed its own customs through the centuries. Farming, seafaring, local costumes and furnishings are featured, with special emphasis on the strawberry (introduced from Virginia in the 17th century), scallop-dragging and the Breuriez apple festival (tel: 02 98 40 21 18; *open* Jul–Aug Mon–Fri 10–12.30, 2–6.30, Sat–Sun 2–6.30; Sep–Jun Tue–Fri, Sun 2–6. *Admission moderate*).

▶ Plougastel, Presqu'île de   116B2

The ragged tatters of land that jut into Brest harbour were very isolated until the modern Albert-Louppe bridge was constructed over the Elorn estuary in 1930; even today, they are not much visited by tourists. Most of the region consists of dull countryside devoted to market gardening, particularly the luscious strawberries that are celebrated throughout Brittany and exported in vast quantities.

Strawberry growing, though, is not a spectacular activity, and most of it goes on invisibly behind hedges and plastic cloches. Other products of this mild, fertile area are shallots, tomatoes and hothouse flowers.

A few scattered chapels make focal points for excursions down the long lanes to the waterfront, from which there are attractive, but hardly obligatory, views of Brest and the Crozon peninsula. Lauberlac'h is a pretty fishing port, but there are no real resorts or good beaches here. The village of Kersanton may ring a bell as this is where much of Brittany's best monumental granite comes from: malleable, but hardening over time.

The history of the region is more interesting than its landscapes, and the best place to learn about it is in **Plougastel-Daoulas▶** itself. Most of the town is fairly dull, but the early 17th-century **calvary▶** is justly famous for its impassive granite tableaux of over 180 figures. Christ steps from his tomb, as though from a bath; the thieves' souls are greeted, one by an angel, the other by a devil; and as at Guimiliau (see page 129), poor Catell Golett is again torn asunder for her sins. The calvary was built to remember a terrible epidemic that ravaged Plougastel in 1598, and the bumps on the cross-shaft are said to represent the blisters of the plague, not the stumps of branches as on other calvaries.

▶▶ St.-Herbot   117D1

The unusual square-towered church stands proudly in a wooded dell, a sheltered oasis in otherwise desolate countryside deep in Brittany's *argoat*. Outside, a lichen-mottled calvary and a Renaissance ossuary catch the eye, but the church is more interesting inside. Carved saints whirl round the main door at the top of the horseshoe staircase. A superb wooden screen surrounds the chancel, topped by a crucifixion scene where angels bear Christ's arms up, and skulls are piled on rocks below the crosses. Tufts of hair from cattle tails lie on the plain granite tables by the chancel, an offering to St. Herbot, the patron of horned beasts. Lift up the choirstalls for some lovely misericords, and notice the saint's tomb, a simple block with low-relief carving.

▶▶▶ St.-Thégonnec   117D2

St.-Thégonnec was one of Brittany's richest parishes in the 17th century and its close is one of the highpoints of this curiously specialized form of Breton art. Through its massive triumphal arch stands a complete set of parish close accoutrements.

The multibranched **calvary▶▶▶** is one of the later versions, constructed in 1610. The biblical scenes are vividly captured. Christ's tormentors set about their sadistic work with gusto (one of them is alleged to be the Protestant king, Henry IV), angels mop up the Redeemer's blood, and the little-known St. Thégonnec puts in an appearance on a low niche. Legend has it that when a wolf ate his donkey, St. Thégonnec tamed it and harnessed it to his cart, where it looks like a little dog. The funerary chapel in the close contains a poignant piece of sculpture by Jacques Lespaignol: an **Entombment**▶▶ scene painted on oak.

The church interior is equally sumptuous, with statues adorning every nook and altarpieces bustling with detail. St.-Thégonnec's pride, however, is its **pulpit**▶▶, a *tour de force* in wood, encrusted with saints, angels, evangelists, cardinal virtues and God himself, giving Moses the tablets of stone inscribed with the words of the Ten Commandments.

After this, anything else in the village is an anticlimax, except perhaps the food at its celebrated *auberge* (see Hotels and Restaurants, page 271).

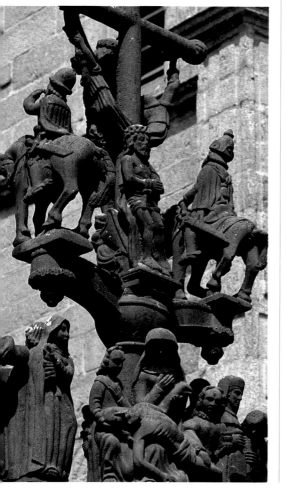

WOLF COUNTRY
The story of St. Thégonnec, whose donkey was eaten by a wolf, is made a little more credible by a local stationmaster in the late 19th century who mentioned the wolves that visited the village in winter—'one of which has killed my favourite dog.' Until the 20th century wolf-hunting was a popular and necessary sport in Brittany from October to January, when hungry wolves were a real threat to local communities.
The **Musée du Loup**, an exhibition on wolves, can be seen in the church cloisters at St.-Thégonnec (tel: 02 98 79 73 45; *open* Jul–Aug daily 2–6; low season, Sun pm. *Admission inexpensive*).

139

HENRY THE APOSTATE
The Protestant King Henri IV was the archetypal pragmatist. His cynical conversion to Catholicism in 1592 ('Paris is worth a Mass') gained him little respect among the villagers of St.-Thégonnec, where he is immortalized on the calvary as one of the principal tormentors of Christ. But Henri's expediency averted national insurrection, and when the Edict of Nantes was signed two years later, the debilitating Wars of Religion came (at least temporarily) to an end (see pages 38–39).

Details on the calvary at St.-Thégonnec: Christ Reviled (above) with Roman soldiers and (below) the Deposition scene

Cornouaille

Crozon
Presqu'île de Crozon 330m
Trégarvan
Aulne
St-Ségal
Ple
St-Hernot
Morgat
Pointe de Dinan
Argol
St-Sébastien
Parc Naturel
Régional
d'Armorique
Menez Hom
D887
Port-Launay
Châteaulin
Pentrez-Plage
Cap de la Chèvre
Plomodiern
Plomodiern
Baie de
Douarnenez
Ste-Anne-
la-Palud
D107
Cast
Kervel
Kergoat
Réserve du
Cap Sizun
Pte de
Beuzec
Pte du
Millier
Tréboul
Douarnenez
Locronan
Plogonnec
le Juch
Kervel
N165-E60
E
Pte du
Van
B. des
Trépassé
Pte de
Brézellec
Notre-Dame
de Kérinec
D765
FINISTÈ
Raz de Sein
Goulien
Pont-Croix
D765
Ile de
Sein
Pointe
du Raz
Plogoff
D784
Audierné
Notre-Dame
de Confort
Guengat
la
St-Tugen
Ste-Evette
Plouhinec
Goyen
QUIMPER
Er
Ga
Plozévet
Landudec
D785
Baie
Pouldreuzic
Pluguffan
Plomelin
d'Audierne
Penhors
Chapelle de
Languidou
Plonéour-
Lanvern
Chapelle de
Languivoa
Odet
la Forêt-
Fouesnant
Tréguennec
Combrit
Fouesnant
Pont-l'Abbé
Bénodet
Perguet
Cap-
Coz
Notre-Dame
de Tronoën
Ste-Marine
Plage de la Torche
St-Guénolé
Manoir de
Kérazan
Ile-Tudy
Loctudy
Pointe de
Mousterlin
Phare d'Eckmühl
Penmarc'h
Lesdonil
Pointe de Penmarc'h
le Guilvinec
Léchiagat

Iles de Glénan

see drive page 157
see drive pages 158–159
see drive page 173

A   B   C

Breton costumes proudly worn at Pont-l'Abbé, one of the most traditional of all the Cornouaille towns

Cornouaille

CORNOUAILLE Cornouaille is in many ways the most typically Breton part of Brittany, and its natural and cultural features contribute to its immense popularity as a holiday destination. With a southwesterly maritime location, it is alternately soothed by the mild Gulf Stream and battered by Atlantic storms, and its landscapes offer both bleakness and welcoming havens. Its Celtic heritage, the most apparent and carefully preserved in Brittany, and the strip of coastline between Pont-l'Abbé and le Pouldu attract vast numbers of holidaymakers during the season.

Inland, the large town of Quimper acts as regional headquarters and is well worth a day's exploration. On a smaller scale, Locronan and Quimperlé shouldn't be missed. A tour of the Montagnes Noires, which straddle the borders of three *départements*, makes an interesting picnic outing. Aside from these, Cornouaille's interior is unexceptional, and its attention focuses steadfastly on the sea. A blend of idyllic sheltered beaches, picturesque wooded estuaries, apple orchards and quaint fishing towns gives this area its distinctive charm. The Sizun and Penmarc'h peninsulas add more rugged ingredients to coastal excursions, though their relative lack of creature comforts make them less suitable as resort bases. Beaches, too, can be dangerous on these exposed shores and are less than ideal for children or anyone who is an unsure or weak swimmer.

▶▶▶ REGION HIGHLIGHTS

Cap Sizun
pages 172–173

Concarneau
pages 148–149

Locronan *page 156*

Montagnes Noires
page 157

Pont-Aven
pages 162–163

Port-Musée, Douarnenez
pages 152–153

Quimper *pages
168–170*

Cornouaille

THE GLÉNAN DAFFODIL
St.-Nicolas, one of the
Glénan islands (see page
154), claims the smallest
nature reserve in France,
a tiny plot of land protecting one of Europe's rarest
flowers. Le Narcisse de
Glénan was allegedly
brought to the island by
Phoenician sailors, and
first identified as a unique
species in 1903. It is a
tiny plant, so fragile that
it is easily swamped by
more rampant vegetation.
A flock of sheep grazes
the reserve, and visitors
are asked to keep dogs
on leashes. Though a host
of silvery flowers can be
seen blooming in April,
picking them is, of course,
strictly forbidden.

*Fishing boats take
on a festive air at
Douarnenez, one of
Brittany's major
fishing ports*

LIVING FROM THE SEA Cornouaille has a historic and
venerable pedigree. It was once a kingdom—according to
legend the seat of King Gradlon, whose great city of Ys lies
beneath the waves in the bay of Douarnenez (see pages
18–19). When Ys was submerged, Gradlon set up his court
in Quimper, which is still the regional capital. During the
Middle Ages, Cornouaille was a Duchy whose boundaries
stretched as far north as Morlaix. After the union of
Brittany and France, the region's importance diminished,
and it suffered economic decline and isolation over the
following centuries. Its people retained their fiercely independent streak, however, and stood their ground bravely
against the monstrous taxes imposed by Colbert to finance
Louis XVI's extravagance. Linen-weaving and the manufacture of hempen sailcloth made the merchants of
Locronan wealthy for a while, but even these industries
eventually slid into sharp recession.

Fishing, too, has suffered serious decline, but even today
Cornouaille's ports are among the foremost in France,
notably le Guilvinec, Douarnenez and Concarneau. These
unpretentious working towns still earn their living from
the sea, as generations have done before them, albeit with
state-of-the-art technology these days. Several good museums in each of the major ports (Haliotika, Port-Musée and
Musée de la Pêche) reveal more about the fishing industry.
Visit an early morning *criée* (fish auction) by the harbour,
where the night's catch is sold and distributed to markets
throughout France. Visitors are welcome at these events,
but *criées* these days are businesslike affairs in modern
sheds rather than picturesque market scenes. Keep your
wits about you or you may be bowled over by a crate of
haddock on a fork-lift truck. Local seafood, needless to
say, is excellent, complemented by rich dairy produce
from the interior and the best Breton cider, produced
mostly around Fouesnant.

LOCAL TRADITIONS Cornouaille is the most Celtic region
of Brittany, and culturally it is enormously rich. Here

A HEAD ABOVE THE WAVES
In his book, *The Horse of Pride*, Pierre-Jakez Hélias recounts a fascinating anecdote from the 1930s, when Brittany was opening up to seaside tourism in a big way: '…one day, mark my words, a girl wearing a tall Bigouden *coiffe*, dressed all in black velvet bordered with glass beads, arrives by the jetty. When a moment later she gets out again, she is wearing a black bathing costume, but she has kept her *coiffe* on her head. She runs to the sea, plunges into it, and begins to swim. And it's an astonishing sight to watch the girl's *coiffe* sailing lightly on the bright swelling sea.'

143

Quimperlé and its church of Notre-Dame-de-l'Assomption

particularly in the Pays Bigouden (Penmarc'h peninsula), you can find traces of a rural lifestyle that is centuries old, epitomized most memorably in the remarkable *coiffes*, or headdresses, of the region, which are exaggerated here into enormously tall towers of lace. Known as *bigoudènes*, they are increasingly rare nowadays, and are seen mostly in museums or at festivals to impress tourists. In remoter byways, though, you may still glimpse older women wearing them behind net curtains as everyday garments. Such hats are said to be character-forming, and indeed, keeping them on in anything above the lightest breeze must require great ingenuity.

For a detailed look at the folk history of the region, visit Pont-l'Abbé's castle museum, followed by a tour of Penmarc'h. Quimper also encapsulates much local Breton culture (see the regional museum and, if possible, the Festival de Cornouaille in July). For more background, track down Pierre-Jakez Hélias's autobiographical account of his Bigouden childhood near the village of Plozévet, *The Horse of Pride* (Yale, 1978). A rich social tapestry woven against a canvas of backbreaking work and poverty brings this region to life more forcefully than any museum.

Cornouaille's culture is not all *coiffes* and costumes, however. In the late 19th century it fostered the famous Pont-Aven School of artists, whose most talented exponent was Gauguin. To follow the artists' trail, visit Quimper's Musée des Beaux-Arts, followed by Pont-Aven and le Pouldu. Local people and landscapes were the main sources of inspiration for these painters, as they are for many resident artists and craftworkers today.

The charming houses of Pont-Croix are well worth exploring

▶ Audierne   140B2

The Goyen estuary meets the sea at Audierne, a fishing port sheltered from the open sea by an obliging triangular headland, the Pointe de Lervily. Audierne's extensive river frontage gives it breathing space and the town spreads itself handsomely along the west bank beneath a wooded hill. Moored boats blend appropriately with the wealthy shipowners' houses ranged along the quayside. The main beach is some way downstream at Ste.-Evette.

Audierne's prosperity was built on fishing, and there was once a thriving tuna fleet here which sailed as far as Africa. Douarnenez's modern port facilities attract the deep-sea fishermen now, and today Audierne's daily catch is more likely to consist of langoustines, lobsters and crab, conveniently available in the local *viviers* (enclosed fish-breeding tanks). These form one of the largest fish farms in France, and visitors are welcome.

A major new attraction in Audierne is the **Planète Aquashow▶**, on the riverbank, containing a comprehensive collection of Breton marine life (tel: 02 98 70 03 03; *open* Apr–Sep daily 10–7; Oct–Mar 2–5. *Admission expensive*).

You can walk beside the wooded Goyen, but there are no boats upstream. From Ste.-Evette, however, there is a regular boat service to the Île de Sein (see page 172). The chapel of **St.-Tugen▶**, 4km (2.5 miles) west of Audierne, is a Gothic building renovated in the 17th and 18th centuries, with an elegantly traceried south porch and a fountain dedicated to its patron. St. Tugen can also be found in the chancel in sculpted form, bearing his miraculous keys to keep rabid dogs at bay. During the Middle Ages, pilgrims paid handsomely for copies of these leaden keys,

144

Audierne's picturesque harbour

ıoping the saint's blessing would work the same magic.
Notice the chimney and firedogs in the baptismal chapel,
ınd the odd catafalque bearing statues of Adam and Eve.

▶ Beg-Meil   140C1

This peaceful resort is immensely popular with families
who eschew the brighter lights of Bénodet. Today, Beg-
Meil seems well established and its setting is undeniably
pretty with sandy coves, dunes and rockpools. It occupies
ı corner site, one aspect facing the sheltered bay of
Concarneau, the other towards the open sea. Bright boats
pring lobsters ashore, but there is nothing much else to
distract from the simple pleasures of the seaside.

You can sail and dive here, or take boat excursions to the
Îles de Glénan (see page 154), up the Odet River, or across
the bay to Concarneau. Footpaths follow the wooded
shoreline north towards Cap-Coz, a sandy nose jutting
out into the Baie de la Forêt, where houses and simple
hotels are shaded by a promenade of surviving pines.

*One of Cornouaille's
smartest and most
comfortable hotels is
at Audierne*

*Paddling in the shallows
at Beg-Meil, an ideal
family seaside resort*

▶ Bélon   141D1

The main reason to search for this tiny hamlet scattered
over the wooded mud flats of the Bélon estuary is to eat
oysters, which outnumber the human population by an
astronomical factor. It's a confusing place, spanning both
panks of an unbridged and serpentine river. To find the
oysterbeds, head for the north bank via Riec-sur-Bélon.

Bélons are the original native flat oysters, farmed here
from their spat stage to supply the beds of Cancale on
the Emerald Coast (see page 51). You can taste these in the
region's exceptionally good selection of seafood restaurants, all of which offer the prized local molluscs on their
menus. Deceptively simple bar-restaurants, such as Chez
Jacky (see page 280), and upmarket hotels tucked into
quiet, leafy creeks cater for sophisticated gourmet tastes.
Typical examples include Les Moulins du Duc, and the
Manoir de Kertalg (see pages 272).

The quiet, scattered hamlets of Moëlan-sur-Mer, around
the Bélon estuary, attract an increasing number of
visitors. The countryside is deeply rural, with low-lying,
sometimes waterlogged pastureland divided by screens
of elms. The village of Moëlan (no longer *sur mer*) acts
as the regional centre and has some useful food shops and
a helpful tourist office. Glance at the 15th-century
calvary in the chapel of St.-Philibert if you are passing
through.

THE OYSTER PRINCE
Maurice Sailland, a
celebrated gourmet and
bon viveur who wrote
several gastronomic
tomes under the pen-name
of Curnonsky, adopted the
little hamlet of Riec-sur-
Bélon as a wartime retreat
between 1914 and 1918.
He is believed to have
attended more than 4,000
public banquets during his
life, and his appearance in
any French restaurant
commanded hushed
respect and terror among
the kitchen staff. At Riec,
however, he enjoyed the
relaxed hospitality of
Madame Mélanie Rouet,
who had the reputation of
being the best cook in
Brittany, possessing
special ways with oysters.

Cornouaille

SUNSET STRIP
Bénodet faces due west and enjoys spectacular sunsets from its sheltered location. A late stroll by the river beside the lighthouse and the port when some of the summer crowds have dispersed is one of the best ways to appreciate the resort.

▶▶ Bénodet

140C1

Bénodet's glorious location and fine amenities make it one of Cornouaille's leading beach resorts. However, its popularity and fashionable image make it very crowded in summer, especially at its campsites.

Boat trips galore Apart from its natural setting and an odd scrap of fortress, Bénodet has no unmissable sights or historic buildings. However, for seaside activities it is hard to beat. There are tennis courts and swimming pools, a public golf course a short distance inland at Clohars-Fouesnant, clean Blue Flag bathing beaches (see page 126) and a magnificent sailing school at le Letty, in the tidal lagoon sheltered by a strange long dune. You can windsurf or canoe, rent bicycles or horses, and take a bewildering range of boat trips.

146

There is no shortage of summer activities at Bénodet (above and below)

One excursion not to miss is a trip up the Odet River, confidently trumpeted in Bénodet's tourist literature as the prettiest estuary in France; artists have frequently considered its green shores and clear water a worthy subject. The best part is the wooded gorge-like scenery around les Vire-Court (literally 'short-tack') where sailboats must weave skilfully back and forth to avoid the banks. About half a dozen river cruisers leave Bénodet each day during the high season, these taking about an hour and a quarter to reach Quimper. Contact Vedettes de l'Odet (tel: 02 98 57 00 58).

By day, the charm of Bénodet's setting is best admired from St.-Gilles Point to the south and the viewpoint on the Avenue de Kercreven over the port. Far out into the bay of Concarneau you can just make out the shapes of the Îles de Glénan, like stepping stones in the sea.

Even after dark there are places to go in Bénodet (nightlife is a rare commodity in Brittany), including a couple of nightclubs and a casino. None of the resort's activities could be described as rowdy, however, and it still retains something of a village-like air despite much speculative tourist development.

Bénodet, at the mouth of the Odet estuary

In the same building as the tourist office, the **Musée du Bord de Mer▶** is an exhibition tracing the development of Bénodet as a seaside resort and sailing centre since the beginning of the 20th century (tel: 02 98 57 00 14; *open Jun–Sep Mon–Sat 10–7, Sun 10–6. Admission moderate.*

Escaping the crowds To do this, take the graceful modern road bridge (Pont de Cornouaille, with excellent views) or the little shuttle ferry across the Odet to the picturesque backwater of **Ste.-Marine▶▶**, a tranquil scene of old cottages, pine-clad rock and sand beaches and small fishing boats. One simple but charming shuttered hotel-restaurant (La Ste.-Marine) occupies pride of place on the waterfront, and an elegant restaurant called L'Agape stands on the road leading down to the beach (see pages 272 and 280).

A glorious pale sandy beach (Plage du Teven) of almost tropical beauty stretches west towards Île-Tudy. Other long beaches stretch out towards the **Pointe de Mousterlin▶**, where camping is popular and there are extensive views of the whole bay.

Inland, the little 12th-century chapel of Ste.-Brigitte at **Perguet** has an excellent example of Finistère's typical church architecture, with an exterior roof staircase leading up to the belfry.

Nature and tradition The village of **Combrit**, 4.4km (2.5 miles) northwest of Bénodet, has lovely, quiet sandy beaches and a mild microclimate.

The **Parc Botanique de Cornouaille**, a 5ha (12-acre) natural park off the D44 road, between Pont-l'Abbé and Combrit, is a continuous feast of colours nearly all year round as its camellias, rhododendrons, magnolias, azaleas, heather and rosebushes flower in turn. A mineral collection is also on display (tel: 02 98 56 44 93; *open Jul–Aug 10–7; Mar–Nov, daily 10–12, 2–7. Admission moderate*).

ENGLISH LOCUSTS
'No Egyptian ever dreaded the approach of a swarm of locusts more than the native residents of the little towns of France do the settling down of a flight of English. For the result in both cases is the same—scarcity and dearness of every article of consumption…I met, in the remoter parts of Britanny [*sic*], three or four old Englishmen, many years resident in the country, who constantly retreat before the advancing flood of their countrymen like the squatters, those pioneers of civilization in the western forests of America, knowing that to live cheaply they must find some part of the country where English gold has not yet penetrated.'
—Thomas Adolphus Trollope, *A Summer in Brittany*, shows that mass tourism is nothing new. He wrote this in 1839 about Dinan; today it could apply to Bénodet.

Cornouaille

CRIÉES

Concarneau's celebrated fish auctions, or *criées*, are held by the Arrière-Port in the early morning. The fishing boats unload their catches between midnight and 6am, after which they are rapidly sold to the highest bidder. Don't expect any *folklorique* fishwives crying cockles and mussels on the quayside; fish auctions are a serious and highly competitive affair these days, and the proceedings resemble an anglers' stock exchange. Visitors are welcome to the large modern sheds (guided tours can be arranged in summer). Arrive before 7am if you want to see any action.

148

Concarneau takes on a festive air in high season

►► Concarneau 141C1

This is still one of France's most important fishing ports, on the east flank of a deep bay where shipping takes refuge from Atlantic storms. Whales and sardines have all figured in its former prosperity, although West African tuna is its main catch today. At its *criée* (fish auction), a huge variety of sea creatures can be found. Concarneau combines its piscatorial role with tourism now, offering boat trips up the Odet or to the Îles de Glénan (a 25-minute hydrojet service) and capitalizing on the sandy beaches that lie both north and south of the town in the sheltered Baie de la Forêt. These are not Brittany's best as the Plage des Sables Blancs look a bit tired in high season, and others near the Pointe du Cabellou to the south can be covered in seaweed at certain times.

Island stronghold The best part of Concarneau is its lively old port. The **Ville Close►►**, or walled town, separates the pleasure craft in the marina from the serious business of the inner harbour. This charming citadel measures little more than a kilometre (half a mile) across, and can easily be explored in an hour or two.

Like St.-Malo's *intra muros* quarter (see pages 66–67), Concarneau's Ville Close is on an island, linked to the rest of the town by a fortified bridge and gateway. The town was first fortified in the 11th century, then steadily beefed up by the Normans until, by the 14th century, it was thought impregnable. The English held it for over 30 years after the War of Succession. Even Du Guesclin (see pages 34–35) had to besiege it three times before it fell and the English were driven out. During Louis XIV's reign the military strategist Vauban altered and strengthened it still further, erecting the great ramparts that protect the Ville Close from maritime invasion. Although it was restored in the 19th century, the Ville Close looks much the same today as it did in Vauban's time.

The fortified entrance has a friendlier aspect today. Sundials and tubs of geraniums decorate the clock-tower gate, and the cannons are now merely ornamental. Today the invading hordes of tourists who cram into the picturesque narrow alleys during summer are bombarded more seductively with handmade chocolates and biscuits. Less welcomingly the town charges a small entrance fee to climb the ramparts, but views from the top are impressive, and gateways piercing the walls give satisfying glimpses of the port beyond. An enterprising company called À l'Assault des Remparts (tel: 02 98 50 55 18; www.alassaultdesremparts.fr) organizes guided tours of the old town (some in English), including visits to the harbour, a working

LA FÊTE DES FILETS BLEUS
In late August Concarneau holds its famous Blue Nets Festival. Originally set up in 1905 to help the families of distressed sardine fishermen whose catches were failing, the mix of music, parades, and folk events is similar to many summer festivals held in Brittany. The nets used for Concarneau's sardine fishing fleet were traditionally blue, hence the name, but modern nets are usually brown.

149

The fortress entrance gate to Concarneau's walled Ville Close

trawler and the quayside fish auction. The evening tours are particularly interesting, when you can see the boats arrive to unload their catches sometime after midnight.

Fishy business Do not miss the excellent **Musée de la Pêche▶▶** (*Open Jul–Aug daily 9.30–8; Sep–Jun 10–12, 2–6. Admission moderate*) in the Ville Close, housed in the former arsenal on the main street. Every kind of net, line, block, and tackle seems to be on display, along with some old sardine tins, and also model fishing craft. Clog-wellingtons made of wood and leather, a monster coelacanth and giant scooping nets help enliven informative displays on the movements of fish stocks through the oceans, and the operation of drag nets. Outside, spry visitors can explore an old 34m (112ft) trawler called *Hémerica* moored by the walls, not exactly a comfortable or luxurious workplace.

Concarneau does a brisk trade in matelot *gear (above)*
The sundial on Concarneau's walls (left) reminds visitors that time flies

Brittany is still France's most important fishing region, but where former generations braved the eternal perils of storm and shipwreck, today's fishing communities face less tangible threats: the depletion of fish stocks and competition from foreign imports.

A DANGEROUS LIVING

The *Terre-neuvas* (Newfoundlanders) and *Islandais* (Icelanders) brought prosperity to north Breton shores from the end of the 15th to the 19th centuries. The fleets left Brittany in early March and returned in August via the coast of Gascony, where they sold their fish for a good price and replenished their stocks of salt. Life on board was hard and dangerous, and whenever a shoal of cod was discovered, sleep was abandoned and the crews worked day and night without pause.

150

Business or pleasure Fishing is both a serious, hazardous industry and a pleasurable pastime in Brittany. For centuries a large proportion of the region's inhabitants have made a living from the sea, setting sail from their homes, sometimes for six months of the year, to face terrible dangers and hardships. Less riskily, whole families spend happy Sundays ferreting through rockpools with hoes and trowels in pursuit of edible molluscs and crustaceans. Others sit patiently on riverbanks waiting for bobbing floats or twitching lines. Cradle nets dangle from bamboo poles attached to stilt-huts on the Rance and Vilaine, and in the Grande Brière marsh-eels are harpooned from flat-bottomed barges. Altogether, Brittany has about 9,600km (6,000 miles) of river bank and shoreline for recreational fishing. Fishing for pleasure is immensely popular throughout the region, and discarded tackle can be a minefield for wildlife and leisure sailors.

Deep-sea fishing Until the beginning of the 20th century, hundreds of boats from North Brittany worked the rich fishing grounds around Iceland and Newfoundland. Pierre Loti's novel *Pêcheur d'Islande* (see panel on page 81) gives a flavour of Paimpol's fishing industry in the late 19th century; today, only St.-Malo still sends vessels to trawl the cod and haddock banks of the North Atlantic. From Cornouaille, summer fleets head south, chasing tuna, mackerel and sardine shoals around West Africa and the Azores. In winter the boats are used for other types of fishing. Today only a handful of fleets are truly ocean-going. Most deep-sea fishing from Brittany is done in the Bay of Biscay or the Irish Sea. To compete effectively, boats must be rigged out expensively with the latest refrigeration equipment and computerized navigational

Net-mending is still done the old way in some of Brittany's fishing ports

aids. Both salt- and smoke-curing have given way to ice as a method of preservation. The catch is graded, filleted, and packed for market on board, and then swiftly distributed in efficient containerized lorries as soon as it is landed. Le Guilvinec, Concarneau, Douarnenez, Lorient and St.-Malo are Brittany's largest fishing ports, though there are many smaller fishing towns all around the Breton coast, whose fleets hug inshore waters for sole and turbot, mullet and skate. More than 10,000 Bretons earn their living by fishing, or in associated shore-based industries such as canning and processing. About two-thirds of France's canned fish is produced in Brittany.

Dispatching the fish The best way to get a feel of this vital industry is to visit the fishing harbours when the boats arrive, and attend one of the *criées* (fish auctions—see panel on page 148). The night catch is unloaded very early in the morning and sold from about 6.30am onwards in large warehouses by the quayside. Plastic crates overflow with all kinds of grotesque sea creatures, and forklift trucks dart everywhere. The auction process is fast and furious, with loudhailers and frantic telephoning. The best and biggest *criées* are held at Concarneau and Douarnenez, and the excellent fishing and boat museums

Breton shellfish is often farmed today

151

Bright boats

n these towns provide further background. Other Penmarc'h fishing towns (le Guilvinec, Lesconil, Loctudy and Audierne) also hold *criées*, some in the afternoon.

Fish farming Increasingly, fish farming satisfies the voracious appetites of the restaurant trade. Oysters now spend their lives preparing for the table in sacks of plastic mesh, while mussels attach themselves guilelessly to conveniently accessible ropes hung from wooden posts. Salmon and trout no longer swim oceans and leap waterfalls, but flap listlessly in overcrowded ponds. If you enjoy Brittany's glorious variety of seafood (and there are few who do not), try visiting a *vivier* (fish farm) to see what goes on behind those *cotriades* and *assiettes de fruits de mer*. Cancale, Roscoff and Audierne have some of the largest artificial breeding grounds in France for oysters, lobsters, crab and *langoustines*.

WHALING
Breton whalers ventured into the northern seas from the 15th to the 17th centuries. 'Whaling was not then the safe, mechanized slaughter it has since become: the harpoon was hand-thrown at close quarters, with considerable risk to life and limb...The Bretons were renowned for their endurance and quiet determination, though at times of danger they were capable of sublime eccentricity,' wrote Jules Michelet in the 19th century.

The Île Tristan, just off Douarnenez

ST. TUTUARN'S ISLAND
One explanation of the origin of Douarnenez's name is that it is a corruption of *Tutuarn-Enez* (St. Tutuarn's island), after a 6th-century hermit who lived on the offshore rock known as Ile Tristan.

DAHUD
The legend of Ys (see pages 18–19) is really a Christian morality tale. Douarnenez was sacred to the Celtic horse-god Marc'h, a Druidic deity. King Gradlon's daughter, Dahud, had apparently remained faithful to the old pagan beliefs while her father had been converted to Christianity by St. Guénolé. Dahud's downfall symbolizes the conquest of paganism in Cornouaille.

►► Douarnenez

140B3

Ranking just after Concarneau in France's fishing port league, Douarnenez has a similarly workmanlike atmosphere. The older, pinkish-beige buildings around the Port du Rosmeur give it some character, though it lacks any picturesque old quarter to rival Concarneau's Ville Close. It has a significant sardine fleet, but also deals in lobster and deep-sea fishing. The port's prosperity soared in the latter half of the 19th century, after François Appert invented a technique of preserving food by sterilizing and hermetically sealing it in tins. Today canning factories surround the quays, where a *criée* (fish auction) is held early in the morning.

The drowned city The modern facilities of the Nouveau Port attract trawler fishermen from afar, but Douarnenez is a very ancient town, pre-dating Roman times when it was a famous production centre for *garum* (fermented fish oil), an important ingredient in Roman cuisine. In the Dark Ages the town became associated with King Mark and the Tristan legend. It was also one of the disputed sites of Brittany's mythical Atlantis; the Lost City of Ys, drowned by King Gradlon's daughter (see pages 18–19). As in most of these tales, church bells ring beneath the waves of Douarnenez bay for those with ears to hear them. There may be a grain of truth in the legend somewhere, for sea levels certainly did rise sharply in this part of Brittany at some stage around the 6th century.

Boats and beaches As with most of Brittany's seaside towns, Douarnenez puts in a bid for its slice of the tourism trade. The resort area lies in Tréboul across the Port-Rhu River, linked by a 24m (79ft) high steel bridge. Tréboul is a renowned sailing spot with a large, modern marina, and also offers thalassotherapy. Sea-fishing trips and excursions round the bay leave from Rosmeur in the summer, when a ferry service also links Douarnenez with Morgat on the Crozon peninsula (see page 135).

Douarnenez has comparatively few sights, though the **Port-Musée**►►►, a maritime complex on the old harbour of the Port-Rhu River, is definitely worth a detour.

This vast museum, which occupies the whole harbour area, has a wonderful collection of sailing and fishing craft moored on the banks: steam tugs, sand dredgers, tuna boats, a lightship and even a Thames barge. Several of these boats can be visited in summer. Many maritime events, regattas and ship-handling demonstrations are organized, and the floating harbour of Port-Rhu welcomes historic ships. A covered section of the museum (accessible on the same entrance charge) occupies a handsome old sardine cannery on the quayside. It contains France's largest collection of over 40 small vessels from all over the world, ranging from a simple Welsh coracle to an Inuit kayak and a flat-bottomed Brière barge. Craftsmen demonstrate traditional maritime skills such as sail-making, net-mending and wood-carving (tel: 02 98 92 65 20; open mid-Jun to mid-Sep daily 10–7; off-season Tue–Sun 10–12.30, 2–6; closed Nov–Mar. *Admission moderate*; guided tours, workshops for all age-groups; www.port-musee.org).

Douarnenez bay has many beaches, but some of them are dangerous for swimming. Tréboul's main beach is the Plage des Sables Blancs. A pleasant footpath, the Sentier des Plomarc'h, leads from the old harbour 2km (1 mile) eastwards to the Plage du Ris, backed by pinewood cliffs. Ile Tristan, at the mouth of the Port-Rhu river, is the subject of many legends and was the haunt of the 16th-century bandit, La Fontenelle (see panel). The surrounding villages have several notable churches. L**e Juch**, for example, out on the Quimper road, contains some fine old glass and a statue of St. Michael subduing the Devil. Years ago local fishermen about to set sail would pop an old cigarette butt or tobacco quid in the Devil's mouth for luck, hoping that this would grant them a safe voyage.

LA FONTENELLE

This vicious bandit terrorized the Pays Bigouden from his lair (Ile Tristan) in the late 16th century, using his Catholicism as an excuse to attack the mainly Protestant population of the Penmarc'h peninsula. He killed more than 5,000 peasants and carried off 300 boatloads of booty. At first Henri IV dealt with him surprisingly leniently, demanding only that his private army should be disbanded, but eventually he was accused of plotting against the king and broken on the wheel in 1602.

153

Traditional sailing boats (above) can still be seen occasionally on the Breton coast, sometimes restored as pleasure craft, sometimes in maritime museums

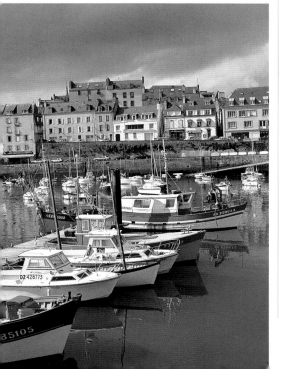

Douarnenez harbour combines business with pleasure (left), with sailboats in the marina and fishing smacks in the port

Cornouaille

154

FOUESNANT
This is a pleasant enough town, though it has little of great interest except its 12th-century church, where a modern war memorial by the Breton sculptor, Quillivic, depicts a woman in local costume mourning for the dead. Fouesnant is in the heart of a very fertile fruit-growing region. It is well known for its apples and cherries, and it is reputed to produce the best cider in Brittany. If you turn up in summer you may get a chance to taste the produce at the *pardon* of Ste. Anne at the end of July, or at the Fête des Pommiers (Apple Tree Festival), when religious ceremonies merge into bibulous celebrations.

WET-WET-WET
Les Balneïdes, on the Beg-Meil road out of Fouesnant, is a well-designed indoor water park with the longest water-slide in Brittany. If there's too much water outside, try this aquatic paradise, maintained at a comfortably steady 29°C (84°F). Saunas, whirlpools, cascades and waterchutes provide a range of both gentle and exhilarating fun for the whole family (tel: 02 98 56 18 19; *open* daily 10–8 in summer, low season pm only. *Admission moderate*).

A poignant war memorial by the Breton sculptor Quillivic at Fouesnant's old church

▶ La Forêt-Fouesnant   *140C2*

Smart yachts clank their rigging in the vast 1,000-berth marina here at the end of a beautiful wooded inlet, the fjord-like creek of the St.-Laurent river. At high tide the water forms a spectacularly scenic looking-glass, inverting boats and trees with sharp-edged perfection; at low tide it disintegrates into a snake of mud. Needless to say, the marina is a Mecca for keen sailors, the old fishing port seeming dead in contrast. Campers also flock here, though the best beach is at Kerleven, about 2km (1 mile) away.

In the village of la Forêt-Fouesnant, the 16th-century **church▶** has an unusual calvary with four corner pilasters. Local walks and drives along the wooded coast road make for attractive tours, and there are boat trips to the Îles de Glénan and up the River Odet.

▶ Iles de Glénan   *140C1*

The Glénans are famous for their birdlife (terns, cormorants and the like) and for a prestigious sailing school based around three of the islands. You can see this compact archipelago on clear days from most of Cornouaille's south coast, and it makes enough of an impact to attract 2,000 visitors a day in high season. The island group consists of some nine islets ranged around a lagoon of calm water called la Chambre, about 18km (11 miles) south of Concarneau. Several resorts run regular boat services to the islands, allowing a day, or half a day, to explore. Concarneau's hydrojet service whisks you here in 25 minutes; longer boat services ply from Bénodet, Beg-Meil, Loctudy, Quimper, Ste.-Marine and la Forêt-Fouesnant. Since facilities on the islands are limited, it is a good idea to pack a picnic. Visitors can only land at St. Nicholas, which is small enough to be explored on foot in half an hour.

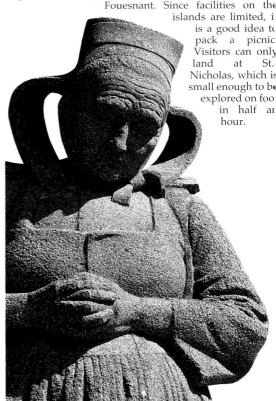

Very little wine is produced in Brittany today. Muscadet, the wine of the Nantes region, now comes officially from the Pays de la Loire. Brittany's more authentic tipple is cider, which makes an excellent accompaniment to crêpes.

Cider and other drinks Cider in shops is sold in corked bottles as *cidre bouché*, and may be still or sparkling. In more traditional bars or restaurants you may be offered local rough cider from a bowl (beware: it can be extremely strong). Pear cider (*poiré*) is made in small quantities around Pontivy, and a fierce cider brandy (*lambig*) is distilled in some areas. The best cider is alleged to come from around Rennes and the Rance valley, or Fouesnant in Cornouaille. Several cider producers have opened little exhibitions or museums on cider-making (at Pleuhiden, la Forêt-Fouesnant and Argol).

155

Beer is also a local drink. The traditional brew was Cervoise, a barley beer. Now real ale is produced in Carhaix-Plouguer, which visitors are invited to inspect and sample at the Coreff brewery (see page 122). Mead, or *chouchenn*, also known as *hydromel*, is a sweet, honey-based drink, best served chilled. Various local *eaux-de-vie* (fruit-flavoured spirits) are also available, perhaps the most unusual of which is a strawberry liqueur that is produced in the Plougastel region.

Cider is still made in traditional presses in a few places; this one can be seen in the Rance valley

Vines A few truly Breton vines still struggle on the Rhuys peninsula, as they have done since Roman times. The resulting wine, however, doesn't match the standard of the vines produced in the 12,000ha (30,000 acres) of vineyards near Nantes. Best of these is the AOC Muscadet de Sèvre et Maine, a crisp, dry white wine ideal with seafood.

Look for the words *sur lie* on the label, meaning the wine is fermented 'on the lees' (in other words, on the grape pips and skins, which produces a much better flavour). Lesser wines of the Pays Nantais include ordinary Muscadet, Muscadet des Côteaux de la Loire, Côteaux d'Ancenis (white, red or rosé), and the widely available white VDQS Gros Plant, a companion for dishes such as shellfish or *galettes*.

THE HARD STUFF
Cynics say that you need three people and a wall to help you drink the potent wine from the Rhuys peninsula: one to pour it out, one either side to stop you keeling over, and the wall behind to prop you up as you collapse backwards.

Muscadet de Sèvre et Maine

Cornouaille

156

SHOPPING IN LOCRONAN

Several of the old buildings on the main square now house craft shops and studios selling tasteful souvenirs. The Maison des Artisans, next to the church, is the most obvious of these, with local linen (fashioned into napkins and tablecloths nowadays rather than galleon sails), ceramics, wood-carvings and wool-lens ranged on three floors of a lovely old house. Flax and wool are spun and woven here, while other residents make a living from tea shops, antique trading, or health foods. A glass-works can be visited on the Châteaulin road.

▶▶ Locronan   140C2

Some claim that this is the prettiest town in Brittany. Roman Polanski thought it evoked Thomas Hardy's Wessex, and used it as a film-set for his mud-spattered version of *Tess of the d'Urbervilles*. The 'old town' is actually very small, confined mainly to a magnificent cobbled square surrounded by a perfectly preserved assembly of Renaissance merchants' mini-mansions, all pedimented dormers and lopsided timbering.

Locronan's prosperity derived from sailcloth manufacture. It cornered the market in the 17th century, supplying not only the French navy but also Spanish and English merchant shipping. However, when Louis XIV abolished Locronan's monopoly on hempen sailcloth the town's economy soon collapsed, leaving it fossilized in its glamorous heyday like an insect in amber.

The small **museum▶▶** (tel: 02 98 91 70 14; *open* Jun–Sep Mon–Sat 10–1, 2–7, Sun pm. *Admission inexpensive*) outlines the town's historic and artistic links (Surrealist painter Yves Tanguy lived in rue Lann). Today Locronan has recovered some of its affluence through tourism, crowds flock here and are requested to leave their cars outside and walk. A select handful of hotels and restaurants make Locronan an attractive, if pricey, touring base.

Traditional wood carvings on sale in Locronan

THE *TROMÉNIES* OF LOCRONAN

Every year the locals of Locronan celebrate their patron, St. Ronan, by re-enacting his daily penitential climb up the hill near the town. This is known as La Petite Troménie. Every sixth year, however, there is a longer 9.5km (6 miles) Grande Troménie right round the hill, stopping at 12 points representing the Stations of the Cross. The next Grande Troménie takes place in July 2007.

The **church▶▶** is the most striking building on the square: a stalwart 15th-century construction in a style known as Ogival Flamboyant. It is dedicated to St. Ronan, an Irish missionary who converted much of the local area during the 5th century. The lively carved pulpit inside the church depicts many scenes from his life, and his tomb lies in the 16th-century Chapelle du Pénity, built on the south side of the church. After St. Ronan's death, Locronan became an important place of pilgrimage and even St. Yves paid homage here; the local *pardons* (called *troménies* in Locronan) continue the tradition (see panel). Rue Moal (the old weaving quarter) leads to a smaller but equally charming church, **Notre-Dame-de-Bonne-Nouvelle▶**, which has a calvary, a 17th-century fountain, and a Christ Reviled, inside.

DOMAINE DE TRÉVAREZ

The extensive grounds of the Château de Trévarez have been turned into a country park, with rose gardens, shrubberies and forest walks. The ruined 19th-century mansion was commandeered by German U-boat crews during the last war and bombarded by the RAF, but now the grandiose architecture of the Belle Epoque château has steadily been restored (tel: 02 98 26 82 79; *open* Jul–Aug daily 11–6.30; low season pm or weekends. *Admission: moderate*).

Many of Locronan's old mansions now house shops and restaurants

Drive

The Montagnes Noires

See map on pages 140–141.

A 90km (55 miles) inland tour through green, rounded escarpments along the course of the Nantes–Brest canal. Wayside chapels and calvaries and quiet country towns are the main focal points. Allow the best part of a day, with a picnic or lunch-stop in Châteauneuf-du-Faou.

The Montagnes Noires (Black Mountains) are gentler and greener than the parallel Arrée range to the north. Wooded paths lead by streams and houses of dark slate; every so often the locks and sluices of the Nantes–Brest canal come into view.

Starting at the little town of **Rostrenen**, first see the castle chapel of Notre-Dame-du-Roncier (porch and fountain), site of a miraculous ever-flowering hawthorn bush where a statue of the Virgin was found. Then head for **la Trinité-Langonnet▶**, a

Flamboyant church with Renaissance beam decorations. **Gourin** is an old slate-quarrying town, now an agricultural centre with dairy and stud farms. Its 16th-century church has a polychrome *Pietà*. Detour north briefly to the chapel of **St.-Hervé**, in the Flamboyant Gothic style, then across to the **Roc de Toullaëron▶**, at 326m (1,070ft) the highest point in the Montagnes Noires. Continue via **Spézet** and the chapel of **Notre-Dame du Crann▶ ▶**, with its 16th-century stained glass and shuttered wooden altarpieces.

Follow signs for St.-Goazec, deviating to the canal at the **Écluse de Gwaker** (lock), where a waterfall tumbles into a pool. Retrace your steps to the D36 to the **Domaine de Trévarez▶** (see panel above).

Châteauneuf-du-Faou▶ is a pleasant canal town on a wooded ridge, famous for salmon fishing, and has a good hotel-restaurant (see page 272). The church contains frescoes by the Pont-Aven artist, Paul Sérusier. Continue towards **Carhaix-Plouguer** (see page 122), calling at the parish closes of **Cléden-Poher▶** (16th-century altarpieces and calvary) and **St.-Hernin▶** (calvary with St. Michael and the dragon, and the thieves being cruelly punished).

Cornouaille

The tall bigoudène coiffe *is one of the most striking in Brittany*

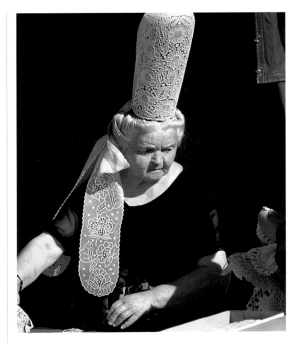

▶▶ Penmarc'h, Presqu'île de　　140B1

This desolate Cornouaille extremity was once a prosperous and populous region. Over the centuries, economic disasters struck in the shape of a vicious bandit called La Fontenelle (see panel, page 153), the disappearance of the cod shoals from its shores, and periodic tidal waves that threatened to engulf the whole low-lying region. Today Penmarc'h seems a grim place to earn a living, the vast shingle beaches of the bay of Audierne exposed to the full brunt of Atlantic storms. Scattered white houses lie like spilt sugarcubes over the bleak farmland, and dour little fishing ports stud the south coast. However, despite the absence of local cod, Penmarc'h is still a significant fishing region. Behind the majestic sweep of Audierne bay lies an attractively varied landscape of dunes and brackish lagoons creating a rich habitat for unusual flora and fauna. Some 300 species of migrant birds have been identified, including hoopoes and sanderlings.

Crêperies, galette shops and potteries are steadily proliferating to cater for tourism. Sheltered Loctudy most closely resembles a seaside resort, offering boat trips to the Îles de Glénan and up the Odet River. Although it may lack visual appeal, Penmarc'h is, however, full of interest. Marketed keenly by the tourist authorities as the Pays Bigouden, it is one of the most tenacious repositories of Breton culture. Here you will still see old-fashioned methods of farming and spot the older women wearing their curious tall *coiffes.*

Pont-l'Abbé is the regional centre, and is a good place to find touring information. Sightseeing is classic Breton fare: churches, megaliths, calvaries and lighthouses.

PENMARC'H BEACHES
The notorious Plage de la Torche is best seen in a gale. Skilled wind-surfers practise here, but it is a fantastically dangerous beach and cannot be recommended for swimming; warning notices abound. The long rocky nose of Pointe de la Torche separates the beach from nearby Plage de Pors-Carn, a more welcoming but still hazardous crescent of sand.

Dramatic coastline

Drive

The Penmarc'h peninsula

See map on pages 140–141.

This is a quiet 50km (30-mile) drive through a cultural time-warp of fishing ports, salt marshes and sand dunes. Pont-l'Abbé is the most convenient base. Allow about half a day.

Start in Pont-l'Abbé (see pages 166–167) at the tourist office. Head south, stopping off at the **Manoir de Kérazan**, a château set in parkland with a fine art collection. **Loctudy▶** stands at the mouth of Pont-l'Abbé's estuary, almost bridged by the curved sandy causeway of Île-Tudy. The church is its finest feature, hiding a beautiful Romanesque interior behind a nondescript 18th-century facade. Good beaches lie west of the port.

Lesconil is the next real port, with an evening *criée* (fish auction). Several large beaches lie to the west. The twin ports of **Léchiagat** and its much larger sibling, **le Guilvinec**, form France's fourth fishing port, a scene of bustling commerce. Set beside the *criée*, **Haliotika** is an exciting multimedia discovery centre devoted to the local fishing industry (tel: 02 98 58 28 38; *open* mid-Mar to mid-Oct Mon–Fri 2.30–7, Sat–Sun 3–6.30. *Admission moderate*). **Penmarc'h**, farther west,

is a scattered parish with a fine late-Gothic church (St.-Nonna). Notice the ships and fish carved on the porch, signifying the church's patronage. Right at the tip of the peninsula, the **Phare d'Eckmühl** (lighthouse) beams its signals over 50km (30 miles) from a granite tower (worth climbing for the views). **St.-Guénolé**, an unlovely sardine-canning centre, has a long beach and a reef of black rocks where the sea pounds. The town's **Musée de la Préhistoire▶** helps to put some of the local antiquities into perspective.

Nearby stands one of Brittany's most venerable calvaries, **Notre-Dame de Tronoën▶▶** (1450), now striped with lichen. The biblical and secular mingle, with unusual scenes of cudgelling dimly discernible to the south, and Mary (who has very long arms and hair) to the north.

North Penmarc'h is scattered with interesting churches, notably at **Languivoa**, **Languidou▶** (ruined), and Plozévet. Penhors is the scene of a famous September *pardon*.

Calm water at Loctudy

The embroidered aprons and starched lace caps of traditional Breton costume become so familiar from postcards and tourist literature that it takes a while to realize hardly anyone actually wears them any more. Sadly, the buckles and bows of yesteryear are now mostly consigned to folk museums or festival days.

Out of fashion It is hardly surprising that few people in Brittany dress traditionally today. The cost, in time and money, of making and maintaining these costumes, trimmed extravagantly with lace, velvet or satin, has simply become too great for modern practical lifestyles. A Breton wedding outfit used to take about three months to make; there are other things to do on dark winter evenings these days. Besides, as Pierre-Jakez Hélias bluntly remarks in his autobiography, *The Horse of Pride*, local costumes of this type are 'a typical feature of peasant civilizations' and hence something that modern Bretons may prefer to forget about. None the less, the sentimental tourist may lament the loss of these bright garments, and those who market Brittany lose no opportunity to squeeze them into the picture somewhere in the glossy brochures they produce.

Costumes appear on high days and holidays now, especially in Cornouaille

160

Regional variety You will still have plenty of opportunity to see traditional costumes if you attend any of Brittany's many summer folk festivals or *pardons*, and just occasionally you may spot one or two of the older women wearing a *coiffe* at Mass or on market day. Virtually any *écomusée* or museum of local history contains a few examples, and there are extensive collections in Quimper, Rennes, Guérande, Nantes, Dinan and Pont-l'Abbé. Cornouaille generally had the most cheerful costumes, and is still the region where you are most likely to come across them.

The Pays Bigouden (Penmarc'h peninsula) has one of the most striking *coiffes* of all, a tall tower of starched linen, supposedly representing a menhir. Fixing these hats on to the head was an amazingly complex performance and keeping them on in a high wind even more so, though they are pierced like Finistère steeples to allow the wind through. Until comparatively recently, the *bigoudène* was an unexceptional *coiffe*, but between 1880 and 1950 it gradually increased in size to its present height of 32cm (12in). Wearing these coiffes was alleged to show strength of character, but they are scarcely flattering garments for most apple-cheeked Breton faces.

Other regional *coiffes* show a remarkable variety of shapes and sizes: some with ribbons and streamers, others with starched wings, peaks and lacy edgings. Men generally wore short, dark jackets with broad lapels, and bright waistcoats and wide-brimmed black felt hats trimmed with buckles and ribbons. Trousers or breeches (known in Breton as *bragonbras*) were usually extremely baggy.

Vive la différence The traditional costume dates back to the 16th century, when Breton clans developed subtler ways of expressing their differences than banging each other over the head. This was born from the same spirit that produced the great parish closes of the region, built at about the same time; an ostentatious statement of rivalry and one-upmanship.

About 70 distinct styles of costume eventually developed, signifying membership of a particular regional group or family. The richness of the costume revealed individual status or wealth within that group, and many

fine distinctions were made about the precise number of skirts a woman should have in her multi-tiered dress. Costumes began to represent a significant proportion of a family's assets, and were often inherited or passed on at marriage. Richer families would have several complete outfits, for weddings, funerals, and the like.

More often than not, plain black was worn for everyday dress, but ceremonial costumes were highly elaborate and richly embroidered. Over the years these have inevitably been modified, and modern versions are worn with shorter skirts and fashionable shoes. But the *coiffe* used to be *de rigueur* at all times, in all weathers. Fixing it on was the first thing a woman did in the morning, and removing it was the last thing she did at night.

CLOGS
The local *sabotier*, or clog-maker, was once a pillar of society in every Breton community. Today they've all but disappeared, but a small factory in Riec-sur-Bélon still makes a modern version. Visitors can watch the partially mechanized process on a guided tour (Fabrique de Sabots Le Roy; tel 02 98 06 40 69; *open* Jul–Aug Wed 10.30. *Admission inexpensive*. www.sabot-breton.com).

Traditional costumes from all over Brittany can be seen at Pont-l'Abbé's annual Fête des Brodeuses (embroidery festival)

161

Sabots (clogs) were once everyday wear in Brittany

Cornouaille

162

THE GORSE-FLOWER FESTIVAL

Painting was not the only art that Pont-Aven fostered. The poet and song-writer, Théodore Botrel (1868–1925) was born here in a red-tiled house near the main square. In 1905 he founded Brittany's first folklore festival, La Fête des Fleurs d'Ajoncs, which is still held annually on the first Sunday in August. Many other towns have developed their own festivals along very similar lines.

►► Pont-Aven   141D1

Mills in the landscape '*Pont-Aven, ville de renom; quartorze moulins, quinze maisons*' goes the rhyme ('Pont-Aven, that famous town; 14 mills and 15 houses'). The mills can still be seen today, though only one of them is still working. One has been transformed into a celebrated hotel-restaurant, while others are occupied by art galleries, with which the town is now overburdened in memory of the famous colony of painters, among them Gauguin, who settled here in the 1880s.

Despite its sometimes wearisome commercialization and the summer crowds, Pont-Aven is a remarkably attractive place, still recognizably the scene captured in so many well-known wood and water landscapes of the late 19th century. The tumbling river rushes past the mills over granite boulders, some of which form slippery stepping-stones. Cambry, an 18th-century writer, wrote: 'The noise of the river, the roar of twenty waterfalls deafen the traveller.' Riverside walks lead away from the madding crowds past wash houses and ruined mills to Pont-Aven's pretty port, once used for shipping oysters and wine. Those keen on watersports can rent canoes and kayaks from the port.

Pont-Aven is a good place to look for souvenirs. Worthwhile art may be discovered among the mass-produced tourist items, and imaginative ceramics as well

as the ubiquitous Quimper *faïence*. Toothsome *galettes de Pont-Aven* (biscuits) are a local delicacy, along with cider and *chouchenn* (mead), and *kouign amann* (a delicious butter cake with caramel topping). The Gauguin connection is well-mined, and souvenir prints and T-shirts featuring his works abound. Staying or eating locally can be either memorable and expensive, for example, at the Moulin de Rosmadec (see Hotels and Restaurants, pages 273and 281), or unmemorable and expensive, so always choose your billet with care.

Pont-Aven's art museum attracts visitors from all over the world

Art and artists The tourist office provides full details of the local walks and painting trails. Don't miss the walk through the Bois d'Amour, a well-liked artist's spot in the beech and chestnut woods above the village. The charming **Chapelle de Trémalo**►► contains the rugged inspiration for Gauguin's *Christ Jaune* (now in the Albright-Knox Art Gallery in Buffalo, US), a vividly carved sallow crucifix in the nave. The lopsided eaves of this woodland chapel nearly touch the ground; inside, the roof is propped with buttresses, the beams studded with decorative bosses and curious beasts. At nearby **Nizon**, the calvary provided another of Gauguin's models, this time a *Christ Vert*. Bright, modern glass splashes the dark interior, where a wooden Christ suffers patiently.

To see more works of the Pont-Aven School, be sure to visit Pont-Aven's **museum**►► (tel: 02 98 06 14 43; *open* Jul–Aug daily 10–7; Sep–Jun daily 10–12.30, 2–6.30 (6 in winter); *closed* Jan. *Admission moderate*) where four galleries house grainy old photos of the town and its bohemian visitors in a startling array of headgear. Pont-Aven's most glittering star, Gauguin, is represented by a mere couple of canvases, *La Crique* and *Le Sabotier*, which are heavily protected behind toughened glass. Other noteworthy paintings include Paul Sérusier's *Ramasseuses de Fougères* (*The Heather-gatherers*) and Monet's *Falaises à Ouessant* (*Cliffs at Ouessant*). Returning fishing fleets, *pardons* and country folk dressed in traditional Breton costume provided an endless source of inspiration for the resident artists. There are also some modern works on display, and temporary exhibitions are held at the museum.

Sailing downstream Downstream from Pont-Aven, the River Aven is one of the most beautiful in Brittany, winding through wooded banks and past picturesque villages. The best way to see it is by boat, perhaps in *La Belle Angèle*, a replica 19th-century coastal vessel known as a *caboteur*. Alternatively, try one of the regular trips operated by Vedettes Aven-Bélon (tel: 02 98 71 14 59). Pick-up points include Moëlan-sur-Mer.

Alternatively, try a drive down the west bank on a fine evening. **Kerdruc** presents a delightful scene, with views east towards the white yachts of **Rosbras**' sailing school on the opposite bank. **Névez**, a little way to the west, has some quaint painted wooden statues in its Ste.-Barbe chapel. This is to be found tucked away from the middle of the village among old stone houses.

You are never far away from the sound of running water in Pont-Aven; the town's only working watermill is now carefully preserved as a tourist attraction

Pont-Aven's rich artistic heritage is conspicuous in the high street

Brittany's cultural heritage shows such clear evidence of creative talent, particularly in its church architecture and furniture-making, that it seems odd so few artists were known by name until the 19th century. Even then, most of them were not native to the region but hailed from outside.

CAREER MODELLING
The Pont-Aven School artists found no great difficulty in obtaining subjects for their paintings: 'The peasants, both men and women, are glad to sit for a franc for the greater part of a day; it is only at harvest time, when field labourers are scarce, that the demand may be greater than the supply, and recruits have to be found in the neighbouring fishing villages. Once or twice a week in the summer, a beauty comes over from Concarneau in a cart, her face radiant in the sunshine, the white lappets of her cap flying in the wind.'
—Henry Blackburn, *Breton Folk* (1880)

Gauguin was one of the more famous exponents of the Pont-Aven School

The Pont-Aven School Brittany's most famous group of artists is known as the Pont-Aven School, whose most illustrious exponent was Paul Gauguin (1848–1903). But these were by no means the first painters to be inspired by the Breton landscape and inhabitants. Writers and artists had trampled through Brittany since the late 18th century, and several books about the region achieved popular acclaim and helped to put it on the Victorian map. One influential travelogue was *A Summer in Brittany*, written in 1839 by Thomas Adolphus Trollope, brother of the novelist Anthony Trollope. A later book, *Breton Folk* (1880), by Henry Blackburn, described the already burgeoning artistic scene in Pont-Aven in the 1870s: 'Its inhabitants in their picturesque costume have learned that to sit as a model is a pleasant and lucrative profession...On approaching Pont-Aven the traveller notices a curious noise rising from the ground and from the woods around him. It is the flickering of the paint brushes on the canvases of the hardworking painters who come into view on leafy nooks and shady corners.'

Gauguin and the Synthetists Gauguin first arrived in Pont-Aven in 1886, where he discovered an established coterie of artists, many of whom were English or American. Their reasons for choosing Brittany were not simply a love of the landscapes and an everlasting supply of biddable local models; they could also live very cheaply there, and the Pension Gloannec in the main square was soon colonized by a bohemian clientele.

Most of their talents were modest, and Gauguin soon tired of their derivative outpourings. But the artist did find Brittany unexpectedly congenial for his work: 'When my clogs strike the granite underfoot, I hear the dull, matt, powerful tone that I'm after in my painting.'

In 1888 a kindred spirit arrived at Pont-Aven in the shape of Émile Bernard, who was experimenting with an innovative technique called *cloisonnisme*. Together, Bernard and Gauguin developed an earthier, less naturalistic style that became known as Synthetism. Their techniques involved abandoning conventional perspective, and instead painting from memory in a bold, bright, two-dimensional manner with heavy outlines. Religious subjects gave their work a spiritual and emotional depth, for example, Gauguin's *Christ Jaune,* based on the sculpture in the Chapelle de Trémalo at Pont-Aven (see page 162).

In 1889 Gauguin abandoned Pont-Aven for a quieter life in le Pouldu, where a band of like-minded followers (Sérusier, Filiger and Bernard) soon joined him to develop their artistic ideas still further: 'Paint what you see, not what is there!' was their motto. A few years later Gauguin left Europe for the South Seas, where he

endured great hardship and poverty. But he never forgot Brittany; when a heart attack mercifully curtailed the final ravages of syphilis, the last painting on his easel was *A Breton Village Under Snow,* now in the Louvre.

Other artists Gauguin overshadows the rest of the Pont-Aven School. Disappointingly little of his work remains in Brittany, but his fellow-artists are much better-represented, and provide a fascinating insight into Brittany as it used to be. The major collections are in Pont-Aven, Quimper, Rennes, Nantes and Brest. Vannes' la Cohue museum and the Musée de Morlaix also have

good art sections, and le Faouët displays works by little-known 20th-century Breton artists. Two native artists who deserve a mention are Mathurin Méheut (1882–1958), whose animated paintings, drawings and ceramics feature animal scenes, and Emmanuel de la Villéon (1858–1944), an Impressionist. Their works are on display in their home towns of Lamballe and Fougères.

ANNA THE JAVANESE
Gauguin's time in Brittany was not entirely happy. When he lived in Pont-Aven he kept an Indonesian mistress, who always had a tame monkey on her shoulder. When Gauguin tried to prevent children from taunting and throwing stones at her in Concarneau, he became involved in a brawl with some drunken sailors, who kicked him savagely with their wooden clogs: 'My leg is broken level with the ankle, and the bone has pierced right through the skin,' he wrote. While he was recovering, his mistress plundered his Parisian studio and made off with all she could find.

Little of Gauguin's work can now be seen in Pont-Aven

EMERALD EYES
An artists' trail along the Emerald Coast has been prepared by the tourist authorities, pinpointing the exact locations various artists chose for landscape paintings. The locations, mostly between Dinard and Cap Fréhel, include scenes by Picasso, Renoir and Émile Bernard. Bernard wrote of his artistic summers in St.-Briac: 'We all had a debt to pay to Brittany. It was she who lit up our youth, she who brought us so many poetic emotions and kindled Faith and a love of Art. It is wonderful to think that she will never forget us.'

Pancake-making is a fine art in Brittany

CHAPELS NEAR PONT-CROIX

Notre-Dame de Confort, 6km (3.5 miles) east of the town, is a 16th-century church with a galleried belfry. The glass is particularly fine, especially the Tree of Jesse in the chancel. On the final arch in the nave is a carillon wheel with 12 bells, traditionally rung to restore speech to dumb children. The calvary outside was restored in 1870. Notre-Dame de Kérinec, a little farther northeast, was struck by lightning in 1958, but its lovely 17th-century bell tower has been rebuilt in the same style.

Pont-Croix's hilly streets contain some well-restored old buildings

► Pont-Croix — 140B2

The Goyen river, which meets the sea at Audierne, ceases to be tidal at Pont-Croix, a pretty inland port of medieval gold-stone houses and narrow streets. Its most interesting building is the church of **Notre-Dame-de-Roscudon► ►**, which has three beautiful lacy gables over its south porch. Inside, the weighty nave distorts some of its massive lozenge-shaped pillars. Notice the remarkable woodcarving of the Last Supper in the chapel behind the altar, and the fine old glass intermingled with more modern windows.

► Pont-l'Abbé — 140B1

The capital of the Pays Bigouden commands a strategic bridging point at the head of a complex inlet where the River Pont-l'Abbé joins the sea. The town was established by the monks of Loctudy and fortified in the 14th century. Its castle houses a **museum►** of local history with a fine collection of *coiffes* and costumes. Other exhibits include Breton furniture and model ships (tel: 02 98 66 09 03; *open* Jun–Sep daily 10–12.30, 2–6.30. *Admission inexpensive*). About 2km (1 mile) southeast of Pont-l'Abbé lies the **Maison du Pays Bigouden► ►** (tel: 02 98 66 09 09; *open* Jun–Sep Mon–Sat 10–12, 2–6. *Admission inexpensive*), a traditionally furnished farmhouse of limewashed stone. The outbuildings and agricultural tools give it an earthy reality sometimes lost among endless displays of box beds and linen presses. While in the town, see the domed 14th-century church of **Notre-Dame-des-Carmes►** (once the chapel of a Carmelite monastery) and its pretty rose window.

Aside from this, Pont-l'Abbé's attractions are limited, though it does have one or two good-value hotels which make it worth considering as a touring base. It is a busy market town and the main shopping centre for a large area (Thursday is market day). Local and regional offices

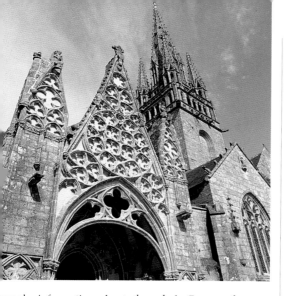

supply information about the whole Penmarc'h area. If you visit the town in July you may be lucky enough to see the Fête des Brodeuses, celebrating the well-known Pont-l'Abbé embroidery. Doll-making is another local craft.

Port-Manec'h 141D1

This tiny resort stands at the mouth of two lovely estuaries, the Aven and Bélon. Though somewhat overwhelmed by a crassly designed modern hotel on the waterfront, the setting is undeniably pretty. A private château shares an eye-catching span of pine-strewn coast with a small beach in a sandy cove. The beach-huts date from Belle Epoque days, when Port-Manec'h became a chic watering hole. Paths lead from the beach to the port, where watersports are well catered for at the Centre Nautique. You can also walk from the lighthouse along the cliffs to **Raguenez-Plage▶**, a little hamlet straggling down to an unspoilt sandy beach punctuated by a tidal island. Still farther west, the **Pointe de Trévignon** has more coastal views, on clear days extending as far as the Île de Groix.

Le Pouldu 141E1

The last resort on Finistère's south coast, le Pouldu has expanded greatly with characterless holiday homes and campsites in recent years, and has lost some of its former fishing-village appeal. Its long beaches look south, sheltered by low, grassy cliffs. Some way from the sprawling beach development, le Pouldu's port on the pretty Laïta estuary offers boats for rent.

Gauguin retreated here in 1889 along with a select band of talented artists (see pages 164–165). They all lodged at a local inn which is now the Café de la Plage. Nearby, the **Maison Marie Henry▶** has been carefully re-created with period furnishings and copies of the paintings the artists left behind on the walls in lieu of rent (tel: 02 98 39 98 51; open for guided tours Jun–Sep Wed–Sun 10.30–12.30, 3–7; Oct–May Thu–Sun 2–6. *Admission moderate*).

GAUGUIN'S MORTGAGE
When Gauguin decided to quit French shores for the warmer climes of Polynesia he could not (as usual) raise the rent he owed his landlady, Marie-Henry. Instead, he left her a few paintings as a surety against his debt. When he returned out of the blue some years later, his reputation firmly established, he somewhat meanspiritedly demanded his pawned canvases back, and even started legal proceedings to retrieve them. Today the pictures are scattered worldwide in famous art collections, and a single one of them would raise many times the 300 francs that Gauguin originally owed.

[Map of Quimper city centre with scale 0–200 m / 0–200 yards. Labels include: PLACE DE LA TOURBIE, RUE DE LA PROVIDENCE, Steir, RUE DU PICHERY, RUE ÉLIE-FRÉRON, RUE DES DOUVES, PL DE LOCRONAN, Temple, RUE DU CHAPEAU ROUGE, R DE FALKIRK, Église St-Mathieu, R DU SALLE, RUE DU GUÉODET, Hôtel de Ville et Musée des Beaux-Arts, PL A MASSE, RUE DE BREST, PLACE TERRE-AU-DUC, RUE KERÉON, RUE ST-MATHIEU, RUE ASTOR, RUE ST-FRANÇOIS, PL ST-CORENTIN, R DU FROUT, RUE E GOURMELEN, R DES RÉGUAIRES, RUE LUZEL, RUE LAENNEC, R R MADEC, Musée Départemental Breton, Cathédrale St-Corentin, R DE JUNIVILLE, BLVD DE KERGUÉLEN, RUE AMIRAL RONARC'H, RUE DU PARC, Odet, BLVD DUPLEIX, R T LE HARS, BLVD DUPLEIX, RUE A BRIAND, PL DE LA RÉSISTANCE-ET-DU-GÉN-DE-GAULLE, Préfecture, Théâtre, QUAI DE L'ODET, Odet, R STE-THÉRÈSE, Bois et Promenades du Mont Frugy, Mont Frugy, ALLÉES DE LOCMARIA, RUE DE PEN-ARSTANG, RUE JEAN JAURÈS, Musée de la Faïence, Locmaria]

168

QUIMPER *FAïENCE*

An abundance of fresh water, fuel, and suitable clay made Quimper a centre of the pottery industry over 300 years ago. Quimper pottery is now sold all over Brittany in a distinctive blue and yellow *paysan* design of flowers, birds and costumed figures. True Quimper-ware is all hand-decorated and individually signed before firing, though many cheaper imitations are mass-produced these days. Good-quality seconds can be purchased in a shop near the factories. The most famous and oldest *faïencerie* is the factory set up by H.B. Henriot, which still produces tradi-tional styles (it offers guided tours Mon–Fri, Mon–Sat in Jul and Aug; tel: 02 98 90 09 36; www.hb-henriot.com. *Admission moderate*).

Market day in Quimper

►►► Quimper

140C2

One of Brittany's most charming cities, Quimper is not to be missed if you are anywhere in Cornouaille. Its only serious weakness is a lack of pleasing old-town hotels which makes it less than ideal as a touring base. For a day trip, however, Quimper will entertain you royally as it is excellent for shopping, strolling, eating and sightseeing. The old quarter, near the junction of the Odet and Steir rivers, is quite compact and easy to explore on foot. Leave your car near the cathedral if you can, or by the tourist office on the south bank of the Odet. To visit the pottery workshops, walk or drive downstream to Locmaria.

Continued on page 170.

Walk

The old town of Quimper

See map opposite.

A stroll through the old city in the shadow of St.-Corentin's twin spires. Allow half a day, including museum visits. Add an extra hour or two if you wish to do justice to the Locmaria *faïence* potteries.

Start by the tourist office in Place de la Résistance, a well-stocked regional information point. Rising sharply behind are the wooded, landscaped slopes of Mont Frugy, worth the 80m (265ft) climb for a city overview (and a good place for a picnic). Cross the river, heading for the cathedral spires in the old quarter. The **Cathédrale St.-Corentin▶▶** dates from the 13th to 15th centuries, though its lacy steeples were erected only in 1856, now blending well with the original fabric. Restoration has improved the interior, whose nave is oddly out of true with the 13th-century chancel. Stained-glass windows and works of art line the aisles and side-chapels, and St. Corentin's life is carved on the pulpit. From the pleasant gardens behind, you can survey the cathedral's Gothic exterior.

Next door in the bishop's palace is Quimper's history museum, the **Musée Départemental Breton▶▶** (tel: 02 98 95 21 60; *open* Jun–Sep daily 9–6; *closed* Mon, Sun am in winter. *Admission moderate*), containing a great selection of costumes, pottery, worm-eaten sculpture and furniture. Notice the fine spiral staircase in the Rohan tower. Quimper's other central museum is the **Musée des Beaux-Arts (Fine Arts Museum)▶▶** (tel: 02 98 95 45 20; *open* Jul–Aug daily 10–7; low season *closed* Tue. *Admission moderate*) in the town hall, with samples of the Pont-Aven School and local artists Pierre de Bellay and Max Jacob.

After this, wander westwards through the pedestrianized old town past quaint stone and timber mansions, such as the ornately decorated **Maison des Cariatides▶** in rue Guéodet. Traces of the ramparts can be seen in rue des Douves and the boulevard de Kerguélen. The modern covered market (*halles*) by rue Astor replaces one destroyed in a fire in 1979. Bridges over the Steir give good views of old flower-decked buildings. The **Place Terre-au-Duc▶**, by the southernmost bridge, has one of the best concentrations of Quimper architecture, and the church of **St.-Mathieu▶** at the west end of the walk has a fine 16th-century chancel window.

Now head south, over the Odet, and follow the river a short distance downstream to Locmaria (off the map). Visit the Romanesque church, with its glory beam, and the earthernware *faïence* **factories▶** (see panel opposite). The **Musée de la Faïence▶▶** contains a fascinating display of Quimper ware and ceramic techniques through the ages (*Open* Apr–Oct Mon–Sat 10–6).

An overview of the town and the spires of St.-Corentin

169

Cornouaille

*Water rushes through
the lower town of
Quimperlé*

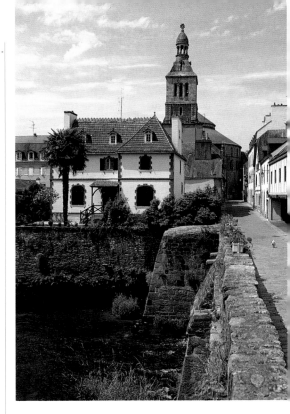

ST. CORENTIN'S FISH
Corentin was King
Gradlon's first bishop in
Quimper, and founder of
the city's great cathedral.
He was alleged to have
lived by means of a
miraculous immortal fish
which swam in the pool
near his hermitage.
Whenever Corentin was
hungry he would simply
catch the fish and carve a
chunk off it, then toss it
back into the water where,
unharmed, it instantly
renewed itself ready for
the next meal.

THE GLASS CEREMONY
A statue of King Gradlon
on horseback stands
between the spires of
Quimper's cathedral. In
the past, a July festival
honoured the town's royal
founder. An official would
climb up to the statue and
drink a toast of wine to
the king; then he would
throw the glass down into
the square below, where
the assembled citizens
would try to catch it.
Anyone who could deliver
the glass intact to the
mayor would receive a
hefty prize of gold coins.
No one ever managed it,
though a good many
hands were cut trying.

Continued from page 168.

Once Quimper was the capital of the medieval Duchy of Cornouaille, whose boundaries stretched as far as Morlaix. It became the legendary seat of Gradlon's court after Ys sank beneath the waves (see pages 18–19), and developed into a place of influence and prestige. After Brittany's union with France, Quimper was largely eclipsed, even serving as a place of exile in Louis XIII's reign. In World War II the town was a hub of Resistance activity, but was fortunate enough to avoid most of the destruction that savaged other Breton cities.

For centuries, poor communications have hampered development, but Quimper now has an international airport and greatly improved road and rail links. There is some industry on its outskirts, but it is mostly a market and tourist spot. Quimper is the most overtly Celtic city in Brittany, and market days still attract stallholders in *sabots* and *coiffes*. Its three-day July folk festival (Festival de Cornouaille) is huge, attracting visitors from all over Europe. A month later, the annual Seminaires Musicales attract a more classical following.

South of Quimper is the château of Lanniron, whose formal gardens on the banks of the Odet were laid out by Le Nôtre in the 17th century, and contain an exceptional collection of plants. The château was the summer residence of the bishops of Quimper and Léon (tel: 02 98 90 62 02; *open* for guided tours of the gardens and orangery mid-May to mid-Sep daily 2–6. *Admission moderate*).

▶▶ Quimperlé   141E1

The name of the town comes from the same Breton root as Quimper (*kemper*, a meeting of rivers). In Quimperlé the fast-flowing rivers Ellé and Isole converge noisily to form the Laïta. A steep hill divides the split-level old town.

In the Ville Basse, or lower town, the church of **Ste.-Croix▶▶** makes a prominent, squat, grey statement on its island setting, surrounded by rivers and bridges. It has a most unusual cruciform design, based on the circular church of the Holy Sepulchre in Jerusalem. Like the rest of Quimperlé, Ste.-Croix is on two levels, the arcaded chancel raised on a sort of dais. The crypt and apse comprise some of Brittany's best surviving Romanesque architecture and date from the 12th century, but the remainder of the church was rebuilt after structural damage over a century ago, when the original bell tower collapsed. The new bell tower stands apart from the rest of the church. In the older sections the Celtic carvings and capitals are worth close examination. Other points of interest are the Renaissance stone altarpiece by the entrance and a 16th-century Entombment scene.

The streets near the church contain some venerable houses, particularly along rue Dom-Morice. The timber-framed **Maison des Archers▶** is one of the most striking examples. There are more fine half-timbered and corbelled houses in rue Brémond-d'Ars, along with the ruined church of St.-Colomban and an interesting exterior staircase on the old law courts (Presidial) at No. 15 *bis*.

In the upper town, the church of **Notre-Dame-de-l'Assomption▶** (also known as St.-Michel) makes a complete contrast to its Ville Basse neighbour. This is a solid, Gothic church in the main square, with a large square tower, but perilously constructed on a steep slope, using adjacent buildings as props. In places it is crumbling badly, and its fine porch carvings are weathered. Inside, the nave is gaunt and lacking an aisle, while Our Lady of Good Tidings stands woodenly in the chancel.

QUIMPERLÉ EXCURSIONS
Quimperlé itself has relatively few diversions, but a couple of good picnic expeditions lie within easy driving distance. About 12km (7 miles) northeast is the Roche du Diable, a rocky platform overlooking a steep, cliff-lined valley where the Ellé foams far below. Access is free; it's a short walk through pretty woodland to the viewpoint. South of the town, along the attractive Laïta valley, the Forêt de Carnoët extends over 750ha (1,800 acres). Tracks lead in from the woodland road, and from there you can drive around parts of the forest, or park in clearings and walk beyond the barriers that prevent vehicular access.

171

Quaint back alleyways in Quimperlé reveal many interesting old buildings

The Chapel of Ste.-Anne, focus of pardons

172

KENTOC'H MERVEL

During World War II every able-bodied male on the Île du Sein volunteered to answer General de Gaulle's call to arms. The women and children were left behind singing the 'Marseillaise' from the quayside. After the war, de Gaulle visited the island in person to present its citizens with the Croix de la Libération, the highest honour for services rendered in wartime. A local war memorial captures the spirit of the Senans with the Breton inscription *Kentoc'h Mervel*—'Better to die'.

POINTE DU RAZ

The Pointe du Raz is one of Finistère's most dramatic headlands. On windy days it is unforgettable. A visitor centre near the point organizes walks and talks on the area (tel: 02 98 70 67 18; *open* Jul–Aug daily 9.30–7.30; Sep–Jun reduced hours; www.pointeduraz.com). Technically it is not Brittany's most westerly promontory, but sailors remark that the climate and temper of the sea seem to change once it is rounded.

A much-venerated statue (right) at Ste.-Anne-la-Palud

▶ Ste.-Anne-la-Palud   140B3

St. Anne, mother of the Virgin Mary, is the patroness of Brittany and in certain areas has a great cult following (see page 20). The *pardon* held at this tiny place on the bay of Douarnenez for three days over the last weekend in August is an indication of her importance; pilgrims hail from far and wide to pay homage to a painted granite statue dating from 1548, while torchlit processions celebrate mass at a chapel in fields near the beach. The chapel is not particularly old (19th century), and stands inland from the original site founded by St. Guenolé in the 6th century, which was swamped by the sea. Everyone dresses up, and this is one of the best opportunities to see Breton costumes. At other times of year Ste.-Anne is a peaceful place of quiet beaches, dunes and a wooded headland.

▶ Sein, Île de   140A2

Barely visible above the waterline, Sein presents yet another challenge to mariners navigating the west coast of Brittany. *'Qui voit Sein, voit sa fin'* ('Who sees Sein, sees his doom'), goes the rhyme, and a chain of lighthouses backs up the warning.

The island lies about 8km (5 miles) off the Pointe du Raz, measuring only about 1.8km (1 mile) long at its maximum. It is rather like an iceberg, at times virtually submerged, but its reefs and sandbanks trail far beyond the shore. A lethal tidal race runs between the straits, amply justifying Sein's feared reputation.

In pagan times the island was one of the last refuges of the Druids, who were buried here. Later, its only inhabitants were wreckers preying on lost ships; the bodies of the drowned often washed up on the mainland at Baie des Trépassés. Eventually the Senans developed a more public spirit, and they are now renowned for their intrepid sea-rescue services. Visitors may reach the island by boat from Audierne (a one-hour journey), though there is little to see but birds and lighthouses.

▶▶▶ Sizun, Cap   140A2

The jagged finger of Sizun stretches far into the Atlantic, ending dramatically at the Pointe du Raz. The best scenery lies to the north. Sensible footwear is essential if you want to explore as the paths can be slippery. Take binoculars if you are keen on watching birds.

Sizun is full of legends: Tristan and Isolde shared their star-crossed love at Douarnenez, and King Gradlon's beautiful city of Ys lies somewhere beneath the waves. Farming and tourism are the mainstays of the local economy. Apart from the fishing ports of Douarnenez and Audierne, there are no large towns, and few settlements exhibit much character (Pont-Croix is a pleasing exception). The cultivated scenery inland is unexceptional and not worth detailed exploration.

173

Pointe de Raz, a dramatic, unforgettable headland on Cap Sizun

Drive

Cap Sizun

See map on pages 140–141.

This 100km (60-mile) drive requires repeated cul-de-sac detours from the main coast road and some walking. Allow at least half a day.

Starting from **Douarnenez** (see pages 152–153), head along the north coast road (D7), ducking northwards first at **Pointe du Millier▶**. A few minutes' walk to the point offers a splendid view of the bay. **Pointe de Beuzec▶** (accessible by car) has similar views.

The **Réserve du Cap Sizun▶▶** is a bird sanctuary, best visited in the nesting season between April and mid-July. Farther west, **Pointe de Brézellec▶** offers a magnificent vantage point of serrated rocks and cliffs. Farther still is the **Pointe du Van▶▶**, which requires a lengthy walk to a desolate headland, not as spectacular as Pointe du Raz but less crowded. The cliffs here are dangerous. Southwards is the sweeping crescent of the **Baie des Trépassés▶▶**. Currents here are strong. **Pointe du Raz▶▶▶** is undoubtedly the highlight of the journey (see panel opposite).

Return on the D784 via St.-Tugen, Audierne and Pont-Croix (see pages 144–145 and 166), calling en route at **Notre-Dame de Confort▶** and **Notre-Dame de Kérinec** chapels (see panel on page 166).

Notre-Dame-des-Naufragés (Our Lady of the Shipwrecked), Pointe du Raz

Langonnet
Abbaye de Langonnet
Ploërdut
Séglien
Stival
St-Gérand
Gueltas
le Faouët
Ste-Barbe
St-Nicolas
Lignol
Guémené-sur-Scorff
le Sourn
Pontivy
Noyal-Pontivy
St-Fiacre
Meslan
Kernascléden
Guern
St-Thuriau
Querrien
la Roche du Diable
Inguiniel
Melrand
Bubry
Bieuzy
St-Nicolas-des-Eaux
Site de Castennec
Naizin
Réguiny
FINISTÈRE
Mellac
Ellé
Arzano
Plouay
Quistinic
Pluméliau
Remungol
St-Allouestr
Quimperlé
Poul Fetan
Blavet
Guénin
Châte Kerguéc
Forêt de Carnoët
Cléguer
Pont-Scorff
Inzinzac-Lochrist
Baud
Locmine
Bignan
St-Jean Brévelay
Caudan
Quéven
Hennebont
Languidic
Camors
MORBIHAN
le Pouldu
Guidel
Guidel-Plages
Lanester
Landévant
Pluvigner
le Loch
Grand-Champ
le Fort Bloque
Ploemeur
Larmor-Plage
LORIENT
Locmiquélic
Kervignac
Merlevenez
Landaul
Brech
Ste-Anne-d'Auray
Riantec
Port-Louis
Ploubinec
Pointe de Gâvres
St-Cado
Belz
St-Degan
Auray
Pluneret
Vannes
Ile de Groix
Port-Tudy
Groix
Locmaria
Etel
Erdeven
Ploeren
Arradon
Golfe du
St
Plouharnel
Alignements de Carnac
Port-Blanc
Ile aux Moines
Ile d'Arz
le Galion
Carnac
la Trinité-sur-Mer
Cairn de Gavrinis
St-Arme
Morbihan
Penthièvre
Carnac-Plage
Locmariaquer
Arzon
Tumulus de Tumiac
Fort de Penthièvre
Pointe du Percho
St-Pierre-Quiberon
Port-Navalo
Sarzeau
Presqu'île de
Quiberon
Baie de
Presqu'île de R
Château de Suscinio
Quiberon
Quiberon
St-Gildas-de-Rhuys
Port-Maria
Pointe du Conguel
Pointe des Poulains
Sauzon
Ile d'Houat
le Palais
Bangor
Aiguilles de Port-Coton
Port-Goulphar
Ile d'Hoëdic
Pointe de Kerdonis
Belle-Ile
Locmaria

The cobbled old town quarter of Rochefort-en-Terre

175

MORBIHAN Morbihan is the only one of Brittany's *départements* with a specifically Breton name. It means 'Little Sea', a reference to its most striking geographical feature, the vast, mud-rimmed tidal lagoon known as the Golfe du Morbihan. This strange, landlocked maze of creeks and islands provides a splendid breeding and overwintering ground for enormous numbers of seabirds and wildfowl, and its sheltered microclimate and varied habitats produce a rich, almost Mediterranean plant life.

In summer the gulf hums with excursion cruisers and flurrying sails, as countless boats weave in and out of complex channels that run between pine-topped, grassy

Morbihan

176

VAUBAN (1633–1707)

One of the great military engineer's finest achievements, the citadel at le Palais, can be seen on Belle-Île in Morbihan. Sébastien le Prestre de Vauban rose against all odds of class and birth to become Marshal of France. A gallant soldier, he demonstrated early in his career an uncanny flair for siege warfare, and created an innovative ring of superbly designed fortresses all over France for his master, Louis XIV. Vauban's politics were by no means undilutedly Royalist. He became increasingly uneasy about the lot of the poor, and foresaw the Revolution. He died, out of royal favour, in 1707. Despite his remarkable achievements, rapid developments in military strategy rendered many of his fortifications obsolete by the time he died.

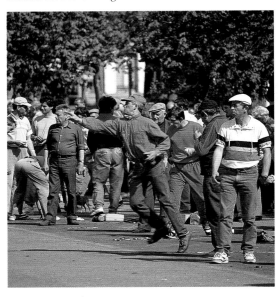

A lively palet *match (right) in Pontivy's town square*

Old schooner at Auray, now a museum

hummocks, and past chapels, ruined villas, and the extraordinary prehistoric cairn at Gavrinis. In 56BC the Golfe du Morbihan witnessed a crucial battle when Julius Caesar defeated the Veneti and confirmed Roman rule in Armorican Gaul (see pages 32–33).

HOLIDAY OPTIONS Morbihan is an important holiday area, and in summer the local population swells to many times its resident size. Sandy beaches and calm muddy estuaries where oysters thrive characterize much of the coast. Beachcombers and yachting folk are prominent visitors, while Quiberon and Carnac, the liveliest resorts, offer thalassotherapy treatments. Messing about in boats is a particularly popular pastime. The apparent gentleness of the seaside scenery may deceive, however. Strong currents make some beaches extremely dangerous, especially along the west coast of Quiberon and around the Morbihan gulf.

Seawards, Morbihan incorporates several islands, including Brittany's largest and most beautiful, Belle-Île. The mainland coastline is generally low-lying and less dramatic than north or west Brittany, but its warmer and more sheltered climate may make summer seaside holidays a more attractive option. Less welcome are the increased humidity, and a large crop of mosquitoes encouraged by brackish expanses of sheltered water.

The whole tempo of this Breton riviera is slightly more Mediterranean, more French, than elsewhere in Brittany, and the locals even produce wine on the Rhuys peninsula. But the season is still short; expect the shutters to come down soon after the school summer holidays end.

The region extends far inland through plateaux of heathy schist and woodland carved by many rivers, and is more or less bounded on its northern fringes by the course of the Nantes–Brest canal. Hedged fields, trout streams and small copses (the last remnants of once-vast forests that cloaked Brittany's interior until medieval times) make for pleasant but not very remarkable scenery.

LOCAL INTEREST The only really large coastal town is Lorient, one of France's most important commercial and fishing ports. For most visitors, smaller ports such as Locmariaquer or Port-Louis, or the historic old city of Vannes, hold many more attractions. Inland, other towns of architectural interest include Josselin, Auray, Rochefort-en-Terre, la Roche-Bernard and Pontivy. The relative prosperity of places able to capitalize on tourism disguises a sadder aspect of Morbihan's declining rural economy. Some of those picturesquely fossilized little *écomusées* are all that remain of once-flourishing villages whose livelihoods have vanished.

Historically, however, the whole of the Morbihan area is packed with interest, from its famous collection of neolithic monuments around Carnac to grand ducal castles and *villes fleuries*. Many aspects of regional life are traced in a selection of excellent modern museums. Specifically Celtic or Breton culture is less apparent than, say, in Cornouaille or North Finistère. You will rarely find *coiffes* or costumes worn here, and there are fewer Breton-speakers. But the religious element still dominates, with dozens of healing fountains, wayside chapels and calvaries, and the most important pilgrimage centre in all Brittany at Ste.-Anne-d'Auray.

The most haunting memories of Morbihan are provided by its oldest monuments: the mysteriously ordered menhirs of Carnac. In high season traffic crawls past the metal fencing protecting thousands of standing stones, neatly arranged in *alignements* (rows). Overrun by visitors during the day, the menhirs seem diminished, almost mundane. But if you see them quietly and in solitude (in an early morning mist, or perhaps by moonlight) the ancient magic returns. At these times the stones seem to stand guard over the landscape like a petrified army, defying all attempts to explain them away.

LEST WE FORGET
In every village, war memorials commemorate the fallen of the Great War, some of them touching portrayals of personal grief: an old Breton couple mourn their lost sons; an infantryman leans disconsolately on his rifle. On many, a jaunty cockerel symbolizes a new dawn. Monuments erected after World War II testify to the horror of hideous atrocities and mass executions committed in retaliation for Resistance sabotage. Not all war crimes were carried out by the Gestapo; Vichy agents were also responsible for some. To find out more about wartime Brittany, visit the Musée de la Résistance Bretonne at St.-Marcel, near Malestroit (see page 192).

177

The wash houses (lavoirs) by the ramparts of Vannes

Waterfront cafés in St.-Goustan

BENJAMIN FRANKLIN
A gale forced a ship carrying the famous American, then serving as ambassador to France, to take refuge at Auray in 1776. Franklin was on his way to Nantes, hoping to enlist France's help against the English in the American War of Independence. He spent the night at No. 8 Place St.-Sauveur (now a popular *crêperie*) and travelled on to Nantes overland.

THE MIRACULOUS VISION
In 1623 a ploughman, Yves Nicolazic, saw a vision of St. Anne telling him to build a church in a place she would show him. The good ploughman unearthed a statue which he took to be a sign from heaven. The church was duly built, and soon became a great place of pilgrimage. The sacred statue was burned by a Revolutionary mob as a graven image, but fragments of it remain inside the base of the present 19th-century version.

Modern pilgrims, Ste.-Anne-d'Auray

▶▶ **Auray** *174B2*

This ancient place illuminates several periods of Breton history. It seems peaceful now but has witnessed some bloody scenes, including the last battle of the 14th-century War of Succession and a terrible massacre of Chouan counter-Revolutionaries in 1795 (see panel opposite). Auray is said to have been the last place Julius Caesar reached in his conquest of Gaul. The Romans set up camp in what is now the St.-Goustan quarter, still the oldest and most picturesque part of the town. A small cluster of harmoniously timber-framed 15th-century houses decorates the quayside Place St.-Sauveur and the hilly streets behind. From the opposite bank (reached over a picturesque medieval stone bridge), the promenade du Loch, by the remnants of the old castle, gives an excellent view. A picturesque restored schooner lies moored on the waterfront. Up the hill in Auray's main centre, the church of **St.-Gildas**▶ has a fine Renaissance porch and a marble altarpiece (1664).

Ste.-Anne-d'Auray▶▶, to the northeast, commemorates the feast of Brittany's patron St. Anne (on 26 July), when thousands of pilgrims gather for one of the region's most spectacular *pardons*. The church itself is of no great interest; a ponderous 19th-century basilica now replaces the original. In the vast cathedral precinct, the **Scala Sancta**▶ is a disembodied double staircase which the faithful climb on their knees. Various museums are housed in the church buildings: a treasury of relics and religious sculpture (including a relic of St. Anne offered by Anne of Austria), a costume museum, and a diorama of the pilgrimage in medieval times.

More stirring than any of this commercialized religiosity is the vast **war memorial**▶▶, raised by public subscription to the 250,000 Bretons who died serving in World War I. Walls over 200m (650ft) long inscribed with the names of the dead enclose a space of paved walks and lawns. Outside the town, a Franco-Belgian cemetery contains row upon row of neat, plain graves.

The French Revolution dashed Breton hopes of independence. Far from promising liberté, egalité *and* fraternité, *the actions of the revolutionary leaders seemed to spell repression, discrimination and intolerance.*

As the excesses of the Revolution worsened, the Breton language was threatened with abolition, churches were vandalized, and people everywhere suffered terrible hardships. In Nantes, the infamous Jean-Baptiste Carrier began a personal Reign of Terror, drowning thousands of suspected Royalists in the Loire. Breton traditionalists responded by banding together in a secret society called the Association Bretonne, popularly dubbed the Chouans (from *chat huant*, the cry of the screech owl, which they used for night signalling).

In Morbihan the Chouan cause rallied around a local farmer, Georges Cadoudal, who had been appalled at witnessing mass executions in Rennes. Dispossessed

aristocrats, many in exile in England, latched on to the Chouans in the hope of retrieving their former power and wealth. In 1795 an expeditionary force of French exiles, backed by the British Navy, landed on the Quiberon peninsula, hoping to team up with the Chouans and stage an insurrection. But their numbers were much smaller than expected, and their cause had been betrayed to the Republican commander General Hoche (see panel on page 197). He trapped the invading force at the tip of the peninsula and took nearly 1,000 prisoners. Some were executed immediately, while others were taken to Vannes and Auray for interrogation and then shot.

The last hero Cadoudal himself got away and lived to fight another day. Again he was defeated, escaping to England in a fishing boat. Impressed by his courage, Napoleon offered him a free pardon and high office but Cadoudal refused, and staged an even more reckless scheme: to kidnap the newly proclaimed emperor. The plot was thwarted, and this time Napoleon showed Cadoudal no mercy. The last Chouan was shot by a firing squad in Paris in June 1804. His body rests in a little mausoleum overlooking his family farm on the outskirts of Auray (see panel).

CHOUAN SHRINES
On the western outskirts of Auray, a glum neo-classical mausoleum contains the tomb of local hero, Georges Cadoudal, the last Chouan. More Chouan history can be traced just north of the town, where a chilling black and white reliquary chapel in the Carthusian monastery pays homage to the 953 exiled Chouans who were executed in Auray after their failed Royalist uprising. The original collegiate church nearby was built in 1364 to commemorate Jean de Montfort's victory in the final battle of the War of Succession (see page 34), and his dead adversary and brother-in-law, Charles de Blois. The Champ des Martyrs, just up the road, was where the Chouan rebels were actually shot.

George Cadoudal, leader of the Chouan cause

HOUAT AND HOÊDIC
Trips to these two smaller, more peaceful islands (whose names mean 'Duck' and 'Duckling' in Breton) east of Belle-Île are also advertised from Quiberon. Journey time 45–60 minutes.

Leaving Quiberon for Belle-Île

►►► **Belle-Île**   *174B1*

Of all Brittany's islands, Belle-Île perhaps has most to offer. It is the largest, at 17km (10 miles) by 10km (6 miles), has attractively varied scenery, and is rich in history. Access to the island is easy, with regular boat services in season making the 45-minute crossing from Quiberon.

Boats dock at Belle-Île's capital, **le Palais►►**, a small bustling port with hotels, shops, cafés and restaurants. Above the harbour looms a mighty star-shaped fortress, originally built in the 16th century and strengthened by Vauban (see panel, page 176). The citadel now houses a **museum►►** showing Belle-Île's history in photos, documents, sardine tins, and seaweed pictures (*Open* daily 9–7 in summer; low season 9.30–6. *Admission moderate*).

The island consists of four parishes, named after its four principal settlements. (One is called Bangor, indicating early occupation by Welsh monks.) After successive waves of Celts, Romans, Saxons and Normans passed through, the island passed to the abbey of Redon in 1006. Later it was owned by Louis XIV's ambitious finance minister, Nicholas Fouquet, who strengthened Belle-Ile's defences mightily and even stationed his own navy here. Unsurprisingly, the king saw him as a threat, and had him arrested by the Three Musketeers in 1661. English and Dutch forces repeatedly attacked the island and the English held it for two years from 1761, after which it was swapped for Menorca.

The interior of the island is a plateau of fertile schist, cut by many valleys in which white houses cluster, sheltering from the wind. Moorland alternates with hedged arable fields, vegetable plots and cattle pasture, and the climate is mild but windswept. The east coast has several safe sandy beaches: les Grands Sables is the largest, with facilities for watersports. Another sheltered beach is at Port-Kérel on the south side, the only safe bathing on the Côte Sauvage.

The scenery on the west side is much more dramatic. **Port-Goulphar▶▶**, where coach parties are usually dropped off for lunch, overlooks a fjord-like inlet with preternaturally blue-green water. Farther north, an obligatory photo stop at **Port-Coton▶▶** provides a splendid view of the sea-gnawed Aiguilles (Pinnacles) rock stacks, which Monet is alleged to have painted 38 times. The lighthouse on this coast is one of the most powerful in Europe, with a beam of 120km (70 miles) (*Open* summer daily 10.30–12, 2–5.30. *Admission free*; 256 steps). **Port-Donnant▶▶** has a beautiful but dangerous beach.

At a road junction inland, two menhirs known as Jean and Jeanne are alleged to be the petrified remains of lovers punished for preempting their wedding night. **Sauzon▶▶**, on the northeastern side, is the prettiest place on the island, a charming fishing port of lobster pots, colour-washed cottages and bright flowers. A fort on Pointe des Poulains was once the holiday home of the celebrated actress Sarah Bernhardt. It was destroyed by the Germans in World War II.

Les Aguilles de Port-Coton

THE CANADIAN CONNECTION
In 1763 Belle-Île (then in English hands) was exchanged for Menorca in the Treaty of Paris. Another condition of this treaty was the expulsion from New England of French settlers who refused to submit to English rule. About 80 of the original French-Canadian families moved to Belle-Île in 1766, bringing with them the potato, a new crop which had not yet found its way to mainland France.

GOOSE BARNACLES
In winter, locals on Belle-Île, roped like mountaineers, clamber down the perilous cliffs of the Côte Sauvage in search of a strange delicacy called *pouce pied*, a large, rudely shaped barnacle which grows on the rocks by the waterline. The French aren't very keen on these salty things, but they achieve a high price in Spain and are mainly exported there (where they are known as *percebes*, a popular snack with drinks).

Carnac's evocative Alignements de Kermario are best seen from a viewing platform at the eastern end of the site

PREHISTORY MUSEUM
Finds from Carnac's megalithic sites are displayed in the Musée de Préhistoire, founded in 1881 by a Scottish archaeologist, James Miln, and enlarged by his local collaborator, Zacharie Le Rouzic. A visit to the museum helps to put the megaliths in context. The presentation is academic (borrow the English explanatory notes) and chronological, from earliest paleolithic (450,000 years ago) to early medieval times. The main emphasis is predictably on the neolithic period (4000–1500BC) to which Carnac's megaliths belong (tel: 02 97 52 22 04; www.muséedecarnac.com; *open* Jun–Sep daily 10–12.30, 1.30–7; Oct–May until 6pm; *closed* Wed am and Jan. *Admission moderate*; combined tickets available for local megaliths).

►►► Carnac   *174B2*

Thousands of visitors invade Carnac every year in order to see the extraordinary and baffling array of megaliths just outside the town (see pages 184–185). Apart from these and the explanatory **museum►►** (see panel), Carnac's only building of interest is its **church►**, dedicated to St. Cornély, patron saint of farm animals, whose statue can be seen on the facade between two oxen. Inside, the panelled vaulting is covered with paintings.

Carnac's seaside resort, **Carnac-Plage►**, occupies a long, gently shelving beach of fine sand, extensively developed with modern hotels, beach and yacht clubs, and thalassotherapy. Smaller, quieter settlements nearby specialize in oysters. Carnac's summer crowding keeps accommodation prices high.

► Etel Estuary   *174B3*

On the map this complex estuary looks even more extensive than Lorient's bustling roadsteads to the west. Once you reach the declining fishing port of Etel at the mouth of the inlet you soon see why the Etel River is left mostly to oysters. A deadly sand-bar almost blocks the entrance to the estuary.

The Etel is not Brittany's prettiest river, but for drivers exploring local megaliths the quiet access lanes to points on its trailing shores make good picnic spots, overlooking grassy islands and oysterbeds. The best place to make for is picturesque **St.-Cado►►** (see panel opposite).

►► Le Faouët   *174A4*

The most striking feature of this attractive little town, watered by rivers from the Montagnes Noires, is its splendid 16th-century covered **market hall►** in the main square. A small **museum** nearby houses a collection of early 20th-century art on various Breton subjects (*Open* Jun–Sep daily 10–12, 2–6. *Admission moderate*). On the town's northern edges is an excellent exhibition on social

The interior of St.-Fiacre chapel at le Faouët

insects called **L'Abeille Vivante et la Cité Fourmis**▶ (tel: 02 97 23 08 05; www.abeilles-et-fourmis.com; *open* Apr–Oct daily 10–6, mid-Jun to mid–Sep 10–7. *Admission moderate*), showing bees and ants in action. Lots of honey-based products are on sale here.

Other places of interest lie scattered around the town and could be strung into a pleasant half-day tour. About 3km (2 miles) to the north is **Ste.-Barbe**▶▶, a chapel in Flamboyant style shoehorned into a rocky crevice in a wooded hillside overlooking the Ellé valley. Legend states that the chapel was built by a knight caught in a terrifying storm, who prayed to Ste. Barbe for protection. Pilgrims today toll the bell by the custodian's house for Ste. Barbe's blessing (you have to be strong to make any sound). The interior is less compelling than the setting. Inside is an unusual carved lord's gallery' and some good stained glass.

St.-Fiacre▶▶, the same distance southeast of le Faouët, is essential viewing if you are at all keen on Breton churches. Inside, a bright **rood screen**▶▶ dating from 1480 depicts some of Brittany's liveliest and laciest Flamboyant woodcarvings. Above athletic angels, who seem to be practising as trapeze artists, the seven deadly sins assume human forms: Sloth is a man playing the bagpipes, avarice an apple-scrumper, gluttony someone being spectacularly sick.

Another fine rood screen can be seen in the **Chapelle St.-Nicolas**▶ some distance east. Continuing north past St.-Nicolas, you reach the mostly modern Cistercian abbey of **Langonnet**▶, a retreat for priests. The chapter house is original, dating from the 13th century. South of le Faouët lies the **Roche du Diable (Devil's Rock)**▶, a well-known beauty spot overlooking the Ellé. Paths from a woodland parking area lead to a rocky platform where steep cliffs drop down to the surging river below.

ST.-CADO
This is a particularly idyllic spot on the Etel estuary, a circular islet anchored to the shore by a slim causeway. On it stands a pretty village of stone fishing cottages. Its Romanesque chapel is dedicated to the island's patron, a mysterious Celtic monk able to cure deafness in all who place their ears to his stone bed. St. Cado's fountain stands below the east end, overlooking the shore. A legend tells how St. Cado persuaded the Devil to build the bridge linking the island to the mainland in return for the first soul to travel across. When it was finished, St. Cado sent a cat across before anyone used it.

183

St.-Fiacre's unusual gable-belfry has three slim spire turrets

Prehistoric monuments exist in many parts of the world, but nowhere are they so numerous as in Brittany. Even the words used to describe them—dolmen (table stone), menhir (long stone) and cromlech (curved stone)—are Breton.

184

VISITING THE STONES
Until 1991Carnac's stand-ing stones were freely accessible, but now the main groups are fenced off to protect them from dam-age. For many centuries the stones have been dug up, removed, reshaped, defaced, and perhaps mis-takenly restored until it is impossible to know precise-ly their original positions, or even how many there were. La Maison des Mégalithes near the Alignements de Ménec has a rooftop view-ing terrace, a video presen-tation and books about the site (tel: 02 97 52 89 99; www.monum.fr; *open* Jul–Aug 9–8; May–Jun 9–7; Sep–Apr 10–5.15. *Admission free*). In winter you can wander freely round some of the *alignements*, but in summer you must join a guided tour, booked at the visitor centre.

Menhir de Champ Dolent, near Dol-de-Bretagne

Enigma variations Most of Brittany's archaeological wonders are clustered in and around Carnac and the Morbihan gulf. Estimates of their numbers vary widely, from 2,500 to over 5,000. Of the two main types the most numerous are the menhirs, or standing stones. You find these all over Brittany, but nowhere are they as dramatically organized as in Carnac, for instead of being isolated totems they are arranged in curious lines (*alignements*), some terminating in curved formations (cromlechs).

The other type is the group consisting of dolmens, cairns, *allées couvertes* and tumuli. These are less numerous, and to some extent less mysterious in that they are clearly burial chambers, presumably for important people such as priests or chieftains. They are generally flat-topped, table-like constructions made of stone slabs, and sometimes covered with mounds of earth (see also pages 30–31).

Current knowledge of the people who built the megaliths is very limited, but they were clearly sophisticated folk capable of organizing vast amounts of manpower and time for these weighty projects. Most of the stones were erected between about 4500 and 1800BC, though some may be even older than this, predating Mediterranean antiquities such as the Egyptian Pyramids or Crete's Palace of Knossos.

Mixed views Many archaeologists regard Carnac as the most important prehistoric site in Europe. Not everyone is equally impressed, however. The Breton stones are numerous but they lack the awesome scale and solitary impact of, say, Stonehenge in the UK. Perhaps the most remarkable thing about them is that they are still there, when virtually all other traces of the civilization that built them (and many subsequent civilizations) have passed away. Some find the absence of conclusive evidence about their purpose fascinating; others are disappointed to discover that one megalith looks pretty much like another. All sorts of theories abound as to what exactly the stones were for, from some sort of astronomical observatory designed to predict times for planting crops, to temples of sun worship or fertility rites.

At some megaliths there is an entrance charge, while others are freely accessible. A torch is use-ful to see the interiors of burial chambers proper-ly; wear robust footwear, as the areas around and in the chambers can be slippery and muddy after rain. Finds from the sites are displayed in egional museums, the most illuminating of which are in Carnac (see panel on page 182) and in Rennes (see page 221).

Pick of the Megaliths

Carnac Menhirs: three main groups of *alignements* just north of the town (free access)—**Ménec**▶▶▶ (11 rows of about 1,200 stones that stretch for 1km/0.6 miles);

Kermario▶▶▶ (about 1,000 stones set out in 10 rows); **Kerlescan**▶▶▶ (555 stones set out in 13 rows, with a cromlech at one end). Dolmens: **Crucuno**▶▶ (a 40-tonne capstone); **Mané-Kerioned**▶ (has engravings). Tumuli: **Kercado**▶▶ (a mound covering a large carved dolmen, topped by a menhir – *open* daily); **Tumulus de St.-Michel**▶ (a 12m/40ft high burial place with several chambers; closed for restoration).

Locmariaquer, Grand Menhir Brise▶▶ (see panel); **Table des Marchands**▶▶ (decorated dolmen protected by a tumulus). Dolmens: **Pierres Plates**▶, **Mané-Lud, Mané-Rethual, Mané-er-Hroech** (free access).

Golfe du Morbihan, Cairn de Gavrinis▶▶▶ (impressively decorated burial chamber on island; see panel, page 193).

Near Morlaix, Cairn de Barnenez▶▶ (11 burial chambers with approach galleries in massive cairn; see page 83).

Near Rennes, La Roche aux Fées▶▶ (20m/65ft covered gallery of purple schist; see panel on page 213).

Many other menhirs and dolmens are sprinkled all over Brittany. There is an important concentration at St.-Just, near Redon, and more *alignements* at Lagatjar, near Morgat (Crozon peninsula), and Quiberon.

GRAND MENHIR BRISE
This monument in Locmariaquer is the largest-known standing stone. Or at least it would be if it were not in several pieces, as it is now on its side, broken into four sections (a putative fifth piece is missing). Experts believe the 20m (65ft) high menhir must have been subjected to some natural calamity such as lightning or earthquake several hundred years ago. The task of manhandling such a colossal piece of granite is truly awesome: more than 12,000 people and 125 teams of oxen would have been required to shift it (*open* Jul–Aug daily 10–7; May–Jun 10–6; Sep–Apr 11–12.30, 2–5.15. *Admission moderate*; combined ticket available for Carnac sights).

THEORIES ON MENHIRS
Over the centuries the standing stones of Carnac have spawned an amazing number of explanations. "Carnac," said Flaubert, "has had more rubbish written about it than it has standing stones." Most experts attribute some sort of religious or ritual element to them, but several go for military theories. Were they perhaps the tentpegs of Caesar's army, or anti-tank devices set up by the Germans during the Occupation (as one apocryphal US Marine is supposed to have concluded during the Liberation of Brittany)? Or were they Roman soldiers, miraculously turned to stone to save Carnac's patron saint, Cornély, as he fled for his life from Rome in the 3rd century?

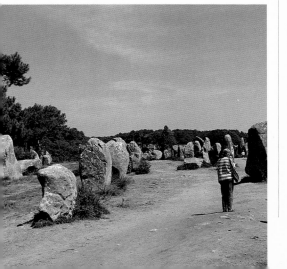

You can still walk round some of Carnac's monuments, though many are now fenced off to prevent damage to the stones and vegetation.

Notre-Dame-de-Paradis, Hennebont

▶ **Groix, Île de**   *174A2*

A popular excursion from Lorient, this island takes about 45 minutes to reach by boat. You can take a car but many visitors prefer to explore by bicycle. The island measures about 8km (5 miles) by 2km (1 mile) and has about 3,000 inhabitants, most of whom live in the capital, Groix, or its pretty harbour town, Port-Tudy.

Île de Groix is a raised plateau fringed by steep cliffs, most dramatic on the north and western sides, where the coastline is indented and pierced with blowholes. Safe bathing beaches can be found on the more sheltered eastern side, notably the convex Plage des Grands Sables.

Parts of the island are cultivated, but most of the inhabitants live on fishing and, increasingly, tourism. Groix had the largest tuna fleet in France up to the 1930s. A sign of these times can be seen in the tuna fish weather-vane on Groix church, but now the industry has declined and its canning factory in Port-Tudy houses an **écomusée**▶ displaying many aspects of island life (tel: 02 97 86 84 60; *open* Jun–Aug daily 9.30–12.30, 3–7; Sep–May reduced hours; *closed* Mon. *Admission moderate*). Groix's last fishing boat, the *Kenavo*, offers summer excursions.

Groix favours the self-sufficient visitor. Geologists find the island fascinating for its unique selection of rare minerals, while ornithologists head to the western tip for resident seabirds and passing migrants.

▶ **Guéhenno**   *175D3*

If an exhaustive tour of Finistère's parish closes has not drained you completely, seek out this charming calvary 10km (6 miles) southwest of Josselin. It dates originally from 1550, but was badly damaged in the Revolution. The local masons demanded such high fees to restore it that

TUNA-FISHING IN GROIX
In his book, *The Six Sailors of Groix*, the Breton novelist Henri Queffelec describes the tuna-fishing scene during the 1930s: 'The boats were crammed in, gunwale to gunwale…Oh, the wonderful confusion of mooring ropes, which crossed over each other, got tangled up in tillers and grappling-hooks, and plunged beneath the keels!'

the parish priest and his assistant decided to have a go at it themselves, which explains the charmingly naïve carvings. A cock crows on a column in front of the cross, symbolizing Peter's denial of Christ. The ossuary behind represents Christ's tomb, guarded by soldiers.

▶▶ Hennebont   *174B3*

Only a small section of this once-proud feudal town remains. Its iron-smelting industry and its proximity to the U-boat pens in Lorient (see pages 190–191) made it a target for heavy attacks in World War II. For all that, Hennebont is not without interest.

The much restored towers of the 14th-century **Porte Broërec▶** (tel: 02 97 36 29 18; *open* Jun–Sep 10.30–12.30, 1.30–6.30. *Admission moderate*) define its earlier fortifications. As well as the small museum within the barbican, the massive belfry and carved porch of the 16th-century church of **Notre-Dame-de-Paradis▶**, demand attention at the top of the hill. The botanic gardens of **Parc de Kerbihan▶** make a pleasant stroll, and also within the town is **Le Haras National▶▶** one of Brittany's most important stud-farms, with around 70 stallions palatially housed (tel: 02 97 89 40 30; *open* Jul–Aug 9–7; Sep–Jun 9–12.30, 2–6; *closed* Sat and Sun am; guided tours 10, 11, 2.15, 3.15, 4.15. *Admission moderate*).

Out of town, the industrial suburb of Inzinzac-Lochrist on the banks of the River Blavet once had a thriving iron foundry, and during the wars it played a significant role in munition manufacture. Despite innumerable strikes and protests, the foundry finally closed in 1966, and an **industrial museum▶▶** now occupies the old smelting works. The **Ecomusée Industriel des Forges** traces the history of the local iron and steel trade and the Blavet canal that was its lifeline (tel: 02 97 36 98 21; *open* Jul–Aug Mon–Fri 10–6.30, Sat–Sun 2–6.30; *closed* Sep–Jun lunchtime and Sat. *Admission moderate*).

Still farther up the Blavet, the abandoned village of **Poul-Fétan▶** (another victim of rural economic decline) has been turned into an *écomusée* of traditional thatched cottages furnished in period style, with incorporated complexes of crafts shops and cider-presses. The village is well signposted from neighbouring roads (tel: 02 97 39 51 74; www.poul-fetan.com; *open* Jul–Aug daily 10–7; Jun, Sep 2–7; Wed and weekends only in winter; guided tours in the morning. *Admission moderate*).

LA FORÊT DE TREMELIN
This 750ha (1,850-acre) expanse of mixed woodland north of Hennebont makes a pleasant place for a stroll. Criss-crossed by footpaths and trails, it contains many species of wildlife, including badgers and deer. The barrage lake of Ty-Mat makes a good picnic site.

187

A well dating from 1623 is one of the earliest surviving examples of Hennebont's wrought-iron industry

►► Josselin

Josselin's mighty **castle**►► (*Open* Jul–Aug daily, guided tours 10–6; Jun–Sep 2–6; Apr, May, Oct Sat–Sun 2–6. *Admission moderate*), mirrored in the waters of the Oust, is an impressive sight and lingers long in the mind's eye. Its walls rise sheer from the rocky riverbanks, culminating in three circular towers topped by witch-hat turrets. Beyond the forbidding exterior, however, the living quarters shelter behind a gloriously delicate facade of Flamboyant Gothic tracery.

The River Oust, canalized at Josselin, is one of the best places for boating in central Brittany

THE BATTLE OF THE THIRTY
In March 1351 the leaders of the opposing sides in the War of Succession, weary of siege warfare, staged a chivalric fight to establish ascendancy. Each side supplied 30 hand-picked knights, and the contestants met halfway between their two camps at Josselin and Ploërmel, where they fought on foot. The English-backed supporters of Jean de Montfort were commanded by John Bemborough, while the French contingent from Josselin (supporting Charles de Blois) was led by Jean de Beaumanoir. The day was won by the French leader. Eight knights lay dead, including Bemborough, and the rest were captured (in true chivalric style they were treated well). Beaumanoir won the battle but not the war, which grated on for another 13 years, culminating in the Battle of Auray (see page 178).

The town was founded in about AD1000 by a nobleman who bestowed on it the name of his second son. In about 1370 the original fortress was superseded by the present version, which was constructed by Olivier de Clisson (Du Guesclin's successor as Constable of France). De Clisson married Marguerite de Rohan, widow of Jean de Beaumanoir, who commanded the victorious side in the heroic Battle of the Thirty during the War of Succession (see panel). Subsequently Josselin passed into the hands of the powerful Rohan family.

Twice the castle was partially dismantled, once in 1488 and later on Richelieu's orders in 1629. The building was abandoned after damage in the Revolution and then finally restored in the 19th century. Descendants of the original Rohans still live in the castle. The grandly furnished rooms on the ground floor are open to the public. One of the castle's prize possessions is the table on which the Edict of Nantes (see pages 238–239) was signed in 1598. The former stables house the **Musée des Poupées**►►, containing over 600 Rohan dolls dating from the 18th century to modern times. Smiling *babuschkas* from Russia and snake-charmers from Asia mingle with modern blue-eyed Barbie dolls, in pottery, wood, wax and plastic. (Combined tickets available for both castle and museum; opening times the same.)

The old town of well-kept timber-framed houses lies behind the castle around the 12th-century basilica of **Notre-Dame-du-Roncier (Our Lady of the Brambles)**►. Most of it is in the Flamboyant style, with wondrously elongated gargoyles and a fretted spire (which you can climb). Inside lies the tomb of Josselin's former lord and master, Olivier de Clisson. From the opposite side of the river the picturesque Ste.-Croix quarter and the **Chapelle Ste.-Croix▶** provide good vantage points of the castle.

▶ Kerguéhennec 174C3

Tel: 02 97 60 44 44; www.artkerguehennec.com. Open mid-Jun to mid-Sep daily 10–7; mid Sep to mid Jun Tue–Sun 10–6. Closed mid-Dec to mid-Jan. Admission free

This estate of wooded parkland and a lake surrounding an 18th-century château is now owned and administered by the Morbihan local authority, which has turned it into an imaginative outdoor gallery for modern sculpture. European artists of international renown exhibit works here, and visitors wander through the grounds as though on a treasure hunt, spotting weird and wonderful *objets trouvés* amid the trees. Strange red plastic forms float in the lake; concrete slabs or circular patios of crazy paving erupt on grassy promenades; a broken skiff dangles in a tree. Check the greenhouse for Jean-Pierre Raynaud's red flower pots (1986). The château's grand *salons,* restored in the 19th century, can be visited in summer.

▶ Kernascléden 174A4

The extraordinary church that dominates this small village was built by the Rohan family, lords of Josselin and Pontivy. Both inside and out, the mid-15th century building is full of interest. Its lichen-mottled exterior is much carved and ornamented with slender crocketed pinnacles and sculpted balustrades, and there is a splendid set of Apostles in one of its porches.

The church's real claim to originality, however, lies inside, where frescoes adorn the walls and vaulting. Some are damaged, but all remain vivid and bright. Scenes from the Virgin's life decorate the chancel, an angelic orchestra plays soundlessly in the north transept, and Christ rises serenely from his tomb. Startling Bosch-like visions of hell disturb the south transept: Eyes are put out and demons rake the damned in cauldrons or barrels turned over raging fires.

THE *PARDON* OF THE BARKING WOMEN
Josselin's September *pardon* is named after the miraculous Virgin found in a bramble bush (Notre-Dame-du-Roncier), which now takes pride of place in the church. A strange legend is associated with it. One day a ragged beggar woman asked for a drink of water at the pump, but the local women drove her off with dogs and harsh words. Immediately their curses changed to a dog-like howl, for the beggar was the Virgin in disguise sent to try their charity. Every year, the women of Josselin must ask the Virgin for forgiveness or the barking curse will take hold again.

189

Josselin's mighty castle guards the waterfront approach to the old town

▶▶ Locmariaquer 174C2

After Carnac, this small oyster port is the most important site in Brittany for megaliths. Its most dramatic prehistoric remains lie in a single fenced compound just north of the village, with on-site information centre (see panel on page 185).

Locmariaquer's charms are not confined to the nearby ancient monuments. It is a pretty place, with less suburban development than Carnac and a friendlier atmosphere. The beaches aren't as good, but they are in a pleasant setting behind pines or dunes (there are also several decent walks). At low tide you can join a host of local families hunting for shellfish among the rocks. In the main village, old stone cottages and a pretty church stand around the harbour, where rival boat companies advertise tours of the Golfe du Morbihan.

Good-value accommodation and eating places also score over Carnac. Locmariaquer's double-aspect location commands both gulf and bay views, including an excellent sighting from the Pointe de Kerpenhir of the strange grassy tumulus on **Gavrinis** in the Golfe du Morbihan (see panel on page 193).

La Trinité-sur-Mer, between Carnac and Locmariaquer, consists of a modern yacht marina serviced by chandleries and smart boutiques. A world-renowned sailing centre, its thousand-plus berths are always full, and it has a sleek and sophisticated air.

▶ Lorient 174A3

Brittany's fourth largest city is almost entirely modern, a blockish place of angular white buildings and functional port facilities. During World War II it was repeatedly pounded by Allied bombs until over 85 per cent of its buildings lay in rubble. The Germans held out here long after there was any military point in doing so. Ironically, the main target of the attacks, the concrete U-boat pens, survived almost intact. Used by the French navy for the

THE MAST POND
The black poles you may spot emerging at low tide from the River Scorff near St.-Christophe bridge are the remnants of a mast pond, where wood used for boat building was stored in water-logged sand to prevent it rotting. It was first started in 1826.

190

The attractive town of Locmariaquer

The Dolmen des Pierres Plates standing over-looking the sea at Locmariaquer

ast 50 years, they are now open to visitors for summer guided tours.

The rest of the port is easily accessible from the new town, including the massive cargo wharfs at the Kergroise docks; the vast modern fishing port of Kéroman (one of the best equipped in France); and the leisure marina of Kernevel. The fishing port is liveliest in the mornings; its business-like daily *criée* (fish auction) can be visited on summer guided tours (Wed at 8am; tel: 02 97 21 07 84).

La Thalassa on the Quai de Rohan is an oceanographic research vessel, now turned into an entertaining, high-tech presentation of life at sea, displayed on four separate decks (tel: 02 97 35 13 00; www.sellor.com; *open* Jul–Aug daily 9–7; low season *closed* lunchtime and weekends pm. *Admission moderate*). A modern visitor centre on the adjacent quayside houses temporary exhibitions on maritime themes.

Lorient's name (from *l'Orient* meaning the East) echoes its purpose. It was once the headquarters of the Compagnie des Indes (India Company), founded here by Colbert, Louis XIV's naval minister, in 1666 when its predecessor across the water in Port-Louis failed. This southerly site was chosen to avoid the hazards faced by Channel shipping during the 17th century because of the depredations of English pirates. Lorient thrived for a century, then declined rapidly after the loss of India and the French Revolution.

Lorient is not an obvious tourist town. Dreary suburbs extend inland up the estuaries of the Blavet and the Scorff, and local pollution makes it no place for a beach holiday. Despite this, prestigious sailing events, boat trips around its three roadsteads, excursions to the Île de Groix (see page 186), plus its blockbusting Festival Interceltique attract many visitors.

The modern concrete church of **Notre-Dame-de-Victoire▶** (usually known as **St.-Louis**) stands in the new shopping area. It is an angular, brutalist structure roofed by a shallow dome, with a dramatically stark interior illuminated by bright, jagged splinter glass. A handful of art nouveau and art deco buildings survived the wartime bombardemnt, mostly in the Quartier de Merville and on the rue de Liège just south of the church.

PONT-SCORFF

This pretty village 7km (4.5 miles) upstream of Lorient has several attractions. The **Cour de Métiers d'Art** is a complex of craft studios in historic surroundings. **L'Odyssaum** is an exhibition on wild salmon (tel: 02 97 32 42 00; www.sellor.com; *open* Jul–Aug daily 9–7; Sep–Jun 9–12.30, 2–6, *closed* Sat, Sun am. *Admission moderate*). The local Zoo has more than 600 animals and is a noted breeding facility for big cats and elephants (tel: 02 97 32 60 86; *open* summer daily 9.30–7; winter 10–5. *Admission expensive*).

LARMOR-PLAGE

Lorient's nearest resort at the mouth of the estuary is also a naval base. Larmor-Plage's parish church dates from the 12th century and has a number of interesting features and a fine interior. Traditionally, any warship leaving Lorient on active service would fire a three-gun salute as it passed Notre-Dame-de-Larmor, and in reply the priest would hoist a flag, ring the church bells, and give the ship a blessing. On the Sunday closest to 24 June, Midsummer's Day, a Blessing of the Waters ceremony is held in the town.

The church at Malestroit

192

ÎLE AUX MOINES
This straggly lump of land measures about 7km (4 miles) at its longest. It is the most populous, and popular, island in the gulf, thronged with day-trippers in summer. The quickest ferry journey is from Port-Blanc (five minutes). Woods and heaths make up most of the interior, and lush plants fill the gardens of stone or thatched houses. You can explore its innumerable paths and lanes on foot or by bicycle, heading for scattered megaliths or a stepped calvary. The beach near the port is one of the best in the gulf.

Strange and humorous carvings decorate the old houses around Malestroit's main square

►► Malestroit   175D:

This baronial town sits at the junction of several majo: roads, and is also on the Nantes–Brest canal. Its historic core is around Place du Bouffay and the church o: St.-Gilles (12th to 16th centuries), a delightful assembly of slate-hung Gothic and Renaissance houses that repay: close inspection for their bizarre carvings, for example a man in his nightshirt beats his wife; a hare plays the bag pipes; and a sow threads a distaff. Edward III of England and Philip VI of France signed a truce in Malestroit dur ing the Hundred Years War, giving England a 40-yea: foothold in Brittany.

Apart from pleasant walks along the canalside there isn't a great deal to see or do in the town itself, but a St.-Marcel, a short distance west, the **Musée de la Résistance Bretonne** ►► (tel: 02 97 75 16 90; *oper* mid-Jun to mid-Sep daily 10–7; mid-Sep tc mid-Jun Wed–Mon 10–12, 2–6. *Admission mod erate*) is essential viewing for anyone interest ed in local history. It stands on the site of a significant wartime operation which started in June 1944, when the local Maquis (Frencb Resistance) successfully diverted many Germar troops from the Allied landings taking place in Normandy.

The first room re-creates Brittany under the Occupation, with the buckled engines of a shot-dowr American bomber amid propaganda posters and ratior cards. In subsequent rooms, Resistance sabotage, the black market and an account of the battle of St.-Marce are covered, while the unforgettable tune of 'Lil Marlene' trickles relentlessly into the visitor's brain fo: the rest of the day. The presentation is generally good, bu pick up the English translation at the desk and follow the numbering system carefully to get the best from the exhi bition. Local monuments and war memorials show hov vividly (and bitterly) memories of war continue to linge: in this area.

The 'Little Sea' which gives its name to the region was formed quite recently in geological terms, between 2,000 and 4,000 years ago, when land levels fell. Over 20km (12 miles) wide and 15km (9 miles) from north to south, the gulf is an area of great natural and historic interest. It has the largest concentration of seabirds on the French Atlantic coast, and a great variety of wildlife habitats: dunes, mud flats, oysterbeds, salt marshes, lagoons, islands, creeks, estuaries, reed beds, heaths and pinewoods. Mediterranean vegetation flourishes in the mild climate of the area.

There are no real seaside resorts on the gulf, apart from Locmariaquer (see page 190), whose main beach faces the open sea and is thua rather exposed. The small settlements along the shore catering for visitors have sailing centres, boat-trips, and watersports rather than bathing beaches. A handful of hotels, restaurants and campsites provide the necessary facilities for quiet waterside sojourns. Fresh seafood, needless to say, is excellent, particularly the oysters.

For all its sheltered position away from ocean storms, the gulf is fiercely tidal, its waters ripping in and out of the narrow neck near Locmariaquer, fizzing like champagne. Currents can make its beaches very dangerous for swimming. At low tide the water generally retreats beyond vast areas of mud or weed, and pollution can be a problem in the built-up area around Vannes. The state of the tide and the weather can make a huge difference to the appearance of the gulf.

One of the best excursions in Morbihan is a boat trip across the gulf, possibly stopping at one of the islands en route. There are more than 300 of these islands, some no more than grassy hummocks barely emerging from the waterline, others much larger and inhabited; some are even privately owned by film stars or other celebrities. Visitors who use public transport may land on only three islands: the **Ile aux Moines**▶▶ (the largest and most varied of the islands, see panel opposite); the **Île d'Arz**, and the **Île de Gavrinis**▶▶, which has the most ornately decorated prehistoric tomb in Brittany and should not be missed (see panel). Several centres offer a bewildering variety of boat trips, notably Locmariaquer, Vannes, Port-Navalo and Auray. Larmor-Baden operates monopoly sailings to Gavrinis. If you have your own boat you can explore at leisure, weaving among the disorientating land-masses and lagoons.

CAIRN DE GAVRINIS
The tomb is buried under a grass-topped stone cairn. Many stones of the burial chamber display ritualistic or realistic shapes of snakes, sun-rays, chevrons, and spirals. Visitor numbers are limited, so book ahead (tel: 02 97 57 19 38; *open* Apr–Oct guided tours daily. *Admission expensive;* includes ferry fare).

Yachts tied up on the tree-lined estuary near Auray

Carvings from the porch at Ploërmel

LIZIO
This pretty place was once a halt for pilgrims on the long journey through France to the Spanish medieval shrine of Santiago de Compostela. The skill of the local stone-cutting industry shows through in the perfectly bonded masonry of its mellow buildings. Weaving was another important industry in the community.

Pontivy splits sharply into two architectural styles: higgledy-piggledy half-timbering in the old town (shown here) and Napoleonic order in the new town to the west (shown opposite)

► **Ploërmel** 175D

Ploërmel's finest hour was probably in the 14th century when the de Montforts, who held the town at the time won the War of Succession and became medieval Duke of Brittany. It is now the market centre of the prosperou Porhoët farming region, and a popular touring base fo the Forêt de Paimpont to the northeast (see page 216–217). The local reservoir (Étang au Duc) caters fo fishing and watersports enthusiasts. A waymarked trai called the **Circuit des Hortensias** follows the tracks of disused railway line around the shore through a super collection of hydrangeas (tel: 02 97 74 02 70; *open* all yea but best May–Sep. *Admission free*).

On 27 March, 1351 the famously chivalric tournamen known as the Battle of the Thirty was fought half-wa between Ploërmel and Josselin (see panel on page 188) The town was damaged during World War II, and com paratively little of the old medieval hunting tow remains, apart from the Flamboyant Gothic church of **St. Armel►**, where the local patron slays a dragon and Duke Jean II and III stand in a side chapel. Notice the carving on the north door; among more biblical scenes, one show a clogmaker sewing up his nagging wife's mouth.

Just a few picturesque houses line Ploërmel's olde streets, notably the **Maison des Marmousets►** on rue Beaumanoir, but a few sights lie south of the town **Lizio** has an **Ecomusée des Vieux Métiers►** (tel: 02 97 74 93 01; *open* Apr–Sep 10–12, 2–7; Oct–Mar 2–6. *Admission moderate*), with over 70,000 farm- and craftworking implements on display. It also has an **Insectarium** full of exotic and startling bugs (tel: 02 97 74 99 12 www.insectarium-de-lizio.com; *open* daily 10–12.30 1.30–6.30. *Admission moderate*).

► **Pontivy** 174C

Like Josselin, Pontivy was a seat of the Rohan family. Its squat fortress of rusty schist at the northeast end of town dates from about 1485, with pepperpot bastions guarding

The town hall at Pontivy, a formal public building typical of the Napoleonic era

deep, dry moat. Now the castle is used for temporary exhibitions (the tourist office stands just outside).

Pontivy's old town around the Place du Martray is the same age as the castle. The main square is busiest on market day (Tuesday). Quaint old half-timbering characterizes the narrow streets near **Notre-Dame-de-la-Joie**, where a revered statue answered local prayers during an outbreak of bubonic plague. Less overtly picturesque but equally interesting is the newer sector to the southwest, which was built by Napoleon. Pontivy's Republican sentiments appealed to the Consul-cum-Emperor, and he modernized the town in formal neoclassical style with wide, grid-like boulevards, landscaped parks and grandiose administrative and military buildings. Later, Pontivy fitted in neatly with Napoleon's ambitions to create a canal linking Nantes and Brest that was far away from coastal marauders. The townsfolk rechristened the town Napoléonville in his honour, but it reverted to its original name when Bonapartism fell out of favour.

Pontivy makes a pleasant touring base for a day or two. Several villages to the south lie within a brief drive. **St.-Nicolas-des-Eaux**▶ stands placidly on the Blavet, its older nucleus of thatched cottages much expanded by modern holiday homes. Just south of the village the river executes a dramatic loop, and at the encircled knoll known as the **Site de Castennec**▶ an excellent view can be had from a roadside belvedere. **Bieuzy**▶ has an attractive church with a knobbly Renaissance chevet (apsidal end). Beside it is an unusual war memorial—an ordinary soldier leaning casually on his rifle. An old well, communal bread oven and fountain can also be seen.

Melrand, down the road, has granite houses and an unusual calvary encrusted with gold lichen, its shaft ornamented with the heads of the Apostles. A **Ferme Archéologique (Archaeological Farm)**▶ dating from about AD1000 has been excavated and reconstructed as a tourist sight, complete with thatched dwellings, rare breeds of sheep and a medieval-style herb garden (tel: 02 97 39 57 89; *open* May–Aug daily 10–7; Sep–May daily 11–5. *Admission inexpensive*).

THE VENUS DE QUINIPILY
The humdrum little town of Baud (some 20km/12 miles south of Pontivy) has just one claim on visitors' attention, a *jolie laide* statue known as the Venus de Quinipily, which can be found in the grounds of the Château de Quinipily, 2km (1 mile) southwest of Baud. Originally discovered at Castennac, the statue is of uncertain provenance, some declaring it to be Roman or Egyptian. Thus suffused with curious pagan legends, the image became the object of various unspeakable practices, and was several times thrown into the Blavet by order of the Church (whereupon it was instantly retrieved). Eventually the local lord of the manor had the statue decently resculpted, with some clothing and a less ample posterior, and placed her on her present dignified plinth.

196

THE BRETON LEAGUE

One of the more confusing patches of Brittany's history occurred during the Wars of Religion in the late 16th century. The Duke of Mercoeur (then Governor of Brittany) plotted against the succession of the Protestant French king, Henry IV. The duke's Catholic supporters, the Breton League, enlisted the help of Philip II of Spain, and in 1590 a force of 3,000 Spaniards arrived at Port-Louis, which they occupied for eight years. A similar Spanish garrison was set up on the Crozon peninsula (see panel on page 124). The insurrection ended in 1598 when Henry signed the Edict of Nantes, which granted freedom of religion to Protestants (mainly Huguenots) throughout France, thus ending the Wars of Religion.

The rocks off the Quiberon coast are a peril to sailors

▶▶ Port-Louis   *174A3*

The history of this sea-port at the mouth of the Blavet estuary is inextricably bound up with Lorient, its huge sibling across the water (see pages 190–191). As the fortunes of one town waxed, the other's waned.

The fortified citadel at the entrance to the roadstead was founded in 1591, when Port-Louis was under temporary Spanish occupation (see panel). It was subsequently reinforced in 1616 and 1641, and used as a prison, barracks, and arsenal. Port-Louis was the original headquarters of the Compagnie des Indes (India Company), set up by Cardinal Richelieu in Louis XIII's reign (when the town took his name). The venture was not a success. Despite the port's previous experience of trade with Africa and Madagascar, it had become corrupt and gangster-ridden, and soon the first Compagnie des Indes failed. It was resurrected in Lorient in 1666 to challenge English and Dutch trading supremacy in the Far East.

Port-Louis achieved minor prosperity from sardine- and tuna-fishing in the 19th century, and is now an attractive little resort. Ironically, it is Port-Louis, not Lorient, that now displays the history of the Compagnie des Indes in the **museum complex**, within the ramparts: **l'Arsenale**, with model ships and naval documents; the **Poudrière** (Powder Factory), focusing on naval armaments, mines, torpedoes and the like; the **Musée de la Marine** (Maritime Museum); and the **Musée de la Compagnie des Indes (India Company Museum)▶▶**, with exotic imports from the Orient, along with documents, maps and models (tel: 02 97 82 19 13; www.lorient.com/musee; *open* mid-May to Aug daily 10–6.30; pm only low season. *Closed* Tue and mid-Dec to Jan. *Admission moderate*). Walks along the ramparts offer excellent views of the Blavet roadsteads, and near the parking area is a gateway that leads to an attrac-

Port-Louis is still a thriving tuna-fishing port

THE BLAVET VIRGINS
A tale from Port-Louis' period of Spanish occupation relates how a group of 40 young girls tried to evade capture by Spanish forces. They set sail in a ship but were pursued. To prevent themselves being seized they joined hands and leapt into the sea, where they all perished.

SHELL PICTURES
Le Galion, a modern replica of an 18th-century vessel built from an old barge, lies beached in Plouharnel at the north end of the Quiberon peninsula. It has an extraordinary display of elaborate shell pictures, including depictions of the Piazza San Marco in Venice, a Japanese pagoda and a Loire château (tel: 02 97 52 39 56; *open* Jul–Aug 9.30–7, Apr–Jun, Sep 10–12, 2–6. *Admission inexpensive).*

GENERAL HOCHE
A crucial turning point of the Chouan rebellion (see page 179) took place in Quiberon in 1795, when General Hoche massively defeated the straggling invasion fleet of exiled aristocrats and their supporters from England. He wrote to his chief of staff: 'The Anglo-French Emigré Chouans are trapped like rats on Quiberon, where the army has hemmed them in. I hope we shall be rid of them in a few days.' This happened more literally than he intended. The 900 beleaguered Chouans surrendered, were taken prisoner and, to Hoche's horror, were all shot without trial at Auray. He protested at this atrocity, but to no avail.

tive, quiet beach of sand and rock. Just south of the town, the enclosed Mer de Gâvres presents a mournful scene of mud flats and ducks.

▶ **Quiberon, Presqu'île de** *174B2*
This curious protuberance from the Morbihan coastline is reached by a causeway of tidal sediment in places scarcely wider than the road. Plouharnel, at the top of the peninsula, offers two unusual attractions: *le Galion*▶, a mock galleon filled with shell pictures of extraordinary elaboration, and the **Musée de la Chouannerie**▶ (*Open* Apr–Sep 10–12, 2–6. *Admission moderate*) recounting the story of the Chouans (see page 179). The main road along the Penthièvre isthmus leads past piles of blown sand and windblasted conifers, with a massive exposed beach on the west side. Eastwards, the sands of Sables Blancs look inviting at high water.

At the **Fort de Penthièvre**, which guards the neck of the peninsula, a monument commemorates 59 Resistance members who were executed here in 1944. To the west the Atlantic beats wildly at the Côte Sauvage, a coast of cliffs, caves, crags and chasms. There are beaches here too, but the undertow is treacherous, as testfied by an awesome list of drownings. Head west to **Pointe du Percho**▶, and walk to the end for views of fractured rocks and wave-sculpted sea-caves. **Beg-er-Goalennec** makes another good belvedere for this exciting coast.

Quiberon▶ is one of Morbihan's liveliest resorts, its harbour area throbbing with shops, restaurants, bars and hotels. Traffic queues form in summer as over 100,000 visitors annually converge, most bent on visiting Belle-Île (see pages 180–181). Beyond the bustling *gare maritime* at Port-Maria, the long beach curves past a massive modern thalassotherapy facility towards the low-lying **Pointe du Conguel**. The east coast consists mostly of low-key holiday development and amorphous little resorts. **St.-Pierre-Quiberon** is the largest, with rows of megaliths (22 in all) on rue des Menhirs. Sheltered from prevailing winds, Quiberon bay is smooth and calm. Marinas and Beg-Rohu's sailing school cater for the local passion.

Market, St.-Gildas-de-Rhuys (above)

Drive

The Rhuys peninsula

See map on pages 174–175.

The Rhuys peninsula is the arm of land cradling the southern side of the Golfe du Morbihan. From its tip, the Locmariaquer headland is only 2km (1 mile) away; by road, it is a 60km (36 miles) drive via Vannes and Auray. Allow three hours or so from Vannes.

The Rhuys peninsula has a very mild microclimate. Figs, camellias, and pomegranates flourish, and the vines produce a wine of legendary potency.
   Starting from Vannes, follow the main gulf road (D780) round to the southeast, skirting the waterfront. Sarzeau is the main community on Rhuys, though it has little to interest visitors aside

from a couple of fine Renaissance houses near the church and a regional tourist office. South of the main road, a signposted turning leads to the peninsula's most interesting sight, the **Château de Suscinio**▶▶ (tel: 02 97 41 91 91; *open* Spring to Sep daily 10–7; low season *closed* Wed and lunchtime. *Admission moderate*), restored in 1995. Dating from the 13th century, it stands in lonely marshes, partly roofless now, but was once moated by the sea. The castle was a summer residence of the Dukes of Brittany, and the Duc de Richemont, victor of the Hundred Years War, was born here.
   Farther west, another detour from the main road leads to **St.-Gildas-de-Rhuys**, where a dour abbey church attracts pilgrims for its associations with Peter Abelard (see panel on page 199). Inside, notice the carved capitals, model ships, and the tomb of St. Gildas, a 6th-century saint.
   To the right of the main road near **Arzon**, a small hillock erupts from the low-lying surroundings. This neolithic monument is the **Tumulus de Tumiac**▶, known as Caesar's Mount, where Julius Caesar is said to have watched the naval battle in which the Veneti were defeated in 56BC (see page 33). The tip of the peninsula is quite extensively developed, the resort of **Port-Navalo** now covered with holiday homes. **Port du Crouesty** is a marina complex of apartments and boutiques.

▶▶ La Roche-Bernard   *175E2*

Originally this attractive town was a Viking foundation. During the Wars of Religion it was a Protestant centre, and its fortunes grew after the Edict of Nantes in 1598, when religious tolerance was granted. Its ship-building industry flourished, and the great warship *La Couronne* was commissioned in 1634. Riverine trade also prospered; cargo boats sailed up and down the Vilaine bearing grain, wine, timber, salt, and spices. This aspect of the town's history is covered in the **Musée de la Vilaine Maritime▶▶** (tel: 02 99 90 83 47; *open* mid–Jun to mid-Sep daily 10.30–12.30, 2.30–6.30. *Admission inexpensive*), housed in the Château des Basses-Fosses on the west bank. During the Revolution la Roche-Bernard was a Republican town, but the Chouans overcame the few stalwarts defending it. They ordered the mayor, Joseph Sauveur, to shout 'Long live the King', but he shouted 'Long live the Republic' and was shot dead.

Since the Arzal dam was built, the river is no longer tidal, and pleasure craft are the only vessels to reach the town. The massive suspension bridge spanning the river replaces an earlier one accidentally destroyed during World War II, when lightning struck a German ammunition dump. In its day, the earlier bridge was the longest

ABELARD'S EXILE

The sad affair of Héloïse and Abelard in the 12th century is one of the great love stories of all time. Abelard was forced into exile as abbot at St.-Gildas-de-Rhuys, 'a wild country where every day brings new perils,' he wrote. When his fellow monks attempted to poison him he managed to escape down a secret passage, and eventually returned to Paris.
The lovers were finally reunited in death and now lie in the same grave in Paris. A museum at Abelard's birthplace, le Pallet near Nantes (just outside the area covered by this book), documents Abelard's life.

199

ever built, and its supporting pillars can still be seen from the new bridge.

A by-pass takes traffic past the town, leaving the centre relatively quiet. The old quarter around place du Bouffay is far less grim today than it was in 1793, when a guillotine stood here. In town hall is a gun from an English warship, the *Inflexible*, which sought refuge here after a battle.

La Roche-Bernard has an excellent range of accommodation and restaurants, and makes a good touring base. On the way to Vannes lies the **Moulin de Pen-Mur**, an old mill where you can watch paper being made in the traditional way (tel: 02 97 41 43 79; www.moulin-pen-mur.com; *open* Apr–Sep Mon–Sat 10–12.30. *Admission moderate*).

Cannons watch over the estuary at la Roche-Bernard, once an important naval dockyard

Rochefort-en-Terre's old centre is best enjoyed on foot

►► Rochefort-en-Terre   *175E2*

The winner of many 'best-kept village' competitions, Rochefort-en-Terre is instantly and conspicuously appealing. It stands high on a spur of schist jutting into the Arz valley, and is surrounded by plunging slopes of woodland and babbling brooks. The old town is best explored on foot. Aristocratic stone mansions, much embellished with carvings and windowboxes, line the cobbled main streets, and some have been turned into shops and restaurants catering for visitors.

The church, **Notre-Dame-de-la-Tronchaye►►**, is a delightful building with an unusual gabled facade and a delicate three-tiered calvary outside. Inside, interesting features include Renaissance altarpieces of white stone and a wrought-iron font. The revered statue of Our Lady of la Tronchaye, discovered in the 12th century apparently hidden from Norse invaders in a tree, stands in the south transept behind a wrought-iron grille. A *pardon* takes place on the Sunday after Assumption Day.

Near the top of the town stands a **castle**. The original fortress was damaged in 1488 and finally destroyed during the Revolution, but at the turn of the 20th century two American artist brothers, Alfred and Trafford Klots, decided to restore and rebuild it, using stone salvaged from various local châteaux. Today the castle belongs to the town, and is open to the public. It is furnished in 16th- and 17th-century style, embellished with tapestries, paintings by the Klots brothers, and a collection of Quimper porcelain madonnas. A small museum of popular folklore stands in the grounds, and the terrace commands excellent views of the surrounding countryside.

A couple of contrived tourist attractions can be found close to Rochefort. A **Parc de Préhistoire** at Malansac relates an everyday story of cavemen in lifesize tableaux (tel: 02 97 43 34 17; *open* Apr to mid-Oct daily 10–7. *Admission expensive*), and an exotic tropical garden flourishes at St.-Jacut-les-Pins, but the local scenery beats both hands down.

Accommodation in town is limited, but to the northwest the Château de Talhouët promises an unusual and delightful stay (see page 275).

Prehistory comes alive at Malansac

SLATE QUARRIES
The terrain around Rochefort-en-Terre shows much evidence of quarrying. The Lac Bleu, just south of the town, makes a pretty spot for a picnic, its waters eerily blue with suspended particles, and the long-disused slate galleries are inhabited by unusual fauna (blind butterflies and long-eared bats).

▶▶▶ Vannes

174C2

Vannes is one of Brittany's best-looking towns, livelier and more cosmopolitan than many and with a Gallic rather than a Celtic air. It has a long and prestigious pedigree and has played an important role in Breton history. The name stems from Veneti, the Celtic tribe that Caesar vanquished. Vannes shared the honour of being the Breton capital with Nantes and Rennes throughout the Middle Ages, finally signing away its status by the Act of Union with France in 1532.

There is plenty to see here and Vannes also makes a good excursion base, particularly for boat trips on the Golfe du Morbihan. The river is canalized and used by pleasure craft, which moor outside the old town. Near the *gare maritime* a leisure complex offers several wet-weather attractions: an aquarium (overshadowed now by better versions at Brest and le Croisic), a butterfly park and an exhibition on the Golfe du Morbihan. Like several otherwise appealing Breton towns, Vannes suffers a conspicuous lack of pleasant central accommodation.

Watching the world go by in Vannes

THE ELVEN TOWERS
The fortress of Largoët, northeast of Vannes at Elven, is an impressive feudal ruin in extensive wooded parkland. It once belonged to the Marshal de Rieux, tutor to Anne de Bretagne. In 1488 the castle was burned down by the king of France, Charles VIII, and now the ruins make an atmospheric setting for summer *son-et-lumière* presentations. During the day visitors are welcome to wander through the woods from the lodge to the gaunt ruins. Two mighty towers and a gateway with a drawbridge over the moat are still intact (tel: 02 97 53 35 96; *open* Jul–Aug daily 10.30–12, 2.30–6.30; *closed* Nov to mid-Mar; guided tours, *son-et-lumière* shows in summer. *Admission moderate*).

One of Vannes' picturesque old houses

Walk

The old town of Vannes

Vannes escaped serious damage in the war, and much of its delightful walled old town remains intact. This stroll round the scenic area surrounding the cathedral offers an agreeable mix of museums and architecture, covering time from prehistory to the present day.

Vannes' ramparts confine traffic to the outskirts of the old town, where it screeches around confusing one-way systems in search of parking places. Try Place de la République or the area by the port, then approach the walled town on foot. **Porte St.-Vincent** at the

southern end is a good place to start, and you can visit the tourist office en route. Nearby **Place Gambetta** consists of a terraced crescent of 19th-century buildings, its cafés and bars especially lively in the early evening.

Beyond the walls, virtually every street or square has buildings of interest. On a fine day, old Vannes is very photogenic. **Place des Lices** was a medieval tilt-yard where jousting tournaments were held. Just off it, on a corner of rue Rogue, is the Maison de Vannes, an old house adorned with carved wooden statues of a jolly rustic couple known as **Vannes and his Wife**. Nearby is the **Musée d'Histoire et d'Archéologie de Vannes** (tel: 02 97 01 63 00; *open* Jun–Sep 10–6. *Admission inexpensive*), in the 15th-century Château Gaillard, once the Breton parliament. The display doesn't do justice to the contents, which include, on the first floor, finds from Morbihan's important megalithic sites.

The **Cathédrale St.-Pierre**▶▶ is unmissable, an eclectic muddle of architecture from the 13th to the 19th centuries, trailing through Romanesque, Gothic and Italian Renaissance. Inside the unusual Rotunda chapel lies the tomb of St. Vincent Ferrier, the town's patron, and there are pictures and tapestries depicting his good works. This Spanish saint, a Dominican monk, achieved great fame as a preacher and performed many miraculous cures. He travelled widely and played a role in ending the Papal schism between Rome and Avignon. Less benevolently, his flamboyant oratory was the cause of anti-Semitic riots in the Spanish city of Toledo, when many Jews were flung over the cliffs to their deaths. When the saint died here in 1419, the people of Vannes refused to give up his body to Spanish or Dominican authorities, and it was laid to rest in the cathedral, where it still lies. Be sure to see his house at 17 Place Valencia, marked by a niched statue. The **cathedral treasury**, housed in the old chapter house, contains a fine collection of religious gold plate.

Virtually opposite the cathedral is **la Cohue**▶▶. This medieval covered market has served many purposes over the years, and once housed the law courts. Today it contains Vannes' museum of art (tel: 02 97 01 63 00; *open* Jul–Aug, daily 10–6, low season 1.30–6. *Admission moderate*) and holds temporary exhibitions.

Wander west to rue Thiers in the newer town to glance at the imposing 19th-century **Hôtel de Ville**▶, with its fine equestrian statue, and the **Hôtel de Limur**, a 17th-century town house. Then walk back through the machicolated Porte Prison and meander past the **ramparts**▶▶, their stern defensive towers softened by brilliant flowerbeds and a passing stream. You get a good view of these from the **Promenade de la Garenne**, a raised walk by well-tended public gardens. Vannes' most picturesque buildings, the medieval *lavoirs* (**wash houses**)▶▶ are near the Porte Poterne, a photogenic assembly of slate roofs and flower-decked dormers.

203

Beautifully kept municipal gardens add cheer to the forbidding ramparts enclosing the old town

The castle at Combourg, where the writer François-René de Chateaubriand spent two emotionally charged years of his adolescence

INLAND BRITTANY Compared with Brittany's overtly attractive coastline, the interior of Haute Bretagne (the easterly section closest to the rest of France) has little charisma. Mostly it is an uneventful 'managed' landscape given over to agricultural pursuits and interspersed with low hills, stands of woodland and sluggish waterways. Mighty fortresses punctuate the marches that once severed Brittany from France, yet at first sight there seems little to distinguish this region from the lush farmland of Normandy or the Loire Valley; there are few of the *coiffes*, *pardons* or parish closes that characterize the far west. The lonely plateau villages north of Mûr-de-Bretagne have preserved more of their traditional culture, and here Breton is still spoken in a few places.

HISTORIC INTEREST Historically, though, Haute Bretagne's hinterland offers rich pickings, from the great bastion towns of Fougères and Vitré to the present provincial capital of Rennes, one of Brittany's most cosmopolitan cities. Rennes is often undersold because of its unattractive industrial sprawl, but its museums and historic middle amply repay a day's exploration. Smaller fortified towns such as Montfort-sur-Meu and Quintin are more easily accessible destinations.

Touring the countryside is not unrewarding, whether by boat along its canal systems, by road through the lonely lakes and gorges north of Pontivy, or on foot through remnants of the virgin forests that once cloaked Brittany's

▶▶▶ REGION HIGHLIGHTS

Fougères
pages 208–209

Gorges around Mûr-de-Bretagne *page 215*

Forêt de Paimpont
pages 216–217

Rennes *pages 218–221*

Vitré *pages 224–225*

Inland Brittany

A SALMON A DAY
In 17th-century Brittany, salmon was very much part of the staple diet. Over 4,500 tonnes of it were eaten every year, and it was no special treat. At one time it was regarded as such dull fare that servants in the great houses of central Brittany made their masters sign contracts promising not to give them salmon more than three times a week.

Grey granite dominates at Combourg

ANIMAL MAGIC
If you have children to amuse, the Combourg area offers several possibilities. The Château de la Bourbansais (12km/7 miles west of Combourg) makes an impressive statement of turrets and pavilions across velvety lawns set with classical statuary, but its contents (Aubusson tapestries and oriental porcelain) may appeal less to younger visitors than the menagerie of wild animals roaming through the park. Cobac Parc at Lanhélin (10km/6 miles northwest) also has more than 200 animals among many other amusements (water park, boat rides and mini golf). Zooloisirs at Québriac near Tinténiac (8km/5 miles southwest), has an unusual mix of rose gardens, mild-mannered livestock (llamas, wallabies, and the like), and an extensive collection of stuffed beasts.

Wherever you go in Fougères, you can't avoid the hills

argoat. Most evocative of these woodlands is the Forêt de Paimpont, the Brocéliande of Arthurian legend.

UNCROWDED RESORTS Apart from in the obvious tourist spots, accommodation and restaurants are scarcer inland than on the coast, and may be geared to commercial visitors. Tourism is big business throughout Brittany and if you choose a base carefully (perhaps in one of the *stations vertes,* or country tourist centres, now promoted as inland resorts) you should have little difficulty in finding somewhere to stay, even at the height of the summer season when coastal resorts are crammed to capacity. Increasingly, farmhouses and private châteaux provide interesting alternatives to conventional hotels. Fougères, Mûr-de-Bretagne and Combourg make pleasant town bases, and there are a couple of excellent hotels conveniently and peacefully set between Vitré and Rennes.

▶ Bécherel
205D2

A thriving linen industry once kept this pretty old hill town prosperous. Now Bécherel's sobriquet is *cité du livre* (city of the book), and second-hand bookshops of all types occupy many of its charming stone houses. A book market is held on the first Sunday of each month, and a major book fair takes place in spring.

A few sporadic castle ruins are left in the town, for Bécherel was once fortified. More noteworthy, though, is the **Château de Caradeuc▶** (tel: 02 99 66 77 76; *open* Jul–Aug daily 12–6; Sep–Jun Sat–Sun 2–6; *closed* mid-Sep–Easter. *Admission moderate*), 1km (0.6 miles) west. Only the landscaped park and gardens are open.

Bécherel stands in attractive wooded walking country, with views to the north over the Rance valley. If you have time, east towards Hédé (see page 212) is the Gothic church of **les Iffs▶**, with beautiful stained glass and sculpture, and the **Château de Montmuran▶** (tel: 02 99 45 88 88; *open* Jun–Sep daily 2–7. *Admission moderate*), where Du Guesclin was knighted in 1354 (see pages 34–35).

▶ Combourg, Chateau de
205D3

Tel: 02 99 73 22 95; www.combourg.net
Open: Jul–Aug daily 11–5.30; Sep–Jun Sun–Fri 2–5; Oct 2–4.30; grounds Jul–Aug 10–6; Sep–Jun Sun–Fri reduced hours; closed lunchtime and Nov–Mar.
Admission moderate

The massive towers of Combourg's feudal fortress, with conical roofs and spiky finials, pierce the town's skyline. Founded by an Archbishop of Dol in the 11th century, it underwent many modifications during the Middle Ages and was once owned by Du Guesclin. In 1761, the castle was bought by Count Chateaubriand, father of one of France's most famous Romantic writers. The young François-René spent his childhood behind these gloomy walls. Downstairs his parents lived in reclusive melancholy, his father pacing the drawing room in silence and his mother incapacitated by hypochondria and religious mania. Visitors are taken to see his haunted bedroom in the Tour du Chat, the chapel, and the archives, and along a parapet walk with a view of the town.

The stately château at Caradeuc

THE MASTER OF CARADEUC
The fine Château de Caradeuc was once the home of a fiery public prosecutor, the Marquis de Caradeuc de la Chalotais, whose pamphlet advocating the dissolution of the Jesuits (a powerfully conservative influence on local government) caused a political stir in 1762. Louis XV opposed his views and had La Chalotais arrested, but the Rennes parliament took his side and won. Many historians believe this clash of wills was a significant spark in the events leading to the French Revolution.

Statuary in the grounds of Caradeuc

Inland Brittany

THE MARQUIS DE LA ROUËRIE
Fougères has seen its share of conflict. The Chouan movement (see page 179) was founded by the Marquis de la Rouërie (1756–1793), a minor scion of Fougères nobility. Instead of fleeing into exile like many of his peers, he organized a form of guerrilla resistance in the Breton countryside, stowing caches of arms and drumming up supporters. However, he died early on in the struggle, which dragged on in Brittany for a further decade. Fougères was used as the setting for both Victor Hugo's *Quatre-vingt-treize* (*Ninety-three*) and Balzac's *Les Chouans*, the classic novels of this period.

►►► Fougères

205E2

Fougères is a frontier town, once capital of the Breton Marches dividing France and Brittany. Duchess Anne dubbed it 'the key to my royal treasure'; for Victor Hugo, Fougères was 'the Carcassonne of the North'. Its promontory setting above a tight loop in the River Nançon is a classically defensible location, though unusually its massive fortress was constructed *below* the town, not above it. The rocky spurs above the castle walls cradle the upper town of mostly 18th-century buildings. Precipitous steps and alleys lead from the back of the church of St.-Léonard down to a much older sector around the Place du Marchix, where tanneries and mills can be seen among an enchanting cluster of 16th-century houses, focused by the slender pencil spire of St.-Sulpice.

Like many Breton towns, Fougères grew wealthy on the textile trades of wool and hemp. Later it turned its historic cattle market and tanning business to good use in a new enterprise of shoe manufacture, supplemented after post-World War II recession by ventures into electronics and robotics. Beyond the modern suburbs a state forest of beech, spruce and chestnut extends northeast, shading megaliths and 12th-century cellars used as hiding places in times of war.

Fougères has one of Brittany's most memorable fortresses

Walk

The old town of Fougères

See map opposite.

Start at the top of the town to get an overview of its huge fortress before you explore inside. Allow half a day, and try to see the local art museum.

Head for the upper town and park in one of the squares near the tourist office, and then walk along the pedestrianized rue Nationale. Don't miss the elegant 14th-century **beffroi**▶ (belfry) behind the covered market. Continue along rue Nationale to reach **Musée de la Villéon** (tel: 02 99 99 19 98; *open* mid-Jun to mid-Sep daily 10.30–12.30, 2–6; low season Wed–Sun 10–12, 2–5. *Admission free*). This museum, in a picturesque 16th-century house, is dedicated to the Impressionist painter Emmanuel de la Villéon (1858–1944), a native of Fougères.

The church of St.-Léonard stands near the Renaissance town hall, its grey austerity lifted by vivid stained glass (traditional and modern) and an ornate north facade. Behind the church, neat municipal gardens give a splendid view over wooded chasms, the Marchix quarter and the huge fortress beyond. Thread your way down the stepped alleys, and across the river via the rue des Tanneurs. In the streets around the Place du Marchix

St.-Léonard's church and gardens

The Marchix quarter (above), as seen from the upper town

are many old buildings. The Flamboyant church of **St.-Sulpice**▶ has as much grace inside as its exterior suggests. Fine woodwork and granite altarpieces catch the eye, as does a 12th-century statue of the Virgin (Notre-Dame-des-Marais) suckling a child.

Visit the **castle**▶▶ next (tel: 02 99 99 79 59; *open* mid-Jun to mid-Sep, daily 9–7; low season 10–12, 2–5; *closed* Jan. *Admission moderate*). This is one of the largest and most imposing in France and is the town's main tourist attraction. The original fortress dates from around AD1000, and despite its stalwart defences it was frequently attacked and often changed hands. Festivals are sometimes held in the grounds. A walk outside the walls is almost as impressive as a tour inside, where you can investigate the tower rooms and walk the ramparts. Notice the foundations of the keep (destroyed in 1166) and the waterwheels by the gatehouse.

Return to the upper town via rue de la Pinterie, a steep climb. More gardens give you a chance to rest, and a final view of the castle and river.

209

After centuries of living with the threat of sea raids or invasion by the kings of France, it is scarcely surprising that Brittany bristles with fortresses, watchtowers and walled towns. Most of them, naturally, stand along the coastline, or on the region's eastern borderlands.

PICK OF THE FORTRESSES

● Walled towns: Vannes, Vitré, Guérande, St.-Malo, Concarneau.
● Military citadels: Port-Louis, Belle-Île.
● Medieval castles: Josselin, Fougères, Dinan, Nantes, Châteaubriant, Hennebont, Pontivy, Kérouzéré, Montfort, Trécesson.
● Coastal fortresses: Fort la Latte, Suscinio, Brest, Fort National (St.-Malo).
● Evocative ruins: Largoët, Hunaudaie, Tonquédec, Ranrouët, Coatfrec, la Groulais (Blain).
● Furnished châteaux: Kerjean, Combourg, Rochers-Sévigné, Rosanbo, Bienassis, Quintin, Kérazan.
● Parks and gardens: Bourbansais, Trémazan, Kergrist, Kerguéhennec, Caradeuc, Rocher-Jagu.

210

Fort la Latte's romantic seacliff setting on the Emerald Coast

Castles through the ages Compared with the stately pleasure domes of the Loire or the doughty strongholds of the Dordogne, Brittany's castles are mostly in a minor league. The Breton nobility were relatively poor, and what resources they had were devoted mainly to spiritual buildings such as churches and parish closes rather than grandiose defensive structures.

Scarcely anything remains of Brittany's earliest fortifications, though a few vestiges of Gallo-Roman hill-camps can be seen here and there. The wooden motte-and-bailey forts of the early Middle Ages have also mostly vanished. Not until castles were constructed of stone did they stand much chance of surviving the test of time, and Brittany's abundant building material, granite, was ideal for the purpose. Islet citadels were built at Port-Louis, St.-Malo and Concarneau, while Vannes, Vitré and Guérande were substantially enclosed by walls. Through the centuries, fortress designs changed as methods of warfare advanced from lengthy sieges to sophisticated artillery attacks. Du Guesclin, hero of the 14th century, fought very different battles from Vauban, Louis XIV's military engineer in the late 17th century.

Gradually, castles began to be built for purely domestic use, with more comfortable interiors, aesthetic facades and decorative flourishes, and landscaped parks or gardens. Wealthy merchants and corsairs formed a new breed of gentry in Brittany, and there was a sudden spate of country manor houses in the 17th and 18th centuries, particularly near St.-Malo and Morlaix. During the 19th century a craze for the medieval past produced a wave of neo-Gothic edifices, sprouting fake battlements and arrowslits at every turret.

Destruction and restoration Many castles and manor houses have succumbed through the ages to military onslaughts, or the slower incursions of time and the elements. Cardinal Richelieu ordered a good many Breton fortresses to be demolished, or at least reduced in size, to dissuade the truculent Duchy from any notions of insurrection. Revolutionaries took great delight in destroying the grand houses of the *ancien régime*, or the hideouts of Chouan Royalists. More recently, World War II added its share of mayhem. Ironically, it was Brittany's allies rather than its enemies who did most of the damage in their attempts to drive out the Nazi occupying forces. The towns of St.-Malo, Brest, Lorient, Hennebont and St.-Nazaire (all fortified in their heyday) were pulverized.

What you see of Brittany's fortifications today is generally a piecemeal reconstruction rather than the original medieval buildings. Some are mere ruined shells, or are still in private ownership and not open to visitors. A few château owners happily accept paying guests into their homes, and these provide a fascinating alternative to conventional hotels.

No longer practical for their original purpose or as converted dwellings, plenty of castles are used as museums, tourist offices, exhibition centres, backdrops for pageants or *son-et-lumière* shows, amusement or wildlife parks and grand hostelries. Many are open to the public and can be visited during the summer. You are free to look around most of them by yourself, although a few insist on guided tours (ask about foreign-language tours). The tourist authorities suggest several touring routes linking major castles, such as the Route des Ducs de Bretagne, the Route du Léon et du Trégor or the Route des Marches. Look out for the leaflets in local tourist offices.

Pepperpot towers adorn the restored castle of Combourg

STAYING IN CHATEAUX
If you want to try a taste of château hospitality, look out for the brochures produced by several like-minded consortia, *Bienvenue au Château, Châteaux et Hôtels de France, Château Accueil*, available in many tourist offices.

A detail from the ramparts of St.-Malo

LES ONZE ÉCLUSES

This famous ladder of locks on the Ille-et-Rance Canal at La Madeleine, near Bazouges-sous-Hédé, attracts many visitors. The Maison du Canal is a visitor centre in an old lock-keeper's cottage dating from Napoleonic times. An exhibition inside uses working models and a video presentation to explain how this ambitious engineering feat was achieved, and shows how the canal has been used since it was opened in 1832 (tel: 02 99 45 48 90; *open* Jul–Aug daily 10.30–12.30, 1.30–6; Apr–Jun, Sep–Oct Wed–Mon 2–6; Nov–Mar Wed, Sun 2–5. *Admission inexpensive*).

▶ La Guerche-de-Bretagne   205E1

Du Guesclin (see pages 34–35) was once the seigneur of this feudal manor, now grown to a small town famed for its cider. A cluster of half-timbered houses with porches can be seen near the church, an unusual building with a triple-sided apse and a stoutly buttressed Romanesque tower. The quaintly carved misericords under the choirstall seats are worth a look.

▶ Hédé   205D2

Woods and water are the lasting impressions of this hill village. Streams, cascades and ponds gleam all around, and lush, terraced gardens almost hide the crumbling stone houses and castle ruins perched on an outcrop of rock. The Romanesque church contains an alabaster statue of the Virgin and a 17th-century wooden altar. In the surrounding grounds modern bronze memorials commemorate heroes of war.

Just north of Hédé, at the tiny village at la Madeleine, the Ille-et-Rance canal passes through a magnificent staircase of 11 **locks▶▶**, with a drop of 27m (90ft).

Tinténiac▶, another pretty canal village to the north, also has an interesting church with lots of curious architectural features. An old wooden grain store by the side of the canal houses the **Musée de l'Outil et des Métiers▶** (tel: 02 99 23 09 30; *open* Jul–Sep 10–12, 3–6. *Closed* Sun am and Mon. *Admission inexpensive*), a collection of craft tools

Trees cloak the buildings in the pretty village of Hédé

and machinery in working order belonging to former blacksmiths, cartwrights, saddlers, cobblers and coopers

▶ Loudéac   204B2

The town itself is of no great interest, merely a web of main roads at the heart of an intensive agricultural region. It holds large markets and is also known for horse-racing. About 10km (6 miles) to the southeast lies **la Chèze**, an attractive village with resort facilities and a museum devoted to country crafts, the **Musée Regional des Métiers▶**, which is housed in an old stone tannery on the banks of the River Lié (tel: 02 96 26 63 16; *open* Jul–Aug Mon–Sat 10–12, 2–6, Sun 3–6; May, Jun, Sep afternoons only. *Admission inexpensive*). The village was a Rohan

The old quarter of Moncontour

stronghold; the remains of its 13th-century castle are still visible. **La Ferrière**, 16km (10 miles) southeast, has a large 14th-century church with fine stained glass and statues.

► Moncontour   204B3

This sudden granite spur between two valleys makes an obvious fortification site. Most of the town walls were destroyed in 1626, though a château was reconstructed in the 19th century on a hill to the north. The historic quarter of hilly alleys and old houses huddles round a fine church, **St.-Mathurin►**, whose splendid windows date from the 16th century.

About 3km (2 miles) southeast of Moncontour, near Trédaniel, stands the **Chapelle Notre-Dame-du-Haut►**, which contains the wooden statues of seven healing saints, typically Breton in style. St. Mamertus cures intestinal disorders; St. Yvertin deals with headaches; St. Léobinus treats eye diseases; Ste. Eugénia helps with labour pains; St. Hubert tackles rabies; St. Méen deals in madness; and St. Houarniaule soothes irrational phobias.

The castle of **la Touche-Trébry**, 6km (3.5 miles) to the east, dates from the late 16th century and was once the home of the governor of Moncontour (*Open* Jul–Aug 2–6, guided tours. *Closed* Sun. *Admission moderate*).

Montfort-sur-Meu   205D2

The unusual purplish-red of the local stone immediately marks Montfort out from its grey neighbours. One of the town's claims to fame is that it is the birthplace of Louis-Marie Grignion (1673–1716), a missionary saint canonized in the 20th century; his birthplace at 15 rue de la Saulnerie is open to the public. Montfort's most imposing building, however, is the 14th-century **Papegaut tower**, the last vestige of its baronial castle. This now houses the small but charming **Ecomusée du Pays de Montfort►** (tel: 02 99 09 31 81; *open* Tue–Fri 9–12, 2–6; Sat 10–12, 2–6; Sun 2–6. *Admission moderate*), whose dolls, *coiffes* and old-fashioned wooden toys are genuinely delightful. Traditional games like skittles can be practised in the courtyard. *Papegaut*, which gives the tower its name, is an archery game (the target is a cockerel on a pole). A film on the legends of Brocéliande is shown in the top room of the tower.

213

LA ROCHE AUX FÉES
Fifteen kilometres (9 miles) west of la Guerche-de-Bretagne lies one of Brittany's largest and most striking megalithic monuments: 42 slabs of purplish schist, each weighing up to 45 tonnes, form what looks like an *allée couverte* (gallery grave), though there is some doubt whether it was ever used as a burial place. You can walk inside easily without crouching. It is a popular meeting place for lovers, and engaged couples traditionally walk around the monument in different directions, counting the stones. If their calculations differ by more than a couple of stones, the marriage is said to be doomed. The site is freely accessible at all times.

Inland Brittany

Lac de Guerlédan, near Quintin

LAC DE GUERLÉDAN

Away from the dam, the lake is most attractive, its glittering surface a constant flurry of boats and windsurfers. To the south stands a last bit of *argoat*, the natural woodland that once covered most of inland Brittany, in the shape of the Forêt de Quénécan, which is an ideal spot for walks and picnics. Focal points for exploration include St.-Aignan, southwest of Mûr-de-Bretagne, which has a lovely old church, and les Forges-des-Salles, a picturesquely fortified hamlet at the far west side of the lake. Beau-Rivage is the most popular leisure spot along the shoreline, while the main watersports base is at le Rond-Point.

Lac de Guerlédan provides ideal conditions for many watersports

▶ Mûr-de-Bretagne   204B2

This popular inland resort attracts visitors for its leisure facilities and surroundings rather than tourist sights. The tourist office's label for the area, *'la Suisse bretonne'* (Breton Switzerland), is absurdly extravagant, but overall this region has more to offer in terms of scenery than most of inland Brittany.

In the village itself there is little to see apart from the oak-shaded chapel of Ste.-Suzanne to the north, once a haunt of the noted landscape painter Camille Corot (1796–1875). Mûr-de-Bretagne stands on the artificial Lac de Guerlédan, a sinuous, multibranched reservoir which stretches 11km (7 miles) from a massive concrete dam across the Blavet, built in the 1920s. This makes the Nantes–Brest canal unnavigable as far as Carhaix-Plouguer by anything larger than a kayak. The advantages of hydroelectric power are more pressing today than British threats to French shipping (the *raison d'être* for the canal in Napoleonic times). Nowadays, pleasure boating has taken the place of heavily laden barges.

Drive

The gorges around Mûr-de-Bretagne

See map on pages 204–205.

A 130km (80 miles) tour of the lonely schist plateau north of Mûr-de-Bretagne, exploring calvary villages and hidden churches in wild countryside. Take a picnic and walking shoes for visiting gorges. Allow most of the day.

From Mûr-de-Bretagne, head west past the lakeshore, turning north via the **Gorges du Daoulas▶**. Much of the woodland that once clothed this valley was damaged by a storm in 1987, and spindly birch is beginning to replace it on the steep slopes. The swift Daoulas River races along the narrow valley floor to join the Blavet.

St.-Nicolas-du-Pélem▶ is a quiet village and an increasingly popular *station verte* (hotel and campsite). The 15th-century church contains a bell which the faithful ring before praying. The church at **Lanrivain▶**, on a large central square, still has fresh flowers on its melodramatic war memorial. The calvary nearby consists of large stone figures (about two-thirds life-size) looking rather like Snow White and the Seven Dwarfs in nightcaps. Through the open slats of the ossuary chapel, paper-thin skulls and wafery femurs glimmer faintly.

West lie the **Gorges de Toul-Goulic▶**, which can be reached via a steep path down through the woods. Here the River Blavet disappears beneath mossy boulders in a deep cleft. **Kergrist-Moëlou▶**, southwest again, has a fine aristocratic 16th-century church containing the crests of the Rostrenen family and a barrel-vaulted ceiling painted with curiously secular figures. The parish close, gloomy with ancient yew trees, contains a two-tier calvary of about 100 carved figures in blue granite. These were badly damaged during the Revolution and replaced haphazardly on an octagonal plinth. A memorial by the post office commemorates lost heroes: '*A la Mémoire des Aviateurs Américains James Stubblefield, William A. Monson…*'.

Farther northwest, on one of the emptiest parts of the plateau, the **Gorges du Corong▶ ▶** make another scenic detour. This is a fairly long walk (half an hour each way), but a spectacular one. A tributary of the Hyère river flows through a rocky chaos of waterfalls in thick woodland.

Head north via **Bulat-Pestivien▶**, where the church has ornate porches and a strange sacristy frieze. Notice the lectern with a peasant in local costume, and the sacred fountains scattered through the village. **Bourbriac▶**, to the north, has yet another worthy church with a pillared crypt and a tower in a mix of Gothic and Renaissance styles. The sarcophagus of St. Briac lies inside. **Avaugour**, eastwards, has more chapels, one with statues of the Apostles, the other (**Notre-Dame-de-Restudo**) with 14th-century frescoes. Head southwards via Plésidy (noting the **Manoir de Toul-an-Gollet▶**) and Corlay, deviating to the *village fleuri* of **St.-Gilles-Vieux-Marché**, which nestles in the Poulancre valley, before returning to Mûr-de-Bretagne.

The main square, Bourbriac

ELUSIVE BROCÉLIANDE
The Forêt de Paimpont is periodically colonized by droves of New Agers claiming Druidic beliefs. They are allegedly responsible for removing many of the signposts directing visitors to the wonders of Paimpont and thus, they claim, preserving some of its mystery. After much fruitless searching for sacred fountains and places of enchantment, modern visitors may well sympathize with Robert Wace, author of *The Romance of the Rose*, who wrote in about 1160: 'I went thither on purpose to see these marvels…but I found none. I went like a fool, and so I came back…and found myself a fool for my pains.'

▶▶ **Paimpont, Forêt de**   *204C2*

This 7,000ha (17,500-acre) forest is a pale echo of the woodlands that once covered this part of Brittany, and much has been commercially replanted since any Arthurian knights could have roamed here. But the Brocéliande of legend recounted by the troubadour poet Chrétien de Troyes still exerts a whimsical tug on the imagination. Every year thousands of visitors arrive not simply to explore the forest's prosaic hiking trails and picnic sites, but in vague, half-serious hopes of experiencing a touch of Merlin's magic, or perhaps of gaining a fleeting glimpse of the Holy Grail itself.

The village of Paimpont stands at the heart of the forest, and acts as its main resort. It dates only from the Revolution, and is an unusual place with an enclosed main town of purplish-grey terraced stone houses. Nearby is a large lake with pedalos and passing waterfowl. The 11th-century abbey church (belonging to a monastery that once stood beside the lake) has within its plain interior a silver reliquary of St. Judicaël and an ivory crucifix (carefully locked away, but you may ask to see them). A surprisingly jolly Virgin relaxes near the altar.

The tourist office by the church (*open* summer only) provides maps and guides through the forest. If you propose to track down any Arthurian secrets, detailed instructions are essential. Otherwise, simply enjoy the pleasant woodland walks through bracken, wild flowers and pools.

None of the forest sights is spectacular, and most of them are more fun for their legends than in themselves. The **Fontaine de Barenton▶**, where a spring bubbles up, is where Merlin fell prey to the beautiful enchantress Viviane and was imprisoned in a circle of air. It is said that if water is sprinkled on the slab next to the fountain (known as the Perron de Merlin, or Merlin's Stone), a great storm will come and a mysterious horseman in black armour will appear. This magic has apparently been invoked to end droughts in recent times.

Another popular destination is the **Val sans Retour (Valley of No Return)**, where a steep path leads to the **Rocher des Faux Amants (Rock of False Lovers)**, a trap set by the evil sorceress Morgan le Fay to ensnare men who have betrayed their lovers. Only Lancelot, ever faithful to his Queen Guinevere, managed to break the spell.

There are two castles in the forest. The **Château de Comper▶** is a mostly 19th-century structure housing the **Centre de l'Imaginaire Arthurien** (tel: 02 97 22 79 96; *open* Jul–Sep Thu–Tue 10–7; Apr–Oct Thu–Mon pm; *closed* Tue and Wed. *Admission moderate*), presenting lectures and film shows about the Arthurian legends. The **Château de Trécesson▶** is more satisfactorily medieval, in red schist with a turreted gatehouse (though not open to the public).

A sacred site in the Paimpont forest: Merlin's Stone

The church at **Tréhorenteuc**▶ combines Christianity with King Arthur, and contains a stained-glass window and frescoes depicting the Holy Grail and the Knights of the Round Table. An entrance fee is charged.

Quintin
204B3

The terraced houses of this attractive old town stand above the Gouët river. Quintin was once famed for its fine linen, used for Breton *coiffes*, collars and veils, and before the Revolution was entirely dependent on weaving.

Amid Quintin's attractive 16th- and 17th-century half-

timbered old quarter stands the town's main building of interest, its basilica. This contains a holy relic of the Virgin's belt, allegedly brought back from Jerusalem in the 13th century. Other notable features inside are the statue of Our Lady of Safe Delivery (revered by mothers-to-be), and the holy water stoups made of giant shells. Below the east end of the church is the Porte-Neuve, the last part of the ramparts that once encircled the town. The **château** in the middle of town dates from the 17th and 18th centuries and houses a museum of local history, displaying linen, porcelain, and fans. The cellars and kitchens of

the castle can also be visited (tel: 02 96 74 94 79; *open* mid-Jun to mid-Sep daily 10.30–12.30, 1.30–6.30; Easter–May daily 12–5; weekends only winter. *Admission moderate*).

THE HOLY GRAIL
This was the legendary cup from which Christ drank at the Last Supper. After the Crucifixion, his disciple, Joseph of Arimathea, collected a few drops of Christ's blood in the Grail and carried it away from Palestine, landing first in Britain and then in Brittany, where he settled in the Forest of Brocéliande before vanishing mysteriously. On hearing of the Grail, King Arthur and 50 of his truest knights set out to find it. Only the purest in heart would be successful, the prize going to Sir Percival.

217

MERLIN AND VIVIANE
Merlin the sorceror came to the Forest of Brocéliande from King Arthur's court. There he met the beautiful enchantress Viviane, who cast a spell on him that Merlin himself had taught her. He fell in love with her and to this day remains in her thrall, willingly caged in a magic circle of air.

Quintin (left)
The Robien Château
(below), near Quintin

Inland Brittany

205D2

CLOUDED MEMORIES
The Panthéon, a large room in Rennes' town hall, salutes the memory of those Rennais who fell in World War I, and the ceiling is studded with the names of the military heroes of that conflict. One name, however, is obliterated by a strip of paper. Maréchal Pétain, the traitor of Vichy, is despised in Brittany for his collaboration with the Germans.

▶▶▶ Rennes

Many regular visitors to Brittany ignore its capital. Rennes stands some distance from the sea, in a swathe of low-lying countryside where the Rance and the Vilaine converge. Apart from a few appealing stretches of the Vilaine valley and some patches of deciduous woodland northeast of the city, the surrounding scenery can best be described as uninspiring. However, if you are touring the Breton marches (the old borderlands between France and Brittany), and in particular the magnificent castles of Fougères and Vitré, give Rennes a day of your time.

Inside its modern industrial carapace, the old centre has a lively charm and several genuinely worthwhile museums that place Brittany's historic and cultural significance admirably in context. Driving and parking within

Dramatic half-timbering in Rennes

the city centre can be a nuisance, but good transport links with other towns in Brittany make it quite feasible to visit Rennes on a day excursion from another base (there are direct bus and train services to St.-Malo, Vitré, Fougères, Dinan and Nantes).

History The Romans developed the town from a Gaulish settlement, and it became a strategic hub of important military highways. During the Middle Ages, Rennes shared parliamentary power with Nantes and Vannes, but it became the undisputed Breton capital during the time of the Duchess Anne. It was at Rennes that the duchess first met Charles VIII, with whom she made her momentously tactical match (see pages 36–37). From then on Rennes was to play a significant role in Brittany's political upheavals, including the uprisings against the monstrous taxation imposed during Louis XIV's reign, the Revolutionary Terror, and the German Occupation.

Walk

The old town of Rennes

See map opposite.

The Breton capital's stripy old houses and grand civic architecture make a pleasant half-day tour, although you could easily spend longer shopping and sightseeing. There is a vast free parking area at Esplanade du Général de Gaulle, south of the river, or you may be lucky in Place des Lices, a shorter walk from the old town.

The imposing Hôtel de Ville on Place de la Mairie is a good starting point, one of Jacques Gabriel's most confident municipal statements after the great fire of 1720. The huge clock tower known as 'Le Gros' connects two curving side-wings. Officials will show you round for no charge. Opposite stands the theatre; to the south is the massively ponderous Palais du Commerce.

Thread westwards now through a maze of old streets lined with picturesque houses around two churches. **St.-Sauveur▶** is built in rococo style. Inside, Our Lady of Miracles is depicted as a pretty woman in a red and gold robe. She saved Rennes from the English in 1357 and is still well patronized. **St.-Pierre▶**, Rennes' cathedral, forms a graceless, lumpish 19th-century building with a colonnaded apse of red marble. The rich, sombre interior

The peaceful Jardin du Thabor

contains one splendid work of art—a 16th-century Flemish altarpiece of gilded wood behind glass in a side-chapel by the south transept. Find the light switch to enjoy its amazing three-dimensional effects.

On the edge of the old town, the **Porte Mordelaise** is the last remnant of the 15th-century ramparts. It was through this entrance to the city that the Dukes of Brittany passed for their coronations. Close by is the **Place des Lices▶**, where jousts were once held. Two art nouveau *halles* (market buildings) now dominate the square, continuing a market tradition that first began in 1622. East of here lies another cluster of half-timbered buildings which survived the fire; the most eye-catching group stands in Place du Champ-Jacquet, a mass of tall, stripy facades dating from the 17th century.

The **Palais du Parlement▶▶** is the former seat of the Breton Parliament, and also predates the fire (1618–1655). Somewhat ironically, it was severely damaged by fire in 1994, and for a while it was feared that the intricate timber-framed roof and beautiful coffered ceilings were too badly damaged to be repaired. After restoration the building is open again, and guided tours in various languages can be arranged through the tourist office (tel: 02 99 67 11 66. *Admission moderate*).

A stroll in the **Jardin du Thabor** makes a pleasant change of pace. These large, varied gardens once formed the grounds of a Benedictine abbey (the church of **Notre-Dame-en-St.-Mélaine** still stands). Finish the walk on the south bank of the river.

*House detail (above)
Some of Rennes' restau-
rants (right) have
antique settings*

220

STEPPING BACK IN TIME
Some way out of town
(follow rue Maréchal-Joffre
8km/5 miles southwards)
is the Écomusée du Pays
de Rennes at Bintinais
farm, which traces the
evolution of agricultural
life in Brittany. There is an
educational trail, and rare
breeds of farm animals
are kept on the premises
(*Open* Tue–Fri 9–12, 2–6,
Sat 2–6, Sun 2–7.
Admission moderate).

HERO OR TRAITOR?
Breton feelings towards
Bertrand Du Guesclin
(see pages 34–35) are
mixed. While he takes
pride of place on
horseback in Dinan's main
square (the scene of his
heroic duel with Sir
Thomas of Canterbury),
his statue in Rennes was
blown up by Breton nationalists in 1946. Some
extreme separatists have
never forgiven him for
taking the French side
against the Breton Duke
Jean IV during the War
of Succession.

Cosmopolitan culture Rennes' population has doubled
since World War II to over 270,000, which makes it the
second largest city in Brittany after its old rival Nantes
(which now belongs technically to the region of Loire-
Atlantique). It is mainly preoccupied with administrative,
commercial and industrial concerns. The Citroën headquarters lie just outside the city, and many of Rennes'
more transient occupants are students attending its two
universities or its prestigious medical school. Economic
mainstays include electronics and telecommunications,
the construction industry, and the manufacture of trans-
portation equipment.

Compared with other Breton towns Rennes feels
atypically urban, even cosmopolitan, and more French
than most. Breton culture, however, is well and truly alive
here, from the destructive antics of political separatists to
the more creative aspects of its great July arts festival, Les
Tombées de la Nuit. Encouraged by its young student
population, French rock and jazz musicians congregate
in the city.

Museums Rennes has two major museums. The **Musée des Beaux-Arts**, housed in a grand neoclassical building along the embankment south of the river, contains one of Brittany's most important collections of paintings, ranging

from 14th-century primitives to Impressionists and members of the Pont Aven School. Works to look out for include an *Étude de Draperie* (*Drapery Study*) by Leonardo da Vinci, Rubens' weltering wildlife scene *La Chasse au Tigre* (*The Tiger Hunt*), Georges de la Tour's *Le Nouveau-Né* (*The Newborn*), and Gauguin's *Nature Morte aux Oranges* (*Still Life with Oranges*). An emotional 19th-century canvas by Luminais depicts the legend of Ys, with Dahut slipping into the waves from King Gradlon's galloping horse. Twentieth-century artists such as Picasso and Tanguy are also represented, along with many minor Breton painters (tel: 02 99 28 55 85; www.mbar.org; *open* Tue–Sun 10–12, 2–6. *Admission moderate*).

The **Musée de Bretagne**'s permanent collections, on Breton history and culture, are being relocated to brand

THE GREAT FIRE
One event that changed the face of Rennes for ever was a disastrous fire in 1720, apparently started accidentally by a drunken carpenter. The fire raged for almost a week, and nearly 1,000 houses were destroyed, though luckily very few lives were lost. Eventually a rainstorm extinguished the flames. Rennes' inflammable timbers were subsequently replaced with the dignified, spacious stone buildings that can currently be seen.

More elaborate facades in Rennes (left)

new premises on the Cours des Alliés, not far from the railway station, in 2006 (www.musee-bretagen.fr). This streamlined complex also includes the **Espace des Sciences**, a high-tech interactive science museum (www.espace-sciences.org), which includes a planetarium and displays on the geology of Brittany. Temporary exhibitions and many varied events will take place at these venues.

The Musée de sBeaux-Arts holds some of Brittany's most famous works of art

Brittany has changed dramatically since World War II. The land of coiffes *and* lits clos *has been supplanted by a progressive, forward-looking society that is eager to cast aside its peasant lifestyle. Ironically, tourism, a prime source of revenue for the region, encourages a new remembrance of things past.*

222

Collectable items Brittany is still economically deprived compared with some parts of France, and those who make their living directly from the land or the sea, as generations have done before them, know that times can be hard. But the laboriousness of everyday life and the humiliating anguish of poverty that Pierre-Jakez Hélias described in his autobiography, *The Horse of Pride*, have largely disappeared. With them went many of the symbols of earlier times such as the furniture and costumes, craft tools and kitchen utensils. Most young Breton couples setting up home in Brittany nowadays would probably find a washing machine more useful than a carved oak linen press. To the Bretons' surprise, however, affluent Parisians are flocking to snap up their box beds and old dressers. Breton furniture is highly collectable, sometimes fulfilling new functions as hi-fi units, drinks cabinets or bookshelves.

Tourists, too, seem eternally fascinated by these vanishing bygones. Today Brittany bursts with folk museums, all anxious to reveal the wholesome qualities of traditional rustic life. The most successful of these *écomusées* give a good sense of the cultural past and are informative about local lifestyles (see panel opposite for a selection of some of the best museums).

Furniture The solid, dark-wood furnishings of traditional Breton homes often show a high level of craftsmanship, but above all they are intensely practical. Everything had a specific purpose, and was designed to fit into as compact a space as possible. The constraints of a small cottage, usually housing a large family, meant that its contents had to be skilfully stowed away. Indeed, the reconstructions of Breton interiors you see in the museums are often reminiscent of a ship's galley.

Stock items were usually built to a set

LITS CLOS
'Ah, those *lits clos*, what a good buy! I have found some that have been converted into a coat-cupboard in the hall, a library in the study, a buffet or drinks cupboard in the living-room, a music-box combining pick-up, radio, and television. I have even seen one that functions as a toilet, to the great satisfaction of its users.'
—Pierre-Jakez Hélias, *The Horse of Pride*

A particularly elegant and refined example of a double-decker box bed at the Ecomusée du Pays de Rennes pattern and turned out in great numbers. Decorations were ornate, though repetitive: circular medallions, religious motifs, flower garlands and geometrical patterns are commonly seen, sometimes interspersed with copper studs.

The most characteristic item found in all respectable households was the box bed (*lit clos*), like a cupboard with a sliding door or curtain. Some were double-decker affairs with bunks for children and a bar where a cradle could be hung and rocked. In poorer homes the bedding would be a layer of broom, the quilts stuffed with oats. A bench chest (*banc-coffre*) or blanket box was often used as a step to climb into the bed. The table (*table-huche*) was another essential piece of family equipment, often constructed with sliding panels so that it would take up less space when not in use. A circular contraption to hold spoons or cutlery could be moved up and down, Heath Robinson-fashion, over the table at mealtimes. Marriage chests (to hold trousseaux), dressers, linen presses, grain chests, wardrobes and long-case clocks were other customary items in richer homes. Comfortable chairs were reserved for heads of households.

Domestic architecture Many Breton towns display a remarkable number of beautiful half-timbered old houses, often jettied or partly slate-hung. Houses that are not timber-framed are still nearly always built of granite, though this may be disguised by whitewash. Dormer windows and turreted gables are common features, and many buildings are decorated with quirky carvings of

PICK OF THE FOLK MUSEUMS
● Moulins de Kérouat, Sizun.
● Ecomusée de Niou Uhella, Ouessant.
● Ecomusée du Pays de Rennes, La Bintinais.
● Musée Départemental Breton, Quimper.
● Musée Bigouden, Pont-l'Abbé.
● Château de Kerjean.
● Maison Cornec, St.-Rivoal (Monts d'Arrée).
● Musée du Pays de Lamballe.
● Musée du Patrimoine, Plougastel-Daoulas.
● Musée de la Vilaine Maritime, la Roche-Bernard.
● Musée de la Cohue, Vannes.
● Ecomusée du Pays de Montfort, Montfort-sur-Meu.

223

animals or human figures. Frequently, an exterior stairway leads to a loft or roof.

Houses in the north and west tend to be lower, often only one floor, with small windows and doors carefully placed to reduce the effects of rain and wind. In dryer Morbihan or Loire-Atlantique, thatch was once a common roofing material, especially around the marshlands of the Grande Brière.

Breton interior reconstructed in the Ecomusée du Pays de Rennes

VITRÉ MUSEUMS
Several museums can be visited in and around Vitré on a combined ticket. Most worthwhile are the museums in the castle: sculpture and plans of the château in the Tour St.-Laurent, and a weird assortment of pickled reptiles, insects and frogs in grotesquely anthropomorphic poses (playing billiards, fencing, on crutches) in the Tour de l'Argenterie; see also the Limoges enamelled triptych in the chapel of the Tour de l'Oratoire (tel: 02 99 75 04 54; *open* Jul–Sep daily 10–6; low season *closed* Tue. *Admission moderate*). About 7km (4 miles) southeast lies the Château des Rochers-Sévigné, a fine Gothic manor with witch-hat turrets, once the home of Madame de Sévigné. The grounds, designed by Le Nôtre of Versailles fame, feature lawns etched with scroll patterns (*Open* same hours and ticket as Château de Vitré).

▶▶▶ Vitré   205E2

The best view of old Vitré can be had from the northeast, as you approach from the Fougères direction. Closer to the town, a hilly belvedere by the banks of the Vilaine known as **Tertres Noirs▶▶** gives a splendid silhouette of bristling turrets, drum towers and ramparts. Within the walls, the town seems just as carefully preserved as distant glimpses promise, and half-timbered, slate-hung houses lurch in all directions on hilly, cobbled streets.

Needless to say, Vitré's prettiness attracts many sightseers, and much of the old town's commercial activity now caters expressly for visitors. In former years Vitré's prosperity sprang from the textile trade (hemp, sailcloth, wool and cotton stockings), and today it still makes clothes and remains a market centre. Varied agricultural and industrial enterprises are based in the modern sector to the south of the railway line. The station is convenient to the historic town, should you visit by train.

The memorable parts of Vitré perch on a promontory overlooking the Vilaine, guarded by a massive triangular fortress at the western tip. The town's strategic position on the frontier between France and Brittany made it a constant target during the struggles of the Middle Ages. During the Hundred Years War, English forces camped for several years in the sector to the northwest until the siege-weary inhabitants paid them a ransom to go away. The present suburb is called **Faubourg du Rachapt▶**, meaning 'repurchased'. Its renovated stone cottages, which were once considered slums, now form an attractive part of the town.

Vitré backed the right horse (the king of France) in the years before the Union, and its prosperity grew rapidly. Many rich merchants settled in the town, and it is their fine mansions that give Vitré its classy architectural stamp. During the 15th and 16th centuries the town became a Huguenot (Protestant) stronghold, and it was besieged by Catholics during the Wars of Religion. Some gratitude for these leanings is perhaps expressed in Henri IV's famous compliment to the town: 'Were I not King of France, I would be a citizen of Vitré'.

A brick and slate corner turret on a house in old Vitré

Above: restored houses along rue Beaudrairie

Walk

The old town of Vitré

See map opposite.

Start at the **castle▶▶**, Vitré's unmissable attraction. The gatehouse entrance admits you to a triangular courtyard surrounded by towers and curtain walls. Two of the towers contain small museums (see panel opposite), while in the heart of the courtyard stands an incongruous town hall built in 1913.

The **rue Beaudrairie▶▶** (which takes its name from the leather-workers who once plied their trade here) contains the greatest concentration of old houses, now tastefully restored. The church of **Notre-Dame▶** dates from the 15th and 16th centuries. It has a daisy-pierced spire and a fine interior, but its most interesting feature is a pulpit on an outer wall from which a Catholic priest harangued the unfortunate Huguenot Coligny family who lived opposite.

If you walk through the Poterne St.-Pierre near the church you can follow a well-preserved section of the ramparts (those on the southern side have mostly disappeared) as far as the

Tour de la Bridolle▶ on Place de la République. Rue Sévigné, rue Poterie, and rue d'Embas all contain quaint old houses. Notice No. 9 rue Sévigné, where Madame de Sévigné once lived, and the turreted Hôtel de la Botte Dorée at 10 rue d'Embas. Beyond the city walls, the church of **St.-Martin** is also worth a glance; inside is a forest of candelabra and Romanesque arches.

Château de Vitré

Loire-Atlantique

A peaceful stretch of the Nantes–Brest canal

LOIRE-ATLANTIQUE An administrative reshuffle in 1973 severed this southeasterly *département* from Brittany and attached it to the neighbouring region, Pays de la Loire. In doing so it snatched away one of Brittany's biggest and most fashionable seaside resorts, la Baule, and its historic capital of Nantes. But Bretons pay little heed to Parisian bureaucrats. For them the logical boundary of Brittany is still the stately River Loire, which flows past Nantes and St.-Nazaire on its final reach to the sea, forming a climatic and cultural watershed. North of it are the grey slate roofs and granite churches of the Breton landscape; southwards lie the red clay tiles and soft tufa stone of warmer climes, where apple orchards and vegetable plots give way to vineyards and fields of sunflowers, and the language and local ways are unmistakably French.

WATERY PLEASURES Most of the area's attractions lie on or near the coast. Beach-lovers have plenty of choice; the vast stretch of sand at la Baule is outstanding in any

Loire-Atlantique

The seafront at La Baule

La Baule's attractive holiday villas lie behind the seafront road

terms, but if small, quiet resorts are more your style you may prefer to head for the Croisic peninsula, or perhaps St.-Marc, that archetypal little place near St.-Nazaire where Jacques Tati's classic 1950's film comedy *Monsieur Hulot's Holiday* was set. If you are looking for completely unspoiled seclusion, make for the sands around Pénestin. The Plage de la Mine d'Or is one of the best of these undeveloped beaches.

Inland, Loire-Atlantique is most interestingly explored by boat: a pleasure cruiser up the Erdre from Nantes, a canal boat around the maze of waterways at Redon, or the traditional *chaland* (flat-bottomed punt) used in the Grande Brière. Unfortunately, the River Loire itself is drearily industrialized for most of its length between St.-Nazaire and Nantes; for better views of it, head upstream towards the town of Ancenis.

UNUSUAL LIFESTYLES Coastal Loire-Atlantique is a typical Breton flatland, which the sea and the Loire have periodically smothered in thick strata of silt and sand. Alluvial deposits and huge beaches trapped the marshlands behind, where the water-covered vegetation decomposed to form another layer of peat. The Grande Brière is perhaps the most spectacular of these ancient bogs, and the regional park of which it forms part is one of the largest wildlife reserves in France. Now drained and tamed with canals, it is still largely inaccessible except by boat. The traditional lifestyle of the people living in the Grande Brière revolved around cutting peat, eel-trapping, gathering reeds for thatch and hunting the marshland ducks. However, many Brièrons now head for the dockyards of St.-Nazaire for their livelihoods, and tourism plays an increasing part in their insular existence.

The salt marshes around Guérande form one of Loire-Atlantique's strangest physical features. Aerial photographs show them as an exquisite mosaic of differently sized lagoons and rectangular pits fringed with white, crystalline heaps. Salt extraction by evaporating sea water is another ancient mainstay, practised since Roman times. Today the industry is less important than it was when Brittany revelled in exemption from the hated *gabelle*, or salt tax, imposed on the rest of France. Looming over the salt marshes are the tall belfry of Batz-sur-Mer and the intact stone ramparts of medieval Guérande.

THE ANCESTRAL HEART Loire-Atlantique has no mean share of fortresses. Châteaubriant guards the marches, another link in the chain of border castles fending off incursions from the east. Grand-Fougeray, just over the *département* border in Ille-et-Vilaine, retains only its keep. Vivid legends haunt both these castles, imbuing them with more charisma than the ruined stones alone. Meanwhile, Ancenis and Nantes mount watch over the Loire, Brittany's natural southern moat.

If you are touring Loire-Atlantique, one place that certainly shouldn't be ignored is Nantes. Brave its discouraging suburbs and make for the old quarter by the castle and cathedral. Modern Nantes may look south and east for its new-found role as capital of Pays de la Loire, but its ancestral spirit is as Breton as the great Duchess Anne, who was born here, married here for the second time to a reigning French king, and whose heart (at least until the chaotic upheavals of the Revolution) rested here in a golden casket (see panel).

THE HEART OF BRITTANY
When Anne died, her funeral ceremony was hugely elaborate. She was buried in the traditional last resting-place of all French monarchs, St.-Denis, near Paris, but her heart was placed in a golden casket in Nantes cathedral. Courtiers present as it was removed from her body marvelled at its exceptional size, and the casket is inscribed: '*En ce petit vaisseau de fin or, pur et munde, Repose ung plus grant cueur que oncque dame eut au munde*' ('In this small vessel of pure gold rests the greatest heart any lady ever had in the world'). During the Revolution the heart (or its ashes) vanished, but the casket can still be seen in Nantes' Palais Dobrée (see page 240).

The Château des Ducs de Bretagne in Nantes

DU GUESCLIN'S AXEMEN
Little remains of the castle at Grand-Fougeray, now a small market town but once a strategic frontier fortress. During the Hundred Years War, the Breton warrior Bertrand Du Guesclin captured Fougeray by disguising himself and a band of 30 of his best soldiers as woodcutters. Once inside the castle defences, they dropped their log bundles and drew arms. The entire English garrison was slaughtered.

A windmill on the salt marshes at Batz-sur-Mer

THE BURNING BUSH
Behind Batz-sur-Mer's church are the ruins of another: Notre-Dame-du-Mûrier. The story goes that Jean de Rieux, lord of Ranrouët castle in the 15th century, was sailing home in bad weather, fearing shipwreck at every moment. He prayed for heavenly guidance and saw a strange flickering light above one of Batz's safe beaches, then when he reached the shore he found a mulberry bush (*mûrier*) had mysteriously burst into flames. He built the Gothic chapel in gratitude for this miracle. The granite gable shows a fine example of a turreted staircase.

Thalassotherapy centre, La Baule

▶▶ Batz-sur-Mer 226A1

At first sight the only thing that marks out the small town of Batz is the striking spire of **St.-Guénolé**▶, which towers 60m (200ft) above the low-lying salt marshes of the Guérande peninsula. Inside, the church is memorably charming, from the large-handed madonna at the door to the off-centre chancel draped with fishing nets. Carved bosses catch the eye, one decorated with the torments of the damned. Also in the village is the **Musée des Marais Salants (Salt-Marsh Museum)**▶▶ (tel: 02 40 23 82 79; *open* Jun–Sep daily 10–12, 2–5; weekends only in winter. *Admission moderate*), a museum dedicated to the local salt-working trade (see panel, pages 234–235).

Batz has several good sandy beaches which are quiet enough to contrast pleasantly with the massive jet-set resort of la Baule to the east. A cliff-path from St.-Michel beach has good views of the rocky coastline. Balzac stayed in Batz and set his novel *Béatrix* here.

▶▶ La Baule 226A1

This huge, purpose-built resort is the largest and most glamorous in Brittany, the nearest it gets to the Côte d'Azur. Less than three hours from Paris by high-speed train, it makes a popular weekend playground for affluent city-dwellers in search of a breath of sea air. Bronzed jetsetters flock here for its excellent facilities and a magnificent beach; 'the most beautiful in Europe', according to the tourist authorities. Stretching for 7km (4 miles), the crescent of golden sand shelves so gently that you can walk out about 100m (328ft) and still be well within your depth. Behind it, modern hotels and apartment blocks line the seafront road with all the charm of a shelf of detergent packets. Here and there, however, the soulless rectangles are leavened by more imaginative architecture. Look for a spirited wedding-cake villa encrusted with mermaids, pink roses and plaster urns.

The history of the resort dates back a mere 100 years. Before that, the seafront was entirely undeveloped apart from an old fishing village called Escoublac. Over the centuries several great storms engulfed it in Loire silt and shifting sand, until in 1840 belts of pine trees were planted to help stabilize the dunes and protect the coast from gales, and a more temperate microclimate developed. Escoublac was relocated inland, and in 1879 the seaside pleasure palaces began to appear.

The west end of the resort is the older and more digni-fied section, with several massive Belle Epoque hotels and a casino. Behind the seafront wall of modern buildings lies a belt of elegant Edwardian chalet villas in shady gar-dens. Eastwards stretches the 1930s development of la Baule-les-Pins, a genteel residential district. The hilly Parc des Dryades offers a peaceful haven, its cheerful flower-picture beds interspersed with more naturalistic land-scaping. Here you can pay homage to la Baule's founder, Louis Lajarrige, commemorated in statue form.

What to do Thalassotherapy centres, marinas and every conceivable leisure or seaside activity are available at la Baule. A constant round of events and entertainments is

OXBLOOD FURNITURE
Traditionally *paludier* (salt-maker's) furniture is painted a rich dark red, reflecting the odd colour the salt pans assume at a certain critical salinity just before the salt crystallizes. Typical examples can be seen in the local museums at Batz-sur-Mer, Guérande and Saillé.

Smart pleasure craft line the marina at la Baule

231

held throughout the season: tennis, golf, horse-riding, bridge, sailing, windsurfing, plus 'Breton Weeks' (festi-vals celebrating all things Breton), reminding visitors to these anonymous and artificial surroundings where they are. The main shopping and restaurant area lies behind the beach on avenue du Général de Gaulle, and here too is the main tourist office, on Place de la Victoire. Campsites are mostly inland. The older resorts of **Pornichet** and **le Pouliguen**, at either end of La Baule's long promenade, have a more traditional, less flashy atmosphere.

In summer fast hydrojet boats ply to Belle-Île (see pages 180–181) and other Morbihan islands from Pornichet. Le Pouliguen's *port de plaisance* (pleasure-boat harbour) lies in a sheltered channel which links the ocean with the salt marshes around Saillé. Its buildings date from a more gra-cious age, and even the Garage de la Plage presents a stylish facade of swirling curlicues.

PEAT-CUTTING

The ancient turbary, or peat-cutting rights, of the Brièrons represented a significant part of their income at one time. The writer Alphonse de Châteaubriant vividly describes in his classic novel *La Brière* (1923) how the local people set to work on the precious few days of the year when they were permitted to extract turf: 'They hurled themselves on the treasure. Bearded men with darting eyes, women with calloused ankles—in teams, in families, in clans, they settled to their 4.5sq m (50sq ft) and turned over the soil, dug it, rummaged in it, carried off the strips of sward.'

232

▶▶ Brière, Parc Naturel Régional de   *226B2*

Created in 1970 and covering about 40,000ha (100,000 acres), this marshland park (one of more than 40 regional nature parks in France) enjoys similar status to the Armorique Nature Park (see pages 117–119) in Finistère. About a sixth of it is known as the Grande Brière, and before the last Ice Age this low-lying basin was thickly wooded. When the sea level rose it flooded and all the vegetation died, forming a layer of peat. Gradually the sea retreated, however, and the marshes were drained.

Duke François II, father of the Duchess Anne, granted the 21 communes of the Brière joint ownership of the marshlands in 1461. The Brièrons developed their own way of life, guarding these ancient rights, and their traditional economy was based on hunting and fishing. They used the local reeds for thatching their cottages and weaving wicker fish traps, and found their way through the waterlogged terrain on flat-bottomed punts. A vital source of revenue came from peat, which they were allowed to cut for just nine days each year (see panel).

Inevitably, the 20th century brought great changes to the marshlands as the coastline developed, new roads were built and tourism consequently increased. Many Brièrons forsook the marshes for city life and higher pay in the shipyards or factories of St.-Nazaire.

Following the creation of the park, the future of the marshes has been assured. Steadily the secretive, inaccessible Brière is opening up to leisure pursuits such as fishing, riding and boating. Campsites, *gîtes* and hotels

Reeds are still used for thatching in the Brière Regional Nature Park

MOCK ORANGE
The making of bridal flower ornaments from wax became an important cottage industry for the women of the Brière during the 19th and early 20th centuries, and the products were exported worldwide. The hub of the industry was St.-Joachim. The Maison de la Mariée in Fédrun shows how elaborate these wedding accoutrements were, and how carefully they were preserved in glass globes (*Open* mid-Jun to Sep daily 10.30–1, 2.30–6.40. *Admission moderate;* guided tours).

233

discreetly emerge around the edges of the marshes, little museums spring up in old cottages, and in season every back garden *curée* (canal) seems to have a *blin* or *chaland* (barge) moored, ready to ferry passengers.

Exploring Embarkation points are easy to find (for example, Bréca or les Fossés-Blancs). You can explore on your own, although it's easy to get lost or stuck in the reeds, so take a short guided tour. If you prefer to explore on foot, the GR3 footpath crosses the eastern marshes (known as les Marais-des-Donges).

A circuit of the roads by car takes about a day. Call at **Kerhinet►**, a tidily restored hamlet of reedthatch. One cottage has been converted into a little *écomusée* called the Musée du Chaume (tel: 02 40 66 85 01; *open* Jul to mid-Sep daily 10–1, 2.30–6.30; Apr–Jun 2–6. *Admission moderate*). Another sells crafts and regional foods. The **Brasserie de la Bière** invites you to sample some local beers. **St.-Lyphard►** church spire offers a panoramic view over the marshes, and **la Chapelle-des-Marais** has the park's main information office. The town hall contains a fine example of a *morta*, or fossilized tree trunk.

Île de Fédrun►►, a granite village set in the marshes, is connected to the main road by two bridges. Several of its cottages have become museums, including the **Maison de la Mariée (Bride's House)►**, displaying a collection of wax bridal flowers (see panel). Farther south, at **Rozé►** is the **Maison de l'Éclusier (Lock-keeper's House)►**, a tiny museum of marsh animals and local history (*Open* Easter, Jun–Sep daily 10.30–1, 2.30–6.30. *Admission moderate*). The **Réserve Ornithologique Pierre-Constant** has hides and information panels to help visitors identify species (*Open* Jun–Sep, Oct daily 9–6; Jul–Aug 9–7. *Admission moderate*).

Visitors explore the Brière in traditional manner

Brittany, the land by the sea, reaps a rich harvest from its maritime location. The fruits de mer are not always shelled or finned, but also include less obvious products such as salt and seaweed.

MORE INFORMATION

To find out more about seaweed, visit Brest's magnificent Océanopolis. Roscoff, home of the first thalassotherapy centre, has an exhibition on seaweed, called Thalado. You can also look round Algoplus, where seaweed is processed for use in foodstuffs and cosmetics. For more on salt extraction, visit the museums at Batz-sur-Mer, Saillé and Guérande.

Seaweed gathering When the tide retreats on many Breton beaches, especially after storms, vast piles of seaweed are left behind. Tractors and trailers converge to scoop it away, but the clearing-up exercise is not carried out merely to remove the smelly substance from the tourist's gaze. Seaweed (*goëmon* in Breton) is a valuable commodity in Brittany. For centuries it has been collected and dried to use as fertilizer, particularly in Finistère and on the western islands. The rich, vegetable-growing soils of the Ceinture d'Orée (Golden Belt) near St.-Pol-de-Léon owe their productivity largely to seaweed. Specially equipped boats sail out towards Ouessant to collect the tangles of drifting weed on a rotating screw-like device called a *scoubidou*. Certain species are even farmed, thereby removing the locals' dependence on the tide and its rather haphazard seaweed retrieval.

Most of the seaweeds washed up on Brittany's beaches belong to the *Fucus* family, and are usually brownish with air-sacs or vesicles that enable them to float, sometimes over huge distances. However, if you peer into rockpools and explore the foreshore carefully you will find many kinds of all shapes, sizes and colours. Hundreds of species occur on the Breton coast and about 90 per cent of France's total production comes from the region. When washed and dried they are decorative enough to frame, and seaweed pictures are a local art form.

Today seaweed is known to contain a huge range of hormones, vitamins, trace elements and proteins, and its range of uses has expanded rapidly as a whole new field of scientific research has opened up; for example, soda and alginates are extracted for use in foodstuffs, cosmetics and pharmaceutical products.

Thalassotherapy treatment centres have sprung up all over Brittany in recent years, specializing in sea-water cures. Many health and beauty treatments are based on seaweed extracts, and you can have the seaweed plastered over you, eat it or bathe in it. How effective these 'cures' are is much debated, but medical research is certainly taking seaweed seriously now, and top chefs are using it in new styles of cooking. Its potential as a source of protein for malnourished people in poorer parts of the world is colossal.

Salt extraction Brittany's salt industry stems back to Roman times. Salt was a precious commodity needed for preserving food, and by the 13th century it had become much prized. A high tax was levied on it, known as the *gabelle*, but for many ears Brittany was exempt. *Marais salants*, or salt marshes, re found in several parts of Brittany, especially around the ay of Mont-St.-Michel, on the Golfe du Morbihan and near a Baule. Because the climate is more favourable in the outh, the salt-extraction plants lie mainly around la Baule.

Sheltered, low-lying bays where the tides are easily controllable, with a high incidence of wind and sun, are most productive.

Today the uses of salt are more limited, and Brittany's production is only a tiny fraction of the huge quantities produced in Mediterranean pans. However, Brittany's salt is prized for its purity. Salt extraction takes place only during the summer, when there are about 30 to 40 so-called 'harvests'. The winter is then spent repairing the salt-pans and canals.

The most dramatic salt-pans can be seen around the Guérande peninsula, a surreal landscape of ools and ponds connected by a complex network of luicegates and drainage channels. Egrets and wading irds explore the pans, stepping through pink tassles of alt-tolerant glassworts and sea lavender. Purified salt is old by the roadside all over the marshes and makes a opular, inexpensive regional souvenir.

ALGUES

ARKOGELULES

Arkopharma

SALT CRYSTALLIZATION PROCESS

Sea water is allowed to flood gently into the larger lagoons at high tide, and from these reservoirs it trickles gradually into smaller, shallower pits, which are clay-lined to prevent the water draining away. As the water evaporates the salinity increases, until eventually the salt crystallizes out at a concentration of about 250g per litre (40oz per gallon). Fine white crystals of table salt (*fleurs de sel*) are raked off the surface of the water, while the coarser greyish crystals that form below the waterline are more suitable for industrial uses or cooking. Each *oeillet* (salt-pan) produces about 70–90kg (150–200lb) of salt at every 'harvest'.

Salt-pans near Guérande

Loire-Atlantique

CARRIERE DES FUSILLÉS
A monument by Châteaubriant's gates commemorates 27 hostages executed by the Nazis on 22 October, 1941 in reprisal for the assassination by the Resistance of Colonel Holtz, commander of the German forces based in the town. All local Resistance suspects were rounded up and shot in a quarry west of the town. The monument stands on a pigeonholed plinth containing earth from the execution site.

DYING OF JOY
One of the legends about Châteaubriant's castle tells how a 13th-century lady, Sibylle, was so overcome when her knight husband returned safely from a Crusade in 1250 that she died of happiness after running to embrace him.

►► Châteaubriant   227D3

Set well inland amid lake-strewn woods, Châteaubriant stands guard on the Anjou border, part of the line of fortified bastions protecting Brittany from invasion. Its church, **St.-Jean-de-Béré►**, is of some interest (the oldest parts of red sandstone date back to the 11th century).

Most visitors make for Châteaubriant's partly feudal, partly Renaissance **castle►** (tel: 02 40 28 20 20; *open* Wed–Mon for guided tours at 11, 2.30, 4.30; Sat–Sun at 3 low season; park daily at 7.30–6 (8 in summer). *Admission inexpensive*). The keep is the oldest section. The Seigneurial Palace was built by the Count of Châteaubriant, and several rooms are associated with the sad story of Françoise de Foix (see panel opposite). A balcony overlooks the gardens of the Court of Honour.

►► Le Croisic   226A1

This fishing village resort occupies a bulbous headland on the shores of the Grand Traict lagoon. The harbour faces north towards the salt marshes, where three islands joined by bridges to the mainland form separate basins. The original town lies immediately behind, slightly shabby but pleasant. The oldest (17th-century) houses are near the lantern-towered church, sporting dormers, shutters and wrought-iron balconies.

If you are an early riser (5am) you may be in time to catch the fish auction in a new building on one of the islets where a visitor's gallery overlooks the bidding floor. On the opposite (ocean) side of the peninsula, Port-Lin acts as le Croisic's resort. Drive right round the headland for a

The port at le Croisic

panoramic view of the dark crags. The low hills near the port are man-made with the residue of ballast unloaded by cargo ships in the 18th and 19th centuries.

Le Croisic's aquarium, the **Océarium►►**, is ideal for a wet day but worth a visit in any case. Arranged in five informative and interestingly themed sections, the building takes the form of a starfish. Both Atlantic and tropical species are displayed. Exhibits include baby eels and fingernail-sized infant turbot, mussel-farming on *ouchots* and gurnards gulping gently at their spectators. The tanks are large and beautifully seascaped; the biggest (with sharks, congers and skates) even has a transparent walk-through tunnel (*Open* Jun–Aug, daily 10–7; low season *closed* Jan and lunchtime. *Admission expensive*).

▶ Guérande 226A2

Guérande's 15th-century ramparts, studded with six towers, completely encircle the town; four gateways provide access. The finely turreted church of **St.-Aubin▶**, at the heart of the old town, contains features from many different periods, including a Merovingian sarcophagus, Romanesque columns and superb stained glass.

One of the gatehouses (St.-Michel, the governor's house) contains a fascinating local **museum▶ ▶**. Many displays are connected with the salt industry, including furnishings, tools and costumes (tel: 02 40 42 96 52; *open* Apr–Sep daily 10–12.30, 2.30–7. *Admission moderate*).

South of Guérande is an odd landscape of neatly kept salt-pans. Roadside vendors sell bags of purified salt and pickled samphire. To find out more about the salt-extraction process, visit two small museums: the **Maison des Paludiers▶** at Saillé, 3km (2 miles) south of Guérande (tel: 02 40 62 21 96; *open* Feb–Nov daily 10–12, 2–5.30. *Admission moderate*), and **Terre de Sel▶ ▶** at Pradel, west of town (tel: 02 40 62 08 80; www.seldeguerande.com; *open* Jul–Aug daily 9.30–12.30, 2.30–7; Apr–Jun, Sep 10.30–12.30, 2.30–6; *closed* Mon in winter. *Admission moderate*). North of Guérande the coastal road leads through the fishing town of **la Turballe** to Pointe du Castelli (with fine views) and the pretty village of **Piriac-sur-Mer▶** which has 17th-century timbered houses).

Châteaubriant's castle was founded in the 11th century

FRANÇOISE DE FOIX

Jean de Laval, Count of Chateaubriant, remodelled Châteaubriant's castle in the early 16th century as a fitting home for his child-bride, Françoise, then only 11. As she grew up, news of her beauty and intelligence spread, and eventually François I requested her attendance at court. The jealous count made excuses, arousing the king's curiosity even farther. François bribed a servant to tell him the signal Jean de Laval used to communicate with his wife, and thus managed to arrange a meeting with her. Dazzled by the splendour of court life, Françoise became the king's mistress, but when he tired of her he sent her back to Châteaubriant, where her husband locked her away in a dark room. After 10 years Françoise died, murdered, some say, by Jean de Laval, who never forgave her.

THE DUCHESS OF BERRY
The bourgeois monarchy of Louis-Philippe (1830–1848), faced a minor rebellion in 1832 when the Duchess of Berry staged an abortive rising in Brittany in a bid for the throne. She arrived in Brittany disguised as a peasant and hid in a house in Nantes. The police arrived and, finding the house chilly, started a fire in the grate. Eventually several soot-covered, spluttering figures landed ignominiously in the hearth. The duchess and her loyal followers had spent 16 hours up the chimney.

238

The church of
St.-Nicolas, Nantes

▶▶ Nantes 227D1

The industrialized outskirts of Brittany's historic capital do not entice, but once you manage to abandon your car safely in the old town, Nantes suddenly becomes a much more enjoyable place. The central areas are compact enough to explore without developing blisters, but if you should tire, an excellent network of buses and trams cuts down the walking (day passes and *carnets* are available).

Orientation Exploring all the city sights takes at least a day, and if you decide to stay on there is plenty to do in the evenings or in wet weather. If you choose Nantes as a base for a short break, the surrounding area also has lots to see and do. Nantes' crowning glory is its cathedral, though its art collections rival any elsewhere in Brittany. Of its dozen-plus museums, few are essential viewing but most have a quirky charm. Monday and Tuesday are bad days for sightseeing (several museums close).

The charm of Nantes lies in its atmosphere and variety rather than any set-piece sights. Its shops and stately buildings have touches of Parisian sophistication, and its youthful university population gives it plenty of cultural energy and evening entertainment, yet it has all the down-to-earth practicality and good sense of provincial France. Today it is a great commercial centre and ranks as France's seventh largest city.

History Nantes goes back a long way, to a Gaulish tribe called the Namnetes, who gave the city their name. After the Romans came and went, the Breton Celts fought off successive waves of invading Franks and Norsemen until AD939, when Alain Barbe-Torte (Crookbeard), a heroic leader, finally drove out the Vikings and became Brittany's last king, choosing Nantes as his capital. After the wars and confusion of the Middle Ages, the Dukes of Montfort restored peace and order. Anne de Bretagne was born in the castle and completed the construction begun by her father. In 1598 the castle witnessed another historic event when Henri IV signed the Edict of Nantes, which granted freedom of worship to the many Protestant Huguenots and ended the religious wars that had torn France apart.

Some of Nantes' older quarters make appealing, traffic-free places to stroll

The edict brought peace for a century, until its revocation by Louis XIV in 1685.

In the great trading years of the 16th to 18th centuries Nantes prospered, firstly from sugar and slaves (the notorious 'ebony' trade with Africa and the Caribbean), later from shipping and sardines. When the Loire silted badly, shipping moved downstream to St.-Nazaire, and Nantes hastily diversified into food processing and other light industries. Dredging techniques now keep the Loire free enough to allow modest cargo vessels as far inland as Nantes, and its quays are still lively with grain silos and derricks. After serious damage during World War II, Nantes' grand townscape of the 18th and 19th centuries around the Place Royale has been restored.

Main sights The **Château des Ducs de Bretagne**▶ ▶ was built by Duke François II in 1466 and used first as a ducal palace, then as the Breton governor's residence. It has been much restored and the moat refilled.

A vast restoration project, launched in 1994, is due to be completed in 2008. The aim of the project is to create a modern museum devoted to the history of Nantes and its region, the restored castle being the first and main exhibit of the museum. Meanwhile the courtyard and ramparts can be visited (*Open* Jul–Aug daily 10–7; Sep–Jun Wed–Mon 2–6). The 18th-century *harnachement* (saddlery) building now holds major temporary exhibitions.

The cathedral of **St.-Pierre**▶ ▶ ▶ (tel: 02 40 41 56 56; *open* daily 9–7), a glorious church of dazzling white tufa, is an amazing tour de force, its deceptively simple lines giving the impression of limitless height and space. The best thing in it is the splendid marble tomb of François II and his wife (parents of the Duchess Anne), carved by the master sculptor Michel Colombe. Just outside stand the

BEAUJOIRE
This large park some way north of Nantes by the banks of the Erdre is the site of France's biggest flower show, the Floralies Internationales. Plants from all over the world are exhibited here, with many countries taking a stand. You can reach Beaujoire easily from Nantes by bus or boat.

239

Porte St.-Pierre, a 15th-century gateway, and la Psalette, another turreted structure from the same period, now part of the sacristy.

Housed in a palatial 19th-century building, the **Musée des Beaux-Arts (Fine Arts Museum)**►► contains a wide range of French and European art, from Italian Primitives and Dutch still life to Impressionists, 20th-century abstracts and modern exhibitions (tel: 02 51 17 45 00; *open* Wed–Mon 10–6, Thu 10–8. *Admission inexpensive*).

The **Palais Dobrée**►► (tel: 02 40 71 03 50) is an eccentric Romanesque mansion, the former home of a Nantes shipowner, Thomas Dobrée (1810–1895), whose patchy collection of art and antiquities is now displayed inside. The **Musée Départemental d'Archéologie Régionale**►► contains a vast array of finds from neolithic times to the Viking raids, including Egyptian sarcophagi, plus Greek and Etruscan ceramics and jewellery. (*Open* Tue–Fri 1.30–5.30, Sat–Sun 2.30–5.30. *Admission inexpensive*).

Nantes' natural history museum, the **Musée d'Histoire Naturelle**►►, is a curious, enthusiastically managed collection. The most bizarre item is the stretched skin of a soldier whose dying wish was to be made into a drum. Unfortunately his skin was too thick to offer any beatable resonance, so here it hangs for all to see (tel: 02 40 99 26 20; *open* Wed–Mon, 10–6. *Admission inexpensive*).

240

MINOR MUSEUMS
The Musée Jules-Verne at 3 rue de l'Hermitage (near quai de la Fosse) celebrates a local son, born in Nantes in 1828 and perhaps Brittany's best-known writer outside his native land. Memorabilia and portraits illustrate Verne's imaginative life and writings (tel: 02 40 69 72 52; *open* daily 10–12, 2–6, except Sun morning and Tue. *Admission inexpensive*). Also on this stretch of quayside is the *Maillé-Brézé*, an escort ship launched in 1957 and taken out of service in 1988. It is now docked permanently on the Loire, and visitors are welcome to look round the living quarters, anti-submarine and anti-aircraft weapons, and detection systems (tel: 02 40 69 56 82; *open* Jun–Sep, daily 2–6; Oct–May Wed, Sat–Sun 2–5; guided tours. *Admission moderate*).

Walk

The old town of Nantes

A walk around Nantes' well-restored centre. Allow a full day, including museum visits and a lunch-stop or drink at the magnificent art nouveau Brasserie la Cigale.

Start at the top of the town, and after visiting the main sights here (castle, cathedral and fine arts museum), relax in the **Jardin des Plantes▶**. Go back along rue de Richebourg, deviating briefly to visit the late-Gothic **Chapelle de l'Immaculée**. Head for the delightful **Ste.-Croix district▶▶**, where 15th- and 16th-century houses line the streets (explore rue de la Boucherie, rue de la Juiverie and

rue Bossuet). Most of the nearby Place Royale was destroyed in World War II but the square has been faithfully restored.

Farther west lies the **Ancienne Île Feydeau▶**, once an island of the Loire. Many of the houses of rich shipowners are here. **Passage Pommeraye▶** is worth a look for its elegant covered 19th-century shopping mall. **Place Graslin▶** has a mix of 18th- and 19th-century buildings, best seen from the tables outside the **Brasserie la Cigale▶▶**.

Cours Cambronne▶ is another fine collection of 18th- and 19th-century houses. Head for the **Musée de l'Imprimerie▶** (tel: 02 40 73 26 55; *open* Mon–Sat 10–12, 2–5.30; guided tour at 2.30. *Admission moderate*), an interesting museum of printing, and the quai de la Fosse. Finish at the Musée d'Archéologie, Manoir de la Touche, and Palais Dobrée.

East end of Nantes cathedral

More than 650km (400 miles) of navigable rivers and canals cross Brittany, and the network provides one of the most enjoyable ways of exploring the interior. Many companies rent out suitably equipped craft for boating holidays, and excursion cruisers ply from many waterside centres.

RIVER TRIPS

Not all canal boats are suitable for the stronger currents of the tidal estuaries, and navigation can be tricky. To enjoy these stretches, therefore, you may prefer to let someone else take the helm unless you are an experienced boat-handler. The Rance, Aulne, Odet, Auray, Aven and Trieux all offer regular boat trips in season. Pick up tariffs and timetables at any tourist office.

History Brittany's canal system was not designed for holidaymakers and its original purpose was much more earnest. The aim was to provide a safe overland passage for freight vessels, which were constantly harassed by enemy ships on the open seas. A scheme to link St.-Malo and Brest via inland waterways was first proposed in 1627, but it took the ambition and foresight of Napoleon to implement it. By this time naval tension between England and France was so acute that a cross-country link became an urgent priority.

The Nantes–Brest canal was begun in 1810, linking the Loire with the Aulne and thus providing access to the open sea via the Rade de Brest. The project took 26 years to construct and represented a fantastic cost in human and economic terms. It was initially very slow to recoup capital expenditure, but by the end of the century its time had come and it enjoyed a brief heyday of shunting coal, slate and fertilizer across the province.

After World War I, improved rail and road connections caused a sharp decline in canal trade, and by 1928 cargo barges were rare. The construction of the Guerlédan dam half-way along its course effectively severed the Nantes–Brest link, and afterwards the central section between Pontivy and Carhaix-Plouguer was navigable only by kayak. In 1945 the last freight barge sailed through Châteaulin, and today the canal is used exclusively for tourism.

Waterways today Brittany's inland waterways fall into three main sections, each a combination of river and canal. The Ille-et-Rance section flows south across eastern Brittany, linking St.-Malo with the Atlantic via Rennes and Redon. The canalized stretch between Dinan and Rennes (49 locks) joins the River Vilaine for the southern part of the journey. It is a popular route for yachts and cabin cruisers cutting through from the Channel to the

The canalized River Oust runs through tranquil scenery near Josselin

Atlantic, avoiding the perilous seas of west Finistère. Some of the most picturesque sections lie near Hédé, with its remarkable staircase of locks, and around Redon. The final section down to la Roche-Bernard and the Arzal dam is also interesting.

Two east–west sections are all that remains of the broken-backed Nantes–Brest canal. One of these links Nantes and Lorient via Pontivy and the River Blavet

MORE INFORMATION
La Roche-Bernard's Musée de la Vilaine Maritime, Redon's Musée de la Batellerie, and Hennebont's Maison de l'Eau make interesting ports of call for more information about canals and rivers. Tourist offices can supply all sorts of practical and tourist information on waterways in Brittany and Pays de la Loire. Main boat-rental towns include Châteauneuf-du-Faou, Josselin, Redon, Hédé, Pont-Coblant, Rohan, Baud, Malestroit and Nantes.

Flower-decked locks at Redon

(135 locks); the other joins Carhaix with Brest via Châteaulin and the Aulne estuary (35 locks). On the eastern section the stretches of Oust around Rochefort-en-Terre and Josselin are perhaps the prettiest, and on the Blavet the section around St.-Nicolas-des-Eaux. Westwards, the calm loops of the Aulne estuary are attractive for most of the journey from Carhaix-Plouguer, but particularly scenic around Châteauneuf-du-Faou.

Hiring a boat Fully equipped boats (cabin cruisers or narrowboats) can be rented at various points along all these routes for varying lengths of time, and you can choose whether to sail back to your starting point or take a one-way trip. Canoes can be hired on certain stretches, though Brittany's waterways favour the placid paddler rather than the whitewater enthusiast.

The maximum draught allowable on the canal system is 1.2m (4ft), and the maximum speed limit is 6kph (4mph). Off-season rates are very much lower than July and August charges. Moorings, waterpoints and chandlery services are available en route. Bicycles can often be rented to take with you on board, and can add a useful and enjoyable dimension to the holiday. Towpaths accompany the routes in some places, though not continuously.

Negotiating a lock on the Nantes–Brest canal

Loire-Atlantique

LA GACILLY

The attractions of this small town north of Redon, pretty enough just to look at, are enhanced by its local perfume factory. La Gacilly is the headquarters of Yves Rocher's cosmetics empire, which is based on biological plant products rather than synthetic laboratory concoctions. The factory here employs over 1,000 workers. Needless to say, Yves Rocher products are also on sale in town, along with many arts and crafts. Visitors can see the **Végétarium**, an original museum entirely devoted to the vegetable world (tel: 02 99 08 35 84; *open* mid-Jun to mid-Sep daily 10–7; mid-Sep to mid-Jun 2–6. *Admission moderate*).

►► Redon 226B3

Not only roads, railways and waterways converge at Redon, but also three *départements* and the two regions of Brittany and Pays de la Loire. Strictly speaking Redon is in Ille-et-Vilaine. It once served as Rennes' seaport; now it is an important agricultural area with a Monday market. Various light industries (computers, children's clothes) have been established in the newer parts of the town.

Pleasure craft have taken the place of the cargo barges that once plied along the River Vilaine, but you can still take river trips with Vedettes Jaunes, going downstream as far as the Arzal dam or upstream to Beslé. Under your own steam you can follow the Nantes–Brest canal, which crosses the Vilaine at Redon in a complex series of locks, bridges and sluicegates. The Oust adds its own tortuous course to this watery complexity, waveringly joining up with the canal to the north of the town. Houseboats, pleasure cruisers, canoes and sailboats all converge on Redon throughout the year.

Floral town For most of the year Redon proudly keeps up its reputation as a *ville fleurie*, with a profusion of window-boxes, hanging baskets and flower tubs to give it a constantly festive appearance. Bars with live music, good-value restaurants, and even a summer theatre

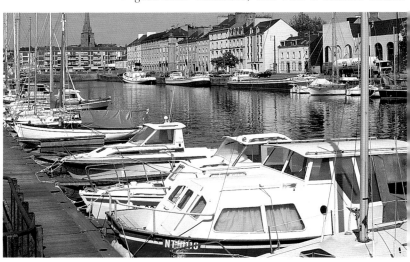

Pleasure cruisers line up for river and canal trips at Redon

provide diversions for its visitors, and it makes a pleasant base for a day or two, with many attractive excursions and walks, especially along the waterfront. Central hotels tend to cluster around the railway station (not the prettiest part of the town), but there are one or two attractive alternatives in more rural settings (see Hotels and Restaurants, page 277). At the end of October the Foire Teillouse festival celebrates the local chestnut harvest with music, dancing and crafts, while the town's chefs cook up imaginative nutty dishes.

Old Redon The oldest and most interesting part of the town lies northwest of the cross formed where the canal meets the river. The church of **St.-Sauveur**▶▶ is the most prominent landmark, an abbey church with a Romanesque tower emerging from its splayed Gothic buttresses. The Gothic belfry nearby was separated from the original church by a fire in 1780, and the adjacent 17th-century cloisters now house a college. One of the best views to be had of the church is from the raised walk of chestnut trees on the other side of rue Richelieu. In the autumn a mini-army of municipal workers arrive on this esplanade with large vacuum cleaners to clear up leaves and fallen conkers. A tidy place indeed.

The main street, **Grande Rue**, takes you through the heart of the old town. If you need picnic provisions, this is a good place to buy them (look for chestnut delicacies in season). On the way you will pass some of its quaintest houses, some corbelled or frescoed. Several old salt-houses can be seen on rue du Port.Down on quai Duguay-Trouin stand the later elegant homes of wealthy shipowners, who were once able to watch their vessels pass by from their living-room windows. Intricate wrought-iron balconies decorate the facades. An inscription on one of these houses reads: *Je suis de 1782, mes voisines de 1783* ('I date from 1782, my neighbours from 1783'). A few scraps of the town's original ramparts remain around quai St.-Jacques.

On the river you may see an unusual method of fishing, whereby large nets are suspended on long poles from a boat.

For more information about the local waterways, visit the **Musée de la Batellerie de l'Ouest**▶▶ (*Open* mid-Jun to mid-Sep daily 10–12, 3–6; low season Sat–Mon, Wed, 2–6. *Admission moderate*) on quai Jean-Bart by the pleasure-boat harbour, its entrance marked by two massive oak lock gates.

The exhibition traces the history of the port and its waterborne traffic from earliest times to its decline in the 20th century with an aquarium of river fish and a film show to supplement the models, photographs and documents on display.

COJOUX COUNTRY
North of Redon, the countryside west of the village of St.-Just (known as the Lande de Cojoux) is liberally sprinkled with megaliths. In fact this part of Brittany has the densest concentration of prehistoric remains outside Carnac. It is poorly documented in tourist literature, but there are guided tours on summer weekends; tel: 02 99 72 61 02. Alternatively, visitors can follow a signposted path that leads across the moor. Among the monuments, the Alignements du Moulin (13 blocks of quartzite) and the Demoiselles de Cojoux (three menhirs, one on its side) are perhaps most impressive.

245

Redon's Grande Rue (left)

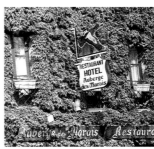

Old Redon (above)

MONSIEUR HULOT'S HOLIDAY

Film buffs may like to make a short pilgrimage to the little resort of St.-Marc, just west of St.-Nazaire, where Jacques Tati made his classic film in 1953. The Hôtel de la Plage is still there, facing the sands from an enticing rocky coast topped with prim villas on wooded cliffs. The film achieved only modest success in its native land, and today the French are still mystified by its enormous popularity among English-speakers, who are the butt of so much its gentle ribbing.

246

▶ St.-Nazaire
226B1

This unfortunate place took a terrible pounding during World War II. Like Brest and Lorient it has been rebuilt in a bleak, blockish style. To discover its fascinating maritime past, head for the port to visit the **Ecomusée de St.-Nazaire▶** (*Open* Jul–Aug, daily 9.30–7; Apr–Jun, Sep–Oct daily 9.30–12.30, 1.30–6; Nov–Dec, Feb–Mar Wed–Sun 10–12.30, 2–6; *closed* Jan. *Admission expensive*), which displays its history from earliest times to the present day, concentrating on wartime bombardment and the postwar rebuilding. The most interesting section of the museum is in the submarine exit, a covered lock which enabled German U-boats to slip out of the harbour unseen. It now houses the French submarine *Espadon*, which sailed beneath the polar ice-cap; a tour of the submarine's interior is included in the museum ticket. **Escal'Atlantic**, an impressive discovery centre, recreates the glamorous world of ocean liners, with multimedia special effects and historic movie footage (*Open* similar hours to Ecomusée).

In 1840 St.-Nazaire handled mail bound for Mexico and the Antilles. Formerly, however, St.-Nazaire's connections with the Caribbean were less innocent; it participated in the notorious slave trade which made Nantes prosper. Shipbuilding has long been one of its main industries. It took up the slack when the Loire silted so badly that deep-draughted shipping could no longer reach Nantes. The Blue Riband liners *Normandie* and *France* were built here, and in 2003, the *Queen Mary 2* (currently the world's largest cruise liner) was launched from its docks. Its shipyards suffered badly during the recession, but are picking up again. Associated industries such as oil-refining help to keep the town going.

St.-Nazaire's most striking architectural feature is its massive suspension bridge (3,356m / 11,687ft long) over the Loire, a graceful curve topped with red and white pylons. For a large toll, it provides a fast link to the south.

The docks at St.-Nazaire

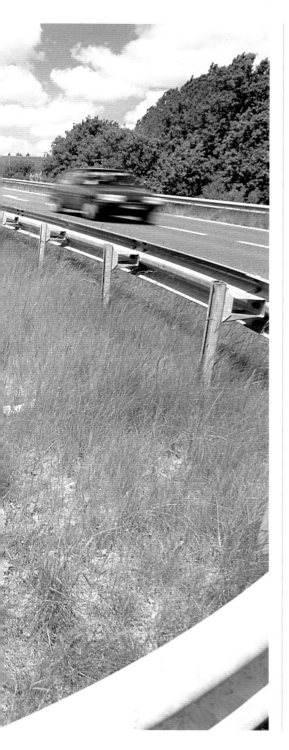

Arriving

Getting there

By air Air connections to northwest France change regularly, so check routes before booking. At the time of writing, the national carriers **Air France** (tel: 0845 0845 111; www.air-france.co.uk) and **British Airways** (tel: 0870 850 9850; www.ba.com) both serve Nantes from the UK. Budget airline **Flybe** (tel: 0871 700 0123; www.flybe.com) operates to Brest and Rennes from Southampton and other UK airports; **Ryanair** (tel: 0871 246 0000; www.ryanair.com) flies to Dinard from Stansted and Dublin. The Irish airline **Aer Lingus** (tel: 0818 365 000; www.aerlingus.com) serves Rennes from Dublin, while **Aer Arann** (tel: 06170 44 28; www.aerarann.ie) flies to Lorient from Galway and Waterford (tel numbers are in the Republic of Ireland). **Aurigny Air Services** (tel: 0871 871 0717; www.aurigny.com) serves Dinard from the Channel Islands. Holiday and charter flights are operated by short-break specialists to popular cities such as Rennes, Quimper and Nantes.

To reach other destinations in Brittany by air, you generally have to travel via Paris or other major cities in France. If you are arriving from North America or Australasia, you may have a choice of using London or Paris as your route-hub. The main domestic operator is Brit'Air (a subsidiary of Air France; same contact details), which flies to Quimper, Brest, Rennes, Nantes and Lorient. Other small domestic airports available in north-western France include Morlaix, Lannion, St.-Brieuc, St.-Nazaire and La Rochelle.

By sea Brittany Ferries (tel: UK 08705 360 360; www.brittanyferries.com) operates year-round sailings to St.-Malo and Roscoff from Portsmouth, Plymouth and Cork. Seasonal catamaran services by **Condor Ferries** (tel: 0845 345 2000; www.condorferries.co.uk) go from Poole or Weymouth to St.-Malo via the Channel Islands, though these may be affected by bad weather. **Irish Ferries** (tel: 01 610 511; www.irishferries.com) serves Roscoff

The modern architecture of the airport at Rennes, also well served by the TGV

The granite mound of Mont Dol

from Cork and Rosslare. Crossings take 7–9 hours from the UK, longer from Ireland.

Shorter, cheaper sea-crossings to the ports of Caen and Cherbourg (with fast, toll-free road links to Brittany) are also worth considering. **Brittany Ferries** (see contact details above) run Poole-Cherbourg and Portsmouth-Caen services.

From the eastern Channel ports you have a choice of other operators, but savings on shorter crossings are generally offset by the additional time and cost of motoring through France. Check www.ferrysavers.com to compare ferry prices.

By train The advent of the TGV (*Train à Grande Vitesse*) has revolutionized travel within Brittany. You can reach Rennes in 2 hours from Paris (Gare Montparnasse); St-Malo, St.-Brieuc or Vannes in about 3 hours; and Brest, Lorient or Quimper in 4 hours. Through-fares are available from Britain via the Channel Tunnel and Lille or Paris (including good-value air/rail deals).

By road Excellent motorway links (A11 and A81) connect Brittany with Paris and the rest of the French road network. Fast expressways (*voies express*) connect all the major cities and towns near the Breton coast converging at Rennes and Nantes. There are no toll roads (*autoroutes á péage*) in Brittany.

Customs regulations

Since 1 January, 1993 there has been virtually no restriction on duty-paid goods taken from one EU country to another, provided they are carried personally and intended for personal use. If you exceed reasonable limits you risk confiscation of the goods and/or a fine. Goods bought in duty-free shops (at airports and on ferries) are still subject to restrictions. Non-EU residents should check relevant allowances before they travel. Visitors from out side the EU may currently import the following quantities into France: 200 cigarettes or 50 cigars; 1 litre of spirits or 2 litres of fortified wine or 4 litres of table wine; 50g perfume; and 250ml toilet water.

Travel insurance

Adequate insurance cover is essential for peace of mind. Many policies are similiar, but read the small print to see if any exclusions would affect you. Certain credit cards provide insurance for cardholders and their family when tickets are bought with their card.

All EU citizens are in theory entitled to reciprocal health care, provided they take a valid European Health Insurance Card (EHIC) issued by local health authorities, but reimbursement can be a time-consuming and bureaucratic procedure and may leave you out of pocket. Check to see whether your existing house contents or health insurance covers you for losses abroad. If you do suffer a loss report it to the police within 24 hours (you need to obtain a copy of your statement for any insurance claim you make). Collect receipts for all expenses incurred.

Visas

All foreign visitors to France require a valid passport or excursion document. European, North American, Australasian and Japanese visitors require no visa for stays up to three months. Check entry requirements with your nearest French consulate if you hold any other non-EU passport. Several types of visa are available, but allow at least two months to apply.

Essentials
When to go

Brittany's tourist season is short and intense. In July and August beaches, campsites and *gîtes* burst at the seams, but by the end of September many resorts may already be closing. In winter the tourist scene is quiet. Hotels and all but the largest museums and attractions are closed, and very few boat trips or sports activities take place. Festivals and events are nearly all geared to the summer season between Easter and October.

If you have a choice, try to avoid visiting in the peak school holiday season, when prices are high and resources are stretched. May/June and September are good times to go, neither crowded nor moribund, although the sea is still cold. The weather is always unpredictable.

Climate

Brittany's climate is maritime, like the southwest coast of Britain, but a little warmer and drier in summer, and wetter in winter. Be prepared for rain at any time of year. Winter sees few extremes of temperature, and frost and snow are rare. Average daytime temperatures in summer are about 21°C (70°F), a little warmer and drier on the south coast than in the north. Near the sea there is usually a breeze, which may blow up to storm force occasionally on the exposed ocean coast. High winds have wreaked havoc with Brittany's native woodlands in recent years.

National holidays
- **New Year's Day** 1 January
- **Easter Sunday**
- **Easter Monday**
- **Labour Day** 1 May
- **VE Day** 8 May
- **Ascension Day**
- **Whitsun (Pentecost)** (and following Monday)
- **Bastille Day** 14 July
- **Assumption Day** 15 August
- **All Saints' Day** 1 November
- **Armistice Day** 11 November
- **Christmas Day** 25 December

Time differences

France is on Central European Time, one hour ahead of GMT for most of

Lighthouse at Perros-Guirec

NANTES

September–January

April–August

BREST

October–January

May–August

the year, six hours ahead of US Eastern Standard Time, nine hours ahead of Pacific Standard Time and nine hours behind Sydney. French summer time begins on the last Sunday in March and ends on the last Sunday in September.

Money matters

Currency The euro is the official currency of France. There are seven banknotes (5, 10, 20, 50, 100, 200 and 500 denominations) and eight coins (1, 2, 5, 10, 20 and 50 cent and 1 and 2 euro coins). Traveller's cheques are the safest way to carry large amounts of money, but it's advisable to take some cash, especially if you arrive on a weekend (many banks also close on Mondays). Larger notes (€500, €200) may be difficult to change, so ask for smaller denominations, and take some coins for parking meters, supermarket trollies and the like. Since the advent of the euro, fewer banks in France offer conventional exchange facilities, and now there is a much greater reliance on ATMs and plastic cards for monetary transactions.

Credit cards Cards belonging to the Carte Bancaire scheme (Visa/Access) are widely accepted in shops, hotels, restaurants and petrol stations. Carte Bleue (Visa/Barclaycard) is the most popular card in France, closely followed by Eurocard (Access/MasterCard). American Express and Diners Club are less readily accepted in certain outlets. Check your receipt carefully (there is no decimal point between euros and cents; a comma is used instead).

DINARD

September, November–January

May–August

Some retailers are reluctant to accept credit cards for small amounts (less than €15 or so). Many banks now have multilingual ATMs, but you must have a PIN (personal identification number). Alternatively, you can draw cash advances at any bank that displays the Carte Bleue (Visa) or Eurocard (Access) sign. Remember you will be charged a fee for this service, and for any transaction using a credit card, with interest accruing on a daily basis. It can be difficult to use some overseas credit cards in France, as they do not incorporate the same security microchip system. It is advisable to ensure that you have an alternative method of payment.

Driving

Car rental
Except for very short breaks, hiring a car in France is unlikely to be cheaper than bringing your own vehicle across the Channel or from elsewhere in Europe. However, some inclusive holiday packages offer good value and may be worth considering. It is generally less expensive to arrange rental before you travel, but all the major international rental firms have desks at airports, ferry terminals and main railway stations. Some insist that drivers should be at least 21 years old or levy higher insurance charges on young drivers. Your current driving licence is usually acceptable, but some require an international driver's permit. If you don't have a credit card you will have to produce a substantial cash deposit when booking. Make sure you sign for collision damage waiver when you take out a contract. You will only need to take out personal accident insurance if it is not covered by your general travel insurance.

Accidents and breakdowns
If your car breaks down, try to move it off the main highway and flash your hazard warning lights or place a red triangle 30m (100ft) behind your car. Emergency phones (*postes d'appel d'urgence*) linked to the local police station are placed at 4km (2.5 miles) intervals on main roads and every 2km (1.5 miles) on motorways. If you have an accident, you must call the police (tel: 17, which also summons an ambulance if necessary). You must also complete and sign an accident statement and exchange insurance details. If possible, try to enlist witnesses at the scene of an accident.

Insurance
Before leaving home, check you have comprehensive insurance and extend your cover if necessary. Many companies offer breakdown cover abroad. Check with your travel agent if you are booking a package holiday.

Driving regulations
To drive in France you must be at least 18 years old and carry a full valid national driving licence. If you are taking your own car, you must have the vehicle registration document (plus a letter of authorization from the owner if the car is not registered in your name), insurance documents and a car nationality sticker. Seat belts must be worn by the driver and all passengers. Children under 10 must sit in the back using a proper restraint system.

Driving is on the right, and headlamp beams must be adjusted on right-hand-drive cars. Carry spare headlamp bulbs, and a red warning triangle in case of breakdown. Drink-driving limits (0.5g/litre) are strictly enforced by the police; if you fail a breath test, expect a heavy fine or driving ban.

Fines
Hefty on-the-spot fines are imposed for contravening traffic regulations. If you consider yourself innocent, you

can pay a deposit (*amende forfaitaire*) and the police will issue a receipt.

Priority

Priorité à droite (priority to traffic coming from the right) is gradually being phased out. Signs may indicate that you have right of way (*passage protégé*) on a major road. On round-abouts *priorité à droite* no longer applies and you must give way to any car already on the roundabout. Watch for the signs '*Vous n'avez pas la priorité*' and take great care.

If an oncoming vehicle flashes its lights, this is likely to mean the driver thinks he or she has priority and you should give way. It's safest to do so.

Roads

France has three types of roads: A stands for *autoroute* (motorway); N is a *route nationale* (main road); D is a secondary road. Brittany has no true motorways (*autoroutes à péage*) but its fast divided highways (*voies express*) are just as efficient and toll-free.

Most roads in Brittany are D (or secondary) roads, but are well maintained and often seem like main roads. Speed limits are 130kph (78mph) on toll motorways, 110kph (66mph) on dual carriageways, 90kph (54mph) on other roads and 50kph (30mph) in towns (lower in wet or foggy conditions).

Parking

Don't park where kerbs are marked with yellow paint. Major towns often have *zones bleues* where parking discs must be used (obtain one from the tourist office). Elsewhere there may be meters (50c coins are useful) or complicated signs indicating *Côté du stationnement, jours pairs/impairs* (meaning you can park on one side of the road on alternate days of the month). In towns, public parking areas may be the answer.

Fuel

There are four basic grades: *gazole* (diesel), *super* (98 octane), *sans plomb* (95 octane unleaded) and *super sans plomb* (98 octane unleaded).

The least expensive place to buy fuel is usually at large supermarkets.

Cruising along on the open road

Route planning

In high season (July and August) main coastal routes in Brittany can get very congested.

Maps showing the *Bis* network are available free from roadside kiosks or tourist offices. *Bis* is short for *Bison Futé* (wily buffalo), a government scheme recommending fast through-routes for holiday traffic.

Road signs

International European traffic signs are steadily replacing the older ones in Brittany, though you may still find old-fashioned placename signs hewn from granite or set in concrete.

253

Translation of road signs:
Chaussée déformée: uneven road surface
Gravillons: loose chippings
Nids de poules: potholes
Déviation: diversion
Rappel: watch your speed (literally, reminder)
Cédez le passage: give way
Absence de marquage: no road markings
Ralentir: slow down
Route barrée: road closed
Passage protégé: right of way
Priorité aux piétons: pedestrian right of way
Sens unique: one-way street
Sens interdit: no entry
Toutes directions: route for through traffic

Public transport

A useful summary of Brittany's public transport network, *Guide Envie*, is available free in tourist offices. Colour-coded, area-by-area route maps with contact details cover coach, bus, train, boat and air transport.

Rail

A decent railway network runs east–west, connecting all Brittany's main bases. North–south travel is more complicated. The flagship trains are the high-speed TGVs, for which a reservation is needed. There are *rapide* and *express* trains, and local services.

Deals are available if you plan to make extensive use of the rail network, but if you remain only within Brittany a rail pass is unlikely to be worthwhile. Some tourist passes are only available outside France, and must be purchased before you travel. Contact **RailEurope** (the overseas arm of SNCF, the French National Rail Company; www.raileurope.com):
• **UK** 179 Piccadilly, London WIV 0BA (tel: 08705 848 848)
• **US** 226 Westchester Avenue, White Plains, NY 10064 (tel: 1-800 942-4866).

Bus

Buses cover a far wider network than the railways and generally cost less. There is no national network, and they are mostly useful for short hops rather than long hauls. The main bus station in a town is usually next to the railway station, and some coach services connect with trains. Tickets should be bought on the bus and cancelled (*compostés*) in a machine near the driver.

Boat

Trips to Brittany's islands are highly recommended, as are cruises along its estuaries. The following companies operate regular summer services:
• **Compagnie Corsaire** (tel: 08 25 16 80 35; www.compagniecorsaire.com) Rance Valley, Chausey islands, Channel Islands and Fréhel coast from St.-Malo and Dinard.
• **Condor Ferries** (tel: 08 25 13 51 35; www.condorferries.co.uk) Channel Islands from St.-Malo and Dinard.
• **Vedettes des Bréhat** (tel: 02 96 55 79 50; www.vedettesdebrehat.com) Trieux estuary and Île de Bréhat from Erquy, le Val-André, Port Dahouet, Binic, St.-Quay-Portrieux and Pointe de l'Arcouest.
• **Armor Découverte** (tel: 02 96 61 10 00) the Pink Granite Coast and the bird sanctuary of les Sept Îles from Perros-Guirec.
• **Compagnie Finistérienne de Transporta Maritimes (CFTM)** (tel: 02 98 61 78 87; www.vedettes-ile-de-brehat.com) Île de Batz and Morlaix Bay from Roscoff and Morlaix.
• **Vedettes Armoricaines** (tel: 02 98 44 44 04) Rade de Brest and Crozon peninsula from Brest and le Fret.
• **Compagnie Maritime Penn ar Bed** (tel: 02 98 80 80 80 or 02 98 70 70 70; www.penn-ar-bed.fr) Ouessant and Molène islands from Brest and le

A bus in the centre of Brest

254

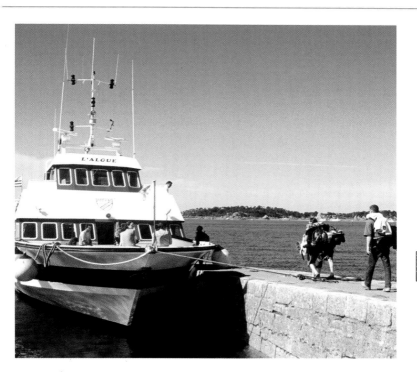

Conquet; Île de Sein from Audierne.
• **Vedettes Rosmeur** (tel: 02 98 92 83 83)
bay of Douarnenez and Crozon pen-
insula from Morgat and Douarnenez.
• **Vedettes de l'Odet** (tel: 08 25 80 08
01; www.vedettes-odet.com) Odet
estuary from Bénodet, Loctudy,
Beg-Meil, Port-la-Forêt, Concarneau
and Quimper.
• **Vedettes Glenn** (tel: 02 98 97 10 31)
Odet estuary and Îles de Glénan from
Concarneau.
• **Batobus** (tel: 02 97 21 28 29;
www.ctrl.com) Rade de Lorient and
Blavat estuary from Lorient, Port-
Louis and Hennebont.
• **Societé Morbihannaise de
Navigation** (tel: 08 20 05 60 00;
www.smn.navigation.fr) Belle-Île,
Houat and Hoëdic from Quiberon;
Île de Groix from Lorient.
• **Navix** (tel: 02 97 46 60 00;
www.navix.fr) Golfe du Morbihan
from Vannes, Ile d'Arz, Ile aux
Moines, Port-Navalo, Locmariaquer, le
Bono, Auray; Belle-Île from la Trinité-
sur-Mer.
• **Izenah Croisières** (tel: 02 97 26 31 45;
www.izenah-croisieres.com) Golfe

du Morbihan from Port-Blanc and Île
aux Moines.
• **Vedettes Jaunes** (tel: 02 97 45 02 81;
www.vedettesjaunes.com) River
Vilaine to Arzal dam from Redon.
• **Compagnie des Iles** (tel: 02 97 46 18
19; www.compagniedesiles.com) a
grand tour of the Golfe du Morbihan
from Vannes.
• **Vedettes Blanches Armor** (tel: 02 97
57 15 27) trips from Larmor-Baden to
Île de Gavrinis (Golfe du Morbihan).
• **Compagnie Maritime Armein** (tel: 02
98 61 77 75) Île de Batz from Roscoff,
Morlaix Bay.
• **Societé Maritime Azénor** (tel: 02 98
41 46 23; www.azenor.com) Rade de
Brest from Brest, le Fret and Camaret-
sur-Mer.
• **Finist'Mer** (tel: 02 98 89 16 61;
www.finist-mer.fr) Ouessant from le
Conquet and Camaret-sur-Mer.
• **Vedettes Aven-Bélon** (tel: 02 98 71 14
59) Aven estuary from Pont-Aven and
Port-Bélon (Moëlan-sur-Mer).
• **Vedettes Bigoudènes** (tel: 02 98 66
23 46) Odet estuary, Pont l'Abbé and
Îles Glénan from Bénodet and
Loctudy.

Student and youth travellers

A valid International Student Card may entitle you to discounts on travel, accommodation, admission charges and so on. Enquire about reduced rail or coach fares (*tarifs jeunes*) if you are under 25. Various youth passes are available for travellers under 26 (Inter-Rail, Eurail, etc). A booklet called *France Youth Travel* is available from the French Government Tourist Office (free with a stamped addressed envelope).

Communications

Media

Foreign newspapers are available in most towns and cities during the tourist season. *Le Monde* and *Le Figaro* are France's biggest national dailies, but the most widely read regional newspaper in France is Rennes-based

Catching up with the news

Ouest-France, which gives details of local events, listings and the other goings-on. *Télérama* lists French radio and television programmes.

Besides French national stations such as France Inter (87.8FM; English-language news bulletins in summer on weekdays at 9am and 4pm) or Radio France Bretagne Ouest (93FM; English holiday news at 10am and 5pm), the BBC's Radio 4 and the World Service, plus Voice of America, can be received in most parts of Brittany. Many of the more expensive hotels provide a

variety of cable and satellite television channels.

Post offices

Bureaux de poste can be recognized by the initials PTT or just *Poste*. Correspondence marked *poste restante* may be addressed to any post office in France and collected on proof of identity (passport) for a small fee. You can buy stamps (*timbres-poste*) at tobacco shops (*tabacs*) and post offices. Post boxes are yellow (free-standing or set into a wall). Use the *département étranger* slot for foreign mail. Many post offices have photocopying and fax machines as well as internet connections (Cyberposte). (See also Opening times on page 262.)

Telephones

Public call boxes in France are usually very efficient and fully operational. There are very few coin boxes left and most booths now operate with a *télé-carte* (phone card) available from post offices, rail stations and *tabacs* (newsagents). In rural areas look for a blue sign saying *téléphone public* on private houses. If you use a phone in a café or restaurant you will probably be surcharged, and if you call from a hotel room you will pay a hefty premium.

Telephone numbers in France are written and quoted in pairs. They contain 10 digits which are always dialled in full. Cheap rates apply 7pm–8am weekdays, and all day at weekends.

Dialling abroad You can make international calls from most call boxes but it may be more convenient to use a post office booth. To make an international call, lift the receiver, insert the money or card, dial 00, wait for the tone to change, then dial the country code followed by the STD number (omitting the initial 0). You must dial the international code if you are using a British-based mobile phone in France.

The international dialling codes are:

- **Australia** 61
- **Canada** 1
- **Ireland** 353
- **New Zealand** 64
- **UK** 44
- **US** 1.

Dial 13 for the operator, 12 for directory enquiries (information). For reverse-charge calls (collect) ask the operator for a PCV (*pay-say-vay*) call (available only to destinations outside France).

Language guide
Despite nationalist dreams and ambitions, the language of Brittany is French. English is spoken widely in Channel port towns (St.-Malo and Roscoff) or resorts popular with the English such as Dinard or Bénodet. You don't need to speak Breton to get by in Brittany, but a few words may add to your enjoyment of a visit.

Everyday Breton expressions
good day	*demat*
goodbye	*kenavo*
thank you	*trugarez*
festival	*fest-noz*
Brittany	*Breizh (BZH)*
good health	*yermat*

Breton place-names
aber	estuary
aven	river
beg	peak
dol	table
enez	island

Painted wood carvings, Locronan

iliz	church
kastell	castle
ker	village, house
lann	hermitage
lech	flat stone
menez	mountain
meur	important, big
mor	sea
penn	head, summit
plou	parish
pors	port
roc'h	rock
ti	house

Basic phrases in French
yes	*oui*
no	*non*
thank you	*merci*
please	*s'il vous plaît*
hello	*bonjour*
good evening	*bon soir*
good night	*bonne nuit*
goodbye	*au revoir*
can you show me…?	*pouvez-vous m'indiquer…?*
the way to…?	*la direction de…?*
where is…?	*où se trouve…?*
I would like	*je voudrais*
we would like	*on voudrait*
how many / much?	*combien?*
this one	*ceci*
that one	*cela*
that's enough	*ça suffit*

left	*à gauche*
right	*à droite*
near	*près*
straight on	*tout droit*
opposite	*en face de*
what time?	*à quelle heure?*

Emergencies

Crime and police

Brittany is generally safe and peaceful but, as in all holiday areas, opportunist theft is a problem, especially at the ferry ports. Take out adequate insur-

Policing the pardon

ance before you go and don't tempt crime by leaving valuables on view in your car or unsupervised on beaches. Be wary of pickpockets on public transport and in other busy places. If anything is stolen from you, report it immediately to the police. They will ask you to sign a statement. Police stations are called *commissariats de police* in towns and *gendarmeries* in rural areas
In emergencies, tel: 17.

Embassies and consulates

All the main national embassies are in Paris. You should contact them only in dire emergencies, such as the theft of your passport. Dial the appropriate 10-digit number.
• **Australia** 4 rue Jean-Rey, 75015 Paris (tel: 01 40 59 33 00).
• **Canada** 35 avenue Montaigne, 75008 Paris (tel: 01 44 43 29 00).
• **Ireland** 4 rue Rude, 75016 Paris (tel: 01 44 17 67 00).
• **New Zealand** 7 ter rue Léonard-de-Vinci, 75116 Paris (tel: 01 45 01 43 43).
• **South Africa** 59 quai d'Orsay, 75007 Paris (tel: 01 53 59 23 23).
• **UK** 35 rue du Faubourg-St.-Honoré, 75008 Paris (tel: 01 44 51 31 00). Consulate: 18 bis rue d'Anjou, 75008 Paris (tel: 01 44 51 31 00).
• **US** 2 avenue Gabriel, 75008 Paris (tel: 01 43 12 22 22). Consulate: 2 rue St.-Florentin, 75001 Paris (tel: 08 92 23 84 72 for visa information).

Emergency telephone numbers

For police or ambulance call 17, for the fire service (*pompiers*) 18. In cities you can also call for the 15 SAMU (Service d'Aide Medicale d'Urgence) ambulance service.

Lost property

If you are unlucky enough to lose something, contact the nearest police station (*gendarmerie* or *commissariat de police*) within 24 hours of discovering the loss. Take your passport (if you still have it). Obtain a copy of the police report if you intend claiming on your insurance. If you lose your credit cards, contact the nearest bank displaying the appropriate sign (Carte Bleue/Visa or Eurocard/Mastercard).

Lost card hotlines (24-hour) If you

lose your credit card, call:
• **Carte Bleue/Visa**, tel: 08 00 90 11 79
• **Eurocard/Access**, tel 08 00 9013 87
• **American Express**, tel: 01 47 77 72 00.

Health, vaccinations and pharmacies

No specific vaccinations are required or recommended for visitors to France. Rabies is still technically endemic in France but it is very rare in Brittany. To be absolutely safe, however, don't touch any local animals, and if you are bitten seek medical attention however minor the wound. Aside from this, the worst ailment you are likely to suffer in Brittany is an occasional mosquito bite, or (if you are unlucky) an upset stomach, particularly if you enjoy shellfish. Tap water is safe to drink.

Accidents and illnesses can strike anywhere, however, so you need to be prepared. EU residents are entitled to reciprocal health treatment in France (take a European Health Insurance Card), but only part of the expenses incurred are reimbursed (repatriation is excluded), and this is no substitute for adequate medical insurance. Non-EU residents should check the validity of their personal health insurance carefully before travelling.

Pharmacies (*pharmacies*) are recognizable by a green cross and are usually open six days a week. Pharmacists are trained to diagnose and treat minor complaints and can give first aid (they may charge a fee). They can also provide the name of a doctor or dentist. They are not allowed to dispense prescriptions from foreign doctors, so take a good supply of any medicines you need regularly. A rota of local pharmacies on duty (*pharmacie de garde*) outside normal hours should be posted on the doors of the shop and in local newspapers, or ask at the police station.

Other information

Camping and self-catering
Brittany has numerous campsites and a huge number of *gîtes*. The

A picturesque pharmacie *at Landerneau*

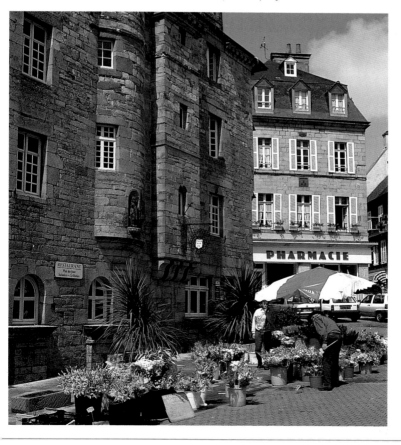

Gîte de France Handbook lists over 2,500 self-catering holiday homes in France (see also page 266). Brittany Ferries is now the official representative of Gîtes de France in the UK.

Camping organizations
• **Camping Plus**
Plobannalec-Lesconil BP28–29740 (tel: 02 98 87 87 86; www.campingplus.com).
• **Eurocamp**
Hartford Manor, Greenbank Lane, Northwich, Cheshire CW8 1HW (tel: 01606 787878; www.eurocamp.co.uk).
• **Canvas Holidays**
East Port House, 12 East Port, Dunfermline, Fife KY12 7SG (tel: 01383 629000; www.canvasholidays.co.uk).
Self-catering organizations
• **Maison des Gîtes de France**
59 rue St-Lazare, 75439 Paris Cedex 09 (tel: 01 49 70 75 75; www.gites-de-france.fr).

• **Brittany Ferries**
Millbay Docks, Plymouth, Devon PL1 3EW (tel: 08705 360360; www.brittanyferries.com).

Visitors with disabilities
Facilities for the disabled have improved somewhat in Brittany. Useful organizations:
Association des Paralysées de France (APF), 17 boulevard Auguste-Blanqui, 75013 Paris; tel: 01 40 78 69 00; www.apf.asso.fr . Regional branches offering advice.
Association France-Handicaps, 9 rue Luce-de-Lancival, 77340 Pontault-Combault; tel: 01 60 28 50 12. Produces the *Guide Rousseau* detailing accessible venues throughout France.
Holiday Care Service, tel: 08451 249 971 (UK); www.holidaycare.org.uk. Travel and holiday information for disabled visitors.
Mobility International USA, PO Box 10767, Eugene, OR 97403; tel: (503) 343

Camping at Rothéneuf

CONVERSION CHARTS

FROM	TO	MULTIPLY BY
Inches	Centimetres	2.54
Centimetres	Inches	0.3937
Feet	Metres	0.3048
Metres	Feet	3.2810
Yards	Metres	0.9144
Metres	Yards	1.0940
Miles	Kilometres	1.6090
Kilometres	Miles	0.6214
Acres	Hectares	0.4047
Hectares	Acres	2.4710
Gallons	Litres	4.5460
Litres	Gallons	0.2200
Ounces	Grams	28.35
Grams	Ounces	0.0353
Pounds	Grams	453.6
Grams	Pounds	0.0022
Pounds	Kilograms	0.4536
Kilograms	Pounds	2.205
Tons	Tonnes	1.0160
Tonnes	Tons	0.9842

MEN'S SUITS

UK	36	38	40	42	44	46	48
Rest of Europe	46	48	50	52	54	56	58
US	36	38	40	42	44	46	48

DRESS SIZES

UK	8	10	12	14	16	18
France	36	38	40	42	44	46
Italy	38	40	42	44	46	48
Rest of Europe	34	36	38	40	42	44
US	6	8	10	12	14	16

MEN'S SHIRTS

UK	14	14.5	15	15.5	16	16.5	17
Rest of Europe	36	37	38	39/40	41	42	43
US	14	14.5	15	15.5	16	16.5	17

MEN'S SHOES

UK	7	7.5	8.5	9.5	10.5	11
Rest of Europe	41	42	43	44	45	46
US	8	8.5	9.5	10.5	11.5	12

WOMEN'S SHOES

UK	4.5	5	5.5	6	6.5	7
Rest of Europe	38	38	39	39	40	41
US	6	6.5	7	7.5	8	8.5

1248 (US); www.miusa.org.
International travel and exchange
schemes for visitors with disabilities.
**Royal Association for Disability and
Rehabilitation (RADAR)**, 12 City
Forum, 250 City Road, London EC1V
8AF; tel: 020 7250 3222 (UK);
www.radar.org.uk.
**Society for Accessible Travel and
Hospitality (SATH)**, 347 Fifth Avenue,
Suite 610, New York NY 10016; tel:
(212) 447 7284 (US); www.sath.org. For
people with special travel needs.
SNCF Accessibilité, tel: 0800 15 47 53.
Advice for rail passengers with
disabilities.
Tripscope, tel: 0845 7585 641 (UK);
www.tripscope.org.uk. Phone infor-
mation service.

Opening times

Shops Food shops generally open
Monday to Saturday 8am–8.30pm,
while other shops open later (at 9 or
9.30). *Boulangeries* (bakeries) open on
Sunday too. Half-day closing varies
but is often Monday. Lunchtime
closing is usually 12–2 but supermarkets stay open all day and may be
open later too. Nearly every town in
Brittany holds a weekly market.

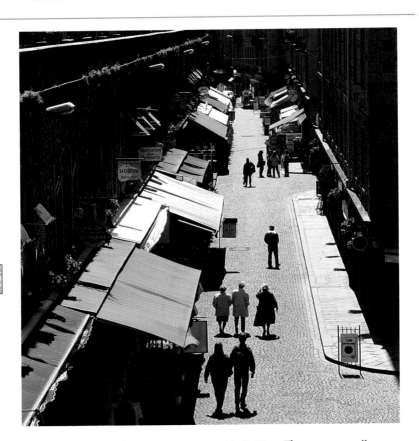

Restaurants by St.-Malo's ramparts

Banks Banks open 9–12 and 2–4. Some open Saturday mornings but may close on Monday. Watch for national holidays; banks close early the day before. *Bureaux de change* at international airports operate daily 6am–11pm.

Museums and other sights National museums close on Tuesdays, others often on Mondays. Most close on major public holidays. In Brittany, opening hours for tourist sights are complex and seasonal, with much longer summer hours. Many sights close at lunchtime (12–2 or 2.30), and completely during the winter (October to Easter). Check opening hours at the local tourist office if you wish to visit something in particular. (Ask about entry fees too, as these vary greatly.)

Souvenirs for sale in Dinan

Post offices These are generally open 8–5, 6 or 7 on weekdays, and 8–12 on Saturday. Smaller offices close at lunchtimes.

Places of worship
Brittany is a strongly Catholic region and every town or village has a thriving church community. Check noticeboards to see what time Masses start. Protestant churches can be found in large towns. Other denominations or faiths may be less well represented. Ask at the tourist office or town hall.

Toilets
Public toilets can be found in filling stations, hypermarkets, large shops and so on. Men are *Messieurs*; women are *Dames*. Unisex autocabins can be found in central urban streets; they take 20c coins. Standards are variable, so take advantage of facilities when you are in cafés, restaurants, hotels or museums, as these are often better kept than average.

Electricity
Nearly everywhere in Brittany operates at 220 volts, 50Hz. Electric sockets take plugs with two round pins. Take an adapter for non-continental appliances. US and Canadian visitors may require a transformer too.

Tourist offices
Overseas offices of the French Government Tourist Office (FGTO) are now promoted under the name 'Maison de la France' (MDLF). Some printed literature is available in these, but more is on its official website www.franceguide.com, and those of the regional tourist boards. Note that the following telephone numbers are

The cider museum at Argol

263

The Maison de la Reine Anne is one of Morlaix's most attractive buildings

generally charged at a premium rate.
• **Australia** French Tourist Bureau, 25 Bligh Street, Level 13, Sydney NSW 2000 (tel: 02 9231 5244).
• **Canada** 1981 Avenue McGill College, Suite 490, Montreal, Québec H3A 2W9 (tel: 514 288 2026).
• **Ireland** 30 Upper Merrion Street Dublin 2 (tel: 1 560 235 235).
• **UK** 178 Piccadilly, London W1V 0AL (tel: 09068 244 126).
• **US** 444 Madison Avenue, 16th Floor, New York, NY 10022 (tel: 514/288-1904).

Tourist offices in Brittany
Nearly every small town or resort has its own *Office du Tourisme* or *Syndicat d'Initiative* (recognisable by a large letter **i**). Many of these are seasonal.

• **Regional tourist office** (Comité Régional du Tourisme) 1 rue Raoul Ponchon, 35069 Rennes, Cedex (tel: 02 99 28 44 30; www.brittanytourism.com or www.tourismebretagne.com).
• **Côtes-d'Armor** 7 rue St-Benoît, BP 4620, 22046 St.-Brieuc (tel: 02 96 62 72 00; www.cotesdarmor.com).
• **Finistère** 11 rue Théodore le Hars, BP1419, 29104 Quimper, Cedex (tel: 02 98 76 20 70; www.finisteretourisme.com).
• **Ille-et-Vilaine** 4 rue Jean-Jaurès, BP6046, 35060 Rennes, Cedex 3 (tel: 02 99 78 47 47; www.bretagne35.com).
• **Morbihan** PIBS, allée Nicolas Leblanc, BP 408, 56010 Vannes (tel: 01 97 54 06 56; www.morbihan.com)
• **Loire-Atlantique** Comité 2 allée Baco, BP 2-5-2, 44005 Nantes (tel: 02 51 72 95 30; www.cdt44.com or www.paysde-laloire.fr).

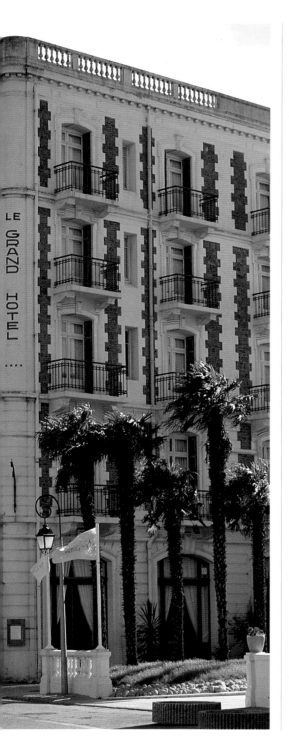

Hotels and Restaurants

Accommodation

Brittany offers a vast range of accommodation to suit all tastes and pockets. Much of it is self-catering in campsites and *gîtes* (see page 260). Besides conventional hotels you have a choice of staying in luxurious châteaux, practical hotels and hostels, or *en famille* in France's expanding network of working farms or *chambres d'hôtes* (bed and breakfasts). Many selective accommodation guides are available.

Generally speaking, accommodation in Brittany caters for families. It is unlikely to be dauntingly exclusive, or bursting with priceless antiques and designer furnishings. Summer bookings are heavy, especially during the peak French holiday season (July and August), so it's best to book in advance to make sure of a place. It is usually easier to find a bed inland than on the coast. Some hotels have online booking facilities or will accept a credit card reservation, but you may be asked for a deposit (*arrhes*); send an international money order to avoid bank charges. Several agencies will organize bookings in registered chains for you. For a small fee, tourist offices will make reservations for up to a week ahead if you visit them in person.

Hotels Brittany has about 1,000 registered hotels though some excellent ones are not listed in the official regional guide. French hotels are officially graded from one to four stars, with an additional "luxury" category, depending on the level of facilities offered. A full list of registered hotels is available from the tourist office. Another tourist office publication is *Hôtels de Charme et de Charactère en Bretagne* (a handpicked list of indivually owned places of distinctive merit). Other groups of hotels produce separate brochures (often available free in tourist offices). One of the best known and most popular is the *Fédération des Logis de France*, consisting of small, inexpensive, family-run hotels, often of considerable character. There are nearly 200 *logis* throughout Brittany, many with good home cooking. The *logis* guide is available in bookshops. Another fast-growing trend is the expansion of inexpensive chains like Campanile and Ibis, all with efficient if rather characterless facilities.

By law, hotel tariffs must be clearly visible in the reception area and in each bedroom. Prices are seasonal and usually quoted per room (top-range hotels sometimes whack on an obligatory 15 percent service charge when you settle the bill) and do not include breakfast. A tourist tax (*taxe de séjour*) is sometimes levied by local authorities; rarely more than €4 per person per day. Hotel breakfasts are in any case generally poor value. You are much better finding a local café or *pâtisserie* to satisfy early-morning hunger pangs. In high season many hotels specify half-board

terms (*demi-pension*). This may be good value, and no hardship if there's a decent cook, but you may prefer to eat out sometimes. On the other hand, if you particularly wish to try a hotel restaurant it can be annoying to find it closed (often the case on Sunday or Monday evenings).

If you are travelling alone you may still have to pay the double-room rate; singles are rare, and often unpleasantly poky or ill-equipped. Negotiate for a discount if you can. Rooms with only a shower are less expensive than those with a bath; if you can make do with a public bathroom you should pay much less.

Gîtes A French *gîte* is a self-catering country holiday home, often in a converted farmhouse or cottage. Many belong to a national government-run scheme called Gîtes de France. These are classified by ears of corn, from one to four depending on the level of sophistication; others are graded by 'nests' (Nids Vacances), from one to three.

To find a good *gîte* you should book well in advance (the previous autumn if possible) by either contacting the owner direct or through the official UK agent, Brittany Ferries, tel: 08705 360 360 (reservations) or 08705 143 537 (brochure line).

Bed linen, towels, teapots, kettles, etc. may not be supplied. You may like to take your own pillows to avoid the dreaded French bolsters.

Gîtes d'étape These are large, communal hostels, often in farmhouses, which have simple, dormitory accommodation for walkers, riders and lovers of the outdoors. There are comparatively few in Brittany, but most sizeable towns have a youth hostel, often on the outskirts.

Chambres d'hôtes The term 'bed and breakfast' as understood in Britain doesn't quite describe the French experience, which is catching on fast as this is a sociable and interesting way to explore France. Establishments vary from grand châteaux to simple rural homes. You are generally provided with an evening meal and are expected to join in family life, so it helps if you can speak a little French.

Local tourist offices provide lists of *chambres d'hôtes*, or you can obtain the FGTO booklet in advance. The associations Château Acceuil and Châteaux et Manoirs de Bretagne cater for the top end of the market. The Maison des Gîtes de France (see page 260) publishes a yearly directory of all the *chambres d'hôtes* in France, classified in the same way as the *gîtes*. The booklet *Bienvenue a la Ferme* lists *gîtes, chambres d'hôtes* and campsites on farms.

Camping Some of France's best campsites can be found in Brittany, especially along the popular holiday coasts of Cornouaille and Trégor. You can find them on lovely beaches, in woods or even in the grounds of châteaux.

Officially they are graded from one to four stars and all are required to have a source of clean running water, daily refuse collection and a telephone. After that you progress through any number of layers to on-site swimming pools, restaurants, supermarkets and entertainment. Most sites have a mixture of free pitches for your own tent, caravan or campervan, and fixed tents, static caravans or chalet-style huts. Camping Plus (see page 260) is a group of high-quality sites (all 3 or 4 star) with about 30 members in Brittany.

If you book a package camping holiday you will probably get a fully equipped tent on one of the better sites and a courier to look after you. Don't expect virgin wilderness or much experience of the great outdoors on such a holiday (these sites are generally both organized and crowded), but it saves you investing in your own equipment and is a good idea for novice or gregarious campers.

Alternatively, you can use a reservation agency; you take your own equipment but bookings are organized for you (see page 260). Independent camping obviously gives you the choice of more peaceful locations and flexibility. If you prefer less organized camping, look for signs saying Camping à la ferme or Aire naturelle de camping. You don't have to use an official site, but camping sauvage is strictly prohibited in nature reserves or regional parks. Some sites require you to present a camping carnet (permit) from various camping organizations.

In July and August many campsites are fully booked, while out of high season facilities may be shut. Useful guides for independent campers include the AA's Caravan and Camping France and Camping à la ferme.

The following list of accommodation has been divided into three price categories, based on starting prices for a double room in high season:

• **inexpensive (€)** under €60
• **moderate (€€)** €60–100
• **expensive (€€€)** over €100

These categories serve as a general guide only. Hotels often have a very wide range of prices, depending on the season and the facilities in each room. If possible, inspect a bedroom before accepting it, or make it clear when booking what facilities you require.

Hotels and restaurants are listed under the nearest main-entry place-name in the gazetteer; this may be some distance from the establishment itself.

THE EMERALD COAST

Cancale
Continental (€€ €€€) 4 quai Thomas (tel: 02 99 89 60 16; www.hotelcancale.com). Cheerful terraced building with bright awnings amid a bustling line of seafood restaurants. Excellently placed overlooking the harbour,

with the oysterbeds almost at arm's length. Choose a room with a sea view if you can. Oysters are served in the restaurant.
Le Château Richeux (€€€) Le Pont du Jour, St-Méloir-des-Ondes (tel: 02 99 89 64 76; www.maisons-de-bricourt.com). This grand and gorgeous villa commands splendid views from its clifftop position. Inside, it's luxurious but understated in a elegantly contemporary style, with friendly staff and an informal atmosphere. Its in-house bistrot marin serves top-notch seafood (see restaurants).
Pointe du Grouin (€€) Pointe du Grouin (tel: 02 99 89 60 55; www.hotelpointedugrouin.com). Popular pitstop for walkers and birdwatchers on a scenic headland overlooking Île des Landes. Overrun with passing trade at summer lunchtimes, but its setting is hard to beat (see restaurants).
Tirel-Guérin (€€ €€€) gare de la Gouesnière, St.-Méloir-des-Ondes (tel: 02 99 89 10 46; www.tirelguerin.com). Classic railway hotel about 4km (2.5mi) inland, well modernized. Charming owners, large bedrooms and excellent food (see restaurants). Indoor pool.

Dinan
Arvor (€ €€) 5 rue Pavie (tel: 02 96 39 21 22; www.destination-bretagne.com). Very central, pleasantly furnished in a former convent building near the tourist office. Parking tricky.
D'Avaugour (€€ €€€) 1 place du Champ (tel: 02 96 39 07 49; www.avaugourhotel.com). Delightful hotel overlooking place Du Guesclin in the heart of historic Dinan. Smartly refurbished, but retains some old-world charm. Very convenient for sightseeing. Lovely rear gardens overlook the castle ramparts. No restaurant.
Le Challonge (€€) 29 place Du Guesclin (tel: 02 96 87 16 30; www.lechallonge.fr.st). A neat, cheerful hotel with attractive, modern rooms. Good brasserie-restaurant.
Jerzuel (€€ €€€) rue quai des Talard, port de Dinan (tel: 02 96 87 02 02; www.bestwestern-jerzual-dinan.com). Tastefully designed in a spacious modern idiom, this purpose-built hotel has a lot in its favour, notably a superb waterfront setting on the Lanvallay side of the Rance. Furnishings are pleasing, if bland, and facilities extensive.

Dinard
Grand Hôtel Barrière (€€€) 46 avenue George V (tel: 02 99 88 26 26; www.lucienbarriere.com). A seafront institution from Dinard's glamorous fin-de-siècle heyday that still hogs the best views over the mouth of the Rance.
Printania (€€) 5 avenue George V (tel: 02 99 46 13 07; www.printaniahotel.com). A charmingly idiosyncratic place with friendly staff and lovely Rance views. The waitresses dress in Breton costume.
Reine Hortense (€€€) 19 rue Malouine (tel: 02 99 46 54 31; www.villa-reine-hortense.com). Another civilized turn-of-the-20th-century house set in a refined residential area above the central beach. It has a lovely secluded gardens with a breakfast terrace.

Hotels & Restaurants

La Vallée (€€) 6 avenue George V (tel: 02 99 46 94 00; www.hotel-de-la-vallee.com). Peacefully situated by the sea, yet only a short walk from the middle of town, this simple family hotel makes an excellent base. The restaurant menu offers lobster and other seafood.

Erquy

Beauséjour (€–€€) 21 rue de la Corniche (tel: 02 96 72 30 39; www.beausejour-erquy.com). Very good small *logis*, overlooking the sea. There is a garden, parking facilities and a choice of good-value menus featuring seasonal scallops.

Plancoët

L'Écrin (€€–€€€) 20 les Quais (tel: 02 96 84 10 24; www.crouzil.com). Seven smart, spacious rooms furnished with antiques, plus Jean-Pierre Crouzil's formidable cooking at this acclaimed hotel-restaurant a short drive inland (see restaurants).

Rance Valley

Manoir de la Rance (€€€) Pleurtuit, la Jouvente (tel: 02 99 88 53 76; www. chateauhotels.com/rance). Converted manor overlooking the Rance estuary in peaceful countryside. Garden where breakfasts, teas and drinks are served. Friendly owners. Relaxing, eclectic furnishings. No restaurant.
Manoir de Rigourdaine (€€) Route de Langrolay, Plouer-sur-Rance (tel: 02 98 86 89 96; www.hotel-rigourdaine.fr). A rambling stone property in a tranquil country setting overlooking the Rance estuary. Bedrooms are in the converted courtyard buildings, and are light, spacious and stylish. There is no restaurant, but it is excellent value.

Sables d'Or-les-Pins

Manoir St.-Michel (€€) la Carquois (tel: 02 96 41 48 87; www.fournel.de). Fifteenth-century stone manor house surrounded by velvety lawns overlooking a scenic slab of coastline. Comfortably furnished in local style, with log fires. No restaurant.
Manoir de la Salle (€€) rue du Lac (tel: 02 96 72 38 29; www.linkparis.com/ manoir-de-la-salle.htm). Attractive renovated stone-built 16th-century manor in a rural setting near the coast. Games room, with billiards and table tennis, but no restaurant.
Voile d'Or (€€€)
Allée des Acacias (tel: 02 96 41 42 49). Panoramic views over the sheltered waters of this pretty resort are a strong incentive to choose this elegant hotel-restaurant. The seafood is excellent.

St.-Cast-le-Guildo

Port Jacquet (€–€€) 32 rue du Port (tel: 02 96 41 97 18; www.port-jacquet.com). This attractive stone-built hotel on the hill leading down to the port has wonderful views of the bay. The interior is bright and nautical. The best rooms have sea views. but there is a quiet little garden. Good seafood.

St.-Malo

L'Ascott (€€€) 35 rue Chapitre, St.-Servan (tel: 02 99 81 89 93; www.ascotthotel.com). This 19th-century townhouse in the quiet suburb of St.-Servan has been elegantly renovated, each bedroom in a different contemporary style. Several are large suites suitable for families. It has quiet rear gardens, with breakfast and drinks served outside in fine weather.
Le Beaufort (€€) 25 chaussée du Sillon (tel: 02 99 40 99 99; www.hotel-beaufort.fr). This classy period house overlooks the main Sillon beach from the seaside promenade called La Digue, just a few minutes from the old town. Ultra-stylish, light and airy inside, and the views are breathtaking.
Les Charmettes (€€) 64 boulevard Hébert (tel: 02 99 56 07 31; www.hotel-les-charmettes .com). Little *pension* consisting of two tranquil houses (one simpler and cheaper than the other) overlooking the sea near Paramé.
Cité (€€) 26 rue Ste.-Barbe (tel: 02 99 40 55 40; www.hotelcite.com). If you enjoy being in the heart of town, you couldn't do better than this hotel near the walls; some top rooms have sea views.
Hotel France & Chateaubriand (€€) (tel: 02 99 56 66 52; www.hotel-fr-chateaubriand .com). Seconds from the beach, in the historic part of the city. The rooms are comfortable with views of the sea or yachting harbour. The restaurant serves fresh fish and seafood.
La Korrigane (€€€) 39 rue le Pomellec, St.-Servan (tel: 02 99 81 65 85). Graceful 19th-century mansion in quietish suburb, five minutes from the sea. Many antiques and *objets d'art*. Friendly owners. Garden. No restaurant.
Logis de Brocéliande (€€) 43 chaussée du Sillon (tel: 02 99 20 62 62). Small, stylish hotel facing the long beaches near Paramé, set back from the seafront road. No restaurant.
Manoir du Cunningham (€€–€€€) 9 place Mgr. Duchesne (tel: 02 99 21 33 33; www.st-malo-hotel-cunningham.com). An imaginative newcomer, cleverly converted from a 17th-century timbered house with exceptional views over Port Solidor and the walled citadel. It is handy for the ferry terminal.
Quic en Groigne (€€) 8 rue d'Estrées (tel: 02 99 20 22 20; www.quic-en-groigne.com). A delightful and exceptionally friendly little hotel right in the heart of the walled city. Cosy, well-finished rooms, generous breakfasts served in a conservatory extension, and secure off-street parking.
La Rance (€€) 15 quai Sébastopol, St.-Servan (tel: 02 99 81 78 63). Civilized small hotel near quiet Port Solidor. Clean, well-equipped rooms, some with excellent views. Traditional furnishings and some antiques. Good breakfast; courteous owners. No restaurant.
L'Univers (€€) place Chateaubriand (tel: 02 99 40 89 52; www.hotel-univers-saintmalo .com). Sensitively upgraded after a recent change of ownership, this historic hotel has managed to retain its character yet provide

good facilities in the bedrooms. The bar walls are crammed with pictures and old photos, and the terraced café-restaurant is a popular meeting place (see restaurant section).

Le Valmarin (€€€) 7 rue Jean XXIII, St.-Servan (tel: 02 99 81 94 76; www.levalmarin.com). If you would like to see what a *malouinière* is like, stay here. This former corsair's home has palatially sized rooms in peaceful grounds, and is elegant and restful. No restaurant.

La Villefromoy (€€–€€€) 7 boulevard Hébert (tel: 02 99 40 92 20; www.villefromoy.fr). On the Paramé side of town, a beautiful old mansion (actually two houses joined together) of great distinction. Furnishings are luxurious, rooms bright and tasteful, some with sea views. Garden for drinks and breakfasts.

Le Val André

De la Mer (€) 63 rue Amiral Charner (tel: 02 96 72 20 44). Simple, unpretentious and on the road behind the beach. Friendly staff. Excellent seafood (see restaurants). A functional motel annexe called Nuit et Jour offers overnighting for families, though you probably wouldn't want to spend your holiday here.

Grand Hôtel du Val André (€€) 80 rue Amiral Charner (tel: 02 96 72 20 56; www.grand-hotel-val-andre.fr). Unchallenged views of Le Val André's superb beach are the main attraction of this large and well-managed hotel. Inside and out it is comfortable, elegant and seasidey, its sun-decks and shady gardens set with stripy parasols and cane chairs. Courteous English-speaking owner.

Villa Marguerite (€€) 34 rue des Garennes (tel: 02 96 72 85 88). High on a hillside in a residential backwater behind the beach, just four bedrooms enjoy sea views. The house is a private home and full of character, with antique furnishings and personal belongings.

THE PINK GRANITE COAST

Armorique Corniche

Grand Hôtel des Bains (€€€) 15 bis rue de l'Eglise, Locquirec (tel: 03 98 67 41 02; www.grand-hotel-des-bains.com). An inspirational renovation of a delightful Belle Epoque residence in an idyllic fishing village that has been used as a film-set. The setting is magical, its terrace overlooking the wooded shores through a perfectly pollarded lime-walk. Inside, the décor is elegantly contemporary.

Le Ty-Pont (€) place Robert le Meur, St.-Jean-du-Doigt (tel: 02 98 67 34 06). One of those delectable French finds that are all too rare: a simple, friendly and good value family-run seaside hotel with generous home cooking.

Bréhat, Ile de

Bellevue (€€–€€€) Port Clos (tel: 02 96 20 00 05; www.hotel-bellevue-brehat.com). A simple but delightful place not far from the landing stage,with lovely views of the rocky shores and the sea. Tables in its flower-filled gardens are always popular.

Guingamp

Château de Brélidy (€€–€€€) Brélidy (tel: 02 96 95 69 38; www.chateau-brelidy.com). This carefully restored 16th-century building, which is tastefully furnished in period style, promises an interesting sojourn. Extensive parkland.

Paimpol

Le Barbu (€€–€€€) pointe de l'Arcouest (tel: 02 96 55 86 98; www.lebarbu.fr). Right by the Bréhat ferry terminal, overlooking a marvellous stretch of coast. Comfortable modern furnishings. Pool and a seafood restaurant.

K'loys (€€–€€€) 21 quai Morand (tel: 02 96 20 40 01). A fascinating old house from the late 19th century directly by the port, this has become a smart period hotel. Breakfast is served in rooms on the verandah.

Le Repaire de Kerroc'h (€€) 29 quai Morand (tel: 02 96 20 50 13). Imposing former corsair's house on the harbour, refurbished in smart traditional style. Very comfortable spacious bedrooms and courteous, affable service. (See also restaurant section.)

Perros-Guirec

269

L'Agapa (€€€) 12 rue des Bons Enfants (tel: 02 96 49 01 10; www.lagapa.com). Clearly in the luxury bracket, this renovated 1930s villa enjoys panoramic views of the Pink Granite Coast from the cliffs above Trestraou beach. Gourmet seafood restaurant.

Les Feux des Îles (€€€) 53 boulevard Clemenceau (tel: 02 96 23 22 94; www.feux-des-iles.com). Tall stone house in gardens overlooking the bay. Rooms vary in style and size but are well furnished. Panoramic sea views and a tennis court. The emphasis is on the food (see restaurant section).

Hermitage Hotel (€€) 20 rue Frères Le Montréer (tel: 02 96 23 21 22). A friendly, relaxed town-centre hotel surrounded by a large garden. Comfortable, well-equipped rooms.

Manoir du Sphinx (€€€) 67 chemin de la Messe (tel: 02 96 23 25 42). Belle Epoque stone house perched on clifftops in a residential area. Good sea views from terraced bedrooms and open-plan bar-restaurant. Light, modern furnishings.

Villa Cyrnos (€€–€€€) 10 rue de Sergent l'Hévedere (tel: 02 96 91 13 36). This handsome granite mansion in the heart of town has splendid views of the harbour. The large, comfortable, tastefully furnished rooms are let on a *chambre d'hôte* basis, and sleep up to four. Breakfast (included in the price) is exceptional.

Plougrescant

Manoir de Kergrec'h (€€€) (tel: 02 96 92 59 13; www.bbfrance.com/kergrech.html). One of the most successful and delightful of all Breton hotel-châteaux—a tasteful period interior with no wrong notes. Peaceful setting in extensive grounds by the sea. Charming and unassuming owners (a viscount and his wife). Dinner by prior arrangement only.

St.-Quay-Portrieux

Le Gerbot d'Avoine (€) 2 boulevard du Littoral (tel: 02 96 70 40 09; www.gerbotdavoine.com). Though rather old-fashioned in some public areas, this modest establishment has high standards of hospitality in the best *logis* tradition. Bedrooms are spacious and comfortable.

Trébeurden

Auberge de Jeunesse (€) 60 corniche Goas-Trez (tel: 02 96 23 52 22; www.fuaj.org). Quietly positioned just outside the resort, near the Marais du Quellen nature reserve, this modern youth hostel is pleasantly equipped and overlooks the splendid coastline. Good bird-watching and megaliths.
Ker An Nod (€–€€) 2 rue de Pors Termen (tel: 02 96 23 50 21; www.kerannod.com). This simple stone-built *logis* couldn't be much closer to the sea. Simple inside, but the welcome is friendly and rooms clean and neat.
Manoir de Lan Kerellec (€€€) allée Centrale (tel: 02 96 15 00 00; www.lankerellec.com). Peaceful manor in the resort overlooking marvellous coastal scenery. Expensive, exclusive catering for hedonists. Nautically themed dining room with excellent views.
Ti al Lannec (€€€) 14 allée de Mézo-Guen (tel: 02 96 15 01 01; www.tiallannec.com). One of Brittany's most appealing hotels; a stay here is a real treat. Wonderful views from all bedrooms, which are individually decorated and luxurious. Health club. Children welcome.

Tréguier

Aigue Marine (€€) port de Plaisance (tel: 02 96 92 97 00; www.aiguemarine.fr). An airy modern hotel down by the marina, but within easy reach of the historic cathedral quarter. Some of the stylish. spacious bedrooms have private balconies overlooking the port. There's a pool terrace, an acclaimed restaurant and good leisure facilities.
Kastell Dinec'h (€€) route de Lannion (tel: 02 96 92 49 39). Handsomely converted farmhouse in a rural setting about 2km (1.3 miles) from the town centre. Stylish bedrooms with a mix of period and modern furniture. Relaxing and family-orientated. Swimming pool.

NORTH FINISTÈRE

Brest

Citotel de la Gare (€–€€) 4 boulevard Gambetta (tel: 02 98 44 47 01; www.hotelgare.com). A neatly kept, welcoming chain hotel within easy reach of the arts centre and the bus and railway stations—a convenient, good-value option with glimpses of Brest harbour from some upper rooms. Modern, functional style.

Brignogan-Plages

Castel Régis (€€) promenade du Garo (tel: 02 98 83 40 22; www.castelregis.com). Superbly located by lovely rock and sand beaches.

Furnishings are fairly plain but the bedrooms (mostly in rustic bungalows) are spacious and peaceful. Swimming pool, tennis and mini-golf. Good, if pricey, restaurant.

Carantec

Carantec (€€€) 20 rue du Kelenn (tel: 02 98 67 00 47; www.hoteldecarantec.com). A charming hotel with stunning views over the beach and picturesque gardens. Several rooms have balconies. See restaurants.

Le Conquet

Le Relais du Vieux Port (€) 1 quai Drellac'h (tel: 02 98 89 15 91; www.lerelaisduvieuxport.com). Restaurant-with-rooms by the harbour (see restaurants). Stylish rooms with views.

Morlaix

L'Europe (€€) 1 rue Aiguillon (tel: 02 98 62 11 99; www.hotel-europe-com.fr). Well-run, slightly old-fashioned central hotel. Conventional furnishings enlivened by a few historic touches (17th-century panelling, baroque plasterwork). Well-placed for exploring the old town.
Du Port (€–€€) 3 quai de Léon (tel: 02 98 88 07 54; www.hotelduport.com). Inexpensive hotel in a pretty, pinkwashed building by the port and viaduct. The modern interior has been attractively renovated.

Ouessant, Île d'

Roc'h-ar-Mor (€–€€) Lampaul (tel: 02 98 48 80 19). Of the three more-or-less basic hotels in the village, the Roc'h-ar-Mor has the attraction of a grassy walled garden overlooking the sea, where bar lunches can be enjoyed.
Ti Jan Ar C'hafe (€€) Kernigou (tel: 02 98 48 82 64). A peaceful haven in a stylish modern idiom of seagrass and natural wood. Bedrooms are bright but soothing in reds and greens. Leisure activities arranged.

Plouescat

La Caravelle (€) 20 rue de Calvaire (tel: 02 98 69 61 75; www.hotel-logis-caravelle.com). Just 15 minutes from Roscoff ferry terminal, this comfortable, simply-furnished establishment is ideal for an overnight stop. The restaurant has a high standard of home cooked dishes with seafood specials.

Plouguerneau

Baie des Anges (€€–€€€) 350 route des Anges, Port de l'Aber Wrac'h, Landéda (tel: 02 98 04 90 04; www.baie-des-anges.com). Classic location overlooking one of the tidal sea inlets known as *abers* in northwest Finistère. Very stylish. Breakfast is a treat.

Roscoff

Le Brittany (€€€) boulevard Ste.-Barbe (tel: 02 98 69 70 78; www.hotel-brittany.com). An extended 18th-century manor house at the east end of the bay near the ferry terminal. Tastefully furnished with antiques, it has a sophisticated but relaxing air. Welcoming owners. Pool. Notable food (see restaurants).

270

Gulf Stream (€€–€€€) rue Marquise-de-Kergariou (tel: 02 98 69 73 19; www.hotel-roscoff.com). A smart, modern resort hotel at the quiet west end of town. Large gardens, sea views, thalassotherapy and a swimming pool.
Hotel du Centre (€€) le Port (tel: 02 98 61 24 25; www.chezjanie.com). Ultra-modern, simple, bright, chic accommodation in greys and reds above a popular long-established seafront bar called Chez Janie (see restaurant section). Excellent value for ferry travellers. Lively atmosphere, friendly staff and good food.
Talabardon (€€–€€€) place de l'Église (tel: 02 98 61 24 95; www.talabardon.fr). Gracious stone building amid the corsairs' houses around the church. Smartly furnished interior; some sea views. Restaurant.
Temps du Vivre (€€€) 19 place de l'Eglise (tel: 02 98 19 33 19; www.letempsdevivre .net). This imaginatively renovated slate-and-grantie corsaire's house provides a truly stylish waterfront annexe to one of Roscoff's top-flight restaurants (see restaurants).

St.-Mathieu, Pointe de
Hostellerie de la Pointe St.-Mathieu (€€–€€€) (tel: 02 98 89 00 19; www.pointe-saint-mathieu.com). Bits of stone cladding and crypt-like vaulting take the modern edge off this somewhat bleak hotel-restaurant by the ruins of the old abbey. Smartly refurbished, the hotel has an excellent seafood restaurant (see restaurant section).

ARMORIQUE

Arrée, Monts d'
Le Clos de 4 Saisons (€) 2 rue de la Paix, Sizun (tel: 02 98 68 80 19). Peaceful accommodation in a building with plenty of character, surrounded by a pretty park. The restaurant, housed in the oldest part of the building, offers inventive cuisine using local produce.

Crozon, Presqu'île de
Julia (€) 43 rue du Tréflez, Morgat (tel: 02 98 27 05 89). A good traditional hotel-restaurant with sea views. Interior furnishings are attractive and modern.
Hostellerie de la Mer (€) 11 quai du Fret (tel: 02 98 27 61 90; www.hostelleriedelamer.com). Pleasing stone logis overlooking the harbour where boats arrive from Brest. Simple bedrooms. (See also restaurant section.)
Pors-Morvan (€) Pors-Morvan, Plomodiern (tel: 02 98 81 53 23). Nineteenth-century stone farm buildings cleverly converted into stylish motel accommodation. Crêpes and snacks served. Tennis. About 6km (4 miles) from the sea.
Presqu'île (€–€€) place de l'Église (tel: 02 98 27 29 29; www.chez.com/mutingourmand). Lovely, airy hotel in seaside blues and yellows, both relaxing and vaguish. Next door to one of Finistère's best restaurants under the same friendly management (Le Mutin Gourmand, see restaurant section).

Le Faou
Beauvoir (€€) place aux Foires (tel: 02 98 81 90 31; ww.hotel-beauvoir.com). A handsome building on the main square with an acclaimed restaurant, La Vieille Renommée (see restaurant section).

Huelgoat
Hôtel du Lac (€) 9 rue du Général de Gaulle, (tel: 02 98 99 71 14). Huelgoat has little to offer its visitors in the way of accommodation, except this small logis overlooking the picturesque lake. Good restaurant serving Breton cuisine. (See also restaurant section.)

Lampaul-Guimiliau
Hostellerie des Enclos (€) route de Saint-Jacques (tel: 02 98 68 77 08; www.lenclos.com). Modern functional logis beside one of the region's most famous churches. Friendly welcome.

Landerneau
Le Clos du Pontic (€€) rue du Pontic (tel: 02 98 21 50 91; www.clos-pontic.com). Unusual turreted house in peaceful gardens some way from the town centre, providing an impersonal but agreeable stay. Most of the well-equipped bedrooms are in a pleasant modern wing with good facilities (such as a coffee bar). Attractive restaurant.

St.-Thégonnec
Auberge St.-Thégonnec (€€) 6 place de la Mairie (tel: 02 98 79 61 18; www.auberge-saintthegonnec.com). Spacious, well-equipped bedrooms, some overlooking quiet gardens. Celebrated cooking (see restaurant section). The famous parish close is directly opposite.

CORNOUAILLE

Audierne
Le Goyen (€€–€€€) place Jean Simon (tel: 02 98 70 08 88; www.legoyen.com). Imposing building, overlooking harbour and estuary. Furnishings are stylishly traditional; the atmosphere refined but relaxed. Celebrated for its food (see restaurant section).

Beg-Meil
Belle Vue (€–€€) 30 descente de Belle Vue, Cap-Coz (tel: 02 98 56 00 33; www.ifrance .com/hotel-belle-vue). Pleasant, well-kept, family-oriented logis close to the beaches of Cap-Coz. Simple rustic furnishings. Garden, terrace and restaurant. Cliff walks.
La Pointe du Cap Coz (€–€€) 153 avenue de la Pointe, Cap-Coz (tel: 02 98 56 01 63; www.hotelcapcoz.com). Simple family hotel in a lovely position on a narrow spit with the sea on either side; direct access to pine-shaded sandy beaches.
Thalamot (€€) 4–6 Chemin-Creux (tel: 02 98 94 97 38; www.hotel-thalamot.com). Relaxing and idiosyncratic hotel near the beach in a shady garden. Simple bedrooms in a newer wing, with a restaurant available.

Hotels & Restaurants

Bélon

Manoir de Kertalg (€€€) route de Riec-sur-Bélon, Moëlan-sur-Mer (tel: 02 98 39 77 77; www.manoirdekertalg.com). Delightful granite manor house, hidden in a vast forested park high above the Bélon estuary, close to Pont-Aven and fine, sandy beaches. River fishing, forest walks, art exhibitions.

Les Moulins du Duc (€€€) Moëlan-sur-Mer (tel: 02 98 96 52 52; www.hotel-moulins-du-duc.com). Luxury hotel converted from a 16th-century mill in deep countryside. Ponds and streams cover much of the extensive grounds. The bedrooms are in stone cottages picturesquely modernized but retaining bits of mill machinery and antique furnishings. Excellent food (see restaurant section).

Bénodet

Armoric (€€–€€€) 3 rue de Penfoul (tel: 02 98 57 04 03; www.armoric-hotel.com). This excellently-managed and welcoming hotel is surrounded by peaceful flower-filled gardens and has a pleasant bar and terrace where visitors can relax. The rooms are smartly furnished and have very good bathrooms.

Ker-Moor (€€–€€€) corniche de la Plage (tel: 02 98 57 04 48; www.kermoor.com). A large and well-equipped complex with extensive leisure facilities, set back from the beach in peaceful grounds.

Ste.-Marine (€€) 19 rue du Bac, Ste.-Marine (tel: 02 98 56 34 79; www.hotelsaintemarine.com). Delightful, stylishly renovated house in a lovely position overlooking the harbour. Stunning views. Tables set outside. It's popular with the sailing fraternity, so book ahead.

Concarneau

Auberge de Jeunesse (€) quai de la Croix (tel: 02 98 97 03 47; www.ucrif.asso.fr). Beautifully located youth hostel by the water's edge. The marine biology institute is next door. A short stroll to the Ville Close.

Les Grandes Roches (€€–€€€) rue des Grandes Roches, Trégunc (tel: 02 98 97 62 97; www.hotel-lesgrandesroches.com). Just east of Concarneau, in extensive grounds on the edge of a village, this attractive rambling old Breton house feels surprisingly countrified. It is a popular place for lunch.

Douarnenez

Le Clos de Vallombreuse (€€–€€€) 7 rue d'Éstienne-d'Orves (tel: 02 98 92 63 64; www.closvallombreuse.com). A distinguished mansion in secluded grounds, right in the heart of the town, converted into a sophisticated hotel-restaurant. Bedrooms, furnished in a variety of styles, have views over the bay. It has a swimming pool and private parking.

Ty Mad (€–€€) place St.-Jean (tel: 02 98 74 00 53; www.hoteltymad.com). Tall, shuttered, well-kept hotel in a quiet corner at the top of the town, with a garden and views of the church and sea. Though accessible only via tortuous back-streets, it is well sign-posted from the port.

La Forêt-Fouesnant

De l'Espérance (€) place de l'Église (tel: 02 98 56 96 58; www.hotel-esperance.com). A modest stone-built house by the church in the village centre. Lush gardens behind. The rooms are of variable quality and price; the quieter ones are at the rear.

Fouesnant

L'Orée du Bois (€) 4 rue Kergoadig (tel: 02 98 56 00 06; www.oree-du-bois29.com). Modest, family-run *logis*, still offering good value and a warm welcome. Several family rooms are available.

La Pointe de Mousterlin (€€–€€€) 102 route de la Pointe de Mousterlin (tel: 02 98 56 04 12; www.hotelmousterlin.com). A stone's throw from the splendid beaches at Mousterlin point, an ideal choice for a relaxing family holiday. Some of the larger rooms have balconies. Fresh local fish is served in the restaurant.

Locronan

Manoir de Moëllien (€€–€€€) Plonévez-Porzay (tel: 02 98 92 50 40; www.moellien.com). The name recalls Chateaubriand's lover, Thérèse de Moëllien, whose home this lovely 17th-century manor once was. Now carefully restored, thriving and peaceful, it has attractive rooms, some in an annexe.

Le Prieuré (€€) 11 rue du Prieuré (tel: 02 98 91 70 89; www.hotel-le-prieure.com). This attractive granite *logis* on the edge of the lovely old town makes an excellent base, though it lacks interesting views. Some refurbished bedrooms and an imposing arched and beamed dining room. Expect crowds in season.

Montagnes Noires

Le Relais de Cornouaille (€) 9 rue Paul Sérusier, Châteauneuf-du-Faou (tel: 02 98 81 75 36). Down-to-earth central hotel-restaurant adorned with flower-filled window-boxes. A good place to have lunch or to use as a base for exploring the Montagnes Noires.

Penmarc'h, Presqu'île de

Le Poisson d'Avril (€€–€€€) rue de Men Meur, le Guilvinec (tel: 02 98 58 23 83). Sophisticated restaurant-with-rooms near the *criée* of one of Brittany's most active fishing ports. Sparkling interiors, superb seafood and stunning sea views.

Pont-Aven

Ajoncs d'Or (€€) place Hôtel de Ville (tel: 02 98 06 02 06; www.ajoncsdor-pontaven.com). Very central and friendly: the best value in this overrun tourist town. Old-fashioned, sensible furnishings and plenty of appropriate artworks.

Les Mimosas (€–€€) square Théodore Botrel (tel: 02 98 06 00 30). Small, family-managed place at the far end of the harbour. Nautical theme and cosy bedrooms, all with river views. Appetizing cooking, informally served.

Moulin de Rosmadec (€€€) (tel: 02 98 06 00 22). Easy to find by the bridge in the village centre, this appealing restaurant-with-rooms has been converted from one of the original watermills for which the town is famous. Just four rooms—book ahead. Splendid cooking (see restaurant section).

Pont-l'Abbé

De Bretagne (€–€€) 24 place de la République (tel: 02 98 87 17 22). Central hotel on the main square (plenty of parking). Smart, civilized rooms, the most peaceful ones at the rear, and excellent food (see restaurant section).

Port-Manec'h

Ar Men-Du (€€–€€€) Raguenez-Plage (tel: 02 98 06 84 22; www.men-du.com). White-painted building in splendid isolation overlooking the beach and a tidal island. Now smartly renovated, it has an attractive all-day brasserie (see restaurant section), and stylish, practical rooms.

Chez Pierre (€€) 27 rue des Îles, Raguenez-Plage (tel: 02 98 06 81 06; www.hotelchezpierre.com). Stone house in the village centre with attractive gardens and a popular restaurant. Comfortably furnished bedrooms and lounge areas.

Du Port (€) 30 rue de l'Aven (tel: 02 98 06 82 17; www.hotelduport.com). Agreeable family *logis* with partial sea views over scenic coastline. Simple furnishings. Garden. It operates in collaboration with another similar hotel just up the hill, the de l'Aven.

Quimper

Dupleix (€€) 34 boulevard Dupleix (tel: 02 98 90 53 35; www.hotel-dupleix.com). Comfortable riverside business hotel a short stroll from the old town. Spacious, quiet interior. Cathedral views form some rooms; private parking.

Gradlon (€€) 30 rue de Brest (tel: 02 98 95 04 39; www.hotel-gradlon.com). Solid, comfortably furnished hotel a short walk from the cathedral. Garden for summer, log fires in winter.

Ste.-Anne-la-Palud

La Plage (€€€) (tel: 02 98 92 50 12; www.plage.com). Isolated, luxurious beach hotel at high-water mark. Comfortably furnished and equipped, it attracts a notably well-heeled (and generally older) clientele. Excellent food.

Sizun, Cap

Baie des Trépassés (€–€€) Plogoff (tel: 02 98 70 61 34; www.baiedestrepasses.com). Lonely seaside spot on a scenic bay near Pointe du Raz. Rather spartan inside, but excellent coastal scenery and sandy beaches.

Kermoor (€€) Plage du Loch, Plogoff (tel: 02 98 70 62 06; www.hotel-kermoor.com). Simple hotel overlooking a lovely stretch of sand, with good seafood restaurant.

MORBIHAN

Auray

L'Auberge (€€) 56 route de Vannes, Ste.-Anne-d'Auray (tel: 02 97 57 61 55; www.auberge-larvoir.com). Attractive, old-world inn, traditionally furnished with dark wood and candelabra. Light, fresh fabrics in the bedrooms. (See also restaurant section.)

La Croix Blanche (€) 25 rue de Vannes, Ste.-Anne-d'Auray (tel: 02 97 57 64 44). Pleasing older-style building on the edge of town, decently furnished. Popular with pilgrims.

Le Marin (€–€€) 1 place du Rolland, port de St.-Goustan (tel: 02 97 24 14 58; www.hotel-lemarin.com). This delightful little place just behind Auray's historic harbour has trim modern bedrooms in an old timbered house. Spacious bar-lounge, and limited river views.

Belle-Île

Atlantique (€–€€) quai de l'Acadie (tel: 02 97 31 80 11; www.hotel-atlantique.com). Perhaps the most appealing of the three attractive and well-kept hotels just below the citadel by the landing stage in le Palais. An elegant yellow-washed building with dormers, comfortably furnished rooms and an animated bar-restaurant, Le Grand Café, downstairs.

Castel Clara (€€€) Anse de Goulphar (tel: 02 97 31 84 21; www.castel-clara.com). Luxury hotel-restaurant overlooking one of Belle-Île's most picturesque sections of coastline. A substantial modern white and grey block with balconied rooms. Many facilities, including tennis, swimming pool and thalassotherapy.

La Desirade (€€€) Le Petit Cosquet, Bangor (tel: 02 97 31 70 70; www.hotel-la-desirade.com). A charming cluster of little buildings set in gardens round a heated pool, this complex promises a memorable stay. Bedrooms decorated in a range of styles.

Phare (€) quai Guerveur, Sauzon (tel: 02 97 31 60 36). Right by the lighthouse in this charming fishing port. A simple, pretty building of great appeal.

Belz

Relais de Kergou (€) route d'Auray (tel: 02 97 55 35 61). Well-modernized farmhouse accommodation in a relaxing, rural location. A good base for exploring the south Breton coast. It has a restaurant and private parking.

Carnac

Celtique (€€) 82 avenue des Druides, Carnac Plage (tel: 02 97 52 14 15; www.hotel-celtique.com). Quie position among pine trees at Carnac Plage. Close to the beach and with a heated outdoor pool, sauna and Jacuzzi.

Hostellerie les Ajoncs d'Or (€€) Kerbachique, Route de Plouharnel (tel: 02 97 52 32 02; www.lesajoncsdor.com). An old stone farmhouse in a tiny village a short drive from the town. It is warm and rustic inside, with well maintained gardens.

La Marine (€) 4 place de la Chapelle (tel: 02 97 52 07 33). A good-value base in the town

273

centre, useful for visiting the Musée de Préhistoire. A well-kept building with modern blue and white furnishings, clean rooms and a terraced seafood restaurant.

Les Rochers (€€) 6 boulevard de la Base Nautique (tel: 02 97 52 10 09; www.les-roches.com). One of the more agreeable options in Carnac's beach resort. Notably welcoming, and attractively furnished with cane rattan chairs and plants, in a prime sea-facing position near the yacht club.

Le Faouët

La Croix d'Or (€) 9 place Bellanger (tel: 02 97 23 07 33; www.lacroixdor.com). A handsome building on the main square, overlooking the splendid covered wooden marketplace. A reliable traditional base for exploring places of interest in this attractive town.

Josselin

Château (€–€€) 1 rue Général de Gaulle (tel: 02 97 22 20 11; www.hotel-chateau.com). Imposing dormered building occupying a prime site on the bank opposite the castle. The interior is traditional and well-kept. Helpful staff.

274

Locmariaquer

Les Chambres Marines de L'Azimut (€€–€€€) 1 rue du Men-Du, la Tinité-sur-Mer (tel: 02 97 55 71 88; www.charme-gastronomie.com). Delightful conversion of a Breton house overlooking the harbour; streamlined, cabin-like bedrooms have private terraces and luxury fittings. Superb seafood in the attached restaurant.

Lautram (€) place de l'Église (tel: 02 97 57 31 32). Well-kept small hotel opposite the church, close to the harbour. Some garden rooms in the rear annexe. Seafood restaurant.

Ostrea (€–€€) cours des Quais, la Trinité-sur-Mer (tel: 02 97 55 73 23; www.hotel-ostrea .com). A simple but chic *logis* decorated in blues and creams just behind the marina. Seafood terrace brasserie and pizzeria attached (see restaurant section).

Petit Hôtel des Hortensias (€€€) place de la Mairie, la Trinité-sur-Mer (tel: 02 97 30 10 30). An exclusive little haunt just above the port, unobtrusively set in a fine old stone house. The rooms are furnished with flair.

Les Trois Fontaines (€€€) route d'Auray (tel: 02 97 57 42 70). A comfortable and elegant place, surrounded by gardens. It is very close to the megaliths.

Morbihan, Golfe du

Auberge du Parc Fétan (€–€€) 17 rue de Berder, Larmor-Baden (tel: 02 97 57 04 38; www.hotel-parcfetan.com). Neatly refurbished hotel a few minutes from the waterfront. crisp modern rooms in blue and white, and some apartments with kitchenettes. Heated pool.

Le Logis de Parc et Gréo (€€–€€€) 9 rue Mane Guen, le Gréo, Arradon (tel: 02 97 44 73 03; www.parcergreo.com). A relaxing place in quiet grounds not far from the Golfe du Morbihan, with an all-weather swimming pool.

Les Vénètes (€€€) la Pointe, Arradon (tel: 02 97 44 85 85; www.lesvenetes.fr). Peacefully set west of Vannes on the Golfe du Morbihan, understandably popular in summer. The restaurant and most bedrooms have tranquil views of boats and islands. Smartly furnished

Ploërmel

Le Cobh (€€) 10 rue des Forges (tel: 02 97 74 00 49; www.hotel-lecobh.com). Well-run town-centre hotel of unusual character. Attractively furnished public areas and well-equipped bedrooms. Parking and restaurant.

Roi Arthur (€€) Le Lac au Duc (tel: 02 97 73 64 64; www.hotelroiarthur.com). Set beside the legendary forest of Broceliande and overlooking the Lac au Duc, the largest natural lake in Brittany. Facilities include a 9-hole golf course, indoor swimming pool and gym.

Pontivy

Le Rohan Wesseling (€€–€€€) 90 rue Nationale (tel: 02 97 25 02 01; www.hotel-le-rohan.com). This comfortable business hotel in a typical period building in the Napoleonic quarter is well managed and fairly quiet. Good facilities and a small garden set with tables. Park and old town nearby.

Le Vieux Moulin (€) St.-Nicolas-des-Eaux (tel: 02 97 51 81 09). Attractive, simple village inn overlooking the River Blavet. Comfortable, well-equipped rooms and a restaurant.

Port-Louis

Commerce-Les Magnolias (€) 1 place du Marché (tel: 02 97 82 46 05; www.hotel-magnolias.com). A commercial *logis* in the heart of this peaceful town, a suitable base for a night or two, with a pleasant garden and plenty of local atmosphere. The restaurant is worth considering, as you may not find anywhere else to eat.

Quiberon, Presqu'île de

Le Neptune (€€) 4 quai de Houat, Port-Maria (tel: 02 97 50 09 62). A well-managed, friendly *logis* on the harbourfront, being upgraded. All rooms have bath and shower. some with balconies overloking the port.

La Petite Sirène (€€) 15 boulevard René Cassin, Quiberon (tel: 02 97 50 17 34). Well-appointed hotel at the southern tip of the Quiberon peninsula, overlooking the sea and close to the thalassotherapy centre. The restaurant serves good meals at moderate prices. Short walk to the beach and casino.

Rhuys, Presqu'île de

Miramar (€€€) Port de Crouesty, Arzon (tel: 02 97 53 49 00; www.miramarcrouesty.com). Designed like an ocean liner, this huge modern hotel lies by the waterline in this purpose-built pleasure port.

Le Mûr du Roy (€–€€) Penvins (tel: 02 97 67 34 08; www.lemurderoy.com). Low, slate-roofed cottage in a coastal setting; attractively furnished. Excellent restaurant.

La Roche-Bernard

Auberge Bretonne (€€€) 2 place Duguesclin (tel: 02 99 90 60 28; www.thorel.fr). Celebrated restaurant-with-rooms (see restaurant section) in the town centre. Well-kept exterior with blue shutters and window-boxes. Very smartly furnished.

Auberge des Deux Magots (€–€€) 1 place du Bouffay (tel: 02 99 90 60 75). Pretty stone and white-painted building in an enclave near the town hall, with cheerful awnings. Rooms more urbanely grand. See restaurants.

Domaine de Rochevilaine (€€€) pointe de Pen-Lan, Billiers (tel: 02 97 41 61 61; www.domainerochevilaine.com). Unusual, rambling, village-like complex right by the sea, originally converted from old watch-post buildings. Inside it is luxurious and relaxing, with magnificent views. Expensive restaurant.

Manoir du Rodoir (€€) route de Nantes (tel: 02 99 90 82 68; www.lemanoirdurodoir.com). A stone house (once an old forge) set off the road in its own grounds. Furnished like an English country house inside, it is tasteful and comfortable throughout. See restaurants.

Rochefort-en-Terre

Château de Talhouët (€€€) off Molac road, NW (tel: 02 97 43 34 72; www.chateaudetalhouet.com). Classy *chambres d'hôtes* in a stone château with fine gardens. Inside all is peace, good taste and understated luxury. Rooms vary greatly in style and price, but all are immensely comfortable.

Vannes

Manche Océan (€€) 31 rue du Lieut. Col. Maury (tel: 02 97 47 26 46; www.manche-ocean.com). Peaceful, comfortable accommodation in a friendly, family-run establishment in the historic centre of the town. Convenient for shops, restaurants and major sights.

Marina (€–€€) 4 place Gambetta (tel: 02 97 47 22 81). Simple rooms above a popular brasserie on the main square by the port, handy for tourist office and old town. Lots of cafés and restaurants within easy reach.

Le Roof (€€) presqu'île de Conleau (tel: 02 97 63 47 47). A modern building occupying an enviable waterfront site some way from the old town. Family-run and much praised for its friendly staff. Good facilities and comfortable rooms. The restaurant overlooks the bay.

Villa Kerasy (€€€) 20 avenue Favrel et Lincy (tel: 02 97 68 36 83; www.villakerasy.com). Flamboyantly decorated bedrooms evoke the spirit of East. This quiet villa unexpectedly tucked near the railway station even has a Japanese garden to help you unwind.

INLAND BRITTANY

Combourg

Du Château (€–€€€) 1 place Chateaubriand (tel: 02 99 73 00 38; www.hotelduchateau.com). Well-established hotel near the castle, comfortably furnished throughout. Annexe bedrooms are modern and well equipped.

Du Lac (€–€€) 2 place Chateaubriand (tel: 02 99 73 05 65; www.hotel-restaurant-du-lac.com). Less expensive and simpler than the Hôtel du Château across the road, this enjoys fine lake views. Good restaurant and a garden (summer barbecues).

Fougères

Balzac (€) 15 rue Nationale (tel: 02 99 99 42 46). Central to the upper town, with a pleasant welcome and old-fashioned furnishings in the rooms. No restaurant.

Hédé

Vieux Moulin (€) La Vallée des Moulins (tel: 02 99 45 45 70). Old inn in a lovely setting. Simply furnished, with good dining room.

Montfort-sur-Meu

Château du Pin (€€) Iffendic (tel: 02 99 09 34 05; www.chateaudupin-bretagne.com). This lovely country house in rural surroundings has lots of style and decorative panache. The enthusiastic owners share their artistic interests and dine *en famille* with guests.

Mûr-de-Bretagne

Auberge Grand' Maison (€€–€€€) 1 rue Léon le Cerf (tel: 02 96 28 51 10; www.auberge-grand-maison.com). Stylish, if slightly cramped, inn. Ambitious food (see restaurant section). Bedrooms vary greatly in standard and price and some are quite small.

Auberge Kreisker (€) 11 place Kreisker, St.-Nicolas-du-Pélem (tel: 02 96 29 51 20; www.hotelkreisker.com). Small hotel in the village with creaking floors and quasi box beds in some rooms. A useful touring base.

Beau-Rivage (€) Caurel, Lac de Guérledan (tel: 02 96 28 52 15). Modern building overlooking the lake. Take a room with a view. Terrace restaurant. Watersports facilities nearby.

Du Blavet (€) Gouarec (tel: 02 96 24 90 03). Tall and interesting, overlooking the point where the Nantes–Brest canal meets the River Blavet. A busy road runs close by; otherwise the surrounding countryside is very peaceful. Period Breton furniture. Good food.

Quedillac

Relais de la Rance (€) 6 rue de Rennes (tel: 02 99 06 20 20). This classic, well-kept *logis*, run by the same family for generations, makes a useful touring base for the Forêt de Paimpont. The emphasis is on the cooking, but the refurbished interior has character.

Rennes

Ar Milin (€€) 30 rue de Paris, Châteaubourg (tel: 02 99 00 30 91; www.armilin.com). Large, comfortable roadside hotel (a converted flour mill) between Rennes and Vitré. Many facilities and extensive gardens landscaped around the river bank.

Hotel Lecoq-Gadby (€€€) 156 rue d'Antrain (tel: 02 99 38 05 55; www.lecoq-gadby.fr). Quite an institution. This elegantly furnished establishment, which provides a comfortably

relaxing stay, is patronized by famous person-
alities. Enjoy the open terrace and solarium. *A
la carte* and fixed-price menus in the restaurant. Easy access to the expressway.
Hôtel des Lices (€€) 7 place des Lices (tel:
02 99 79 14 81; www.hotel-des-lices.com).
Modern, thoroughly civilized and small; on the
edge of the old town. Parking available nearby. Excellent, neat little bedrooms, friendly
welcome and good breakfast.
Pen'Roc (€€–€€€) La Peinière-St.-Didier (tel:
02 99 00 33 02; www.penroc.fr). Excellent
modern hotel. Smart, stylish furnishings,
unfailingly courteous staff and ambitious food.

Le Vitré
Le Petit Billot (€) 5 bis place du Général
Leclerc (tel: 02 99 75 02 10; www.petit-bil-
lot.com). A neat, shuttered building on the
edge of the old town, comfortably modernized
with efficient showers and attractive interiors.
It's a welcoming place, offering good-value
half-board terms with nearby restaurants.

LOIRE-ATLANTIQUE

Batz-sur-Mer
Le Lichen (€–€€€) Baie du Manérick (tel: 02
40 23 91 92; www.le-lichen.com). Well-cared-
for detached house along the seafront road.
Solid, traditional furnishings and good views.
Separate restaurant l'Atlantide.

La Baule
Le Castel Marie-Louise (€€€) 1 avenue
Andrieu (tel: 02 40 11 48 38; www.castel-
marie-louise.com). One of la Baule's most
exclusive hotels, in an imposingly turreted
Belle Epoque mansion. Immaculate gardens
and celebrated food.
La Lutetia (€€) 13 av. des Evens (tel: 02 40
60 25 81; www.lutetia-rossini.com). Close to,
reputedly, Europe's finest beach. The building
retains its original facade; the interior has
comfortable rooms. An elegant restaurant
creates regional cuisine using local produce.
La Palmeraie (€€) 7 allée des Cormorans (tel:
02 40 60 24 41; www.hotel-lapalmeraie-
labaule.com). One of la Baule's best-loved
hotels, a *logis* set in a quiet corner of the
residential belt between beach and high
street. Traditional and reassuringly reliable.
Palm-shaded terraces.
La Mascotte (€€) 26 avenue Marie-Louise
(tel: 02 40 60 26 55; www.la-mascotte.fr). A
large, white-painted building in big gardens
shaded by pines, near the beach and casino.
St.-Christophe (€€) place Notre-Dame (tel: 02
40 62 40 00; www.saintchristophe.com). A
substantial creeper-covered villa in a quietly
desirable residential street in the heart of
the resort. Elegantly furnished period interior.
St. Pierre (€–€€) 124 avenue de Lattre de
Tassigny (tel: 02 40 24 05 41; www.hotel-
saint-pierre.com). A charming, friendly place
with prettily decorated rooms, quite close to
the beach and tourist office.

Ty-Gwenn (€) 25 avenue de la Grande Dune
(tel: 02 40 60 37 07). Simple, pretty family-
run guest-house. Quiet surroundings, short
walk to the beach.

Brière
Auberge de Kerhinet (€€) Kerhinet (tel: 02 40
61 91 46). Typical thatched cottage converted
into an attractive (if somewhat *touristique*)
logis. Dining room (see restaurant section).
La Mare aux Oiseaux (€€–€€€) 162 Ile
de Fedrun (tel: 02 40 88 53 01;
www.mareauxoiseaux.fr). A handful of simple
but charming bedrooms enhance this popular restaurant set in a thatched cottage in
one of la Grande Brière's best-loved villages.

Le Croisic
L'Estacade (€) 4–5 quai du Lénigo (tel: 02 40
23 03 77). Bustling bar-hotel on the waterfront by the *criée* and busy harbour. The bar
area is traditional; the best bedrooms are
modern and stylish. (See restaurants.)
Le Fort de l'Océan (€€€) pointe du Croisic (tel:
02 40 15 77 77; www.fort-ocean.com). Now
firmly on Europe's 'most fashionable hotel'
circuit, this sophisticated place at the far end
of the Croisic peninsula is distinguished by its
quirky architecture, its designer interior and
its stunning coastal setting.
Grand Hotel de l'Océan (€€€) plage de Port-
Lin (tel: 02 40 62 90 03). Port-Lin's smartest
hotel, a boxy, low-rise white block occupying
a prime site by the Atlantic. Spacious, traditionally furnished public areas with big
picture-windows. (See restaurant section.)
Les Nids (€–€€) 15 rue pasteur, Port-Lin (tel:
02 40 23 00 63; www.hotellesnids.com).
Civilized *logis* peacefully set a block back from
Atlantic seafront; partial sea views. Separate
restaurant nearby (see restaurant section).

Guérande
Loscolo (€€–€€€) Pointe de Loscolo, Pénestin
(tel: 02 99 90 31 90). Beautifully situated on
one of Loire-Atlantique's prettiest stretches of
coast, overlooking the Plage de la Mine d'Or.
Quiet, friendly, well-run and attractively
furnished—in short, a charmer.
De la Pointe (€) 1 quai de Verdun, Piriac-sur-
Mer (tel: 02 40 23 50 04). Daudet stayed
here, says a plaque outside. A useful,
modest base in a pretty fishing town of old
half-timbered houses. Good beaches nearby.
Roc Maria (€) 1 rue des Halles (tel: 02 40 24
90 51; www.hotelcreperierocmaria.com). A
15th-century gem tucked in the heart of the
old walled town. Attractively furnished, with a
lovely *crêperie*.

Missilic
Hôtel de la Bretesche (€€€) Domaine
de la Bretesche (tel: 02 51 76 86 96;
www.bretesche.com). Set in the grounds of a
truly breathtaking château picturesquely mirrored in a lake, these smart accommodation
units in the former stableblock are well kitted
out for a luxurious stay.

Nantes

Amiral (€€) 26 bis rue Scribe (tel: 02 40 69 20 21; www.hotel-nantes.fr). A neat, practical, modern hotel near Place Graslin, with attractive furnishings and welcoming staff. Plenty of restaurants, shops and nightlife all around, and nearby parking (but tricky to find by car).

Duchesse Anne (€€) 3–4 place de la Duchesse Anne (tel: 02 51 86 78 78). Grandiose, old-fashioned hotel overlooking the castle. No-frills, but spacious rooms, helpful staff and (not least of Nantes' wonders) garage parking. Good value.

L'Hôtel (€€) 6 rue Henri IV (tel: 02 40 29 30 31; www.nanteshotel.com). This is *the* place for a sophisticated stay in Nantes. A chic interior of cane and cashmere, *objets d'art* and beautifully co-ordinated colour schemes. Prices are geared towards business people but are surprisingly reasonable at weekends. No restaurant.

Le Jules Verne (€€–€€€) 3 rue du Couëdic (tel: 02 40 35 74 50). All is sleek, black and minimalist in this hotel in the heart of the old town near Place Royale. Bedrooms are well equipped.

Novotel Cité des Congrès (€€) 3 rue de Valmy (tel: 02 51 82 00 00). A modern establishment in the heart of town, with well-equipped rooms. A good choice if you anticipate a late arrival as food can be ordered at any time. Guests with disabilities are well catered for.

Pornichet

Sud-Bretagne (€€€) 42 boulevard de la République (tel: 02 40 11 65 00; www.hotel-sudbretagne.com). The phrase *hôtel de charme* is no overstatement here. A dream of a place, full of individuality and character yet thoroughly relaxing and comfortable too. Each room is different, each as delightful. The garden and pool add to the charm.

Villa Flornoy (€€–€€€) 7 avenue Flornoy (tel: 02 40 11 60 00; www.villa-flornoy.com). An elegantly converted villa a block or two back from the beach in a quiet street. It is refined and civilized, but welcoming too.

Redon

Jean-Marc Chandouineau (€€) 10 avenue de la Gare (tel: 02 99 71 02 04). A fairly charmless location by the railway station but conveniently near to the old town. Inside it has character, quite grand furnishings and large, smartly furnished rooms. Its restaurant is a high spot (see restaurant section).

RESTAURANTS

The following restaurants are divided into three price categories, based on the cost of a meal excluding drinks:

- **inexpensive (€)** under €30
- **moderate (€€)** €30–€50
- **expensive (€€€)** over €50

These should be viewed as a rough guideline only; many restaurants have an enormous range of menus and individual dishes. Even famous and august places may have a set-lunch menu well within your budget, and it would be a shame to leave Brittany without tasting some really first-class seafood.

THE EMERALD COAST

Cancale

Continental (€€) 4 quai Thomas (tel: 02 99 89 60 16). An excellent place to sample Cancale's oysters, preferably on the terrace towards sunset. See also hotel section.

Le Coquillage (€€) Le Pont du Jour, St-Méloir-des-Ondes (tel: 02 99 89 64 76). The seafood bistro at the grand and elegant sea-view Château de Richeux makes a splendid setting for some stratospheric Breton cooking at affordable rates. Book ahead, as residents get first pick of the tables (see hotels).

Grain de Vanille (€) 12 place de la Victoire (tel: 02 23 15 12 70). Modest premises at the back of town house this outpost of local master-chef Olivier Roellinger's gastro-empire—a delightful bakery and tea room full of irrestible treats, all made on-site. Eat in among parlour palms, or buy to enjoy later.

Maisons de Bricourt (€€€) rue Du Guesclin (tel: 02 99 89 64 76). The memorable food in this smart establishment earns consistent awards in the food guides, and some consider it Brittany's top restaurant.

Le Surcouf (€€) 7 quai Gambetta (tel: 02 99 89 61 75). One of the best of the restaurants ranged along the quayside. Besides wonderful seafood, there is home-baked buckwheat bread, and menus to suit all budgets.

Tirel-Guérin (€€–€€€) gare de la Gouesnière, St.-Méloir-des-Ondes (tel: 02 99 89 10 46). Plush dining room of drapes and tassels. Famous for lobster. (See also hotel section.)

Dinan

Café Terrasses (€€) 2–4 rue du Quai (tel: 02 96 39 09 60). Delightful waterfront setting at the port by the bridge.

Le Cantorbery (€€) 6 rue Ste.-Claire (tel: 02 96 39 02 52). A popular haunt in one of the old town's most attractive timbered buildings. Delicacies include *pré-salé* lamb and potted fish.

Chez la Mère Pourcel (€€–€€€) 3 place des Merciers (tel: 02 96 39 03 80). Lovely 15th-century house with a magnificent oak staircase. Copious helpings. Tables outside.

Le Léonie (€–€€) 17 rue Rolland (tel: 02 96 85 47 17). Central but quiet, with a keen following of locals who apreciate this inventive but unpretentious fare. Good-value *plats du jour* at lunchtime, with coffee and a pudding.

Le Romarin (€) 11 place des Cordeliers (tel: 02 96 85 20 37). A splendid *salon de thé* in the heart of the old quarter, known for its sweet and savoury tarts, flans and pies, served with imaginative salads and excellent house wine. Open evenings May–Sep.

277

Hotels & Restaurants

Dinard

Didier Méril (€€) 6 rue Yves Verney (tel: 02 99 46 95 74). An enthusiastic chef gives his name to this place, whose reputation goes from strength to strength. Seafood, excellent bread and desserts.

Erquy

L'Escurial (€€) boulevard de la Mer (tel: 02 96 72 31 56). Local scallops (coquilles) are the speciality in this deceptively plain but highly regarded place by the workmanlike harbour.

Fréhel, Cap

La Fauconnière (€) (tel: 02 96 41 54 20). Spectacular cliff-edge restaurant, serving simple fare such as omelettes and fresh fish.

Plancoët

L'Écrin-Jean-Pierre Crouzil (€€€€) 20 les Quais (tel: 02 96 84 10 24). Plancoët is famed for its pure, natural mineral water, but the chef-patron at this smart hotel-restaurant can offer you some 450 vintages if you prefer something a little stronger, as well as some of the best cooking in Brittany (see hotel section).

St.-Cast-le-Guildo

Belle-Meunière (€) 18 rue du Duc d'Aiguillon (tel: 02 96 41 82 22). This is a delightful salon-de-thé behind the main beach, in a smart, traditional setting amid shops and restaurants. You can have breakfast here, or a light lunch as well as an afternoon coupe glacée or kouign amann tatin.

St.-Lunaire

Le Décollé (€€) 1 pointe du Décollé (tel: 02 99 46 01 70). Plenty of visitors make their way to the scenic rocky promontory in this resort. Enjoy the views from the elegant glazed dining room or the summer terraces.

St.-Malo

Le Bénétin (€€) Les Rochers Sculptés, Rothéneuf (tel: 02 99 56 97 64). Another reason to track down Rothéneuf's strange clifftop rock carvings is this understated but quietly chic restaurant and tea room with marvellous coastal views, right beside the entrance. Tables outside in good weather.

La Brigantine (€) 13 rue de Dinan (tel: 02 99 56 82 82). An excellent crêperie-glacier in the heart of the old town, serving an imaginative range of well-prepared pancakes in a bright little dining room.

Le Chalut (€€–€€€) 8 rue de la Corne de Cerf (tel: 02 99 56 71 58). This smart nautical-looking bistro near the old walls hits all the right buttons, handling the catch of the day with care and refinement.

L'Univers (€€) place Chateaubriand (tel: 02 99 40 89 52). A popular place within the walls of the old town specializing in seafood. Late dinners served. (See hotel section.)

À la Duchesse Anne (€€–€€€) 5 place Guy La Chambre (tel: 02 99 40 85 33). One of St.-Malo's most celebrated eating places,

always bustling, by the rampart walls. It specializes in grilled lobster and tarte tatin. No set menus but not outrageously expensive. Book well ahead.

Le Val André

Art & Saveur (€) 28 quai des Terre-Neuvas, port de Dahouët (tel: 02 96 63 19 17). An atmospheric old sail-loft overlooking the picturesque harbour is the setting for this imaginative venture, a mix of art gallery, café and wine-bar serving interesting snacks and light meals. Books, board games and even a bit of live jazz may accompany your visit.

De la Mer (€€) 63 rue Amiral Charner (tel: 02 96 72 20 44). Wonderful moules here, hence its popularity with locals, but all is simple, friendly and cheerful. (See also hotel section.)

THE PINK GRANITE COAST

Binic

Rive Gauche (€) place du Port (tel: 02 96 73 34 79). Tables certainly fill up at this popular waterfront salon de thé. Besides delicious cakes and ices, there's a wide choice of light bites (salads, paninis, sandwiches). Terrace tables in summer.

Bréhat, Île de

L'Oiseau des Îles (€) rue du Port (tel: 02 96 20 00 53). Look for the puffin outside this popular crêperie, a blue-shuttered building a short walk from the port. Specialty fillings include andouille (Breton sausage).

Lannion

Ville Blanche (€€–€€€) route de Tréguier (tel: 02 96 37 04 28). Serious stuff on offer here, with seasonal delicacies like scallops and lobster. Good wines available by the glass.

Paimpol

L'Écluse (€–€€) quai Armand Dayot (tel: 02 96 55 03 38). This airy building among the chandleries and boatyards near the lock-gates serves wonderful fresh seafood, some grilled on an open hearth. The atmosphere is casual, but service and cooking are hard to beat at these prices.

Morel (€) 11 place du Martray (tel: 02 96 20 86 34). Delicious crêpes filled with regional delicacies and accompanied by excellent cider. Be warned, it is always popular.

Aux Pesked (€€–€€€) 59 rue du Légué, St.-Brieuc (tel: 02 96 33 34 65). Classy, with a moderately priced weekday menu; fish specials.

Vieille Tour (€€–€€€) 13 rue Église (tel: 02 96 20 83 18). Set in a small stone house. Good set meals (à la carte can be pricey).

Perros-Guirec

La Crémaillère (€–€€) 13 place de l'Église (tel: 02 96 23 22 08). On the main square by the church, this cosy 17th-century building creates a rustic scene. Seasonal menus include seafood and chargrills.

278

Crêperie Hamon (€) 36 rue de la Salle (tel: 02 96 23 28 82). Widely known to locals, the rustic setting and the skilful pancake-tossing draws in the crowds. Book ahead.
Les Feux des Îles (€€) 53 boulevard Clemenceau (tel: 02 96 23 22 94). The dining room takes full advantage of the views but don't be distracted too much: the food is excellent. (See also hotel section.)

St.-Quay-Portrieux
Ker–Moor (€€) 13 rue du Président le Sénéchal (tel: 02 96 70 52 22). With a garden and panoramic view of the Bay of St.-Brieuc; close to the beach. The house special is scallops.

Tregastel
Auberge de la Vieille Église (€€) place de l'Église (tel: 02 96 23 88 31). This flower-decked restaurant in the hub of the old town makes a delightful spot for lunch or dinner. Excellent service and accomplished cooking.

Tréguier
Le Hangar (€) port de Plaisance (tel: 02 96 92 47 46). This battered old boatshed down beside the harbourmaster's office serves no-frills dishes such as mussels and stuffed clams. It's naturally popular with yachties—the local Dremmwell beer goes down well.
Poissonerie du Trégor (€€–€€€) 2 rue Renan (tel: 02 96 92 30 27). A combination of fishmonger and restaurant. You can take away or try upstairs in the tasting rooms. Special children's menus are available, but no desserts.
Les Trois Rivières (€€) port de Plaisance (tel: 02 96 92 97 00). The restaurant belonging to the Aigue Marine hotel earns high praise. You dine in light, modern surroundings overlooking the port. Service is prompt and affable (see hotel section).

NORTH FINISTÈRE

Brest
Ma Petite Folie (€€) port du Moulin Blanc (tel: 02 98 41 43 68). An old crayfish boat permanently moored by the yacht marina (near Océanopolis) makes an unusual setting for a smart gourmet restaurant. Dine on either deck, but book ahead in high season.

Carantec
Carantec–Patrick Jeffroy (€€€) 20 rue de Kelenn (tel: 02 98 67 00 47). This imposing buttermilk-coloured hotel has a fine restaurant; great for coquilles St.-Jacques fresh from Morlaix bay (see also hotel section).

Le Conquet
Le Relais du Vieux Port (€) 1 quai Drellac'h (tel: 02 98 89 15 91). A variety of snacks, crêpes and salads is served in a simple but stylish setting. Live music. (See hotel section).

Morlaix
Brasserie de l'Europe (€–€€) place Emile Souvestre (tel: 02 98 88 81 15). A bright and breezy café-restaurant producing elegant grazing food in sophisticated modern surroundings. The downstairs wine bar is popular at happy hour (6–8pm).
L'Hermine (€) 35 rue Ange de Guernisac (tel: 02 98 88 10 91). Many restaurants line this quaint steep lane, but you won't go wrong in this charming crêperie. Interesting house specialties include a seaweed filling. Friendly service.
La Marée Bleue (€€) 3 rampe St.-Mélaine (tel: 02 98 63 24 21). Near the tourist office in one of Morlaix's picturesque venelles (alleys). Traditional cooking, good set menus and interesting wines.

Ouessant, Île d'
Crêperie Ti à Dreux (€) Le Bourg (tel: 02 98 48 83 01). This old house has a vast choice of pancake fillings and some imaginative desserts. The experience is enhanced by the family atmosphere.

Roscoff
Chardons Bleus (€–€€) 4 rue Amiral Réveillère (tel: 02 98 69 72 03). Friendly hotel-restaurant a block behind the port. Children's menus available.
Chez Janie (€–€€) le Port (tel: 02 98 61 24 25). This much-loved watering-hole sharing premises with the Hôtel du Centre (see hotel section) attracts both locals and visitors for an appetizing range of drinks, snacks and full meals. Children's menus and good-value plats du jour. Informal but friendly service.
Crêperie de la Poste (€) 12 rue Gambetta (tel: 02 98 69 72 81). Serves a wide range of pancakes in a plain, workaday dining room popular with ferry travellers.
Le Temps de Vivre (€€) place de l'Église (tel: 02 98 61 27 28). Possibly the best place in town, with excellent views of the Île de Batz. Seafood and local vegetables are served in an attractive dining room. (See hotel section.)

St.-Mathieu, Pointe de
Hostellerie de la Pointe St.-Mathieu (€€) pointe St.-Mathieu (tel: 02 98 89 00 19). Crowds head to this scenic spot for the views, and the elaborately prepared seafood in this attractively modernized old Breton house. Atmospheric decor of vaulted stone. (See hotel section.)

ARMORIQUE

Arrée, Monts d'
Milin Kerroch (€) Sizun (tel: 02 98 68 81 56). At the entrance to the village, in the Centre de Loisirs, a converted watermill serving a wide variety of crêpes.

Camaret-sur-Mer
Côté Mer (€–€€) 12 quai Toudouze (tel: 02 98 27 93 79). Seafood menus are chalked on the blackboard in this delightful yellow-painted brasserie with a heated lamplit terrace.

279

Hotels & Restaurants

Carhaix-Plouguer
Auberge du Poher (€€) route de Lorient (tel: 02 98 99 51 18). Pretty, rustic restaurant serving regional Breton food with earthy dishes such as *tripes* and *andouilles*.
Brasserie Coreff (€) 2 place de la Gare (tel: 02 98 93 00 70). Learn how this renowned real ale is produced on a brewery tour, then taste some of it accompanied by a range of traditional Breton fare at the on-site brasserie.
Crêperie Les Salines (€) 23 rue Brizeux (tel: 02 98 99 11 32). Innovative ways with pancakes, using organic flour and interesting seafood. It is good value.

Crozon, Presqu'île de
Hostellerie de la Mer (€€) le Fret (tel: 02 98 27 61 90). Terraces and picture windows make the most of the views, though the food is worth concentrating on too. (See hotel section.)
Le Mutin Gourmand (€€) place de l'Église (tel: 02 98 27 06 51). Consistently praised for its imaginative and skilful use of whatever's best from the market. Unusual creatures swim on to the menus here.

Le Faou
La Vieille Renommée (€€) place aux Foires (tel: 02 98 81 90 31). The restaurant of the Beauvoir Hotel on the main square has a reputation for quality and value.

Guimiliau
Ar Chupen (€) 43 rue du Calvaire (tel: 02 98 68 73 63). This *crêperie* near the church deals with any sudden appetite worked up in the parish close. A *crêpe du pagan* sounds a good antidote to spiritual thoughts.

Huelgoat
Crêperie de l'Argoat (€) 12 rue du Lac (tel: 02 98 99 71 72). A small, rustic place with lake views and a terrace. Fillings range from seafood to chitterling sausage with mustard.

Lampaul-Guimiliau
L'Escapade (€–€€) 8 place du Villers (tel: 02 98 68 61 27). An attractive traditional house near the town hall, producing interesting menus at reasonable prices, including *crêpes*.

Landerneau
L'Amandier (€€) 55 rue de Brest (tel: 02 98 85 10 89). Traditional hotel with an excellent restaurant and brasserie.
La Mairie (€–€€) 9 rue de la Tour d'Auvergne (tel: 02 98 85 01 83). Attractive bar-restaurant overlooking the scenic Pont de Rohan.

St.-Thégonnec
Auberge St.-Thégonnec (€€) 6 place de la Mairie (tel: 02 98 79 61 18). Some of the region's most accomplished cooking is served here in the gardens in summer. (See also hotel section.)

CORNOUAILLE

Audierne
Le Goyen (€€€) place Jean Simon (tel: 02 98 70 08 88). The lovely restaurant at this hotel overlooks a splendid sweep of estuary and serves a mix of traditional and *nouvelle* cuisine. Stick to set menus or you may be in for a shock when the bill arrives.

Bélon
Chez Jacky (€€) Riec-sur-Bélon (tel: 02 98 06 90 32). Oyster farm-cum-restaurant overlooking the River Bélon.
Le Kerfany (€€) Blorimond, route du Port de Bélon, Moëlan-sur-Mer (tel: 02 98 71 00 46). Serving several menus over a wide price range Specialities include seafood and *far Breton*.
Les Moulins du Duc (€€–€€€) Moëlan-sur-Mer (tel: 02 98 96 52 52). Top-quality food is served in two candlelit dining rooms, one non-smoking. (See also hotel section.)

Bénodet
L'Agape (€€–€€€) route de la Plage, Ste.-Marine (tel: 02 98 56 32 70). A lovely old house quietly set near the beaches: elegant, with expensive menus carefully presented.
La Cabane du Pêcheur (€) 37 rond point du Poulquer (tel: 02 98 66 27 97). An attractive seafront *crêperie* with streamlined nautical decor near the casino. Excellent pancakes incorporating regional produce such as cider and andouille de Bretagne, plus pizzas, omelettes, salads and children's menus too.
La Ste.-Marine (€€) 19 rue du Bac, Ste.-Marine (tel: 02 98 56 34 79). The tables outside this delightful hotel are a good place to enjoy views of the Odet estuary.

Concarneau
L'Amiral (€–€€) 1 avenue Pierre Guéguin (tel: 02 98 60 55 23). Very close to the Ville Close on the harbourfront, this handsome bar-restaurant has loads of character, and the food is excellent. Wines by the glass, fresh bread and classic seafood concoctions.
Chez Armande (€) 15 bis avenue Dr. Nicolas (tel: 02 98 97 00 76). Old-fashioned family-run place serving simple fish dishes.
La Coquille (€€) quai Moros (tel: 02 98 97 08 52). Classy but down-to-earth fish restaurant by the new port.
Le Petit Chaperon Rouge (€) 7 place Du Guesclin (tel: 02 98 60 53 32). There's a Little Red Riding Hood theme to the interior at this little place hidden in a tiny square behind the Ville Close. The *crêpes* can't be faulted, and the welcome is warm.

Locronan
Ty Coz (€) place de l'Eglise (tel: 02 98 81 70 79). This long-established, family-run *crêperie* and *glacier* is set in a gorgeous Renaissance building with flower-decked window boxes on the main square. Its beamed dining rooms give an excuse to linger in this good-looking town.

Penmarc'h

Le Chandelier (€€) 16 rue de la Marine, le Guilvinec (tel: 02 98 58 91 00). If you like seafood, this is one of the best bets to sample the catch at one of France's most important fishing ports. The setting is an old fisherman's cottage; the cooking much more *nouvelle*.

Pont-Aven

La Taupinière (€€€) route de Concarneau (tel: 02 98 06 03 12). Locals consider the trek out of town worth it for prime regional cooking. Elegant dining room and good service.

Café des Arts (€) 11 rue du Général-de-Gaulle (tel: 02 98 06 07 12). This lively brasserie is a popular with the young, with live music, good beer and simple, well-prepared dishes like Lyon sausage and potatoes or Thai chicken.

Moulin de Rosmadec (€€€) (tel: 02 98 06 00 22). This lovely old mill in the middle of the racing Aven River provides a good excuse to splash out. Interior combines elegance with old-world Breton charm. (See also hotel section.)

Port-Manec'h

Ar Men-Du (€€–€€) rue des Iles, Raguenès-Plage (tel: 02 98 06 84 22). This beautifully located hotel's bright restaurant draws plenty of daytime trade. It has spectacular sea views. (See hotel section.)

Quimper

L'Ambroisie (€€–€€€) 49 rue Elie-Fréron (tel: 02 98 95 00 02). Close to the cathedral, serving excellent fish dishes. Also noted for its delicious desserts.

Crêperie du Sallé (€) 6 rue du Sallé (tel: 02 98 95 95 80). One of Quimper's quaintest buildings makes a charming setting for this welcoming and inventive *crêperie* in the heart of the old town.

La Fleur de Sel (€€) 1 quai Neuf (tel: 02 98 55 04 71). A handy place for lunch if you're visiting Quimper's *faïencerie* factories in Locmaria. Hop over the bridge for riverside views and light fish dishes.

Au Vieux Quimper (€) 20 rue Verdelet (tel: 02 98 95 31 34). Popular *crêperie* in the old town serving food all day.

Quimperlé

Le Bistro de la Tour (€€) 2 rue Dom-Morice (tel: 02 98 39 21 77). An antique-strewn interior in one of Quimperlé's most atmospheric old streets makes a pleasing setting for hearty dishes with local seafood. Friendly service and good wines.

Ty-Gwechall (€) 4 rue Mellac, Haute Ville (tel: 02 98 96 30 63). *Crêperie* at the top of the town. Unconventional fillings such as carrots, chutney and lots of other things too.

Ste.-Anne-la-Palud

La Plage (€€€) (tel: 02 98 92 50 12). Inventive cuisine in luxurious and elegant surroundings. (See also hotel section.)

MORBIHAN

Auray

L'Auberge (€–€€€) 56 route de Vannes, Ste.-Anne-d'Auray (tel: 02 97 57 61 55). Candlelit restaurant using local produce to serve up highly imaginative food. (See hotel section.)

La Closerie de Kerdrain (€€€) 20 rue Louis-Billet (tel: 02 97 56 61 27). Accomplished traditional fare in an attractive Renaissance mansion just outside the town centre. Book ahead.

L'Eglantine (€€) place Saint-Sauveur, Saint-Goustan (tel: 02 97 56 46 55). Down by the waterfront in Auray's atmospheric old port, this attractive place decked with portraits of Chouan heroes is a safe bet for competent Breton dishes at fair prices.

Belle-Île

Café Atlantique (€–€€) quai de l'Acadie, Le Palais (tel: 02 97 31 80 11). The breezy café of this attractive hotel beside the harbour is a good place to watch those arriving from Quiberon. (See hotel section.)

Contre Quai (€€) rue St.-Nicolas, Sauzon (tel: 02 97 31 60 60). Reputable fish restaurant in one of Belle-Île's prettiest coastal villages.

Roz Avel (€€) rue du Lieutenant-Riou , Sauzon (tel: 02 97 31 61 48). Meals served outside in summer; book in advance.

Carnac

Auberge Le Ratelier (€) 4 chemin du Douët (tel: 02 97 52 05 04). Lovely creeper-clad hotel offering inventive cuisine in a quiet corner of the old town. near the church and museum.

Chez Marie (€) place de l'Église (tel: 02 97 52 07 93). A *crêperie* in an old stone house in the town centre near the church and archaeology museum. A good choice of fillings; prompt and pleasant service.

La Côte (€€) alignements de Karmario (tel: 02 97 52 02 80). Very close to the megaliths, this welcoming place caters well for visitors in an elegant but relaxing stone-built restaurant with large gardens. Pierre Michaud's cooking achieves high standards with dishes of subtlety and precision, using both meat and seafood.

Hennebont

Château de Locguénolé (€€€) route de Port-Louis, Kervignac (tel: 02 97 76 76 76). This elegant riverside hotel is dauntingly grand, but its restaurant is highly acclaimed. Eating here in the evening can be expensive; weekday lunches are just about affordable.

Josselin

La Marine (€) 8 rue du Canal (tel: 02 97 22 21 98). A pretty waterfron *crêperie* with a flower-decked terrace. The pancakes ring the changes with seasonal fillings, but there are other things on the menu too.

La Table d'O (€€) 2 rue Glatinier (tel: 02 97 70 61 39). This weclome addition to

Hotels & Restaurants

Josselin's restaurants is a smart dining room with balcony views over the town. Accomplished, dynamic cooking matches attentive service.

Locmariaquer
Bistrot du Marin (€€) cours des Quais, la Trinité-sur-Mer (tel: 02 97 55 73 23). A good choice, overlooking the port, for a plate of well-prepared seafood. Attached is a stylish little *logis*, L'Ostrea (see hotel section).

Lorient
L'Amphitryon (€€€) 127 rue Col Müller (tel: 02 97 83 34 04). Serving elaborate, reverential cuisine (with prices to match), this choice is for serious foodies. Acclaimed for its seafood.
Le Jardin Gourmand (€–€€) 46 rue Jules-Simon (tel: 02 97 64 17 24). Worth tracking down near the railway station, this place has achieved a solid reputation as one of the best in town. Careful preparation of fresh produce and an elegant setting with tables outside, plus good service.
Le Victor Hugo (€€) 36 rue Lazare-Carnot (tel: 02 97 64 26 54). Easy to miss on a dull busy street, but not far from the marina. Family-run, with good set menus served in a spacious, leafy dining room.

Malestroit
Le Canotier (€) place du Dr. Queinnec (tel: 02 97 75 08 69). Excellent value, near the market square. Choose either the terrace tables or the elegant dining room. Seafood and freshwater fish are on the menus.

Morbihan, Golfe du
Les Embruns (€–€€) rue du Commerce, Île aux Moines (tel: 02 97 26 30 86). One of the most reliable choices on the island, run by a local who trained on the mainland but has returned to his roots.
L'Escale (€€) Ile d'Arz (tel: 02 97 44 32 15) Modern hotel-restaurant on the seafront, a popular lunch stopover on gulf cruises. Seafood specials.
Le Gavrinis (€€) Toulbroch-en-Baden (tel: 02 97 57 00 82). A father-and-son team cook up a storm in this well-established, flower-decked hotel-restaurant. Good-value lunches, and home-baked pastries at breakfast time.
Le San Francisco (€€) Île aux Moines (tel: 02 97 26 31 52). This seafood restaurant overlooks the harbour and has splendid views of the Golfe du Morbihan. Specials include fried *gambas* with aniseed sauce.

Ploërmel
Saint-Marc (€€) 1 place St.-Marc (tel: 02 97 74 00 01). A smart hotel-restaurant with a solid local reputation.

Pontivy
La Pommeraie (€–€€) 17 quai du Couvent (tel: 02 97 25 60 09). In the medieval part of the town, close to the castle. Good lunchtime menu.

Quiberon, Presqu'île de
Ancienne Forge (€€) 20 rue de Verdun, Port-Maria (tel: 02 97 50 18 64). Quiet and pretty, tucked away from the seafront in a cul-de-sac.
La Criée (€–€€) 11 quai de l'Océan, Port-Maria (tel: 02 97 30 53 09). Informal, inexpensive quayside fish restaurant, popular with families. What they serve is either scribbled on the blackboard or awaiting inspection on fishmongers' trays.

Rhuys, Presqu'île de
Le Grand Largue (€€–€€€) rue du Phare, Port-Navalo (tel: 02 97 53 71 58). Smart restaurant near the waterfront, serving seafood full of eastern promise.
L'Hortensia (€€) La Grée Penvins, Sarzeau (tel: 02 97 67 42 15). Blue dining rooms in an old granite house provide a foil for superb cooking using regional produce. There is plenty of seafood, naturally.

La Roche-Bernard
Auberge Bretonne (€€€) 2 place Du Guesclin (tel: 02 99 90 60 28). Celebrated restaurant, where ambitious food is served up in sophisticated surroundings that are arranged around a garden courtyard. (See hotels.)
Auberge des Deux Magots (€–€€) 1 place du Bouffay (tel: 02 99 90 60 75). Stylish, country-style decor with lively frescoes. Cheerful, unpretentious menus. See also hotel section.

Rochefort-en-Terre
Le Bretagne (€€€) Questembert (tel: 02 97 26 11 12). This famous *Relais de Campagne* restaurant has ambitious nouvelle cuisine in gracious panelled surroundings.

Vannes
La Huche à Pain (€) 23 place des Lices (tel: 02 97 47 23 76). Popular *pâtisserie* where you can buy delicious Breton cakes such as *kouignamann*.
La Morgate (€€) 21 rue Fontaine (tel: 02 97 42 42 39). Solid gourmet cooking on a hilly street near the ramparts. Good-value weekday menus, with prompt and courteous service.
Le Pressoir (€€€) 7 rue de l'Hôpital, St.-Avé (tel: 02 97 60 87 63). Renowned restaurant in rustic-style Louis XIII setting just north of the town. Menu offers a good range of meat and fish dishes.
Roscanvec (€€) 17 rue des Halles (tel: 02 97 47 15 96). Accomplished dishes change regularly to show off the owner-chef's talent and whatever's best in the market. Excellent wine list available.

INLAND BRITTANY

Combourg
L'Écrivain (€€) place St.-Gilduin (tel: 02 99 73 01 61). Good value menus in this place opposite the church. The choice is limited but only the freshest of ingredients are used.

Fougères

Les Voyageurs (€) 10 place Gambetta (tel: 02 99 99 14 17). The restaurant in this traditional central hotel (under separate management) produces acclaimed food, albeit in a fairly charmless and noisy setting.

Le Buffet (€) 53 bis rue nationale (tel: 02 99 94 35 76). A friendly place in the upper town, decked with memorabilia and photos, and blazing fires on chilly days.The buffets include wine. Fantastic value.

Hédé

Le Genty Home (€€) Vallée de Hédé (tel: 02 99 45 46 07). A charming setting (stone walls, towers and a big open fireplace) complement local produce.

Mûr-de-Bretagne

Auberge Grand' Maison (€€€) 1 rue Léon le Cerf (tel: 02 96 28 51 10). Ambitious modern cooking in smart surroundings. Elaborate dishes, but set menus can be good value. Delicious desserts. (See hotels.)

Rennes

Auberge St.-Saveur (€–€€) 6 rue St.-Saveur (tel: 02 99 79 32 56). Breton lobster and other shellfish and fish dishes served in a traditional atmosphere in an 18th-century building.

Café Breton (€–€€) 14 rue Nantaise (tel: 02 99 30 74 95). Very busy at lunchtime, and with lots of intimate corners. Good chalkboard specials and terrific wines.

Chouin (€–€€) 12 rue d'Isly (tel: 02 99 30 87 86). This smart restaurant is attached to a fish shop. The lunchtime menu is particularly good value.

Le Four à Ban (€€) 4 rue St. Mélanie (tel: 02 99 38 72 85). Very good-value lunch menu in 18th-century surroundings. The chef only uses fresh produce in season. The parking nearby is a real bonus.

Léon le Cochon (€–€€) 1 rue du Maréchal-Joffre (tel: 02 99 79 37 54). A sophisticated, modern establishment with a rustic air. The dining room is decked with dried flowers and chilli peppers. The menu includes interesting ways with offal.

Vitré

Taverne de l'Ecu (€€) 12 rue Beaudrairie (tel: 02 99 75 11 09). A taste of the old town in a pretty 17th-century building, a stone's throw from the castle.

LOIRE-ATLANTIQUE

La Baule

La Ferme du Grand Clos (€) 52 avenue de Lattre-de-Tassigny (tel: 02 40 60 03 30). A smart crêperie offering delicious pancakes and country classics like cassoulet and duck confit.

Brière

Auberge de Kerhinet (€€) Kerhinet (tel: 02 40 61 91 46). A wide range of dishes are served in the attractive beamed dining room of this small hotel. (See also hotel section.)

Brasserie de la Brière (€) St. Lyphard (tel: 02 50 91 33 62). A great place to enjoy some authentic local beers in a setting of real character in the regional park.

La Mare aux Oiseaux (€€) Île de Fédrun (tel: 02 40 88 53 01). Typical thatched cottage where you can sample popular local dishes including pike, eel, tench and duck. Children's menus available. (See hotels.)

Le Croisic

L'Estacade (€€) 4–5 quai du Lénigo (tel: 02 40 23 03 77). Old-fashioned family-run brasserie near the harbour, popular with locals. Copious helpings of seafood. (See also hotel section.)

Guérande

Les Remparts (€–€€) boulevard du Nord (tel: 02 40 24 90 69). Good set menus available in this traditional hotel by the walls.

Nantes

Auberge du Château (€€) 5 place de la Duchesse-Anne (tel: 02 40 74 31 85). Excellent, imaginative food, just opposite the castle. A good choice if you are staying nearby.

Café du Marché (€) 1 rue de Mayence (tel: 02 40 47 63 50). Popular for business lunches, this place serves a simple, inexpensive menu with three or four starters and a dish of the day.

Chez l'Huitre (€€) 5 rue des Petites Ecuries (tel: 02 51 82 02 02). An atmospheric seafood bistro in the old town, offering oysters, salmon and assembled fish platters.

La Cigale (€–€€) 4 place Graslin (tel: 02 51 84 94 94). A must, at least for coffee, if you are exploring the old town. Gorgeous *fin-de-siècle* brasserie with intact interior. Good seafood lunches and cakes.

L'Esquinade (€€) 7 rue St-Denis (tel: 02 40 48 17 22). Elegant little place near the cathedral with a cosy dining room and plenty of choice.

La Mangeoire (€) 16 rue des Petites-Écuries (tel: 02 40 48 70 83). Excellent country cooking using game, meat and fish. Unpretentious good value.

Redon

L'Akène (€) 10 rue de Jeu-de-Paume (tel: 02 99 71 25 15). In a maze of alleys by the port, this quaint stone-built house offers excellent pancakes. Specialty *raclettes* for two people.

La Bogue (€€) 3 rue des Etats (tel: 02 99 71 12 95). Enterprising regional cooking in an appealingly traditional setting near the town centre. Chestnuts feature on the menu in season.

Jean-Marc Chandouineau (€€) 10 avenue de la Gare (tel: 02 99 71 02 04). Accomplished cooking by one of Redon's best chefs, in surprisingly grand surroundings near the railway station. (See hotels.)

283

Index

Index

Index

Index and Acknowledgments

Acknowledgments

The Automobile Association would like to thank the following photographers, companies and picture libraries for their assistance in the preparation of this book.

Abbreviations for the picture credits are as follows – (t) top; (b) bottom; (c) centre; (l) left; (r) right; (AA) AA World Travel Library.
JOHN FISHER 258; **MARY EVANS PICTURE LIBRARY** 34b, 40b, 41b; **GETTY IMAGES** 35t, 43t, 179b; **ILLUSTRATED LONDON NEWS** 42t; **SPECTRUM COLOUR LIBRARY** 186, 187; **WERNER FORMAN ARCHIVE LTD** 33t;

The remaining photographs are held in the AA PHOTO LIBRARY and were taken by: M Adelman 44t; A Baker 11t, 13b, 56t, 59b, 82, 143t, 144, 160t, 168, 169, 171, 177, 203, 215, 243b, 259; S Day 3, 5t, 6/7, 7, 9, 10b, 13t, 14b, 16c, 16b, 17, 24/5, 25, 29, 35b, 36t, 38t, 38b, 40t, 45, 46, 48, 49t, 49b, 50, 51b. 52, 53, 54t, 54b, 55, 56b, 57t 57b, 58, 59t, 62, 63, 64t 64b, 65a, 65t, 67t, 67b, 68t, 68b, 69t, 69b, 113t, 113b, 126t, 151b, 155c, 176t, 184b, 194b, 195, 204, 206b, 207t, 207b, 208, 209t, 209b, 210t, 210b, 211t, 211b, 214t, 214b. 217t, 217b, 218, 219, 220tl, 220tr, 221t, 221b, 222t, 222b, 223, 224, 225t, 225b, 247, 248, 249, 262t, 262b 265; P Bennett 255; J Edmanson 150b, 231, 235; P Kenward 44b, 51t, 253; A Kouprianoff 32b, 77t, 77b, 87t, 99, 112t, 180, 181, 192t, 250; R Moore 61b; T Oliver 16t; K Paterson 256; C Sawyer 60, 61t; B Smith 116, 127b, 139; T Souter, 18t, 18b; R Strange 2, 4, 5bl, 5br, 8, 10t, 11b, 12t, 14t, 15, 19b, 20b, 21, 22t, 22c, 22b, 23, 24/5, 26t, 26b, 27t, 27b, 30t, 30b, 31t, 31b, 42r, 43b, 44c, 72t, 73, 74, 75bl, 78t, 78b, 79t, 79b, 80, 81t, 81c, 84, 85t, 85b, 86, 87t, 88t, 88b, 89c, 89b, 90t, 96, 97t, 97b, 100, 101t, 101b, 104, 106, 107, 109, 111t, 111b, 114, 115t, 115b, 117, 118, 119t, 120t, 121, 122, 123, 124t, 124b, 125, 126b, 127t 128b, 129t, 129b, 130t, 131, 132t 132b, 133, 134, 135t, 135b, 136a, 136b, 137t, 137c, 137b, 140, 142, 143b, 145t, 145b, 146t, 146b, 147, 148, 149t, 149c, 149b, 150t, 151t, 152, 153bl, 153br, 154, 155t, 155b, 156c, 156b, 157, 158, 159t, 159b, 160b, 161t, 161b, 162, 163t, 164t, 164b, 165t, 166t, 166b, 167, 170,172t, 172b, 173t, 173b, 174, 175, 176bl, 178t, 178b, 179t, 182, 184t, 185b, 188, 189, 190, 192b, 193t, 194t, 197, 198t, 198b, 199, 200t, 200b, 201t, 201b, 226, 228t, 228b, 230t, 230b, 233t, 233b, 236, 237, 238, 239, 241, 242t, 242b, 244, 245bl, 245br, 246, 251, 257, 263, 264; J Tims 98, 185t, 254; P Trenchard 89t; R Victor 12b, 19t, 20t, 66, 70, 72b, 75br, 81b, 83, 90b, 91, 92, 93, 94, 102t, 102b, 103t, 103c, 103b, 105, 110, 112b, 119b, 120b, 128t, 130b, 163b, 165b, 183t, 183b, 191, 193b, 196, 206t, 212, 213, 216, 229, 234, 243t, 252, 260; 261; S Watkins 113c.

Every effort has been made to trace the copyright holders, and we apologise in advance for any accidental errors. We would be happy to apply the corrections in the following edition of this publication.

Contributors

Revision verifier: Lindsay Hunt **Revision edit and design:** Bookwork Creative Associates Ltd.